THE CONSTITUTIONAL PROTECTION OF PRIVATE PROPERTY IN CHINA

This timely book reviews the changes in legal reform around the constitutional protection of private property in China since 1949. Using a comparative approach, it analyses the development of property theories and the various constitutionalisation models and practices of private property in representative countries including the United States, Canada, Germany, India and China. It also explores the interwoven social forces that have been driving the evolution of the constitutional protection of private property in China. By comparing China with the United States, Germany and India, the author reveals the unfairness, unjustness and insufficiency in China's application of three constitutional doctrines – public use, just compensation and due process or procedure. The book concludes by predicting future progress and suggests feasible measures for gradual reform that will be compatible with China's existing political system.

CHUANHUI WANG is Associate Professor at Lingnan (University) College, part of the Sun Yat-Sen University in Guangzhou, China. He received a bachelor degree from Yantai University and master degrees from East China University of Political Science and Law and the University of Michigan. In addition to holding a PhD in law from the University of Leuven (KU Leuven), he also has a PhD in economics from the Shanghai Academy of Social Sciences.

THE CONSTITUTIONAL PROTECTION OF PRIVATE PROPERTY IN CHINA

Historical Evolution and Comparative Research

CHUANHUI WANG
Lingnan (University) College, Sun Yat-sen University

CAMBRIDGE
UNIVERSITY PRESS

CAMBRIDGE
UNIVERSITY PRESS

University Printing House, Cambridge CB2 8BS, United Kingdom

Cambridge University Press is part of the University of Cambridge.

It furthers the University's mission by disseminating knowledge in the pursuit of education, learning and research at the highest international levels of excellence.

www.cambridge.org
Information on this title: www.cambridge.org/9781107125438

First published 2016

A catalogue record for this publication is available from the British Library

ISBN 978-1-107-12543-8 Hardback

To my parents,
who taught me about compassion, responsibility,
independence and dignity

CONTENTS

FIGURES AND TABLES

FOREWORD

It is with great pleasure that I recommend to the reader this fascinating book. I had the honour of supervising the doctoral research by its author, Dr Chuanhui Wang, and never regretted accepting that task. There are several reasons why this book is fascinating and could be of interest to many lawyers and scholars. First of all, it provides an excellent insight into the historical development of law, politics and practice concerning the legal status of land and property in land in China since 1949. It explains a lot for anyone interested in the history of China, but also for those interested in the development of law and politics concerning land in any contemporary society, given its interesting analysis of the different social forces that influence this development. Understanding this history is also necessary in order to understand which reforms or developments are likely to be possible or not, or may have success or not, in contemporary China. Second, the book confronts different constitutional models and practices concerning the protection of property – especially the American, Chinese and Indian models and to some extent the German one – and shows their strengths and weaknesses in a comparative analysis, remaining at the same time well aware of the different historical and socio-economic contexts of these models. The author does not limit his analysis – as is often the case – to the law as it is written; he examines the implementation and application of the law in concreto and the difficulties encountered in realising the constitutional principles. The book also develops rather detailed practical reform proposals for China that are at the same time sufficiently ambitious and sufficiently realistic. The author is thus able to make those proposals that may in practice make a real difference for the protection of property in China and many other countries confronted with similar questions. For all these reasons, the book and the author deserve a wide audience.

Professor Matthias E. Storme
Faculty of Law, KU Leuven

ACKNOWLEDGEMENTS

How to achieve your dream? Personal efforts and good luck are not enough. You must rely on others' instructions, assistance and support. When I reflect on the years spent conducting this research, I am grateful to many people for their kind and generous support and assistance. Without them, I am not sure I could have completed this work.

This book is from a doctoral thesis I completed at KU Leuven. To finish this work and receive a doctorate from KU Leuven has been a dream of mine. Why this topic? I am a scholar who has been driven by my research interest. Since before 2006, I have been shocked by a series of incidents and tragedies regarding the government's infringement on individual property in China. Thus, I was strongly motivated to analyse the constitutional protection of private property and to make this the focus of my doctoral thesis. In May 2006, I received an email from Professor Matthias E. Storme of KU Leuven in which he agreed to be my promotor (supervisor). Upon his suggestion, I finished and submitted my proposal, which, unfortunately, was not initially accepted by the doctoral committee. Under the instruction of and with encouragement from Professor Storme, I revised my proposal three times. At the committee meeting held on 22 January 2008, my proposal was accepted and I officially began my research at KU Leuven.

Professor Storme's support and encouragement continued. He afforded me the opportunity to conduct independent research while at the same time inspiring me to overcome difficulties I encountered during my research. Furthermore, he and his family were warm and welcoming during my time at Ghent, leaving me with many pleasant memories.

I am also sincerely grateful to other professors who have inspired or assisted me. Professor Geert van Calster, a member of my supervising committee, reminded me of the comparison between China and India, and there is no doubt that the addition of India's practice definitely enriches the value of my work. I thank Professor Boudewijn Bouckaert, also a member of my supervision committee, for his comments on China's reform issues and his suggestion regarding the holdout issue. These individuals, along with my supervisor, took the time to instruct me, to supervise my progress and to review my thesis for defence.

Sincere thanks are also offered to the members of my examination committee, Professors Andre J. van der Walt, Vincent Sagaert and Yuwen Li, for the time and effort they spent reviewing my thesis. Their feedback and the referred document challenged and inspired me to think deeper about my research, and thereby improved this text. In addition, Professor Sophia Stijns carefully answered my questions about doctoral training, while Professor Peggy Valcke kindly offered me an opportunity to join a competition policy conference in which I had a strong interest. She also offered me generous guidance in the completion of my doctoral training form. Professor Ching Lin Pang allowed me to join her international workshop, which benefitted my research. Professor Luodan Xu has encouraged me to move forward and her words have always warmed my heart.

I must also acknowledge my friends who have supported me throughout this endeavour. Dr Liyang Hou and his wife, Yingjie Li, cared for me when I stayed in Leuven. Dr Hou contributed greatly to the discussions regarding my research, the organisation of my seminars and the introduction of the doctoral training and defence procedure. Dr Yuemei Ji provided encouragement and inspiration. She and her husband, Paul, graciously served me a wonderful dinner in their home in Leuven. I thank Dr Yannan Ding for his workshop on village towns and Dr Haina Lu for her suggestion on my research. Their valuable friendship is one of the many things I gained during my study at KU Leuven. In addition, I thank Mr. Qingsong Zou for helping me to find valuable reference documents in Germany, and Dr Airong Li, an old friend I have known for more than twenty years, for sharing her valuable opinions on China's property law with me.

Special thanks are due to Joe Ng and Claire Wood, editors at Cambridge University Press. I must thank them for guiding and assisting me through the strict review process and the last stages of the revision and production of this book.

The final and most sincere acknowledgement is to my family. They have my love, and they have a warm home in my soul. They have been the sustainable power that has driven me to follow my dreams. A particular mention goes to my parents. Even though I did not become a government officer or a lawyer as they used to expect, they never stopped giving their selfless support and encouragement to me when I chased the life I think meaningful. I dedicate this book to them.

The completion of this work is the beginning of my new dream. I will keep enjoying the mysterious journey of academic research and contributing my creation as an independent researcher. Yes! Always on my mind and in my heart: Ontdek jezelf (discover yourself). Begin bij de wereld (start with the world).

ABBREVIATIONS

ADB	Asian Development Bank
CPC	Communist Party of China
CPI (M)	Communist Party of India (Maoist) (India)
CPPCC	People's Political Consultative Conference of China
C&R	Custody & Repatriation
EGoM	Empowered Group of Ministers (India)
EPZ	Export Processing Zones
FAO	Food and Agriculture Organisation of the United Nations
FCC	Federal Constitutional Court (Germany)
FDI	Foreign Direct Investment
GDP	Gross Domestic Product
HAC	Higher-stage Agricultural Cooperative
HRS	Household Responsibility System
JCER	Japan Centre for Economic Research
LAA	Land Acquisition Act (India)
LAC	Lower-stage Agricultural Cooperative
LAL	Land Administration Law (China)
LARR	Land Acquisition, Rehabilitation and Resettlement
LF	Left Front (India)
LUREA	Law on Urban Real Estate Administration (China)
MAT	Mutual-Aid Team
MLR	Ministry of Land and Resources (China)
NHA	National Highway Act (India)
NPC	National People's Congress (China)
NPCSC	Standing Committee of National People's Congress (China)
PDR	Persons in Charge of Demolition and Removal
RLCL	Rural Land Contracting Law (China)
RRSL	Regulation on Reforming Suburban Land (China)
SEZ	Special Economic Zone
SIA	Social Impact Assessment
SOE	State Owned Enterprises
SPC	Supreme People's Court (China)
TCP	Trinamool Congress Party (India)
UNRISD	United Nations – Research Institute of Social Development

CASES AND INCIDENTS

China

Couple Pan case in Shanghai (2008)
Gushi case in Henan (2004–8)
Jiahe incident in Hunan (2003)
Maiqili case in Shanghai (2005)
Nail House incident in Chongqing (2007)
Qi Yuling case in Shandong (2001)
Sun Zhigang case in Guangdong (2003)
Tang Fuzhen incident in Sichuan (2009)
Zhang Jian case in Liaoning (2008)

Germany

BVerfGE 100, 226 (*Denkmalschutz*, 1999)
BVerfGE 24, 367 (*Deichordnung*, 1968)
BVerfGE 50, 290 (*Codetermination*, 1979)
BVerfGE 52, 1 (*Small Garden Plot*, 1979)
BVerfGE 56, 249 (*Dürkheimer Gondelbahn*, 1981)
BVerfGE 58, 300 (*Naßauskiesung*, 1981)
BVerfGE 7, 198 (*Lüth*, 1958)
BVerfGE 74, 264 (*Boxberg*, 1987)
BVerfGE 89, 1 (*Landlord/Tenant*, 1993)

India

Charanjit Lal Chowdhury v. *The Union of India*, AIR (38) 1951 SC 41
Kameshwar Singb v. *Province of Bihar*, AIR 1951 Pat 246
Kesavanada Bharathi v. *State of Kerala*, AIR 1973 SC 1461
K. Posayya and Ors. v. *Special Tahsildar*, 1995 SC 1641
Krishi Utpadan Mandi Samiti v. *Malik Sartaj Wali Khan and Anr.*, 2001(10) SCC 660
Nandigram violence (2007)
Rustom Cavasjee Cooper v. *Union of India* (*Bank Nationalization Case*), 1970 SCR (3) 530

Singur incident (2006)
Special Land Acquisition, Davangere v. *P. Veerabhadarappa and Ors.*, 1984 (2) SCC 120
State of Gujarat v. *Shri Shantilal Mangaldas & Ors.*, 1969 (3) SCR 341
State of Madras v. *Namasivaya Mudaliar*, 1964 (6) SCR 35
State of West Bengal v. *Mrs Bella Benerjee*, 1954 SCR 558
Vajravelu Mudaliar v. *Special Deputy Collector, Madras & Anr.*, 1965 SCR (1) 614
W. B. v. *Subodh Gopal*, 1954 SCR 587

Ireland

Educational Co. Ltd. v. *Fitzpatrick* (No 2) [1961] IR 345
Meskell v. *CIE* [1973] IR 121

United States

Agins v. *City of Tiburon*, 447 U.S. 255 (1980)
Berman v. *Parker*, 348 U.S. 26 (1954)
Block v. *Hirsh*, 256 U.S. 135 (1921)
Buck v. *Bell*, 274 U.S. 200 (1927)
Cafeteria Workers v. *McElroy*, 367 U.S. 886 (1961)
Catlin v. *United States*, 324 U.S. 229 (1945)
Cherokee Nation v. *Southern Kansas Ry. Co.*, 135 U.S. 641, 658 (1890)
Cohen v. *Beneficial Industrial Loan Corp.*, 337 U.S. 541 (1949)
County of Wayne v. *Hathcock*, 684 N. W. 2d 765 (Mich. 2004)
Dred Scott v. *Sandford*, 60 U.S. 393 (1856)
Gregory Marina, Inc. v. *Detroit*, 378 Mich. 364, 144 N.W.2d 503 (1966)
Hawaii Housing Authority v. *Midkiff*, 467 U.S. 229 (1984)
Jackman v. *Rosenbaum Co.*, 260 U.S. 22 (1922)
Kelo v. *City of New London*, 545 U.S. 469 (2005)
Keystone Bituminous Coal Association v. *DeBenedictis*, 480 U.S. 470 (1987)
Kimball Laundry Co. v. *United States*, 338 U.S. 1 (1949)
Lingle v. *Chevron*, 544 U.S. 528 (2005)
Lochner v. *New York*, 198 U.S. 45 (1905)
Logan v. *Zimmerman Brush Co.*, 455 U.S. 422 (1982)
L Vogeltein & Co. v. *U.S.*, 262 U.S. 337 (1923)
Marbury v. *Madison*, 5 U.S. 137 (1803)
Mathews v. *Eldridge*, 424 U.S. 319 (1976)
Missouri Pacific Ry. Co. v. *Nebraska*, 164 U.S. 403 (1896)
Monongahela Navigation Co. v. *United States*, 148 U.S. 312 (1893)
Morrissey v. *Brewer*, 408 U.S. 471, 481 (1972)
Mt Vernon-Woodberry Cotton Duck Company v. *Alabama Interstate Power*, 240 U.S. 30 (1916)

Mugler v. *Kansas*, 123 U.S. 623 (1887)
Olson v. *United States*, 292 U.S. 246 (1934)
Penn Central Transportation v. *New York City*, 438 U.S. 104 (1978)
Pennsylvania Coal Co. v. *Mahon*, 260 U.S. 393 (1922)
People ex rel. Detroit & Howell R. Co. v. *Salem Twp. Board*, 20 Mich. 452 (1870)
Planned Parenthood of Southeastern PA. v. *Casey*, 505 U.S. 833 (1992)
Poletown Neighborhood Council v. *City of Detroit*, 410 Mich. 616 (1981)
Rindge Co. v. *Los Angeles*, 262 U.S. 700 (1923)
Roe v. *Wade*, 410 U.S. 113 (1973)
Ryerson v. *Brown*, 35 Mich. 333 (1877)
Sadler v. *Langham*, 34 Ala. 311 (1859)
Scudder v. *Trenton Delaware Falls Co.*, 1 N. J. Eq. 694 (1832)
Skinner v. *Oklahoma*, 316 U.S. 535 (1942)
Sweet v. *Rechel*, 159 U.S. 380 (1895)
Thurlow v. *The Commonwealth of Massachusetts, etc.*, 46 U.S. 504 (1847)
Toyosaburo Korematsu v. *United States*, 323 U.S. 214 (1944)
United States v. *564.54 Acres of Land*, 441 U.S. 506 (1979)
United States v. *Carolene Products Co.*, 304 U.S. 144 (1938)
United States v. *James Daniel Good Real Property*, 510 U.S. 43 (1993)
Weeks v. *United States*, 232 U.S. 383 (1914)
West Coast Hotel Co. v. *Parrish*, 300 U.S. 379 (1937)
Western & Southern Life Ins. Co. v. *State Bd. of Equalization*, 451 U.S. 648 (1981)

1

Introduction

A man's house is his castle. This is the most famous expression used to describe the sanctity and inviolability of a person's property or home. It is commonly regarded as an important doctrine originating from and solidly rooted in the English common law system. It is generally traced to the expression of English Jurist Sir Edward Coke in his *The Institutes of the Laws of England* as early as 1671.[1] Following Coke, Blackstone emphasised the castle analogy by saying: 'For every man's house is looked upon by the law to be his castle of defence and asylum, wherein he should suffer no violence', and '[t]he law of England has so particular and tender a regard to the immunity of a man's house, that it stiles it his castle, and will never suffer it to be violated with impunity.'[2] In the United States, the castle metaphor is also regarded as 'the fabric of the Fourth Amendment' of the *U.S. Constitution*, which prohibits government from unreasonably seizing a citizen's property.[3] It is commented that the *Fourth Amendment* confers on individual owners a nearly absolute right over their property, particularly the right to preclude other individuals and the government from seizing it.[4] Although the original expression containing the absolute exclusion right has been eroded by increasing government power to regulate and seize property, the castle doctrine continues to demonstrate the importance of private property protection, which concerns both the security and dignity of property owners. The invasion of government power in a person's home is allowed under specific situations only and must be

[1] Coke's original complete expression is: 'For a man's house is his castle, et domus sua cuique tutissimum refugium [his home is his safest refuge].' See Coke, *The Third Part*, p. 162. In fact, this quotation's origin is found in an earlier time. For example, a similar expression can be found in William Lambarde's *Eirenarcha*, published in 1581. See Cuddihy and Hardy, 'A Man's House', 371. Moreover, in the *Pandects* (Roman Law Digest, 533 AD) can be found the saying, '[o]ne's home is the safest refuge for everyone'. See Green, 'Castles and Carjackers', 4 (fn16).

[2] Blackstone, *Commentaries*, at Book 3: chap. 19; Book 4: chap. 16.

[3] Hafetz, 'A Man's Home', 175. [4] Penalver, 'Property Metaphors', 2972.

subject to strict constitutional principles, legal rules and just procedures. In the case of *Weeks* v. *United States*, the U.S. Supreme Court ruled that '[r]esistance to these practices (searches and seizures) had established the principle which was enacted into the fundamental law in the 4th Amendment, that a man's house was his castle, and not to be invaded by any general authority to search and seize his goods and papers'. This ruling strengthened the constitutional castle value by citing Judge Cooley's words: 'The maxim that "every man's house is his castle" is made a part of our constitutional law in the clauses prohibiting unreasonable searches and seizures, and has always been looked upon as of high value to the citizen.'[5]

In China, a man's house has never been, nor is it now, his castle.[6] A man's house may become his castle in the future, but that day remains distant. By examining Communist China's experience over more than sixty years (from 1949 to now), we can trace a development route from the times of little recognition and protection of private property in the first thirty years after 1949 to the gradual strengthening and even constitutionalisation of private property protection in the second thirty years.

For China, given the country's transformation from planned economy to market economy, the protection of private property is one among several most important and arguable reform issues. Compared with her fast-developing economic growth, the pace of China in strengthening the protection of private property is criticised as unsatisfactory and even laggard. As Dorn points out, although China is the fastest-growing economy in the world, it still needs time to form 'a true market system with widespread private ownership and a political system that respects human rights'.[7] Dorn is correct in observing the mismatch between fast economic growth and slow individual-right-oriented political reform in China. According to Dorn, if the Communist Party government hinders the reform favouring private property, spontaneous market order, free expression and free association, 'the future of China's civil society will be in jeopardy'.[8] In the eyes of many Western scholars, privatisation and strong protection of private property are a premise for developing market economy and civilisation. The notion that private property is the

[5] *Weeks* v. *United States*, 232 U.S. 383, 390 (1914).

[6] In China, people ironically use 'China', the English name of their country, to denote the demolition activities (particularly of houses) concerning expropriation, because the English pronunciation of 'China' is similar to the Chinese pronunciation of 'demolition' (*chai*).

[7] Dorn, 'Trade and Human Right', 81. [8] Ibid., 83.

foundation of civilisation has been rooted in both the academic literature and the legal traditions in Western countries.[9] Private property, as a core component of the institutional framework that influences economic development, plays an important role in stimulating economic growth and efficiency. An empirical study that covers 115 market economies between 1960 and 1980 found that the politically open countries, which are subject to the institutional framework's binding features of private property, rule of law and market allocation of resources, have a growth rate of three times the rate enjoyed by those economies in which such property rights and freedoms are proscribed. As for the measurement of efficiency, politically open countries have 2.5 times that of those with opposite political institutions.[10] However, for China, a country governed by the Communist Party of China (CPC), strengthening private property protection is a politically sensitive issue. Unlike Russia's shock therapy, transitional reform in China has been gradual. Private property reform in China was addressed relatively late compared with other reform issues. China initiated its reform and opening policy in the late 1970s. However, legal reform encompassing fundamental changes in private property law was not instituted until 2004 when clauses were added to the constitution recognising the constitutional status of private property and limiting the government's eminent domain and expropriation powers.

It is difficult to fathom that China has experienced more than thirty years of rapid economic development within a legal framework ensuring the protection of private property which is weaker than that in developed countries. Why have foreign investors flooded into China in the past thirty years despite insufficient protection of their property? To a large extent, the rapid growth of foreign investment has been driven by many stimulating preference policies offered exclusively to overseas investors. However, with China's demand for foreign investment falling in recent years, the number of preference policies that act as motivational factors has been reduced since early 2000. For overseas investors, however, a stable, predictable and rational legal environment in host countries is becoming more important than preference policies. As for domestic citizens, after

[9] As Hagan observed, such a notion was seldom argued in the late eighteenth and nineteenth centuries in the United States. Hagan also pointed out that for the proponents of severalty in India, it is an accepted fact that private property is essential to civilisation. See Hagan, 'Private Property', 127.

[10] Scully, 'The Institutional Framework', 661.

many years of opening up to the outside world, they are demanding stronger protection of private property similarly to overseas investors. With reforms in the economic sector, the Chinese public's request to transform its orthodox communist society into a civil society with wide recognition and strict protection of private property and other individual liberties has quickened. In fact, a 'quiet revolution' towards civil society has been occurring, accompanied by the pace of economic reforms made since 1978.[11] Thus, in the mid-2000s, China began implementing constitutional reforms concerning private property in response to demands for social development. After the revision of the *Constitution* in 2004, the *Property Law* (*Wuquan Fa*) was promulgated in 2007,[12] and a new regulation concerning the expropriation of urban houses was enacted in 2011.

With the quickening pace of urbanisation and industrialisation, the expropriation and taking of land and houses by governments has increased rapidly in recent years. Violent conflicts between the owners of houses and land rights on the one hand and local governments on the other have increased, particularly in the past ten years. The increase in the government's powers of eminent domain leads to a significant and urgent research topic: learning how to restrain the Chinese government's eminent domain powers through the constitutional protection of citizens' private property. Or, more neutrally, learning how the constitutional balance between government power and individual property rights can transform China into a civil society.

I view society as a sea in which various superficial and embedded, inside and outside currents conflict and converge with each other to form the sea's flow. Thus, this book put the research within the historical background and social context to explain how the constitutional protection of private property in China has been evolving to the current situation, and then to answer where it would go on to move in the future. In this book, I have three main objectives. The first objective is to identify the driving social forces that influence the evolution of legal reform in China with respect to private property during the era of globalisation. The second objective is to analyse the main constitutional issues with respect to the protection of private property in China. The third objective is to design

[11] Dorn, 'Trade and Human Right', 77.

[12] *Wuquan Fa* [*Property Law*], enacted by the Fifth Session of the Tenth NPC on 16 March 2007 and put into force on 1 October 2007. The Chinese text is available at www.gov.cn/flfg/2007–03/19/content_554452.htm.

and suggest feasible reform measures for the revision of the constitution and the strengthening of the constitutional review mechanism.

To achieve the research objective, the following three questions are analysed:

1. What are the driving forces behind both globalisation and localisation that influence the evolution of private property protection in China?
2. How do public authorities and courts in China apply the constitutional principles and relevant rules concerning private property (three prongs) in cases regarding the taking of property?
3. What feasible and constructive reform measures can be implemented to improve China's private property protection through the application of the constitution?

Three research methods are used to address these three questions. Through historical analysis, the evolution of private property and its protection in China as well as the forces influencing such evolution are identified. More importantly, through a review, it is determined that the change in the policies of the CPC government has significant influence on both constitutional legislation and on its adjudication. When analysing the three prongs of the 'taking clause', a comparative method and case study are employed. I compare China with the United States, a representative common law country; with Germany, a representative continental law country; and with India, which, similar to China, is a leading developing country plagued by serious conflicts caused by land expropriation. Through these comparisons, while the discrepancies in both their constitutional stipulations and their applications are found, the experiences of these countries are helpful in identifying the problems within China's system and in offering inspiration for China's further reform. A case study is used to examine private property protection in its social context. An important aspect of my research is that it links relevant legislation and its application to social change and observes legal reform in action. By so doing, the complicated conflicts of interest among individuals, collectives, government and private developers can be identified. Accordingly, the attitudes and practices of public authorities and courts can be analysed. Furthermore, the application of the constitution and the type of institutional mechanism that should be incorporated to guarantee that the constitution is being effectively and appropriately applied are explored. Figure 1.1 exhibits the overall framework with respect to the research objectives, questions and methods in this book.

Method	Research question	Nature	Objective
Historical Method	What forces are driving the evolution of private property protection in China?	Exploratory	To identify the social context
	⇓		⇓
Comparative Method + Case Study	How and why do governments and courts in China address the constitutional issues concerning private property?	Explanatory	To identify the problems and their causes in the social context
	⇓		⇓
Institutional Analysis	How can China reform the constitutional review and adjudication system to improve private property protection?	Constructive	To design the institutional resolutions and evaluate their effect

Figure 1.1 Research Framework

After the introduction in this chapter and the outline of basic theories about and the constitutionalisation models of private property in Chapter 2, this book makes a historical review of the constitutional protection of private property in China first, especially linking China's evolution of the constitutional protection of private property with its path of immerging itself into globalisation to analyse the change in conflicting social forces that have been influencing the constitutionalisation of private property and relevant legislative reform. Then, after the detailed analysis on the three prongs of the taking clauses in the constitution –public interest, just compensation and procedural guarantee – I suggest some feasible and enforceable reform measures with the aim of strengthening the protection of private property, with a premise that such measures do not conflict with the current fundamental political system of Communist Party government.

Chapter 2 begins with the theoretical perspectives of property. The understanding of property from 'right' and 'relationship' perspectives is especially helpful in analysing China's property system, which is characterised by the division of public rights and private rights. Through the comparison of these two concepts (commons and anticommons), the tension between the justification of private property protection and the social function of property is identified and its resolution is reflected in the three-prong design in the constitution. Thus, the constitutionalisation is then analysed, and Germany and the United States are characterised as having a constitutionalisation model. Although China moved towards the constitutionalisation of private property after its opening and reform, compared with India, which removed the constitutional protection of private property in the late 1970s, it is still very weak with respect to the practical protection of private property. The research in this chapter is normative.

Chapter 3 traces the history of the tumultuous fate of private property in China's constitutions. After a short-term recognition of private ownership in the 1950s and prior to China's opening and reform, private ownership of land and other productive means was eliminated. Beginning in the late 1970s, private property rights began a slow revival. Finally, with the adoption of the *2004 Amendment*, the inviolable status of private property was entrenched in the *1982 Constitution of China*, and three limits on expropriation were fully established. However, individuals were still not allowed to have full ownership of the land they held; they were given only limited use and transaction rights. This then resulted in a 'public ownership–private use right' division of land. To explain this twisted structure and its evolutionary path, the relevant social forces are analysed, and globalisation and localisation form the context of the analysis. The social forces influencing the reform of property law in China are distinguished and analysed first from the perspective of globalisation and then from that of localisation. The interaction among the forces and their influence on Chinese property law reform are then illustrated. A popular understanding is that globalisation pushes forward the process of the rule of law in China. In fact, however, the real situation is more complicated as the social forces include pressure from the global society, the demands of the FDI investors, the reform behaviours of the CPC, the citizens' rights consciousness, the rent seeking of the developers and the expansion of fiscal revenue at the level of the local governments. The historical review of the change to the constitutional and legal status of private property in China reveals two facts. The first of these inspirations is that the globalisation process in China in the past more than thirty years has produced a stronger demand for a higher level of private property protection from both overseas investors and domestic citizens. The second fact is that the globalisation process strengthens the motivation of local governments to take private land right and houses. More accurately, the extent to which the constitution restricts eminent domain is decided by the change of the interaction between various social powers in the globalisation process. Moreover, these forces changed and will change during different stages of transitional development, thus resulting in the dynamic character of such interactive social forces. The analysis in this chapter is descriptive.

Chapters 4, 5 and 6, which are based on the preceding normative and positive research and apply comparative method and case study, respectively examine three prongs of the eminent domain or taking clause in the constitution, which are public interest, compensation and procedural restraint.

Chapter 4 opens with an analysis of the explanation of public interest, or a similar principle, in Germany and the United States. Through the division of eminent domain and other government powers, the mode of 'authorised by law' in Germany and that of 'statutory deference' in the United States are compared. In both countries, when explaining and applying the public interest doctrine, the proportionality principle is used in limiting the possible misuse of the power of eminent domain. However, in China, the doctrine of public interest has very little influence in practice and is instead merely symbolic of a constitutional doctrine. The focal issue regarding economic development as public interest is then analysed. By comparing China and India, it is determined that because of the ruthless scope of land expropriation caused by the weak limits of public interest, violent incidents and social unrest have plagued both countries. In turn, both countries responded by implementing reforms that restrained the scope of public interest. China, however, made minimal progress in clarifying the scope of public interest with respect to the expropriation of only urban houses. Moreover, such clarification did not exclude or substantially limit economic development projects. Through the analysis of the *Gushi* case, it is found that the enclosure movements driven by the motivation of economic growth and the enlargement of local revenue slowed the pace of reform in restraining the expansion of expropriation through the narrowing of the scope of public interest.

Chapter 5 examines the compensation issue. In Western countries, the market value based on the comparable sale price is the main compensation standard. However, in China, this standard currently applies only for the calculation of compensation of the expropriated urban houses. For the expropriation of rural land, this standard is not applicable for two reasons. One is that the lack of an effective transaction market of land and land rights results in it being impractical to apply such a standard. The second reason is that the local governments are motivated to lower rather than to raise compensation levels because of their need to enlarge local revenue through land expropriation. The recent reform with respect to the uniform land section price may result in insufficient compensation to those farmers who produce more output than the average in a specific area. In addition to inefficiency, the discrimination in the compensation standards between urban residents and farmers appears to violate the equal treatment doctrine in the constitution. To borrow from India's experience and consider China's reality, two feasible and exact reform measures – 'market value + going-up adjustment' for urban houses and 'minimum standard + solatium' for rural land – are suggested.

Chapter 6 reviews the U.S. due process doctrine and its application in eminent domain cases. The authorisation modes adopted by Germany and India are then analysed. It is found that, compared with the popular practice in the procedural guarantees of private property in democratic countries, even after China's reform in 2004, the expropriation procedures in China remain greatly flawed. This can be reflected in the lack of full information made available to property owners, the inefficient nature of hearing opportunities, the lack of opportunity to challenge the public nature of the concerned project and the lack of advance payment before compulsory occupation. With respect to the institutional mechanism for enforcing constitutional doctrines, China has adopted neither the U.S. nor the European mode, as the Chinese courts play essentially no role in applying the constitutional provisions when trying cases. Accordingly, the review mechanism under the Standing Committee of National People's Congress (NPCSC) is useless in correcting lower-level unconstitutional regulations and rules.

Chapter 7 ends the whole research with concluding remarks and reform suggestions. Considering the CPC political system, which is characterised by public property control and centralised governance power, I am not optimistic about the advocation of substantial privatisation of state-owned enterprises (SOEs) or about publicly and collectively owned lands and resources. In the end, some feasible and constructive suggestions are offered. As to the amendment to the constitution, it is suggested that it be revised. First, it must propertise land use rights; second, it must fundamentalise private property; third, it must ensure the equal treatment of all property rights; fourth, it must establish much clearer limits on compensation such that it be 'full' or 'just' compensation. Regarding the revision of legislation, a main improvement would be the authoritative explanation of public interest and compensation by the NPCSC. The most difficult reform is that of the institutional mechanism of constitutional review. As the total transplantation of the U.S. or European mode is nearly impossible in the near future, partial improvement is, at the very least, suggested. A specific review body under the auspices of the National People's Congress (NPC) can be established to be responsible for the constitutional review, and it should, upon any court's request, give timely response with respect to the constitutionality of the inquired legal rules. The Supreme People's Court (SPC) should be given the power to interpret, independently or with a joint review body, the constitution. The jurisdiction level of the court that hears expropriation cases should be raised to reduce the interference of the local governments.

2

Private property and its constitutionalisation

In this chapter, the basic theories about and the constitutionalisation models of private property are outlined. The old absolutist view of private property has switched to the modern relationship view, which is in essence relativist and is reflected by the governments' increasing power executed to regulate and even invade private property. The constitutionalisation of private property is aimed at restricting the government's threat and thus guarding the domain of private property.

2.1 The perspectives of property

It is difficult to define the term 'property' because its definition is varying and contradictory. Cribbet notes that the question of the definition of property is 'unanswerable' because the definition changes frequently with changes in time and space.[1] Property can be understood from several perspectives, and the complexity of explaining property is profound. However, this can facilitate the understanding of property from a systematic set of levels.

2.1.1 Understanding property: three levels

The starting point is to understand property as things or resources which are physical or intangible and owned or held by a human being. This is the most common and oldest understanding. In essence, it refers to the objects of property rights. Among academics, this physicalisation view of property was advocated by the great English jurist William Blackstone in the eighteenth century. He defined property as the thing in which rights are rooted.[2] As objects to be regulated by rules, the things are

[1] Cribbet, 'Concepts in Transition', 1.

[2] In Book 1 of his famous *Commentaries on the Laws of England*, Blackstone discusses the 'rights of persons' (*jura personarum*). In Book 2 about property, he discusses the 'rights of

classified into different categories to which different rules or laws are applied. The most popular classification in most countries results from distinguishing movable things from immovable things. Immovable things largely consist of land and the buildings on that land, which are always considered the most important or dominant type of property. In the past, particularly in feudal society, the control of land formed the basis of political sovereignty.[3] Land is also called 'real estate' to show its dominant status as the most valuable human asset. Correspondingly, movable things are called personal property. This book largely examines land and houses attached to land. It is also important to categorise property as things according to the capability of private ownership in the law: things that can be privately owned (*in commercium*) and things that cannot be privately owned (*extra commercium*).[4] In fact, this is the classification based on the nature of property and is particularly pertinent to the title of this book.

The second level entails understanding property as the right to things that are recognised and protected by the law. In the continental law system, ownership (full ownership) is distinguished from the limited property rights attributed to things.[5] In the Anglo-American system, which de-emphasises ownership, the law refers to property to rights, which may be attributed to things. Or, in other words, property as the right to things is anatomised to be a bundle of rights or a bundle of 'sticks'. The most important rights in the bundle include the right to possess, the right to use, the right to transfer and the right to exclude.[6] Rights concern the relationship among people. The ownership perspective of continental law observes the relationship between owners and other property rights holders, and the common law's bundle perspective focuses on the relationship among right holders without focusing on such holders' owner or non-owner identities.

The third level is to understand property as a regime or system design, or in terms of the intriguing relationships around property. This understanding regards rights as part of constitutional and other legal arrangements concerning property. It includes the public-private property

things' (*jura rerum*) or 'right of property'. See generally Blackstone, *Commentaries*, Book 1 and Book 2.

[3] Sprankling, *Understanding Property Law*, p. 8.

[4] Storme, 'Property Law', 5. [5] Ibid., 7.

[6] Sprankling, *Understanding Property Law*, p. 5. Cribbet says that the term 'bundle of sticks' is a traditional metaphor for property, which is liked most by property teachers. Cribbet also points out that the contents of such bundles have been changing with changes in time and space in society. See Cribbet, 'Concepts in Transition', 1.

division, the institutions of constitutional protection, civil law arrangement and enforcement procedures and review institutions. We may also regard all legal and institutional arrangements about property as a social system or regime. As for the constitutional arrangement of private property, Michelman comments that two possible senses – holding sense and regime sense – 'cannot in practice be held quite apart', and that 'every judicial intervention to protect an alleged lawful property holding must have an effect on what we understand to be the regime, in both an empirical and a normative sense'.[7] In economics, property as a regime can be analysed in terms of the efficient distribution of resources (things and their rights). The private property title can help an owner to exclude others. This exclusive nature of private property is used to avoid the problems of overexploitation and internal conflicts that may be caused by common property. With a privately owned title, owners can exchange one another in the market to make the allocation of resources or properties efficient. Based on historical and recent privatisation reforms in many countries, Kasper points out that all of these privatisation measures are for 'a more effective, less conflict-ridden way of allocating scarce goods'.[8] In fact, the analysis can be made more comprehensive by including political and social analysis. We may also regard the property regime as institutions supplied by the government to the public or as a component of a modern democratic system. Corresponding to this understanding, the theory of social contracts asserts that the government, as the agent of individuals, should protect its principals' private rights, including property rights.[9] However, the positive view is that the government grants private rights and offers protection by setting the relevant political and legal regime to gain individuals' support.[10]

[7] Michelman, 'Socio-Political Functions', p. 449. [8] Kasper, *Economic Freedom*, p. 60.

[9] Epstein, advocating Locke's natural law view, points out that property is a natural right. However, it is uncertain whether there is appropriate governmental protection and regulation. In civil society, people mutually authorise governments to regulate and preserve their property. Thus, '[t]he question of governance is how the natural rights over labour and property preserved in form and enhanced in value by the exercise of political power.' See Epstein, *Takings*, p. 3.

[10] Itai Sened criticises the views of Marxist and Neoclassical scholars that exclude governments from social order and regard society as having a more natural order. Rather, Sened regards governments as 'necessary players' from which the protection of private rights cannot depart. He uses the interaction – or, in economic terms, the supply and demand – between governments and individuals to explain the existence of political institutions of property rights and other private rights. The government, as a political entrepreneur, produces law and order for individuals, who actively petition the government to supply institutional protection of their rights. See Sened, *The Political Institution*, pp. 3–8.

2.1.2 *From Blackstone to Hohfeld: the evolution of property concepts*

The understanding of property changes as time passes. Although the long-term historical evolution of property concepts is complicated, a general path of change can be generalised to run from the physicalisation and the absoluteness view of property in the eighteenth century to the right and relationship view in the nineteenth century and later. To compare the old concept of property with the modern one, we can clearly observe this direction.

In his *Commentaries*, Blackstone imbues 'property' with the concept that was popularly accepted in the common law system in the eighteenth century:

> There is nothing which so generally strikes the imagination, and engages the affections of mankind, as the right of property; or that sole and despotic dominion which one man claims and exercises over the external things of the world, in total exclusion of the right of any other individual in the universe.[11]

Judging from this paragraph, Blackstone defines property as the 'external things' for which owners have the right to 'in total exclusion' of others. First, the weight of defining property is put on the side of 'things'. This can be called the physicalisation view of property. Second, this definition establishes the absolute rights of property owners to the exclusion of others. This is the absoluteness view.

Entering the eighteenth century, the physical premise for property defined by Blackstone was broken by the courts' practice. Property rights were extended from rights over things to rights over any valuable interests even if no physical things exist – for example, goodwill.[12] With the removal of such an indispensable requirement for things, the concept of property swiftly began to focus on things instead of on rights over things or on other non-physical values.

The second change in the concept of property is relationship-oriented. It was achieved through the limits imposed on property and is defined as a nearly absolute right to exclude others or as any limit, including limits on community interest.[13] The switch to focusing on the rights

[11] Blackstone, *Commentaries*, Book 2: chap. 1.

[12] This movement is generalised as 'Dephysicalization of Property' by Vandevelde. See Vandevelde, 'The New Property', 333–5.

[13] Ibid., 332. Blackstone listed three absolute rights: life, liberty and property. See Blackstone, *Commentaries*, Book 1: chap. 1.

or values of property finally led scholars to consider the new relationship perspective of property. In essence, Blackstone's absolutist definition also refers to relationship, but the one between property owners and the things owned. Furthermore, in this relationship, property owners have a 'sole and despotic dominion' or a kind of absolute power over their properties.[14] However, the new 'relationship' view of property refers to the relationship between people or between property owners and others.

In 1913, Hohfeld proposed a new scheme for outlining the term 'property'. He criticised the ambiguity and inaccuracy of the traditional use of the term 'property' by saying:

> Both with lawyers and with laymen this term has no definite or stable connotation. Sometimes it is employed to indicate the physical object to which various legal rights, privileges, etc., relate; then again-with far greater discrimination and accuracy-the word is used to denote the legal interest (or aggregate of legal relations) appertaining to such physical object. Frequently there is a rapid and fallacious shift from the one meaning to the other.[15]

Hohfeld suggested that the legal concept of terminology be distinguished from the non-legal, physical and mental concepts. Hohfeld used the term 'legal relation', which accommodates the rights or legal interests that carry legal significance rather than physical or mental things, which do not embody a truly legal concept, to formulate the legal concept.[16]

The switch from Blackstone's physicalist and absolutist view to the modern relationship view concerning the concept of property is influenced greatly by the occurrence of new properties, which are defined as valuable rights that may not concern things.[17] The new relationship perspective of property is designed by legal commentators to include such new properties into the realm of property.[18] This new concept of property is apparently meant to loosen the strict limits of physicalisation and the absoluteness of property set by Blackstone.

[14] Blackstone, Book 2: chap. 1.

[15] Hohfeld, 'Some Fundamental Legal Conceptions', 21–2.

[16] He used four jural opposites and four jural correlatives to accommodate various relations. Such jural opposites include: rights/non-rights; privilege/duty; power/disability; immunity/liability. The jural correlatives include: right/duty; privilege/non-right; power/liability; immunity/disability. Ibid., 30.

[17] Vandevelde, 'The New Property', 357–8.

[18] Ibid., 359.

2.1.3 *Application to this book*

This book mainly focuses on land and houses and their attendant rights. Property law is concerned with relationships between individuals and between individuals and the community. In the former relationship, civil law governs. In the latter relationship, however, constitutional law governs, which is the research focus of this book. Land, as the most valuable and scarcest type of property, usually creates tension between individual interest and community welfare.[19] For China, a country with a large population, land is the scarcest resource, and the fierce interest conflict between individuals and governments is reflected in a series of recent violent incidents. In China, houses are emphasised as property, and they are considered more important than empty land because individuals cannot currently own land. However, although citizens can own houses in urban areas, they are given only limited land use rights for the land on which those houses are built. Thus, the governments' expropriation of urban houses mainly targets the ownership of houses. When the word 'property' as it relates to land is used, both the ownership and bundle perspectives can be combined to better understand China's land property system. In China, the dichotomy between land ownership and land property right exists. For urban land, the state holds ownership, and citizens can hold some land rights, such as use rights and limited transaction rights. The ownership of rural land largely goes to collectives, and individual farmers can hold a limited scope of land rights, which include cultivation, interest collection and leasing. This leads us to further clarify the targets of government expropriation in the context of China. Unlike expropriation, which targets the ownership of land in countries with private property as the most popular landed property system, in China, expropriation targets some land rights, which are privately held by individuals. Moreover, expropriation targets the collective ownership of land that, although not private property in a strict sense, is linked with collective members' (farmers') individual property rights. Thus, referring to land as 'private property' also refers to the limited scope or bundle of land rights that can be enjoyed by individuals. The public-private division of property as a social system is particularly significant to research on China's property system. As a country transitioning from a socialist public property system

[19] For abundant resources, the corresponding laws in governing their allocation are simple and stable. For scarce resources such as land, however, the related property laws are complicated and easily changeable. See Cribbet, 'Concepts in Transition', 3.

to a system comprised of both public and private property, the relationship between public and private property is a leading issue identified by the constitution, which greatly influences the status and protection of private property in constitutional institutions.

2.2 Private property and its justifications

2.2.1 Common property, private property and public property

From the perspective of ownership or holding qualification, we observe three types of property: common property, private property and public property.

Common property is open to everyone in society. It is both everybody's property and nobody's property. This is the popularly used definition of common property in the literature. However, there is a definition of common property in a narrower sense, which refers to 'a distribution of property rights in resources in which a number of co-owners are co-equal in their rights to use the resource'.[20] In essence, this narrowly defined concept is about the membership right to use the resource that is collectively owned by a collective, such as a tribe or village. Such collectively controlled property can be regarded as 'collective property', which is a limited form of common property or an early limit on the access to common property.

Private property is conferred to individuals for their personal holding. Public property, as the opposite extreme of private property, means that the state owns or holds property rights. Unlike common property, public property is not necessarily open to everyone but is controlled by the agents representing the state or all people in the state.

In ancient societies, common property was the main form of property. It has been stated that common property exists in the early stages of economic development.[21] Currently, in many developing countries, particularly in the least developed countries, common property or the limited collective form common property popularly exists as an important institution governing individual use rights to natural resources. A similar situation can also be found in the early stages of economic development in European countries. Runge pointed out that 'the common property typical of early Western Europe' lasted at least 1,000 years and

[20] Ciriacy-Wantrup and Bishop, 'Common Property', 714.
[21] Ibid., 717.

declined with the rise of the enclosure movement in the fifteenth and sixteenth centuries.[22]

Socialist countries are the representatives of a public property regime, and in capitalist countries, private property is the foundation of the social property system. It is difficult to identify a country that has only a pure, single form of property. Nearly all countries have a mixture of the three types of property. An important task for modern countries is to arrange for a common-public-private division of property in which the most important part is the public-private division. It seems that socialist countries render public property as the dominant type of property and private property as the supplementary type. However, a reverse arrangement is made in capitalist countries.

2.2.2 *The tragedy of the commons*

Private property, compared with common property, is regarded as being a more efficient arrangement of property rights. In his classic article 'The Tragedy of the Commons', Hardin uses an example of a pasture publicly accessed by herders, namely a common property, to illustrate a negative result called 'the tragedy of the commons'.[23] Because each herder who is driven by interest maximisation and cost minimisation enlarges his own herd instead of growing grass and cultivating land, the pasture is depleted. Although this article is written from an ecologist's perspective, Hardin offers a persuasive example, using a modern efficiency argument, advocating private property. Suppose that such a pasture is privately owned by one or more persons. The owners would cultivate and use the pasture in its most efficient way, a sort of long-term use and cultivation that is more efficient than that of common property. The waste result of commons can also be found in the 'first occupancy' situation. In fact, common property is the starting point that leads to private ownership of the first occupier. The 'first occupancy' principle is the traditional common law theory used to decide the ownership or right-holding qualification, namely that an un-owned natural resource (common resource) can be owned by the first occupier. The most representative illustration of first occupancy theory is from William Blackstone. Blackstone argues that natural resources are a gift given to human being by God and thus, 'by the law of nature and reason, he who first began to use it [un-owned resource], acquired therein a kind of transient property, that lasted so long as he was using it, and no

[22] Runge, 'Common Property', 623. [23] Hardin, 'The Tragedy', 1243–8.

longer'.[24] This theory is more persuasive in explaining how private property originates and evolves than in illustrating the justification of private ownership.[25] One strong criticism of this theory is that it could lead to the waste or overuse of natural resources, which is similar to the type of waste found in the tragedy of the commons. To take fishing as an example, each fisherman who is motivated by the principle of first occupancy fishes as much as possible. Such overfishing leads to the exhaustion of fishing resource and to serious environmental destruction.

Hardin's example should not lead to a conclusion that private property should be the only property ownership attribution. Common land is both everyone's land and no one's land and thus represents inefficient land use. To control and manage land, public property or ownership is an alternative option to private ownership.

2.2.3 *The tragedy of the anticommons*

According to Coase, within a world with zero transaction costs, any property form is efficient.[26] Even for common property, herders can achieve an efficient arrangement on the use of pasture if the transaction costs of negotiating and contracting are zero. However, in the 'real world' where positive transaction costs exist, private property is regarded by many economists as a more efficient property arrangement than public property because private property is more efficient in reducing transaction costs than is public property. The major portion of the transaction costs concerning public property is the cost of the agent. Public property with

[24] Blackstone, *Commentaries*, Book 2: chap. 1.

[25] In addition to the first occupancy doctrine, there are two main traditional theories explaining the origin or the acquirement of ownership to things. One is John Locke's labour or labour-desert theory that asserts that one person's addition or contribution of labour qualifies him to acquire property ownership. Another theory is consent theory in which an owner acquires ownership based on the consent of others in society. See Rose, 'Possession', 73–4.

[26] The dominant and popular new institutional economics has been developed on the basis of Coase's illustration of property rights and transaction costs. The famous Coase Theorem tells us the significance of clear definition, allocation and protection of property rights for the optimal use of resources. See generally Coase, 'The Nature', 386–405; Coase, 'The Federal Communications Commission'; Coase, 'The Problem'. Demsetz further points out that property rights are defined to lower the transaction cost. See generally Demsetz, 'The Exchange'; Demsetz, 'Towards a Theory'. Although the Coase Theorem has been revised, supplemented and developed by many new institutional economists, the core value of property rights in modern institutional analysis still holds. See generally Alchian, 'Some Economics'; Williamson, *Markets*; North, 'The New Institutional Economics'.

the state acting as the owner must be controlled and used by agents, who are governments and their officials. The costs of operating and supervising the agents are high on both the operation side and the control of moral hazard side. However, transaction costs can be used to advocate for a public property regime. The most typical example is the holdout problem in land use or the tragedy of the anticommons. Heller used several empty stores in former communist Eastern European countries to conclude that it is nearly impossible for renters or buyers of store space to negotiate successfully because there are too many owners of the store space. Although market demand for the stores was high, many stores were empty and losing money. This phenomenon inspired Heller to generalise the cooperative failure of multi-owners or multi-rights-holders using the term 'the tragedy of the anticommons', mirroring Hardin's 'the tragedy of the commons'.[27]

The holdout problem in land use, which reflects the tragedy of the anticommons, offers a strong argument for the power of eminent domain used by governments,[28] an issue linked closely to this book. The state must build airports, roads, railroads and other infrastructural facilities on a large scale on land that may be owned by several owners. Suppose that the government must negotiate with every owner to purchase land. Even if most owners agree to sell their parcels for construction, just one dissenting owner, referred to as a 'holdout owner', can cause the collective use of all land to fail. The existence of holdout problems results in high transaction costs for this type of land use projects. The corresponding solution for reducing such transaction costs is eminent domain, compulsory taking by government or expropriation.[29]

If we extend government power to force collective or cooperative activity in land use to an extreme situation, the result would be the birth of socialist society with public property as a dominant property

[27] Heller, 'The Tragedy'.

[28] The origin of the term 'eminent domain' can be found in Grotius's academic work, *De Jure Belli Et Pacis* [The Law of War and Peace], which was completed in the sixteenth century. In the English precedents, such power was exercised in two ways: one was the king's use of private property (rather than the taking of property ownership) without compensation for public affairs, such as national defence. The other way was Parliament's taking of private property with compensation paid. See Berger, 'The Public Purpose', 204.

[29] In referring to the state's compulsory taking or seizure of a citizen's private property for the public interest in exchange for compensation, different terms used in different countries. Such terms include 'eminent domain' (U.S.), 'compulsory acquisition' (India/Australia), 'compulsory purchase' (UK/New Zealand) and 'expropriation' (Germany).

form. The justification of eminent domain power in resolving holdout problems or other government intervention power is illustrated and limited by the theory of public goods in economics.[30] Government intervention cannot be used except to resolve market failure problems, one of which is public goods. Consider infrastructure construction, which is a public good that the public needs. However, infrastructure construction cannot be supplied through efficient market operations owing to holdout problems because private builders in the market find it difficult to negotiate with many owners, including holdout owners. As a result, the state uses compulsory power to take the necessary land from those disagreeing individuals for the production of public goods.

The efficiency standard in economics implies an inspiration and even a danger of restricting private property. Although private property is more efficient than public property in most situations except the limited scope of market failure situations, public property can enlarge its domain in the name of increasing efficiency.[31] However, private property can be justified by factors other than economic efficiency.[32]

30 Paul A. Samuelson proposed the theory of public goods in 1954. He defined 'public goods' as those 'collective consumption goods . . . which all enjoy in common in the sense that each individual's consumption of such a good leads to no subtraction from any other individual's consumption of that good'. See Samuelson, 'The Pure Theory', 387. The fundamental characteristic of public goods is their non-rivalry, which can also be called jointness in consumption. Another property of public goods is their non-excludability, which means that to keep individuals from consuming public goods is difficult after the goods are produced. See Holcombe, 'A Theory', 2.

31 A dominant argument is that a secure and stable system of property rights plays a key role in facilitating economic growth and improving welfare. See generally Norton, 'Poverty'. Research focusing on transitional economies, including China, concludes that the first prerequisite for economic development is the creation and protection of private property rights. See generally Clague (ed.), *Institutions*; Rodrik, 'Trade Policy'. However, Stiglitz denies the prerequisite significance of property rights reform in transitional economies and thinks that competition is much more important than privatisation. See generally Stiglitz, *Whither Socialism*.

32 Even for the practical consideration of efficiency or growth, the strengthened protection of private property through the constitution has its significance in facilitating economic development. Sunstein illustrated the relationship between the strong protection of property rights and economic development. He asserts: 'Firm constitutional protection of property rights, combined with an independent judiciary, is an excellent way of encouraging international investment in one's nation. Such devices should spur domestic investment and initiative as well. Without constitutional protection, there will be a serious obstacle to the necessary economic activity from international and domestic enterprises.' See Sunstein, 'On Property', 907–8.

2.2.4 *The justifications of private property: beyond efficiency*

The law of nature perspective espoused by Locke deems private property to be a natural right that 'stands as an Eternal Rule to all Men, legislators as well as others'.[33] Private property, life and liberty are the natural rights with which people are born. As a natural right, private property cannot be legally taken away. The government is created to secure peoples' natural law rights only. Legal positivism, represented by Bentham, regards private property as a right created in the law or through government. As Bentham commented, 'property and law are born together, and die together'.[34] According to Bentham, there is no property before the law.[35] Legal positivism regards property as the creation of positive laws rather than of natural law, which contradicts the natural law perspective. In essence, legal positivism strengthens the importance of country legislation and government enforcement activities in the protection of property. Natural law and legal positivism can be linked together to form an important argument about private property: property is fundamental to humans because it is a natural right and forms the basis of peoples' survival. However, property is nothing without the government's strong protection through justifiable legislation and effective enforcement.

'Survival' is the starting point for understanding the natural law characteristics of private property rights. 'Survival' strongly implies that property is necessary to peoples' survival in both nature and society. However, this argument alone does not justify private property because in communist countries where private property is rare, survival may be satisfied by the government's distribution plan. One more argument supporting private property stems from labour-desert theory, in which one person is entitled to purchasing the objects produced by his labour. This has an implication of fairness.[36]

Compared with fairness and survival, security and freedom are more powerful in justifying private property. With the private occupancy of property, owners can remove themselves from dependence on others or the government and thus be secure, independent and free. As the U.S. Supreme Court Justice Felix Frankfurter commented, 'the free range of the human spirit becomes shrivelled and constrained under economic

[33] Locke, *Two Treatises*, p. 163. [34] Bentham, *The Theory*, p. 69.

[35] Bentham asserts that '[b]efore laws were made there was no property; take away laws, and property ceases'. Ibid.

[36] Siegan, *Property*, p. 10.

dependence'.[37] Among all property, real estate is the most important because it can help people to realise and guarantee their freedom. First, private property renders humans less dependent on the market. One person can satisfy his need through self-production or market exchange. Private property allows its owner to have things to exchange with others. More importantly, private property induces its owner to retain the opportunity to retreat from the market at any time when he finds that he is under unfair exchange conditions or is exploited by monopolies. In other words, a private owner may produce things himself or exchange things through market, or both, to satisfy his needs.[38] For the socialist countries where most productive materials are owned by the state and both supply and demand are arranged for based on plan or command rather than in the market, individuals rely on commanders to survive, and they have neither private production nor market exchange. As a result, human liberty is seriously limited. As Buchanan commented, this type of socialist property arrangement is the fatal conceit mentioned by Hayek, which is caused by economists' overemphasis on efficiency and disregard for liberty.[39] Second, private property and the market exchange derived from the exchange of private property can help individuals to reduce their reliance on the state or government. Where the range of public property controlled by the state is enlarged, the scope of private property shrinks. Where the government's regulation and police power increases, private property rights decrease. The government has potential interest conflicts with private property owners. However, private owners must rely on the government to protect and realise their property rights. How do we restrict the government's threat to private property while facilitating its protection of private property? The constitutionalisation of private property and its corresponding enforcement mechanism should be a main approach.

2.3 Constitutionalising property or not: theoretical analysis

Should property be stipulated as a constitutional right and enjoy legal protection on the constitutional level? The answers to this question and corresponding practice in different countries are numerous.

[37] Frankfurter, *Mr. Justice Holmes*, p. 74. [38] Buchanan, 'Property', pp. 27–31 (chap. 1).
[39] Ibid., pp. 47–8. For the illustration of the concept of 'fatal conceit', see generally Hayek, *The Fatal Conceit.*

The leading argument for the constitutionalisation of private property is security. Securing private property in the constitution, the highest level of the law, helps to maintain the security of private owners in stably possessing, using and dealing with their properties. Even though this is a more practical consideration, it does not answer a premise question: Why is private property important enough to warrant constitutional protection? The main supporting theories can be found in the natural law perspective described in the previous section. Private property is considered a natural right and thus a fundamental or basic right for the human being. In more detail, property, along with other natural rights, including life and liberty, is given by nature or God to one person. John Locke strengthened the natural law nature of property and other natural rights by saying: 'The state of nature has a law of nature to govern it which obliges every one; and reason, which is that law, teaches all mankind who will but consult it that, being all equal and independent, no one ought to harm another in his life, health, liberty, or possessions.'[40] In other words, without these basic rights, how can a person be a surviving and independent person with dignity and freedom?[41] However, the mechanism through which property rights can be practically protected in a country must be examined. According to legal positivism, strong protection is necessary to endow people with practical property rights. Thus, the necessity of constitutional protection as the highest level enters the discussion. Private property protection precludes private owners from infringing on their property rights of others or the government. Civil law, particularly the law of obligations, serves mainly to protect private owners from the infringement by other private bodies; but to counteract the harm of government or public power, constitutional protection is necessary because it is the most effective means for taming unfettered government power.

However, arguments against the constitutionalisation of private property can also be derived from the previously mentioned two sides that support constitutionalisation: the value of property and the relationship between private owners and the government. First, it can be argued that property is second to other fundamental rights or values; therefore, it should not deserve a status equal to that enjoyed by other fundamental rights in the constitution. Thus, private property should not be considered as aligned with life, liberty, equity and other basic values in a constitution.

[40] Locke, *Two Treatises*, p. 107.

[41] Natural right is, as Gibbard commented, 'a right one has independently of institutional arrangements'. See Gibbard, 'Natural Property Rights', 77.

As Nedelsky illustrated, 'property should be held accountable to equality, not vice versa'.[42] Moreover, a role of government is protecting property to make it a tangible right and to regulate and operate a society, which is composed of individuals, to achieve common welfare. The constitutional protection of property as the strictest restraint of government may hinder the effective use of the government's public power for the benefit of the whole society and the individuals in the society. The constitutionalisation of property does not normally affect the current distribution of property; in other words, it does not question the possible injustice of acquiring or distributing property, which may happen before the property comes into existence. For countries that need more government-initiated legal reforms to combat social injustice, the constitutional protection of property may be an obstacle. This view is closely linked to the first one, which regards property as an approach to guarding and achieving the constitution's higher values. Thus, the government is given more power to interfere in private property issues.[43]

Although various theories exist, it is reasonable to say that the previously mentioned theories should be cited and used in practice depending on different situations and periods in different countries. It is more appropriate to say that the constitutionalisation of private property is a dynamic process, particularly in those developing or transitional countries that are still adjusting their property systems. Even in developed countries with more stable property systems, from a historical viewpoint, we may find both models of constitutionalisation and unconstitutionalisation. Additionally, we may find in a country constitutionalising property in some periods and not in other periods or partial or limited constitutionalisation in one period but less limited constitutionalisation in other periods. If we regard property as a regime that allocates resources, we can find that the evolution of the constitutional framework of property is always linked to the dynamic political-social-economic complex, which is created by various social forces. In the following section, I analyse the experiences of the constitutionalisation or the unconstitutionalisation of private property in the United States, Germany, Canada and India. Even though the United States uses a common law system and Germany uses a continental law system, both countries have constitutionalised private property. Canada has refused to constitutionalise private property despite being a developed country. Additionally, like the United States, Canada's legal system has been influenced by its former coloniser, the United Kingdom. Like

[42] Nedelsky, 'Should Property', p. 425.

[43] Ibid., p. 423.

China, India is a major developing economy. It is facing an issue similar to that faced by China of contradiction between private property protection and economic growth. After its independence, India constitutionalised private property but later removed the private property clauses from its constitution.

2.4 Constitutionalising property or not: country practice

2.4.1 Germany: constitutionalising private property as a basic right

Germany can function as a model country for treating property as an independent, constitutional right. Germany's currently enforced constitution, the *Basic Law for the Federal Republic of Germany* (*Grundgesetz*, '*German Basic Law*'), which was enacted in 1949, refers to property as a 'basic right'.[44] However, the *Weimar Constitution* (1919–1933) that preceded the *German Basic Law* did not admit property as a citizen's basic right. Instead, the *Weimar Constitution* dealt with private property in a section titled 'The Economy', declaring that '[l]aws determine its content and limitation'.[45] This strongly implies that property is a right set by the laws of constitution rather than a basic constitutional right.

Leaving the change of the location of property in the structure of the constitution aside, the content of the property clauses in the *Weimar Constitution* and the *German Basic Law* are similar. They both focus

[44] Other basic rights include dignity; personal freedom; equality; freedom of faith, conscience and creed; freedom of expression; marriage and the family; the rights of children born outside of wedlock; education, freedom of assembly, freedom of association, privacy of correspondence, posts and telecommunications; freedom of movement; occupational freedom; inviolability of the home; citizenship; the right of asylum; and the right of petition. See *German Basic Law*, Part I. An English version of the *German Basic Law* is available at www.iuscomp.org/gla/statutes/GG.htm. This translation was done by Christian Tomuschat and David P. Currie and revised by Christian Tomuschat and Donald P. Kommers in cooperation with the Language Service of the German Bundestag.

[45] Article 153 of *Weimar Constitution* stipulates that:

> Property is guaranteed by the constitution. Laws determine its content and limitation.
> Expropriation may only be decreed based on valid laws and for the purpose of public welfare. It has to be executed with appropriate compensation, unless specified otherwise by Reich law. Regarding the amount of the compensation, the course of law at general courts has to be kept open in case of a controversy, unless Reich laws specify otherwise.
> Expropriations by the Reich at the expense of the states, communities or charitable organizations may only be executed if accompanied by appropriate compensation.
> Property obliges. Its use shall simultaneously be service for the common best.

The English version of *Weimar Constitution* is available at www.zum.de/psm/weimar/weimar_vve.php.

on a stipulation concerning expropriation. First, private property rights are guaranteed by the constitution, and the content and limitation of property are determined by law. Second, the legislature is obliged by the 'public good' (*German Basic Law*)[46] or the 'common best' (*Weimar Constitution*).[47] Government expropriation can be executed for the public good (*German Basic Law*) or the public welfare (*Weimar Constitution*). Third, compensation must be given to the person whose property is expropriated. The *Weimar Constitution* required an appropriate amount of compensation and the *German Basic Law* says that, 'such compensation shall be determined by establishing an equitable balance between the public interest and the interests of those affected'.[48]

In addition to the categorisation of property as basic rights, the *German Basic Law* uses positive and affirmative expressions to provide the constitutional guarantee of private property. Its art. 14(1) provides that '[p]roperty and the right of inheritance shall be guaranteed'. To combine this expression with the location of property in the constitution, we can conclude that private property is officially recognised as a basic right that is guaranteed by the constitution. This conclusion is reaffirmed by the Federal Constitutional Court (FCC). In its rulings, the FCC strengthened the status of property as 'an elementary basic right' which shall be guaranteed by the constitutional provisions as legal institution.[49]

The German constitution strengthens the social duties related to property and other basic rights. In the section titled 'Basic Right', the rights, obligations and limits of basic rights are included.[50] In art. 14, which contains the property clause, the *German Basic Law* declares that '[p]roperty entails obligations' and '[i]ts use shall also serve the public good'. The *German Basic Law* also stipulates in art. 15 that to achieve socialisation, land, natural resources and the means of production can be transferred to public ownership or other forms of public control.[51]

[46] *German Basic Law*, art. 14(2)(3).

[47] *Weimar Constitution*, art. 153.

[48] *German Basic Law*, art. 14(3).

[49] The related cases include BVerfGE 50, 290 (*Codetermination*, 1979) and BVerfGE 24, 367 (*Deichordnung* or *Hamburg Flood Control*, 1968). See Alexander, 'Property', 737.

[50] *German Basic Law*, art. 17 'Restriction of certain basic rights by laws respecting defense and alternative service', art. 18 'Forfeiture of basic rights' and art. 19 'Restriction of basic rights'.

[51] The art. 15 of *German Basic Law* stipulates: 'Land, natural resources, and means of production may for the purpose of socialization be transferred to public ownership or other forms of public enterprise by a law that determines the nature and extent of compensation. With respect to such compensation the third and fourth sentences of paragraph (3) of Article 14 shall apply mutatis mutandis.'

In Italy, another continental law country, the property clause has a structure similar to that of the *German Basic Law*. Italy's constitution (The *Constitution of the Italian Republic*) includes property in Part I, 'Rights and Duties of Citizens'; but the Italian constitution further divides citizens' rights and duties into four categories: 'civil rights', 'ethical and social relations', 'economic relations' and 'political rights'. Property is included under the category of 'economic relations' with a description of both public and private ownership.[52]

The integration of rights and duties in the same section of the constitution shows that in the *German Basic Law*, property has two functions: individual significance and social function. On the one hand, the constitution recognises the fundamental value of property to individuals and awards protection on the constitutional level. On the other hand, the constitution emphasises the social obligation of property. This integration reflects the efforts of the framers of the *German Basic Law* to harmonise two inherently conflicting state models: the rule-of-law state (*Rechtsstaat*) and the social welfare state (*Sozialstaat*).[53] *Rechtsstaat* advocates individual liberty and is thus politically liberal. *Sozialstaat* focuses more on the realisation of socio-economic justice by limiting individual rights. In post–World War II Germany, ideas called 'ordoliberalism' became popular, advocating the development of a 'properly ordered society', 'one in which a market economy, individual freedom, and social and economic justice existed together in harmony'.[54] Such a market economy incorporating social order is also called a 'social market economy', which should be developed, according to ordoliberals, through laws, with the

[52] Article 42 (Socialisation) of Italian constitution stipulates:

(1) Property is public or private. Economic goods may belong to the state, to public bodies, or to private persons.
(2) Private ownership is recognized and guaranteed by laws determining the manner of acquisition and enjoyment and its limits, in order to ensure its social function and to make it accessible to all.
(3) Private property, in cases determined by law and with compensation, may be expropriated for reasons of common interest.
(4) The law establishes the rules of legitimate and testamentary succession and its limits and the state's right to the heritage.

Article 43 (Expropriation) of Italian constitution stipulates: 'To the end of the general good, the law may reserve establishment or transfer, by expropriation with compensation, to the state, public bodies, or workers or consumer communities, specific enterprises or categories of enterprises of primary common interest for essential public services or energy sources, or act as monopolies in the preeminate public interest.' The English version of the *Constitution of the Italian Republic* is available at www.servat.unibe.ch/icl/it00000_.html.

[53] Alexander, *The Global Debate*, p. 104. [54] Ibid., p. 109.

constitution as the most prominent of those laws.[55] Clearly, the popularity of ordoliberalism greatly influenced the drafting of the *German Basic Law*.

Thus, to understand the 'property' guaranteed by the *German Basic Law*, four perspectives are particularly important: 'purpose', 'context', 'interest' and 'dualism'. First, whether some property can receive constitutional protection is based on its value to its holder. The German constitution does not weigh all property equally. Only those properties that can help to sustain individuals' self-development or achieve the purpose of the constitutional property clause can be protected by the *German Basic Law*. Those properties that do not achieve the constitutional purpose are protected by inferior laws, for example civil law.[56] Second, the analysis on the abovementioned purpose should be contextual. In different social contexts, the various purposes of the same property may differ. A house, when it is used as a residence, can be constitutionally protected because a residence is generally regarded as being necessary for realising the fundamental purpose of an individual's self-development. However, when a house is used as an investment, which is not as necessary to self-development, constitutional protection of the property rights to that house may not be awarded. Third, the term 'property' in the constitution focuses more on 'interest' than on 'ownership'. Thus, in the case of an individual who is not the owner of a property but who has a fundamental interest in that property, his or her property interests can be protected by the constitutional property clause. In a case concerning an apartment tenant, the FCC ruled that the tenant's right of occupancy in the rented apartment was property guaranteed by the constitution, because housing, either by owned property or rented property, is crucial to individual existence.[57] However, this case did not reflect that Germany transferred from its traditional unitary conception of ownership to the concept of a 'bundle of rights'. Alexander comments that the German constitution maintains its ownership-centred conception of property. It is better to understand that 'the tenant had a constitutional property interest that is different from the landlord's private law ownership interest'.[58]

[55] Ibid., p. 108.

[56] Alexander, generalising the rulings of FCC, concludes that 'the court distinguishes among different categories of property, creating a kind of hierarchy among types of resources'. Ibid., p. 138.

[57] BVerfGE 89, 1 (*Landlord/Tenant*, 1993). A brief of this case is available at www.hrcr.org/safrica/property/89bverfge1.html.

[58] Alexander, *The Global Debate*, p. 127.

Nevertheless, this case enlarges the scope of constitutional property to embrace non-ownership property interest.

Finally, there are two property guarantees (dual guarantees) in the constitution. The property clause includes both an individual guarantee in art. 14(2)(3) and an institutional guarantee in the first sentence of art. 14(1). The former guarantee is negatively framed and the latter guarantee is positively framed. In essence, individual guarantee examines the constitutionality of regulatory limits on individual specific property. The concerned legislation or regulation is unconstitutional if it does not conform to the constitutional requirements for the expropriation of individual property. Institutional guarantee scrutinises the constitutionality of the legislation concerning the setting of property contents. The related legislation is unconstitutional if it removes a whole category of property from the private domain without constitutional justification.[59] Thus, the former guarantee protects individuals from governmental interference except where constitutional restraints (such as the public good and compensation) must be satisfied. The latter guarantee strengthens the constitution's ability to maintain and secure a private property system from interference by the government. Combining both of these guarantees and three other perspectives, we obtain a complete and accurate reading of the German constitutional property clause. The property system dominated by private property should be secured by the constitution. Each individual's property entails both fundamental individual value and social obligation. When the property is intended for the achievement of fundamental value, its expropriation should be subject to constitutional scrutiny. When overriding public interest demands it, individual property can be expropriated according to constitutional requirements.

2.4.2 *The United States: overall design of the taking clause*

The United States represents the constitutionalisation model without expressively declaring property as an independent basic right. The *U.S. Constitution* protects private property through a three-pronged taking clause designed to guard citizens' liberty in owning property.

In the foundation document, the *Declaration of Independence*, which was passed by the Continental Congress on 4 July 1776 and which declared the independence of the United States from Great Britain, property is not

[59] van der Walt, *Constitutional Property*, pp. 128–32.

listed with life and liberty as an 'inalienable right'. In the *Declaration of Independence*, we read,

> We hold these truths to be self-evident, that all men are created equal, that they are endowed by their Creator with certain unalienable Rights, that among these are Life, Liberty and the pursuit of Happiness.[60]

'Life, Liberty and the pursuit of Happiness', as one of the most influential phrases in the *Declaration of Independence*, is always regarded as the borrowing of Locke's natural law expression in his famous work *Two Treatises of Government* (1690).[61] In Locke's view, citizens' natural rights include life, liberty and property (estate). However, when Thomas Jefferson borrowed Locke's expression for drafting the Declaration of Independence, 'property' was replaced with 'the pursuit of Happiness'.[62] Was this alteration, namely the removal of property from the list of natural rights, made intentionally by Thomas Jefferson? Without considering the explanations that Jefferson made this substitution because of his flawed memory or the desire to insert a vapid nicety, Gary Wills argued that Jefferson deliberately devalued property because he believed that property should be removed from the list of inalienable rights.[63] In fact, Jefferson shared this opinion with Benjamin Franklin that property was a creation of society and should thus serve social need.[64] There is also argument that Jefferson did not intend to reject the importance of property rights since the pursuit of happiness was a 'widely accepted' end of government and the acquirement and possession of property is necessary to the realisation of happiness.[65]

The subsequent constitution, the *Constitution of the United States* (the *U.S. Constitution*), which was passed in 1787, did not include property as an inalienable right. In fact, the 1787 *U.S. Constitution* mainly regulates the branches of the federal government and the relationship between the federal and state governments. It does not stipulate any individual rights

60 The *Declaration of Independence* is available at www.ushistory.org/declaration/document/.

61 Locke's expression is 'life, liberty and estate'. He wrote: 'Man being born, as has been proved, with a title to perfect freedom and an uncontrolled enjoyment of all the rights and privileges of the law of Nature, equally with any other man, or number of men in the world, hath by nature a power not only to preserve his property – that is, his life, liberty, and estate, against the injuries and attempts of other men'. See Locke, *Two Treatises*, p. 141.

62 Katz, 'Thomas Jefferson', 488.

63 In a letter written to Gary Wills by Thomas Jefferson, an author of the *Declaration of Independence*, Jefferson suggested removing property rights from the list of inalienable rights. See Cui, 'A Comparative Study'.

64 Ibid.

65 Ely, *The Guardian*, p. 29.

or freedoms. This flaw was remedied in 1791 by the ratification of ten amendments.

These ten amendments, as a whole, are called *Bill of Rights*. The *Fifth Amendment* stipulates: '[No person shall] be deprived of life, liberty, or property, without due process of law; nor shall private property be taken for public use, without just compensation'.[66]

In 1868, the *Fourteenth Amendment* was passed to prohibit states from depriving people of life, liberty and property without due process of the law.[67] This amendment extended the constitutional guarantee of private property to limit the states' activities. There are two points worthy of attention. First, after being removed from the *Declaration of Independence*'s list of inalienable rights, property was ranked equally with life and liberty in the *Fifth Amendment* and the *Fourteenth Amendment*. Second, unlike the *German Basic Law*, the *U.S. Constitution* does not expressly declare that property (or life or liberty) is a basic right of citizens. However, it can be reasonably concluded that the equal ranking of property with life and liberty shows that property enjoys an implied status as a basic right in the *U.S. Constitution*.[68]

However, the U.S. Supreme Court's practice tends to reluctantly recognise the equal status that property enjoys alongside life, liberty and various other rights enumerated in the *Bill of Rights*. The court's long-term practice placed all rights into two groups: fundamental rights and non-fundamental rights. For the former group of rights, the strictest judicial review, including substantive due process review, is imposed as the strongest judicial guarantee. The latter group of rights are subject to a lower level of judicial review protection based on the rationality test, which is weaker than substantive due process review. According to Goodpaster's generalisation, these main fundamental rights include the *First Amendment* rights (freedom of religion, press and expression), political participation rights, the rights to due process and the rights to equal protection. In addition, the Supreme Court conferred fundamental status to these rights: the right to travel, the right to privacy, the right of access to the courts and the right to education.[69] Although property has been

[66] The *Fifth Amendment* to the *U.S. Constitution*. The *U.S. Constitution* and its amendments are available at www.usconstitution.net.

[67] The *Fourteenth Amendment* stipulates: 'No State shall make or enforce any law which shall abridge the privileges or immunities of citizens of the United States; nor shall any State deprive any person of life, liberty, or property, without due process of law; nor deny to any person within its jurisdiction the equal protection of the laws'.

[68] The *Fourteenth Amendment* is also called the citizenship or citizen's rights clause.

[69] See Goodpaster, 'The Constitution', 482–3.

denied the status of a fundamental right by the Supreme Court, there is a strong scholarly voice, represented by Richard Epstein and James Ely, supporting the recognition of property as such. Indeed, some cases in the 1980s and 1990s show that the Supreme Court was preparing to give property a higher status. However, the road to this end is still long, and the current court rulings have not yet established the fundamental right status of property.[70]

The lack of clarification of fundamental rights in the *Constitution* by the legislature leaves it to the U.S. Supreme Court's discretion to decide which rights are fundamental, and this judicial discretion can lead to a varying scope of fundamental rights in different times. For example, in the 1905 case of *Lochner* v. *New York*, the 'liberty of contract' was established as a fundamental right by the court, but it was removed from the list of fundamental rights by the 1937 case of *West Coast Hotel Co.* v. *Parrish.*[71]

The *U.S. Constitution* protects private property by controlling governments' taking activity or the exercise of their eminent domain power. That is why the *Fifth Amendment* is also called the Taking Clause. We also find that in the United States, property was not constitutionally protected when the *Constitution* was implemented. However, this defect was corrected by the *Fifth Amendment*, and the Taking Clause was extended to all states in 1868 by the *Fourteenth Amendment.*

The Taking Clause resulted from a compromise between Republicanism and Liberalism.[72] Republicanism, represented by Thomas Jefferson, holds that private property should be subject to social need, but liberal thinkers insist that private property should be the individual's inalienable right and should serve individual goals. Finally, the taking clause ranks property equivalently with life and liberty, two rights that Republicans hold to be inalienable. On the other hand, Republicanism stipulates that government can take private property under the three-pronged limit, which includes public use, just compensation and due process.

2.4.3 *Canada: the unconstitutionalisation of private property*

The entrenchment of property in the constitution has been resisted in Canada. Neither the *1867 Constitution Act* or the *1982 Constitution*

[70] Alexander, 'Property', 734–5.

[71] *Lochner* v. *New York*, 198 U.S. 45 (1905); *West Coast Hotel Co.* v. *Parrish*, 300 U.S. 379 (1937).

[72] Cui, 'A Comparative Study'.

Act established property as a constitutional basic right.[73] In 1960, the House of Commons enacted the *Bill of Rights*, which stipulates human rights and fundamental freedoms, including 'the right of the individual to life, liberty, security of the person and enjoyment of property, and the right not to be deprived thereof except by due process of law'.[74] However, such a bill is technically federal legislation without constitutional status and only operates within the federal jurisdiction.

In the first section of the *1982 Constitution Act*, titled 'The Charter of Rights and Freedoms', property is not on the list of constitutional rights. In April 1983, Prime Minister Pierre Trudeau publicly supported the addition of property in the constitution with the precondition that debate would be limited to one day. This led to the use of severe partisan tactics. Soon, the Conservative Party initiated a motion of non-confidence, taking the resolution of property entrenchment to the Canadian House of Commons. Although this motion was defeated in the House, the proposed amendment of entrenching property into the constitution died during the constitutionalisation process.[75]

Resistance at the society level came from several interest groups, including women's groups, native's groups, labour groups and environmental groups. In the political system, many provincial governments expressed their worries that the constitutionalisation of property would lead to much stricter constitutional limits on the use of government power for the achievement of social interest.[76]

A significant amount of provincial resistance was recorded when most provinces blocked a resolution, passed in 1988 by a vote of 108 to 16 in the House, calling for the entrenchment of property in the constitution. The resolution says:

> That in the opinion of this House, the Constitution Act, 1982 should be amended in order to recognize the right to enjoyment of property, and the right not to be deprived thereof, except in accordance with the principles of fundamental justice, and in keeping with the tradition of the usual federal-provincial consultative process.[77]

[73] *Constitution Acts* 1867–1982, available at laws.justice.gc.ca/eng/Const/Const_index.html.

[74] *Bill of Rights*, Section 1. The *Bill of Rights* is available at laws-lois.justice.gc.ca/eng/acts/C-12.3/FullText.html.

[75] Johansen, 'Property Rights'.

[76] These government activities include, for example, land use planning and municipal laws, real and personal property laws, environmental laws and health and safety laws. Ibid.

[77] House of Commons (Canada), *Debates*, 2 May 1988, 15044.

The federal-provincial process requires the endorsement by seven out of ten provinces with no less than 50 per cent of the population voting. This endorsement was not achieved before the end of a three-year consultative period.[78]

2.4.4 *India: from constitutionalisation to unconstitutionalisation*

Unlike many democratic countries embracing the constitutionalisation of property, India has experienced reverse reform, having removed the property clause from its constitution.

Property rights had been constitutionally protected in India between 1950 and 1978.[79] In 1978, the property clauses were removed from the constitution through the adoption of the *Forty-Fourth Amendment*.[80]

After the *Forty-Fourth Amendment* was implemented, the fundamental right to property ceased to exist in India. Property is a legal and statutory right only. Although the document titled, '*Statement of Objects and Reasons appended to the Constitution (Forty-fourth Amendment) Bill*', declares that the right of persons in holding lands and receiving compensation at the market value 'would not be affected', the negative impact of denying the constitutional status of property rights is significant.[81]

The elimination of the property clause was the result of an approximately twenty-eight-year battle between the judicial system and other government powers, including administrative and legislative branches.

[78] Johansen, 'Property Rights'.

[79] Independent India's constitution (the *Constitution of India*) was enacted by the Constituent Assembly on 26 November 1949 and went into effect on 26 January 1950. Property clauses in the original version of this constitution were derived from the *Government of India Act* (1935), sec. 299 of which stipulates property rights and restraints (public purpose and compensation) against expropriation or acquisition. To follow the structure of the 1935 act in protecting property, the 1950 constitution stipulates that property rights are a freedom in art. 19 (1) (f) and outlines expropriation in art. 31.

[80] See *Constitution (Forty-fourth Amendment) Act* (1978), available at indiacode.nic.in/coiweb/amend/amend44.htm.

[81] Ibid. The *Statement of Objects and Reasons*, in the third paragraph, announces that the property would be changed from a constitutional right to a legal right. In the fourth and fifth paragraphs, it says:

4. Similarly, the right of persons holding land for personal cultivation and within the ceiling limit to receive compensation at the market value would not be affected.
5. Property, while ceasing to be a fundamental right, would, however, be given express recognition as a legal right, provision being made that no person shall be deprived of his property save in accordance with law.

India gained its independence from Britain in 1947.[82] One oppressive and urgent task for the new government after independence was instituting land reform to increase productivity and adjust unjust distribution. However, within no more than two years after the enactment of the constitution, the courts, citing the constitution's property clause, denied the validity of land reform legislation in some cases.[83] Legislative authority responded quickly. It consecutively passed the *First Amendment* (in 1951), the *Fourth Amendment* (in 1955), the *Twenty-Fourth Amendment* and the *Twenty-Fifth Amendment* (in 1971) to restrict the courts' judicial review power of the government's land reform and expropriation measures. The Ninth Schedule and art. 31B introduced by the *First Amendment* clearly expressed the legislative authority's desire to loosen judicial restraint. According to art. 31B,

> [N]one of the Acts and Regulations specified in the Ninth Schedule nor any of the provisions thereof shall be deemed to be void, or ever to have become void, on the ground that such Act, Regulation or provision is inconsistent with, or takes away or abridges any of the rights conferred by, any provisions of this Part (Part III Fundamental Rights), and notwithstanding any judgment, decree or order of any court or Tribunal to the contrary, each of the said Acts and Regulations shall, subject to the power of any competent Legislature to repeal or amend it, continue in force.[84]

The list in the Ninth Schedule has been lengthened since then. It now contains 284 acts concerning land or agrarian reform that are exempted from the judicial review, which is based on the fundamental rights portion of the constitution.

The *Twenty-Fifth Amendment*, born in 1971, substituted the term 'compensation', required for the compulsory acquisition of property in art. 31(2), with the phrase 'for an amount' that can be fixed by or determined according to the law. It also declares that art. 19(1)(f) is inapplicable to the compulsory acquisition stipulated in art. 31(2).[85] Additionally, the *Twenty-Fifth Amendment* added art. 31C to the constitution. Article 31C stipulates that no law securing the directive principles of state policy set

[82] The British Parliament passed the *Indian Independence Act* to allow the independence of India and Pakistan on 18 July 1947.

[83] These cases include: *Kameshwar Singh* v. *Province of Bihar*, AIR 1951 Pat 246; *Charanjit Lal Chowdhury* v. *The Union of India*, AIR (38) 1951 SC 41.

[84] *Constitution of India*, art. 31B. The English version of the Indian constitution is available at lawmin.nic.in/coi/coiason29july08.pdf.

[85] Article 31 (2) states that '[n]othing in sub-clause (f) of clause (1) of article 19 shall affect any such law as is referred to in clause (2)'.

out in Part IV of the constitution (mainly art. 39(b)(c)) 'shall be deemed to be void on the ground that it is inconsistent with, or takes away or abridges any of the rights conferred by article 14, article 19 or article 31', and 'no law containing a declaration that it is for giving effect to such policy shall be called in question in any court on the ground that it does not give effect to such policy'. Considering that art. 39(b)(c) deals with the economic system, the *Twenty-Fifth Amendment* exempts countless numbers of laws advocating economic policies or directives from the restraint of constitutional fundamental rights as well as from judicial review. However, starting with the 1973 case *Kesavanada Bharathi* v. *State of Kerala*,[86] the Indian Supreme Court resisted the legislature's erosion of the constitution. However, the court's majority decision is more compromise than victory. Although the Supreme Court halted the legislature's ruthless expansion by declaring that the legislature's amendment power was limited, cannot alter the basic structure or framework of the constitution and guards judicial review power by declaring void the section in art. 31C that eliminates court review, the provisions in art. 31C that abrogate the fundamental rights are declared valid because the concerned portion of the amendment does not alter the basic structure of the constitution.

The Supreme Court's small battlefield that remained after the *Kesavanada* case was finally occupied by the legislature in 1978, when the property clauses (arts 19(1)(f) and 31) were deleted from the constitution by Parliament. Since then, the only article concerning property left in the constitution has been art. 300A, which says, 'No person shall be deprived of his property save by authority of law.' However, this article, standing alone, leaves the courts with no power to review government taking measures based on the constitution.

2.4.5 *China: the constitutionalisation of private property in a CPC country*

China has been waffling on constitutionalising private property since 1949. In the beginning, the constitution enacted in 1954 allowed the existence of private property within a limited scope. After two years, however, China was reformed into a purely socialist country, and the 1975 and 1978 constitutions solidly affirmed the dominant status of public property in the constitution, and individuals' property rights were largely

[86] *Kesavanada Bharathi* v. *State of Kerala*, AIR 1973 SC 1461.

dissolved. However, when the CPC began to reform domestically and to open to the outside world after 1978, a new constitution was passed in 1982 to revive individuals' rights over land and other real estate to some extent.[87] With these reforms, amendments to the constitution were made to enlarge the scope of private property rights in the following years. A milestone amendment was made in 2004 when the constitution for the first time included a clause declaring the inviolability of private property and the stipulations concerning expropriation and requisition.[88]

However, China's entrenchment of private property in the constitution is limited by two premises. The first is the property system with public property consisting of land and natural resources as the dominant part of that system. This implies that the future reform of private property will be largely limited to the enlargement of private use rights to land. It is difficult to predict whether the reform led by the CPC would lead to the endowment of an ownership of land to individuals. The second premise is the CPC's leadership status, which implies that the reform concerning the design of institutional enforcement of constitutional principles will not be beyond the fundamental controlling power of the CPC and will not be allowed to conflict with the elementary framework of the CPC-centred political system.

The next chapter illustrates the historical evolution of the constitutional protection of private property in China in more detail.

2.5 Comparative analysis on the constitutionalisation of private property

The core issue regarding the constitutionalisation of private property is, as Alvaro argued, 'the tension between property and democracy'.[89] In more detail, the questions of whether 'to constitutionalise or not' and 'to what extent to constitutionalise private property' reflect the option of two different social systems: a propertarian system and a democratic-communitarian system. The former system regards the recognition and protection of property as the supreme principle in the country, and the

87 According to this constitution and the related legislation, farmers can acquire the contracting right of farmland and individuals can acquire the use right of urban land. Such rights are separated from collective and state ownership for the holding of private bodies.

88 For more information about the enactment history of Chinese constitutions, see Chapter 3 of this book.

89 Alvaro, 'Why Property', 310.

government's task is to protect property. In the latter system, 'decision-making is exercised on behalf of at least a majority of adult residents on the basis of democratic will and community values'.[90] The propertarian system reflects a natural law influence in defining the government's role in the protection of property, which is entrenched by the constitution as the supreme principle in society. Instead, the democratic-communitarian system reflects positivism by insisting that private property as a legal right should be defined and may be changed by the government elected by the majority in a country. Clearly, in a propertarian system, governments as democratic institutions 'are subordinated to property ownership'.[91] However, in a democratic-communitarian system, private ownership should be secondary to the community interest represented by democratic government.

It is inspiring to compare the constitutional protection of property in the United States and Canada. These two former colonies of Britain in North America took different paths as to the constitutionalisation of property. The United States adopted a propertarian system facilitating the constitutionalisation of property by a taking clause that indirectly confirms the constitutional status of property as an inalienable right. This reflects the founding fathers' wish to limit the possible disaster that may be produced by democracy through constitutional design. According to Rowley, what is most distinctive about the *U.S. Constitution* is that it places more importance on individual constitutional rights than on government power and strengthens the protection of private property.[92] The constitutional protection of property in the United States also reflects the influence of the former colonising country. Among European countries, Britain is a representative country with a long history of strengthening the protection of private property. In 1215, King John signed the *Magna Carta* to protect the feudal lords' property from being seized arbitrarily by the monarch. Since then, individualist property protection has been endorsed by important legal documents, judicial decisions and academic literature.[93] As Alvaro commented, 'British Institutions were decidedly propertarian in nature'.[94]

Canada took a different path. The current Canadian constitution eliminates property rights and is strongly characterised by community interest.

90 Ibid. 91 Ibid. 92 Rowley, 'Limits of Democracy', p. 17.

93 For example the 1689 *Bill of Rights*, the case of *Entick* v. *Carrington* and the academic contribution by John Locke (1632–1704).

94 Alvaro, 'Why Property', 312.

In the *1867 Constitution Act*, the foundation document of the confederation of Canada, there is no entrenchment of property as a fundamental right or value. The founding fathers of Canada, in drafting this document, realised the possible infringement of the democratic system on private property and designed measures restricting the misuse of government power to erode property rights. At that time, unlike in the United States, which focused more on individual property rights, Canada was balancing the propertarian system and the democratic system through constitutional design. First, this balance was reflected in the institutional design of Parliament. Each senator, a member of one branch of Parliament, was required to have real and personal property worth 'Four thousand Dollars over and above his Debts and Liabilities'.[95] This minimum property requirement was intended to render senators the representatives of property owners with veto power to deny legislation passed by the Commons, another parliamentary branch composed of elected members who were not subjected to a minimum property requirement. Second, balance was struck between federal power and provincial power. On the one hand, the *1867 Constitution Act* afforded the provinces legislative power by stipulating 'Property and Civil Rights'.[96] On the other hand, the federal Parliament was allowed to create uniform laws concerning property and civil rights in the future. This balance is not even, giving more weight to provinces, because the uniform laws, which would be passed by the federal Parliament in the future, 'shall not have effect in any Province unless and until it is adopted and enacted as Law by the Legislature thereof'.[97]

The Senate's function as the guard of property was never successfully fulfilled. For a long time after the *1867 Constitution Act*, the senators became 'a rubber stamp for Commons legislation and a burial ground for political patrons'.[98] The efforts by the federal legislature to unify property legislation were resented by the provinces, which led to the removal of property clauses in the *1982 Constitution Act*.

Although the *German Basic Law* recognises property as an independent right, unlike the United States, Germany runs a democratic-communitarian system similar to that of Canada. Both the *Weimar Constitution* and the current *Basic Law* strengthen the social obligations of property holders. As for legislative intention, the *U.S. Constitution* is more

95 1867 *Constitution Act*, S. 23 (4). 96 Ibid., S. 92 (13).
97 Ibid., S. 94. 98 Alvaro, 'Why Property', 315.

individualist in the protection of property, and the German constitution is more social interest-oriented. Thus, an interesting finding is that the *U.S. Constitution*, without the expressive entrenchment of property's status as a fundamental right, is more akin to a propertarian system, whereas the German constitution, which clearly and positively announces the basic natural right of property, is more communitarian in its strengthening of the social obligations of private property holders.[99]

The framework of the analysis of the property-democracy tension is also helpful in explaining India's experience. The de-constitutionalisation process of private property in India shows that India does not have a propertarian system. Artefacts of the British legal system, the property clauses were written into India's constitution. This continuation was so weak that it could not resist quick and strong erosion by the legislature, which represents the democratic will solidly rooted in society. Similar to Canada, India is a model declaring victory of government power over private property. However, the difference between India and Canada, where the provincial power is the main barrier to the constitutionalisation of property, is that the strong resistance in India stems from the federal legislature. Moreover, unlike Canada, India urgently and strongly pushed social reforms of the property system after its independence. By de-constitutionalising property the Indian government could gain more freedom to initiate reforms,

[99] Alexander commented that in both constitutional provisions and court interpretations, the constitution's treatment of property in Germany 'is functionally dynamic and socially based'. First, private property is perceived to be secondary to the social or public interest. This could be illustrated more clearly by one sentence in a draft of art. 14(2) of the *GermanBasic Law*: 'Its [property's] use shall find its limits in the living necessities of all citizens and in the public order essential to society'. Second, different types of properties entail different social obligations. The type of property that is most important to the public good should be limited more than the types that are less important to the public good. Third, the observance of such social obligation should be dynamic. The type of property that is at first most significant to the social interest may become less important with the passage of time. See Alexander, 'Property', 748–53. The case of *Small Garden Plot* clearly presents how the change of the social function of some property influences constitutional protection. The FCC ruled that a federal statute that limits landowners' rights to terminate the leases of their garden plots was unconstitutional. In explaining why such a limit is disproportionate to the public purpose it achieves, the court mentioned the historical change of the social function of the concerned gardens. Such gardens were significant to older societies as a main food source. However, when this type of decentralised individual agricultural production was supplanted by modern, large-scale commercial agricultural production, the original function of garden plots in society decreased so greatly that it rendered the existing limit unfairly disproportionate. See BVerfGE 52, 1 (*Small Garden Plot*, 1979). See also Alexander, *The Global Debate*, p. 136.

which may substantially change the ownership of current property owners or redistribute the property interest among the rights holders.[100]

Although it was the strong need for reform that drove the Indian government to strengthen its power by challenging the judicial system and the constitutional protection of property, India's case falls within the framework of the property-democracy dimension. Despite China, as one of the largest developing economies alongside India, having a similar urgency to that of India for social reform, the analysis here goes beyond the Western analysis framework. The 'property-democracy' spectrum can only be used to analyse democratic countries, but China is not a Western-style democratic country. China has been a centralised country led by the CPC since 1949. After 1949, the social system in China was largely socialist, with the allowance of private ownership of land and capitalistic industrial and commercial entities for only a few years. After 1978, however, China started to make gradual reform towards market economy by offering individuals more rights to own property and property rights. However, economic reform stimulated peoples' desire for more democracy and stronger protection of property by making political and legal reform integral to constitutional reform.

Between 1949 and 1978, the tension of 'property-party (CPC)' was an appropriate framework for analysing the property system in effect in China at that time. The governance of Communist Party led to public property dominance in the property system, which was present in the former Soviet Union and Eastern European countries. After 1978, however, with more respect for and protection of private property requested by the people and a greater demand for democracy introduced into Chinese society, the basic framework originally used to analyse China's property system changed to the triangle seen in Figure 2.1.

To stimulate economic growth, the CPC must loosen its control of the property system and introduce a degree of democracy. However, the borderline of the tolerable space for the reform of private property and democracy is the leading role of public property in the property system and of the CPC's leadership power in the political system. In tracing back the history of more than thirty years of reform in China, the tolerable

[100] Land reform was implemented in poor agrarian economies to augment access to land or land interests for the poor. The radical reform approach can be accomplished through land redistribution policies that change the ownership structure of the land. For the Indian government, land reform has been important in relieving poverty. However, India used a less radical land reform measure of setting a ceiling on landholding or securing and augmenting tenants' land rights. See Besley and Burgess, 'Land Reform', 389–90.

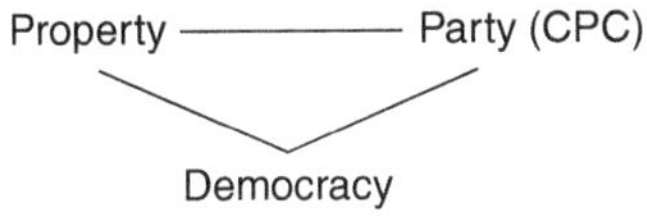

Figure 2.1 Framework of Analysing China's Property System

space for private property reform is much larger than it is for the reform of political democracy.

The tension between property and democracy in Western countries can also be considered in the analysis of the change of China's property system. Although the Communist Party is not substituted by democratic mechanism, it is limited by the growing democratic voice in society. To maintain and solidify its ruling power, the party tends to consider and respond to peoples' voices and requirements in the society, although often passively and slowly. However, with the development of economic reform, interest groups are becoming more diversified and conflicts among them are becoming more complicated. Similar to competing parties in democratic countries, which design policies that benefit the majority to win elections in democratic countries, the CPC tends to follow the majority's willingness to gain more support to stabilise its leading status. Inevitably, some measures reflecting the democratic request in the form of populism may be adopted at the expense of harming individuals' property rights.

Compared to Western countries, India and China both have been more dynamic in their constitutionalisation of private property. In both countries, the property system is unstable, and fundamental reforms concerning the structure of property redistribution are still necessary. However, in developed countries such as the United States, Canada and Germany, government reforms consist of insubstantial adjustments that fail to fundamentally change the current distribution of private property. Interestingly, however, the reform routes towards constitutionalising private property in India and China are contradictory. India discarded constitutional protection of property and has been heading for much stronger reform in the area of government regulation and property reform. Commenting on India's progress in removing property rights from the constitution, the former Chief Justice Subba Rao noted that 'autocratic power was sustained by democratic processes' and 'the amendments in the realm of property substituted the Constitutional philosophy by totalitarian ideology'.[101]

[101] Rao, 'Property Rights'.

However, in China, the route towards constitutionalisation began with the country's earlier totalitarianism and extended through its later transition towards more democracy to the limited constitutionalisation of private property that was implemented in 2004. Perhaps India and China will evolve similar property systems that effectively balance the need for social reform with the protection of individual property. Will India strengthen government power to the extent that it reverts to socialism? Will China break the reform bottleneck to become a country based on competition among democratic parties? The likely answer to both of these questions in the long term is 'no'.

3

The private property protection in China's constitutions

A historical review

The constitutional protection of private property in China evolved with the reform of the property system, of which land is a main part. In this chapter, the historical changes in land reform in the New China are reviewed, and the historical evolution of the constitutional protection of private property is analysed. Based on a historical review, the changes in the social forces that influence the property system and the protection of private property are identified.

3.1 Land reform in the New China

3.1.1 1949–1953: land redistribution in the period of new democracy

The Communist ideology regards private property as a cause of class exploitation. According to Marxism, the capitalist society is an evil one characterised by class exploitation, namely 'a system of domination of men by men, of men by things, and of men by impersonal forces'.[1] The existence of private property institutions renders the capitalist's appropriation of surplus labour or the exploitation of the worker class feasible. The central point of socialist justice is to abolish the private property system and thus to eliminate exploitation through public control of the means of production.[2] Thus, to remove and even eliminate private property in the New China was an urgent job for the Communist Party government after 1949. On 29 September 1949, two days before the establishment of the New China, the Chinese People's Political Consultative Conference (CPPCC) passed the *Common Programme*, which is called the

[1] Husami, 'Marx', 27. [2] Ibid., 46–8.

provisional constitution for the New China.[3] Article 3 of the *Common Programme* declared that bureaucratic capital would be confiscated by the government, rural land would be distributed to farmers and private property owned by workers, farmers, the petit bourgeoisie (*xiao zichan jieji*) and the national bourgeoisie (*minzu zichan jieji*) would be protected.

In June 1950, the government enacted *Land Reform Law*,[4] which initiated nationwide land reform. The *Land Reform Law* revoked rural landlords' land ownership and distributed the majority of their land to individual farmers. A small portion of these landlords' land was reserved for town-and country-level governments.[5] The redistribution of rural land was nearly complete by early 1953, when approximately 700 million *mu* (1 hectare = 15 *mu*) of land was distributed to more than 300 million individual farmers.[6] Land reform also covered the suburban areas of large cities. In November 1950, the central government promulgated and enforced the *Regulation for Reforming the Land in the City Suburbs*.[7] According to this regulation (arts. 3 and 5), the landlords' land in the city suburbs was confiscated, and the farmland owned by persons engaged in industrial and commercial activities was expropriated.

The first Chinese constitution was enacted in 1954 (*1954 Constitution of China*).[8] It kept intact the *Common Programme*'s land ownership

[3] *Gongtong Gangling* [*Common Programme*], enacted by the first Plenary Session of the CPPCC on 29 September 1949. The Chinese text is available at news.xinhuanet.com/ziliao/2004–12/07/content_2304465.htm.

[4] *Tudi Gaige Fa* [*Land Reform Law*], enacted by People's Central Government of China on 28 June 1950. The Chinese text is available at www.npc.gov.cn/wxzl/wxzl/2000–12/10/content_4246.htm.

[5] Ibid., arts. 14–15. The peasants, according to their household wealth, were categorised into three groups: rich peasants (*funong*), middle peasants (*zhongnong*) and poor peasants (*pinnong*). The seized landlords' land was distributed to the middle and poor ones. As to rich peasants, their rented-out land was seized and redistributed. However, they were allowed to own land with a per capita amount which was more than that of middle and poor ones. As commented by Bramall, the rich peasants were treated differently because the CPC 'saw the preservation of the rich peasant economy as a way to promote economic growth and ultimately poverty relief'. See C. Bramall, 'Chinese Land Reform', 111–12.

[6] *Xinhua*, 'Xin Zhongguo'.

[7] *Chengshi Jiaoqu Tudi Gaige Tiaoli* [*Regulation for Reforming the Land in the City Suburbs*], enacted by the State Council (*Zhengwu Yuan*) on 21 November 1950. Its Chinese text is available at news.xinhuanet.com/ziliao/2004–12/13/content_2328565.htm.

[8] After the establishment of the CPC government in 1949, the farmland owned by landlords was distributed to poor farmers. The farmers' ownership of land was recognised by the constitution. See art. 8 of *1954 Constitution of China*, which was enacted by the First Session of the First NPC on 20 September 1954. The Chinese text is available at www.npc.gov.cn/wxzl/wxzl/2000–12/26/content_4264.htm. The English version is available at e-chaupak.net/database/chicon/1954/1954bilingual.htm.

principles and defined four ownership forms: all-people ownership (*quanmin suoyouzhi*), collective ownership (*hezuoshe suoyouzhi*), individual labourer ownership (*geti laodongzhe suoyouzhi*) and capitalist ownership (*zibenjia suoyouzhi*).[9] In essence, this provision in the *1954 Constitution of China* resulted from earlier land reform efforts. In other words, we may say that the land reform movement lacked a constitutional basis. The land redistribution measures, which changed the ownership structure of property, were made before the official constitution was enacted. This phenomenon can be called 'government reform first, constitutional legislation later'. This phenomenon occurred repeatedly in subsequent years and reflects an outstanding feature of party-leading or administration-leading reform in China.

3.1.2 1953–1957: transition towards cooperatives

To increase the efficient cultivation of farmland, the establishment and expansion of cooperatives (*hezuoshe*) was encouraged by the government. There were three stages of farmers' cooperatives, with a sequence from loose cooperation to tight union. The earliest form of the cooperative was the Mutual-Aid Team (*huzhuzu*, MAT). MATs were organised based on individual farmers' willingness and aimed at short-term or long-term cooperation in cultivating land. Although such collaboration was encouraged by the government, farmers had the freedom to form, dissolve and change their teams. The farmers' land ownership was not influenced. The second cooperative form was the Lower-stage Agricultural Cooperative (*chuji nongye hezuoshe*, LAC). The land owned by farmer members was converted to a certain percentage of shares in the LAC. Cooperative members cultivated the land collectively and distributed the farm earnings (*fenhong*) according to their respective percentage of shares. The third cooperative form was the Higher-stage Agricultural Cooperative (*gaoji nongye hezuoshe*, HAC). In a HAC, farmers' dividend rights were cancelled and their income was calculated based on their labour quantity and quality rather than on the percentage of land they owned.

The government advocated rapid collectivisation. The MATs lasted from 1948 to 1953. LACs began to appear in 1954, and by 1956, HACs began to develop.[10] Transitioning through these three stages entailed a process of revoking farmers' individual land ownership rights and other means of production. In the MAT stage, team members' land ownership was still recognised by law. However, in the LAC stage, a portion of

[9] Ibid., art. 5. [10] Wang, 'Complex Households', 534.

farmers' land ownership rights, namely their control and management rights, was revoked, but they were allowed to retain their dividend rights. In the HAC stage, nearly all of the rights in the land ownership bundle were revoked and famers became the nominal owners of their land only. The completion of these three stages served as a foundation for revoking farmers' total land ownership.[11]

3.1.3 1958–1978: the elimination of the private ownership of land

Starting in 1958, HACs were reshaped into People Communes (*renmin gongshe*).[12] Farmers were the members of communes and their land rights were collected and controlled by the commune to which they belonged. In March 1961, the CPC's Central Committee meeting in Guangzhou passed the *Work Regulations on People's Communes in Rural Areas(Draft)*. In the next year, the revised draft was promulgated. According to this regulation (arts. 1, 2 and 21), the People Commune is the basic unit in rural areas, and it can include either two levels (the commune and the production team [*shengchan dui*] or three levels (the commune, big production team [*shengchan dadui*] and production teams). The regulation stipulates that all land under the management scope of production team is owned by such teams.[13] The occurrence of communes eliminated the private ownership of rural land and the collective ownership of rural land was established. People Communes continued until 1978 when China began to open to the world and implement reforms. The People Communes ended formally in 1983 when the CPC issued its *No. 1 Central Committee Document*, which requires the reform of People Communes.[14]

11 After the advanced form of cooperatives was formed, the farmers' land was transferred to the ownership of village collectives and the state. The land tenure system with the feature of unified management of land was established. See Spoor and Shi, 'Cotton', p. 228.

12 China adopted People Communes from the Soviet Union. For the borrowing of the former Soviet Union's experience in communes, see Du and Huang, *Shidi Nongmin*, pp. 69–73.

13 *Nongcun Renmin Gongshe Gongzuo Tiaoli (xiuzheng cao-an)* [*Work Regulations on People's Communes in Rural Areas (Revised Draft)*], passed by the Tenth Plenary Session of the Eighth CPC Central Committee on 27 September 1962. The Chinese text of this regulation is available at www.china.com.cn/cpc/2011–04/15/content_22370613.htm. This document is called the *Sixty Articles for Agriculture* (*Nongye Liushi Tiao*) because there are sixty articles in the regulation. For the historical background and the revision process of the *Sixty Articles for Agriculture*, see Xin, 'Nongye'.

14 *Dangqian Nongcun Jingji Zhengce de Ruogan Wenti* (*1983 Nian Zhongyang Yihao Wenjian*) [*Several Issues of the Current Economic Policies in the Rural Areas* (The CPC's *No. 1 Central Committee Document* of 1983)], passed by the CPC Politburo on 31 December 1982. The Chinese text is available at www.legaldaily.com.cn/zt/2006–02/24/content_271243.htm. See also Sachs and Woo, 'Reform', 115.

On 17 January 1975, a new constitution (*1975 Constitution of China*) was passed.[15] This constitution stipulated two main forms of property ownership: all-people ownership and collective ownership.[16] The constitution passed in 1978 (*1978 Constitution of China*) repeated these two ownership forms in its art. 5.[17] It should be noted that the *1954 Constitution of China* was not cancelled before the birth of the *1975 Constitution of China*. Thus, the revocation of farmers' individual ownership of production materials between 1958 and early 1975 was unconstitutional. In fact, similarly to the *1954 Constitution of China*, which generalised the land reforms of 1950–1953, the 1975 and 1978 constitutions were the generalisation or constitutionalisation of the 1958–1978 land reforms.

3.1.4 1978 and later: the revival of private land rights

The production of farmland is closely linked to the farmers' motivation, which is stimulated by the design of the land tenure system. Although the compulsory redistribution of landlords' land to poor farmers was driven mainly by political motive and lacked a constitutional basis, it is still a redistribution of private property rather than a total denial of private property. The farmers who received land from the government, as owners, had a strong motivation to cultivate the land for high production. This can be proved by the growth of grain production after land reform. In 1949, total grain production was 113.2 million tons. In 1953, total grain production rose to 166.8 million tons. During the MAT and the LAC stages, when farmers' individual ownership was still recognised, grain production continued to grow. In 1956, approximately 192.7 million tons of grain was produced.[18] However, within the twenty years comprising the People Communes' period, grain production growth rates were extremely low. Grain production per capita in 1978 was similar to that in 1957.[19]

The negative outcome of the collectivisation movement in the former Soviet Union is a good example for explaining why the revocation of land

[15] *1975 Constitution of China*, enacted by the First Session of the Fourth NPC on 17 January 1975. The Chinese text is available at www.npc.gov.cn/wxzl/wxzl/2000–12/06/content_4362.htm.

[16] *The 1975 Constitution of China* stipulates that the production means are owned by all of the people or by the collectives. In fact, the production means are the most important part of property collection, with land as a main constituent. Ibid., art. 5.

[17] *1978 Constitution of China*, enacted by the First Session of the Fifth NPC on 5 March 1978. The Chinese text is available at www.npc.gov.cn/wxzl/wxzl/2000–12/06/content_4365.htm.

[18] Zhongguo Gaige Fazhan Yanjiuyuan, *Zhongguo Nongcun*, pp. 31–2.

[19] Du and Huang, *Shidi Nongmin*, p. 76.

ownership rights can lead to low agricultural production. Comparing agricultural production in 1928 (pre-collectivisation level) with agricultural production between 1929 and 1940 (post-collectivisation level), we find a general decline, with some minor fluctuations, as in 1937 and 1940, when the annual total agricultural output was higher than the pre-collectivisation level. The worst performance occurred in the production of animal products. In 1933, the annual output of animal products fell to lower than pre-collectivisation levels.[20] Moreover, at least 5 million people in the countryside died as a result of the forced collectivisation movement – and according to Rosefielde's research, this figure is too conservative.[21] As Hunter commented, an 'absolute shortfall' brought about by the collectivisation 'cut cruelly into rural living standards and lowered urban living standards as well'.[22]

From 1952 to 1958, when the collectivisation movement in China was pushed from the MAT to the HAC, the annual agricultural output continuously increased and the peasants did not resist the gradual erosion of farmers' land ownership. This led some scholars in that period to conclude optimistically that China could avoid the Soviet Union's collectivisation mishaps. This overconfident judgement was soon struck down by the rapid decrease in agricultural output in 1959. Between 1959 and 1961, when the government compulsorily pushed farmers into People Communes, gross agricultural output fell by 14 per cent in 1959, 12 per cent in 1960 and 2.5 per cent in 1961.[23]

In the winter of 1978, Xiaogang Village in Anhui Province initiated an experimental reform called Big Contracting (*dabaogan*) or Land Contracting, which was later developed into an official system called the Household Responsibility System (*jiating lianchan chengbao zerenzhi*, HRS).[24] Under HRS, the land owned by communes was divided into parcels that were then distributed to households for farming within a certain period. Doubtless, the leaders in Xiaogang Village took a great political risk in initiating this measure.[25] The achievement was astonishing. In the first year of HRS reform, grain production in Xiaogang Village was similar to the amount of total grain produced between 1955 and

[20] Hunter, 'Soviet Agriculture', 204. [21] Rosefielde, 'Excess Collectivization', 83–8.
[22] Hunter, 'Soviet Agriculture', 215–16. [23] Lin, 'Collectivization', 1228–9, 1234.
[24] The experiment in Xiaogang Village started China's bottom-up decollectivisation reform. See Li, 'Path Creation', 66.
[25] Eighteen leaders in Xiaogang Village, before starting this contracting system, all left a will which was about the arrangement of the care of their children after their possible arrest.

1970. After Xiaogang's experiment, various forms of HRS were spread throughout China during the following eighteenmonths.[26]

The HRS was officially accepted in September 1980 when the Central Committee of the CPC promulgated an important document titled, '*Several Issues Concerning the Further Strengthening of the Agricultural Production Responsibility System*'.[27] On the one hand, this document reconfirmed the collective ownership of rural land; on the other hand, it pointed out the necessity and importance of HRS in motivating agricultural production. Within one year of the promulgation of this document, by October 1981, 97.7 per cent of China's agricultural units had adopted HRS.[28] The adoption of HRS does not deny the collective ownership of rural land. Farmers are given some important land property rights, such as the rights to occupy land, cultivate crops and receive interest on production, in exchange for signing responsibility contracts with the collective units, which hold legal ownership of the land. Thus, HRS is also called the Land Contracting System. HRS results in the segregation feature of the property structure of collective land.

The HRS initiated by the Xiaogang Experiment is unconstitutional. The *1978 Constitution of China*, which was still in force during the experiment, stipulated that farmers, as individuals, can keep only a small piece of land for individual cultivation and that its main use must be collective.[29] Despite its unconstitutionality when it was adopted, the basic principle

[26] Lin's research compared the agricultural output in four periods: the period of voluntary collectivisation (1952–8), the period of compulsory collectivisation (1959–78), the period of decollectivisation (1979–83) and the period of post-HRS reform (1984–8). During the voluntary collectivisation period, the annual output was rising in small increments. During the following compulsory collectivisation period, however, the annual output had declined. During the third period, the annual output began to recover and reached the 1952 level in 1983. During the period of HRS, the output increased quickly reaching a level 30 per cent higher than the 1952 productivity level in 1987. Based on the empirical evidence, Lin concluded that the main cause for explaining why the annual agricultural output fell sharply in 1959–61 was 'the change in the incentive structure due to the deprivation of the right to withdraw from a collective, that is, the transition from a voluntary to a compulsory collectivisation in the fall of 1958'. The experience in China, the Soviet Union and other countries which initiated the collectivisation movement shows that the initial success of collectivisation movement 'was followed by severe difficulties and a long period of stagnation in agriculture'. See Lin, 'Collectivization', 1245–9.

[27] *Guanyu Jinyibu Jiaqiang he Wanshan Nongye Shengchan Zerenzhi de Jige Wenti* [*Several Issues Concerning the Further Strengthening of the Agricultural Production Responsibility System*], enacted by the CPC Central Committee on 27 September 1980. The Chinese text is available at news.xinhuanet.com/ziliao/2005–02/04/content_2547020.htm.

[28] Du and Huang, *Shidi Nongmin*, p. 78.

[29] *1978 Constitution of China*, art. 7(2).

behind the HRS was incorporated into the constitution enacted in 1982 (*1982 Constitution of China*).[30] Article 11 of the *1982 Constitution of China* declares:

> The individual economy of urban and rural working people, operating within the limits prescribed by law, is a complement to the Socialist public economy. The State protects the lawful rights and interests of the individual economy.

The *Land Administration Law* (*LAL*) was enacted on 25 June 1986.[31] Article 7 of this law further clarifies that the land owned by the state and the collectives can be offered to individuals for use according to the law. Until 1986, however, the laws concerning the land contracting system failed to provide adequate protection of the private and individual rights of farmers under the HRS. The farmers felt insecure with their contracted rights. The collectives, as the contract-issuing parties, often misused their management power to adjust the distribution of the contracted land and even take back the contracted land before contracts expired. Moreover, the contract term of land responsibility was so short that it encouraged overuse by farmers. The contract period of rural land in the first round of contracting, which began in the early 1980s, was usually fifteen years.[32] When it expired, one CPC document, which was promulgated in 1993, required that in the second round of contracting, the contract should be renewed for an additional thirty years.[33] The thirty-year extension was

[30] *1982 Constitution of China*, enacted by the Fifth Session of the Fifth NPC on 4 December 1982. The original Chinese text of this constitution is available at www.npc.gov.cn/wxzl/wxzl/2000–12/06/content_4421.htm. The currently enforced version with the *2004 Amendment* is available at www.gov.cn/gongbao/content/2004/content_62714.htm. The official English version of the *1982 Constitution of China* is available at www.npc.gov.cn/englishnpc/Constitution/node_2825.htm.

[31] *Tudi Guanli Fa* [*Land Administration Law*], enacted by the Sixteenth Meeting of the Standing Committee of the Sixth NPC on 25 June 1986. It was later revised in 1988, 1998 and 2004. The Chinese texts of the 1986 version and the later revisions are available at www.lawyee.org/Act/Act_Display.asp?RID=29466.

[32] *Zhonggong Zhongyang guanyu 1984 Nian Nongcun Gongzuo de Tongzhi* (*1984 Nian Zhongyang Yihao Wenjian*) [*The CPC Central Committee's Notice on the Work in Rural Area in 1984* (*No.1 Central Committee Document of 1984*)], promulgated by the Central Committee of CPC on 1 January 1984. The Chinese text is available at www.ncfz.org/default3242.html.

[33] *Guanyu Dangqian Nongye he Nongcunjingji Fazhan de Ruogan Zhengce Cuoshi* [*Several Policy Measures about Current Agriculture and Rural Economic Development*], promulgated by the CPC Central Committee and the State Council on 5 January 1993. The Chinese text is available at news.xinhuanet.com/ziliao/2005–03/17/content_2709788.htm.

strengthened again by a notice promulgated in 1997.[34] The small adjustment was allowed when the land contract was renewed, but it had to be passed by the villagers or villager representatives with at least a two-thirds vote and approved by government authority at the town and county levels. Local governments were prohibited from using an administrative order to require land adjustment during the renewed contract period.[35] The thirty-year contract term and procedural protection of land contracting term were soon added to the *LAL*, which was revised in 1998.[36]

However, the 1997 notice and 1998 revision of the *LAL* seem to play only a weak role in strengthening the farmers' stable and secure land tenure. A survey conducted in 2001 shows that more than 60 per cent of the surveyed villages made adjustments when they implemented the second round of land contracts, and more than half of these villages made large adjustments, which is prohibited by policy. Approximately 45 per cent of farmers responded that they did not have the chance to sign a land use right contract, and only slightly more than 45 per cent of farmers were issued such contracts. In approximately 55 per cent of the surveyed villages, land use rights certificates were not issued to farmers. As for land use rights contracts, less than 9 per cent of all contracts prohibited land adjustment during the contract term. Approximately 46 per cent of contracts allowed – and even required – future land adjustments.[37]

On 29 August 2002, a specific law for regulating rural land contracts, titled '*Rural Land Contracting Law*' (*RLCL*), was passed by the NPCSC.[38] In addition to securing stricter rural land use rights at the national

[34] *Guanyu Jinyibu Wending he Wanshan Nongcun Tudi Chengbao Guanxi de Tongzhi* [*Notice Concerning the Further Stabilization and Improvement of Rural Land Contracting Relations*], promulgagated by General Office (*Bangong Ting*) of the CPC Central Committee and General Office of the State Council] on 27 August 1997. This notice is available at news.xinhuanet.com/ziliao/2002–03/03/content_2644232.htm.

[35] Ibid.

[36] *LAL* (the version revised in 1998), art. 14. The revision also set strict procedure requirements for the readjustment of contracted land. It requires that any readjustment must obtain the approval of more than two-thirds of village members or village representatives and the approval of government at the town or county level.

[37] The survey concerning the implementation of the thirty-year rural land use rights was conducted by Renmin University and the Rural Development Institute in July and August of 2001. The survey covered 1,617 rural households in seventeen provinces. See Schwarzwalder, Prosterman, Ye and Riedinger, 'An Update', 166–71.

[38] *Nongcun Tudi Chengbao Fa* [*Rural Land Contracting Law*], enacted by the Twenty-ninth Meeting of the Standing Committee of the Ninth NPC on 29 August 2002. It was implemented on 1 March 2003. The Chinese text is available at news.xinhuanet.com/zhengfu/2002–08/30/content_543847.htm.

legislation level, the standing committee aims to strengthen farmers' capacity to enforce their rights and to facilitate the transfer of rural land.[39] First, this law stipulates the contract periods of various types of rural land in greater detail. For arable land (*gengdi*), the contract period is thirty years. For grassland (*caodi*), the contract period is thirty to fifty years. For wood land (*lindi*), the contract period is thirty to seventy years.[40] Second, the *RLCL* prohibits any organisation or individual from illegally infringing farmers' contracted land rights.[41] It declares that the contract-issuing party is prohibited from taking back the contracted land within the contract term.[42] The land readjustment can be performed only under the specific situation of natural disaster and through the required approval procedure.[43] Third, the *RLCL* allows the circulation of the contracted land on the premise that its original agricultural purpose not be changed.[44] Until the enforcement of *RLCL*, which offers strong, long-term protection of land rights to farmers, farmer households' land rights evolved from the fragile rights afforded in the contracts to stronger, systemised rights. In other words, an important bundle of rights was separated from collective ownership, allowing for collective units to be owners of the land, at least in a nominal sense.

3.1.5 The reform path of urban land and houses since 1949

The reform of urban land rights before reform and opening is less complex and winding than that of rural land rights. One term can be used to generalise reform from 1949 to 1978: nationalisation.

In the first four years following liberation, private owners of houses and land were categorised into two groups: the alliance group and the alien group. The former group was composed of poor workers, small dealers or urban petit bourgeoisie and national bourgeoisie. Maintaining the stable and prosperous development of urban industrial and commercial businesses, land, houses and other private property owned by the members of this group were maintained and protected.[45] The alien group

[39] Deininger, Jin and Rozelle, 'Dynamics', 5. [40] *RLCL*, art. 20.
[41] Ibid., art. 5. [42] Ibid., art. 26.
[43] Ibid., art. 27. The approval procedure is the same as that stipulated by art. 14 of the *LAL*.
[44] Ibid., art. 32.
[45] According to the *Common Programme*, in the rural areas, the farmers' private property shall be protected and in the urban areas, the private properties owned by workers, small dealers and national bourgeoisie shall be protected. The purpose of providing so is clarified as being for transferring China from agriculture country to industrial country. See *Common Programme*, art. 3.

includes bureaucratic capital holders and anti-revolution businessmen. Their capital and property including land and houses were confiscated and ownership was transferred to the government representing all citizens.[46]

The removal of private property in cities followed a route similar to that found in rural areas. Before 1953, the industrial and commercial dealers' privately owned property, including real estate, was recognised and protected by law, and confirmed by the *1954 Constitution of China*. Beginning in October 1953, the industrial and commercial dealers' enterprises began to be transferred from original private ownership to public-private cooperatives (*gongsi heying*), a type of joint ownership.[47] In the major cities by the end of 1955, most of the industrial and commercial firms had been turned into cooperatives. However, this was not the end of the story. Cooperatives represented a partial removal of city dealers' private ownership. The final goal of reform was to remove nearly all private property from the means of production, similar to what had been happening in the villages at that time. Before the Cultural Revolution that began in 1966, the privately owned portions of enterprises disappeared and all enterprises were placed under national or collective ownership. As a result, China's bourgeoisie disappeared.[48] The houses owned by rich enterprise owners were distributed to workers and poor urban residents. With the disappearance of private land rights in rural areas and private forms of enterprise in cities, China had become, by the end of the 1950s, a purely socialist country, following the footsteps of the former Soviet Union. The more than ten-year reform movement, characterised by the removal of private property from China's political and legal system, is referred to as Socialist Transformation or Socialist Reconstruction (*shehui zhuyi gaizao*). After the transformation, citizens' individual ownership covered only 'lawfully earned income, savings, houses and other lawful properties'.[49] Before China began to reform, houses in the cities were allocated by governments or units to staff or workers for living mainly, and no exchange, leasing or other transactions concerning these houses

[46] Ibid.

[47] In June 1953, the Central Committee of the CPC drafted a document titled, '*Guanyu Liyong Xianzhi he Gaizao Ziben Zhuyi Gongshangye de Ruogan Wenti*' ['*Opinions on Utilizing, Restricting and Reforming Capitalist Industrial and Commercial Enterprises*']. To follow this document and Chairman Mao's instruction, the All-China Federation of Industry & Commerce called on the movement, which transformed existing privately owned enterprises to become a public-private cooperative by October of that year.

[48] For more information on the short duration of the bourgeoisie after 1949, see generally Yang, 'The Evolution'.

[49] *1978 Constitution of China*, art. 9.

were allowed. In essence, urban residents had the right of occupation or residence rather than of ownership. Workers were given a type of residence right on some real estate. There was also a small group of people who were still the private owners of their houses, but private ownership of these houses was nominal only, because no transactions in the market were allowed at that time.

Under the planned economy system before 1978, houses in urban areas mainly were supplied by the government using fiscal income,[50] which was called the public welfare housing system. Citizens were allocated houses by local governments, state-owned enterprises (SOEs) or collectively owned units. For encouraging industrial growth, the majority of government investment was put into production. The dearth of investment in the living side led to a large shortage in the supply of houses.[51] This is evident in the data concerning average living area per capita. In 1977, the per capita living area was 3.6 square metres, less than the 4.5 square metres seen in 1945.[52]

After 1978, the central government began developing the real estate market. In 1979, it supported some experimental sales of houses in four cities: Xi-an, Liuzhou, Wuzhou and Nanning. The next year, the geographical scope of this reform was enlarged to include fifty cities. In 1982, a subsidised sale began,[53] and in 1984, a reform that raised house rents was implemented in Yantai, a seaside city in Shandong Province.[54] In 1988, the first national housing reform conference held by the central

[50] More than 87 per cent of total housing was built and supplied by the public sector and the collectives between 1949 and 1990. Among the small percentage of private housing, most of it was built after 1978. See Tang and Xie (eds.), *Zhongguo Fangdichan*, p. 1125.

[51] Before 1979, the main portion of capital construction investment in China had been made on the production side. According to data from the State Statistical Bureau of China, between 1950 and 1952, investment in productive construction was 65.6 per cent, and investment in housing construction was only 10.6 per cent. Between 1966 and 1970, the percentage of productive construction investment increased to more than 88 per cent of total investment and only 4 per cent of total investment was made on the housing side. See Zhong and Hays, 'The Transformation', 632–3.

[52] The data is from the State Statistical Bureau of China. In Romania, then also a socialist country, the per capita living area was 9.6 square meters in 1977. As to the former Soviet Union, the per capita living area was 12.7 square meters in 1977. See Ma and Sun (eds.), *Zhongguo Jingji*, p. 6. Additionally, residents paid nothing or only a little rent for the houses in which they lived. Thus, houses were offered to the residents as a type of welfare.

[53] Under this reform measure, the buyer paid only one-third of the total house price. The working unit of the buyer and the state paid one-third each. Thus, it was called the Three One-thirds System. See Zhong and Hays, 'The Transformation', 639–40.

[54] The purpose of raising house rents was to motivate more residents to buy houses.

government decided to augment its pilot experiment by extending it from selected cities to the entire nation, and the decision promulgated by this conference clarified that the purpose of housing reform was the gradual accomplishment of 'housing commercialisation'.[55] Later, housing reform was pushed forward in 1994 and 1998 when the State Council issued important decisions about the development of the housing market and the overall monetisation of the housing allocation system. The 1994 decision announced that the state would facilitate the development of a housing market from both the supply and demand sides.[56] The 1998 document prohibited working units from constructing and buying houses for their staff. Working units were required to convert their funds for financing housing construction and allocation to monetary subsidies for financing employees' buying of houses from the market.[57] This monetisation reform was initiated soon after the 1997 Asian financial crisis, which slowed China's increase of its exports and increased the need to stimulate domestic demand. The real estate industry was selected as a strategic industry to increase economic growth. Additionally, the working units, which were previously responsible for allocating houses to their employees, mainly were state-owned enterprises whose operation and performance were negatively influenced by the heavy load of housing allocation and other welfare. Thus, monetisation reform could stimulate the development of the housing market and release the welfare burden of state-owned enterprises.[58]

All of these reform experiments and measures aimed at separating the right to use land from its ownership. House buyers were given ownership of the houses and the right to use the land underneath them. Thus, a requirement for developing the real estate market is loosening government control of land ownership. The *LAL*, which was passed in 1986, stipulates that urban land owned by the state can be offered to individuals

[55] *Guanyu zai Quanguo Chengzhen Fenqi Fenpi Tuixing Zhufang Zhidu Gaige de Shishi Fang-an* [*The Proposals about the Gradual Implementation of Nationwide Urban Housing Reform*], enacted by the State Council on 25 February 1988. The Chinese text is available at www.gdczt.gov.cn/adminfo/polipub/fgbrowse/comprehensive/201004/t20100415_17329.htm.

[56] *Guanyu Shenhua Chengzhen Zhufang Zhidu Gaige de Jueding* [*Decision on Deepening Urban Housing Reform*], enacted by the State Council on 18 July 1994. The Chinese text is available at www.gov.cn/xxgk/pub/govpublic/mrlm/201011/t20101115_62794.html.

[57] *Guanyu Jinyibu Shenhua Chengzhen Zhufang Zhidu Gaige Jiakuai Zhufang Jianshe de Tongzhi* [*Notice on Deepening the Urban Housing Reform and Accelerating Housing Construction*], enacted by the State Council on 3 July 1998. The Chinese text is available at www.china.com.cn/law/flfg/txt/2006–08/08/content_7058347.htm.

[58] Deng, Shen and Wang, 'The Emerging', 170.

and units (including enterprises owned by all of the people or by collectives) for use. In 1988, the *1982 Constitution of China* was revised to allow the transfer of land use rights, and this set the constitutional basis for developing a transaction market for land use rights.[59] In 1994, the *Law on Urban Real Estate Administration* (*LUREA*) was enacted.[60] The *LUREA* stipulates two methods for acquiring land use rights from governments. The first method is through government allocation (*huabo*), which is mainly for land used for the public interest.[61] The second method is through leasing (*churang*), which is the primary way in which individuals and enterprises can acquire land use rights. Generally, leasing is made through the government auction of land use rights.[62] For residential use, the maximum term of land use rights is seventy years; for industrial use, the maximum term is fifty years; and for commercial, tourism or entertainment use, the term is forty years.[63]

Before 1953, the private property system in both rural and urban areas was reshaped. In rural areas, the private ownership of land held by landlords was substituted by farmers' individual ownership. In urban areas, the alliance group members' private ownership over land and houses was maintained. From 1953 to 1978, the removal of private ownership led to the nationalisation of urban land and the collectivisation of rural land. In urban areas, the individual ownership of most houses was removed and the remaining individual ownership of a small percentage of houses was restricted to the owners' individual or family residential needs. After 1978, market-oriented reforms, although stopping short of reviving the private ownership of land, enabled individuals and firms to obtain long-term use rights to land. Additionally, the private ownership of houses in both rural and urban areas was restored. Although the full privatisation

[59] Through the *1988 Amendment*, the following sentence was added into the art. 10 of *1982 Constitution of China*: The right to the use of land may be transferred according to law. See *1982 Constitution of China*, art. 10(4).

[60] *Chengshi Fangdichan Guanli Fa* [*Law on Urban Real Estate Administration*], enacted by the Eighth Meeting of the Standing Committee of the Eighth NPC on 5 July 1994 and revised by the Twenty-ninth Meeting of the Standing Committee of the Tenth NPC on 30 August 2007. The Chinese text of this law is available at www.gov.cn/flfg/2007–08/30/content_732595.htm.

[61] Ibid., art. 23. [62] Ibid., art. 12.

[63] *Chengzhen Guoyou Tudi Shiyongquan Churang he Zhuanrang Zanxing Tiaoli* [*Provisional Regulation on Land Conveyance and Transfer in Municipalities and Towns*], art. 12. This regulation was enacted by the State Council on 19 May 1990. The Chinese text is available at www.mlr.gov.cn/zwgk/flfg/tdglflfg/200601/t20060119_72175.htm.

of land may not be expected in the near future in China, the partial restoration of private property has led to the rapid development of the real estate market in urban areas and to greater agricultural growth in rural areas.

To comment on China's property system, Walker and Li noted that it is 'too vast, too complex and currently subject to too many changes'.[64] Compared to the Western property system, which is dominated by private ownership, China's current property system is indeed much more complicated. In Western countries, individuals are the main owners of land and houses, whereas in China, landowners are governments (representing the state or all of the people) and collectives. Additionally, individuals and firms can own houses and use rights, as well as a limited scope of land transaction rights. The Western property system can be called a freehold system, and China's system can be called a leasehold system. Is China's property system too complex? Even for individual owners, leasing and other transferrable activities may occur broadly. If we regard ownership as a bundle of rights using the U.S. perspective, we may find that in China, the main rights in the bundle of land ownership – including the rights to occupy, use, derive interest and transfer – are conferred to private owners. Land use rights can also be regarded as private property or a type of quasi-ownership. However, in a freehold system, the leasing relationship mainly occurs between two private subjects. In China, lessees as individuals must face a more powerful owner (the state) or representative of the owner, which is the government. As agents of all the people, government officers may engage in corruption or other rent seeking activities that could harm fair competition in the acquirement of land and houses.[65] Thus, the restriction of government officers' unjust activities creates high transaction costs. For freehold owners, there is no limit of the life term of

64 Anthony and Li, 'Land Use', 210.

65 During the pre-reform period, when the supply of housing was controlled by government and the allocation of housing was mainly made through the working units, which were composed of government agencies and state-owned or collectively owned enterprises, the supply and allocation of housing was criticised for its unequal distribution and the corruption it produced. The allocation of housing units was based on the consideration of household heads' social status or position and had no direct link with the demanders' housing needs and incomes. The persons with higher status in the society could be allocated larger and better houses. The housing units were allocated by the officers in charge rather than through the market, and this created corruption in the housing allocation system. See Wang and Murie, 'The Process', 973.

ownership, but in China, land use rights are set within a certain period. Generally and theoretically, private ownership is clearer than land use rights or lease rights, but this difference can be reduced by clarifying the scope of the lease rights and by stabilising and prolonging the life term of such rights in the law.

What should cause the most worry is the dynamic and changeable nature of China's property system, which influences the predictability of property rights and distorts the long-term rational decisions of rights holders. From 1949 until the present day, China's property system has been undergoing processes of both upside-down and downside-up change. It is argued that 'attempting to put anything in print about China and its land reforms is extremely dangerous'. The danger is twofold: 'the system is so dynamic that whatever one may have written is probably well on the way to being out of date when read'; and, 'things are never quite as they seem.'[66] Is China's property system too easily changeable? Or does this system demonstrate the fragility of any set property that is easily changed? Looking back at the system before 1978, the answer is 'yes'. However, with openness and reform producing greater internationalisation and freedom, the strengthening of laws and their enforcement, and peoples' awareness of their private rights, the changeability and fragility of China's property system is lessening, albeit slowly. It would be correct to say that the current property system will continue to change. However, it can be asserted that the change must be towards the development of the market economy based on stronger private property protection.

Thus, currently and in the future, what is most important for China's individual rights holders is not fighting for ownership in name but advocating a clearer definition of land rights and stronger protections of property rights. These measures will help to reduce the complexity and instability of China's property system.

3.2 The evolution of private property in the constitutions

The dynamic change in private property protection in the New China is reflected in the frequent revision of the country's constitutional provisions. Between 1954 and 1982, China enacted four constitutions, in 1954, 1975, 1978 and 1982.

66 Walker and McKinnell, 'Economic Reform', 39.

3.2.1 *The 1949* Common Programme

The *Common Programme* was passed on 29 September 1949 by the CPPCC, only two days before the birth of the New China. The *Common Programme* is called China's provisional constitution because it was drafted to offer guiding principles for organising and operating a new political system in China.[67] Although it is not an official constitution, the process of negotiating and passing the *Common Programme* was more democratic than was the process of negotiating and passing the subsequent constitutions. The CPPCC is composed of representatives from the Communist Party and other democratic parties and represents various interest groups. Thus, as a result of balancing the various interests of various parties, the *Common Programme* did not announce China as a Socialist country, but as a country of new democracy, although the leadership of the working class was emphasised.[68] Correspondingly, the *Common Programme* does not copy the mature model of the Soviet Union, which established a public property system. Instead, private property was emphasised. Article 3 of the *Common Programme* stipulates that: 'People's Republic of China . . . protects the state's public property and the communes' property and protects the economic interest and private interest of workers, farmers, petit bourgeoisie and national bourgeoisies.'[69]

Persons qualified to own private property were limited to the alliance group. Although the protection of private property is not the fundamental or dominant basis of New China's property system, it was emphasised equivalently with the protection of public property and collective property.

3.2.2 *The* 1954 Constitution of China

Unlike the *Common Programme*, the *1954 Constitution of China* stipulated in its preamble that China should progress from the current new democracy system to a socialist system, and thus, that China was in a

[67] The adoption of the *Common Programme* is regarded as the first important action in building the New China's legal system. See Wu, 'Building The New China's Legal System', 6. The *Common Programme* later became the foundation for the *1954 Constitution of China*. The preamble to the *1954 Constitution of China* states: 'This *Constitution* is based on the *Common Programme* of the Chinese People's Political Consultative Conference of 1949 and is a development of it.' See Hsia, 'The Constitution', 426.

[68] See the preamble to the 1949 CPPCC *Common Programme*. In addition, the leadership of the Communist Party is not specified in this document.

[69] Ibid., art. 3.

transition period. The *Common Programme* also stipulated that Socialist China should be established through socialist industrialisation and reconstruction.[70]

As a country in transition, China adopted the *Common Programme*'s basic principles concerning the property system, namely, the coexistence of public property and private property. The *Common Programme* provided four forms of ownership in China: national ownership (all-people ownership), collective ownership (cooperative ownership), individual dealers' ownership and capitalist ownership.[71]

To meet the transitional goal of turning China into a socialist country, however, the government also stipulated that individual or private ownership shall be encouraged, led or guided towards collective or national ownership. For farmers and independent labourers, their ownership of land and other production means would be protected. At the same time, they were encouraged by the government to form collectives.[72] The *1954 Constitution of China* provided the protection of capitalist ownership. However, it also stipulated that capitalist ownership would be gradually substituted by national ownership.[73] Compared to the *Common Programme*, this constitution emphasised the status of public property over private property.

This constitution included a provision on expropriation. It allowed governments to expropriate land and other means of production for the public interest.[74] However, no compensation is set in this provision. The lack of compensation created a vacant constitutional protection of private properties. In essence, the purpose of the expropriation provision was to offer constitutional assistance to the government in transferring ownership of private property to the national government or to the collectives, or to serve social reconstruction purposes, rather than to protect private property owners.

The socialist reconstruction movement was advanced rapidly under the government's strict orders. Most reconstructions were finished before the end of 1950s. In the fifteen years following its birth, the *1954 Constitution of China* had become meaningless because China had become a purely socialist country with a property system dominated by public property rather than a democratic country with a mixed property system, as stipulated by the constitution.

[70] *1954 Constitution of China*, art. 4. [71] Ibid., art. 5.
[72] Ibid., arts. 8–9. [73] Ibid., art. 10. [74] Ibid., art. 13.

3.2.3 The 1975 and 1978 constitutions

Regarding the property system, the provisions in these two constitutions are nearly the same. They are both of a socialist nature. They stipulate two main forms of ownership: all-people ownership and collective ownership. Although individual economic activity was allowed within a limited scope, it should be gradually collectivized, as specified in the constitution. Individuals were allowed to exercise ownership mainly over their living materials. The government's expropriation of collective land and of individually owned materials was allowed and no compensation was stipulated by the constitution.

3.2.4 The 1982 Constitution of China

The constitution enacted in 1982 is China's current enforceable constitution. It stipulates that individual ownership in rural and urban areas is a supplementary type of ownership of publicly owned property.[75] The *1982 Constitution of China* clarifies again the national ownership of urban land and the collective ownership of rural and suburban land. However, the constitution stipulates that individuals own 'legal property' rather than 'living material', which was stipulated by the *1978 Constitution of China.*[76] This revision means that citizens, as individuals, can own both living and productive materials according to the law. The scope of individual ownership is enlarged in the *1982 Constitution of China.*

As a constitution born in the early stages of openness and reform, it emphasises the significance of public property. Its art. 12 stipulates: 'Socialist public property is sacred and inviolable. The state protects Socialist public property. Appropriation or damaging of state or collective property by any organisation or individual by whatever means is prohibited.'

This constitution allows government to take over land, and no compensation for seized land was stipulated when it was enacted.[77] To compare this stipulation with the taking clause in the *1954 Constitution of China*, the objects to be taken were limited to land. This small revision may demonstrate that during the period of market-oriented reform, the government's taking power should be restrained.

[75] *1982 Constitution of China*, art. 11. [76] Ibid., art. 13.

[77] Article 10 of the original *1982 Constitution of China* stipulates that the state can requisition land for the needs of the public according to the law. This article was later revised by the *2004 Amendment*.

3.2.5 *Amendments to the* 1982 Constitution of China

3.2.5.1 *1988 Amendment*

The first amendment was made in 1988.[78] This amendment allows for the transfer of land use rights, specifying that, '[l]and use right can be transferred according to laws.'[79] Moreover, it legalises the status of private economic sectors by stipulating that, 'the private sector of the economy is a complement to the Socialist public economy', and 'the State protects the lawful rights and interests of the private sector of the economy'.

3.2.5.2 *1993 Amendment*

The most attractive revision made by the *1993 Amendment* was substituting the phrase 'Socialist public ownership economy' with 'Socialist market economy'. Declaring to the world that China is moving from a planned economy based on public ownership to a market economy allowing for the existence and development of a private economy is a milestone revision. Another revision showing China's progress towards a market economy is the replacement of the term 'state-run' (*guoying*) of economy or enterprises with the term 'state-owned' (*guoyou*). This change implies that the state or government will step back from direct operation or control of state-owned enterprises and keep only its identity as their owner.[80]

The outdated rural collectives, including the rural People Communes and agricultural producers' cooperatives, were deleted from the constitution by this amendment. The recently developed rural contracted responsibility system, based mainly on the households, was added to the constitution. These revisions show the constitutional acceptance of the development of a private economy and individual property rights in rural areas.

[78] The *1988 Amendment* was enacted by the First Session of the Seventh NPC on 12 April 1988. The Chinese text is available at www.npc.gov.cn/wxzl/gongbao/2000–12/05/content_5004498.htm.

[79] Before this amendment, the constitution stipulated only that '[n]o organization or individual may appropriate, buy, sell or lease land or otherwise engage in the transfer of land by unlawful means'. See *1982 Constitution of China* (the original version), art. 10.

[80] The *1993 Amendment* was enacted by the First Session of the Eighth NPC on 29 March 1993. The Chinese text is available at www.npc.gov.cn/wxzl/gongbao/1993–03/29/content_1481290.htm.

3.2.5.3 *1999 Amendment*

This amendment inserts the doctrine of 'rule of law' into the *Constitution* by stating that the state shall be governed 'according to law' and that China will be developed as 'a Socialist country under the rule of law'.[81]

Following the *1993 Amendment* that subsumed the rural responsibility system, the *1999 Amendment* further provided for a double operation system characterised by 'the combination of centralised operation with decentralised operation on the basis of operation by households under a contract'.

The status of non-public economies, including individual economies and private economies, was lifted once more. The newer amendment revised the complementary status of the private economy in the *1988 Amendment* to become an 'important component' by stipulating that 'the individual and private sectors of the economy, operating within the limits prescribed by law, constitute an important component of the Socialist market economy'. Although the new wording in this amendment appears to place private and individual economies on a parallel level with the public economy, we cannot say that the private economy enjoys identical protection to that of the public economy because the *1982 Constitution of China* continues to emphasise the dominant position of public ownership. The provision that public ownership serves as the basis of the socialist economic system was removed. The new economic system, according to the *1982 Constitution of China*, includes 'diverse forms of ownership' (with public ownership as the dominant component) that shall be developed side by side. Correspondingly, the system of private property, as the basis for the developing private economy, should be protected more strongly than before. However, the essential constitutional revision regarding private property protection came several years later in 2004.

3.2.5.4 *2004 Amendment*

First, of the four amendments, the *2004 Amendment* most clearly embodies the modern constitutional spirit.[82] In China, this is the first time the

[81] This addition forms the first paragraph of art. 5 of the *1982 Constitution of China*. The *1999 Amendment* was enacted by the Second Session of the Ninth NPC on 15 March 1999. The Chinese text is available at www.npc.gov.cn/wxzl/wxzl/2000–12/10/content_7075.htm.

[82] The *2004 Amendment* was enacted by the Second Session of the Tenth NPC on 14 March 2004. The Chinese text is available at www.npc.gov.cn/wxzl/wxzl/2004–04/19/content_334620.htm.

words 'human rights' have appeared in the constitution: 'the State respects and preserves human rights'.[83] Second, the significance of the non-public economy is further emphasised. According to this amendment, the state 'encourages, supports and guides the development of the non-public sectors of the economy'.[84] Third, this is the first time the words 'the inviolability of private property' have appeared in China's constitutions. The outdated wording of 'lawfully earned income, savings, houses and other lawful property' in former constitutions has been replaced with the phrase 'private property'. This amendment declares that 'citizens' lawful private property is inviolable' and stipulates the compensation required when the government takes private property.[85] For the purpose of public interest, the state may expropriate or requisition land or private property for its use; however, the state must render compensation for the land or private property expropriated or requisitioned. The compensation requirement for the land that is expropriated or requisitioned is inserted into art. 10 of the *1982 Constitution of China* by this amendment.[86]

3.3 The party-leading route of China's constitutional change

In China, constitutional change has been on a party-leading route. This route contains three steps: reform experiment, party generalisation and constitutional absorption. Decisions on major reform issues are first rendered in the form of informal or unofficial party policy guidelines or initiatives when implementing reform experiments. After a period of experiment, the generalised decision is made to replace the old notions or principles in the party constitution or other important party documents with the new notions. The third step is to revise the constitution (and relevant laws) to incorporate the newly changed principles, rules or ideologies. When then party leader Jiang Zemin visited Guangdong Province in February 2000, he delivered an important description of 'three represents' (*sange daibiao*), which later became Jiang's most distinctive political contribution to the theoretical development of the CPC. From 1989 when he took the leadership position in both party and country until 2002 when he retired from his party leadership position, Jiang Zemin had been pushing the notion of ruling the country according to law. The phrases 'three represents' and 'Ruling the Country According to Law' (*yifa zhiguo*) were

[83] This addition is incorporated into the *1982 Constitution of China* as its art. 33(3).
[84] *1982 Constitution of China*, art. 11(2).
[85] Ibid., art. 13. [86] Ibid., arts. 10(3), 13(3).

both added to the party constitution at the Sixteenth Party Congress in 2002.[87] Then, in 2004 and with the stamp of Jiang's personal contribution, these two phrases were added to the *1982 Constitution of China*. China's constitutional revisions always carry the personal stamps of individual leaders. It is also argued, 'as such, that each constitutional revision coincides with the five-year term of the Party Congress, and the NPC reflects in effect the changes in Party leadership'.[88] Constitutional revisions have generally been initiated by the party. For example, the party's central committee in 2003 submitted suggestions regarding the revision of the *1982 Constitution of China* to the NPCSC. Nearly all of the suggestions were later included in the *2004 Amendment* passed by the NPC.[89]

The personal stamp on constitutional progress causes concern that China's constitution cannot be stable because it is too easily changeable. However, because China is in a period of rapid transition from a planned economy to a market economy and requires frequent adjustment of its legal and political system, such changeability is understandable. The most serious problem is that the *1982 Constitution of China* has no promise or guarantees that a market economy or the rule of law should be the permanent and unchangeable doctrine for China. The socialist system remains the basic system of China, and the fundamental feature of China is 'a Socialist state under the people's democratic dictatorship led by the working class and based on the alliance of workers and peasants'.[90] Considering that China is and will be in the primary stages of socialist development for a long time, the socialist market economy should be developed. It appears that a market economy is only a transitional phase on its way to the final socialist stage. Will the market economy system nevertheless be adopted, and will private property protection continue to be emphasised after the passing of the early transition stages of the socialist society? Although the early stage is currently declared to be long term, it could easily be ended soon or within a few years. In addition, the term 'socialist' is linked

[87] *Guanyu Zhongguo Gongchandang Zhangcheng (Xiuzheng-an) de Jueyi* [*The Decision on Revising the Constitution of China's Communist Party*], passed by the Sixteenth CPC National Party Congress on 14 November 2002. This decision is available at news.xinhuanet.com/newscenter/2002–11/14/content_630175.htm.

[88] Chen, 'The Revision', at the 7th para.

[89] *Guanyu Xiugai Xianfa Bufen Neirong de Jianyi* [*Suggestions on Revising Partial Contents of the Constitution*], submitted by the Central Committee of the CPC to the NPCSC on 12 December 2003. This document is available at news.xinhuanet.com/newscenter/2003–12/22/content_1243461.htm.

[90] *1982 Constitution of China*, art. 1.

to nearly every key word or term reflecting reform movement towards the protection of private property or other individual basic rights. These include 'socialist market economy', 'socialist democracy', 'socialist legal system' and 'socialist rule of law'. This implies that the socialist society is based on the dominance of public property and that under the leadership of the communist party, the dominance of public property is the goal or the premise of every political, economic or legal reform. The *1954 Constitution of China* stipulates that China is in the new democracy stage of socialism and that the transition period will be gradual. In addition, the socialist transformation of production means is based on individuals' personal free will.[91] In 1954, it was estimated that the socialist transformation would continue for approximately fifteen years; however, the socialist transformation or reconstruction was quickly driven to completion by the individual requirements of then-leader Mao Zedong within two years after the enactment of this constitution. More seriously, the compulsory deprivation of privately owned land and other production means during the socialist transformation was unconstitutional.[92] For identical reasons, perhaps the current constitution, with cautious progress in pushing a market economy and protecting private property, may at some point be changed, and this type of uncertainty or unpredictability leads to individuals' lack of confidence in owning and using their privately owned property or exercising their property rights. However, it is also argued that after more than thirty years of openness and reform, the people's knowledge of the *Constitution* is broad, and the expectation of the constitutional protection of individual basic rights is deeply rooted in society.[93] This situation is fundamentally different from the environment surrounding the birth of the *1954 Constitution of China* when the CPC strictly controlled people's ideology and most people were supporters of the public property system. Thus, although China is and will be under the leadership of the communist party for the foreseeable future, it will not be easy for the CPC to render a constitutional change that reverts to the original socialist public property system and planned economy. The openness and reform policies that were implemented in the late 1970s had a huge influence on the development of China's economy and society and moved China in the direction of a market economy. This tendency

[91] *1954 Constitution of China*, arts. 8–10.

[92] For a historical review of the change of property clauses in the constitutions in China, see Wang, 'Xinzhongguo'.

[93] Chen, 'The Revision', at the 28th para.

is difficult to reverse because, after many years of market economy development, the power structure that supported a socialist planned economy in the pre-reform stage has changed to one with diversified powers in which the social forces supporting a market economy have become quite powerful.[94] Conversely, any radical or active reform that may lead to the reduction of the party's leadership power is intolerable to the CPC. That is why the constitutional changes in the past years have barely allowed for fundamental political or legal reform although continual bits of progress has been made. This is called the slow, gradual approach or the minimalist approach of China's constitutional revisions.[95]

3.4 The current constitutional framework of private property protection

3.4.1 The ownership structure of property

The ownership structure of property in the Chinese constitution corresponds to the components of the economic system. The economic system comprises the public economy, including the state-owned economy and the cooperative economy; and the non-public sectors of the economy, which are the individual and private sectors of the economy. Correspondingly, the ownership structure comprises public ownership, which includes state ownership (ownership by all of the people) and collective ownership by the working people, and non-public ownership or private ownership. The cooperative economy and the linked collective ownership operate in both rural and urban areas. In rural areas, they concern rural collective economic organisations, and in urban areas, they concern various forms of the cooperative economy in cities and towns, such as those in the handicraft and industrial sectors, and building, transport, commercial and service trades.[96]

94 This can be generalised concisely and precisely by Nee's assertion:

> Despite the political retrenchment in China, the market reforms implemented in the 1980s have lasting consequences that are not easily reversed, even with a hard-line conservative faction in control of state power. Economic reform from 1978 to 1989 brought about changes in power relationships within the state structure and in society, which in turn gave rise to new alignments of interests that champion marketization.

See Nee, 'Organizational Dynamics', 1.

95 Chen argues that 'in this context, there are reasons to be cautiously optimistic about the future of rule of law and constitutionalism in China'. See Chen, 'The Revision', at the 29th para.

96 *1982 Constitution of China*, art. 8.

State ownership covers urban land and most natural resources including all mineral resources and water and the majority of the forests, mountains, grasslands, unreclaimed land and beaches. Some portions of forests, mountains, grasslands, unreclaimed land and beaches can be owned by collectives as prescribed by law.[97] Moreover, collective ownership covers rural and suburban land and also house sites and privately farmed plots of cropland and hilly land.[98] Individual or private ownership covers houses, living materials and production means, except land and natural resources. The most distinctive feature of China's current ownership structure is that individuals are excluded from ownership of the most important or fundamental land.

3.4.2 *The hierarchy of ownership forms*

We cannot assert that all forms of ownership are constitutionally equal. For economic forms, 'the state-owned economy, namely, the Socialist economy under ownership by the whole people, is the leading force in the national economy'.[99] Private economy is defined as 'an important component of the Socialist market economy'.[100] Apparently, in the economic structure, the state-owned economy has the highest status, the co-operative economy is at the next level, and the private economy at the lowest level.

The status of private ownership in the *1982 Constitution of China* is not equal to the status of public ownership. Public ownership is defined clearly and solidly as the basis of China's socialist economic system. In the current and future primary stages of socialism, the status of public ownership is dominant.[101] Although diverse forms of ownership, including individual or private ownership, are allowed to develop side by side, private ownership's status can only be secondary or supplementary although the *Constitution* deems it important.

The inequality between public ownership and non-public ownership is clearly certified by differences in the provisions concerning the protection of property. The *1982 Constitution of China* declares that 'socialist public

[97] Ibid., arts. 9–10.

[98] Specifically, the majority of rural and suburban land is owned by collective organisations except a portion that may be owned by the state according to law. Ibid., art. 10.

[99] Ibid., art. 7. [100] Ibid., art. 11. [101] Ibid., art. 6.

property is sacred and inviolable'[102] and 'citizens' lawful private property is inviolable'.[103] Although neither public nor private properties may be violated according to the *1982 Constitution*, only public property is declared to be sacred.[104]

3.4.3 *Separation between public ownership and its use rights*

Various levels of government control the state ownership of a vast array of properties, the most important component of which is land. However, government officers or agencies are not the appropriate administrators of state-owned properties. In a country that desires to both maintain socialist features and operate public assets efficiently by motivating individual incentive, the separation of use and other operation and transaction rights from state ownership becomes the only feasible option. There are two typical examples of separation of state ownership. One is the separation of state-owned enterprises' ownership from the enterprises' operation. In 1993, the *1982 Constitution of China* was revised to replace 'planned economy' with 'market economy'. To coincide with this transformation, the term 'state-run economy' was changed to 'state-owned economy', and the term 'state-run enterprises' was replaced with 'state-owned enterprises'. Moreover, the requirement that the state do the planning for state-owned enterprises was removed. This revision led to the separation of state enterprises' operation rights from the enterprises' ownership. National or local governments may not operate the state enterprises directly or control the state enterprises' operation fully by state or government planning. Another important separation example is the separation of state-owned land and its use rights. Article 10 of the *1982 Constitution of China* allows that 'the right to the use of land may be transferred according to law'. This constitutional rule is enforced based on the *LAL* and the *LUREA*.

The foremost example of the separation of collective ownership is land use rights, which are separated from land ownership in rural areas. Parcels of rural land are distributed to households for decentralised operation and

[102] Ibid., art. 12. [103] Ibid., art. 13.

[104] What is interesting is that in the official English translation of the *1982 Constitution of China* (with the *2004 Amendment*) promulgated by the NPC, Socialist public property is said to be inviolable only, and the word 'sacred' does not appear with it. Is this omission intentional or negligent?

cultivation within the statutory period. As owners, the collective organisations play a role in the centralised operation in the forms of cooperatives of producers, supply and marketing, credit and consumers.[105] This system is called the dual operation system, comprising decentralised household operations and centralised collective operations. The second separation example of collective ownership concerns operating rights, which are separated from collective enterprises. The collective enterprises can transfer the use or operating rights of such enterprises to individuals by contracts.

3.4.4 *The structure of private property in China*

Currently, according to the *1982 Constitution of China*, private property includes ownership property and non-ownership property. The former refers to property over which individuals can have full or unitary ownership rights or enjoy owner's status. Ownership property mainly includes living materials and houses. Non-ownership property refers to property rights that can be assigned mainly to citizens and includes property rights separated from state or collective ownership, mainly referring to land use and transaction rights. Unlike Western countries in which the expropriation of land targets the private owners of land, the expropriation of rural land in China targets collective ownership and individual use rights. In urban areas, expropriation by government targets mainly the private ownership of houses and the use rights to the land underneath the houses, which is held by citizens.

3.5 The constitutional restraints against governmental taking

Article 13 of the current constitution is the main provision for restraining the use of eminent domain or governmental taking of property. First, this article declares that a citizen's lawful private property is inviolable and the state must protect the rights of citizens to private property and its inheritance according to law. Second, the governmental taking of private property can only be conducted in the public interest. Third, the persons whose private property is taken must be compensated. Fourth, taking and compensation decisions must be made in accordance with the law. These are the four components of the constitutional protection of private

[105] Ibid., art. 8.

property or the taking of private property clause: the inviolability of private property, the public interest purpose, the compensation requirement and the lawful enforcement requirement.

Article 10 (3) of the *1982 Constitution of China* specifically covers the governmental taking of land. Its content is similar to the taking of private property clause (art. 13).[106]

3.5.1 The constitutional status of private property rights: fundamental or not?

Notably, art. 13 – which regards private property protection – is placed in the first chapter titled 'General Principles', rather than in the second chapter titled 'The Fundamental Rights and Duties of Citizens'. This design is different from the popular practice observed in Western countries. In the *U.S. Constitution*, the right to private property is ranked with other fundamental rights, such as life and liberty.[107] In Germany, the *German Basic Law* places private property in the first section, 'Basic Rights'.[108] In Japan, the article concerning private property is found in the section on 'Rights and Duties of the People'.[109] The current enforceable French constitution does not have a clause concerning the legal status of private property; however, it declares the incorporation of basic principles of *The Declaration of the Rights of Man and of the Citizen* (*French Declaration*), a foundation document born in the French Revolution in 1789.[110] According to the *French Declaration*, property rights are defined as one of the 'natural and imprescriptible rights' of man.[111] Although different descriptions such as 'basic' or 'natural' are used, all of these representative

[106] Article 10(3) stipulates that '[t]he State may, in the public interest and in accordance with law, expropriate or requisition land for its use and make compensation for the land expropriated or requisitioned'.

[107] See the *Fifth Amendment* and *Fourteenth Amendment* to the *U.S. Constitution*.

[108] *German Basic Law*, art. 14.

[109] *Constitution of Japan*, chap. 3. The English text of this constitution is available at www.solon.org/Constitutions/Japan/English/english-Constitution.html.

[110] This declaration is titled '*Declaration of 1793*'. It was adopted by the National Constituent Assembly (Assemblée Nationale Constituante) in 1789. In 1793, a lengthier version was adopted. It was considered the first step in producing a constitution for France.

[111] Other natural rights include liberty, security, and resistance to oppression. See *French Declaration*, art. 2. The English text of this constitution is available at www.assemblee-nationale.fr/english/8ab.asp.

Western countries' constitutions directly or indirectly define property as one of citizens' fundamental or basic constitutional rights.

We cannot say that China's incorporation of private property into the chapter that precedes the chapter concerning fundamental rights indicates the state's intention to strengthen the protection of private property or give private property the highest status. In fact, this placement follows past practice during the stage of the planned economy. All of China's constitutions after 1949 include the provisions concerning private property or individual materials in the first chapter. For example, the *1954 Constitution of China* stipulates farmers' ownership of rural land in art. 8, individual workers' ownership of production means in art. 9, capitalists' ownership of production means and other capital in art. 10 and citizens' ownership of living materials in art. 11. All these four articles are in the first chapter, titled 'General Principles'. This type of design originated in the former leading socialist country, the USSR. The *1936 Constitution of the USSR* stipulated citizens' limited ownership of property in its first chapter, entitled 'The Organisation of Soviet Society'.[112] The first chapter in both the Chinese and the USSR's constitutions concern the basic socialist economic system in the countries. Including private property rights in this section purposely weakens private property's status and limits the scope of individual property by strengthening the idea that privately owned property is only a secondary and supplementary attachment to the basic public property system. Although the *2004 Amendment* to the *1982 Constitution of China* declares for the first time the inviolability of private property, the location of private property clauses in the section on the socialist economic system indicates private property's constitutional status, which is lower than the status of public property. This also implies that in a country with a socialist ideology, one function of private property is to help to achieve social development. Another natural conclusion is that the strengthening of private property protection shown in the *2004 Amendment* is only a small amount of progress within a basic socialist economic system in which public property remains the dominant or leading property form.

[112] Article 10 of the *1936 Constitution of the USSR* stipulates that '[t]he right of citizens to personal ownership of their incomes from work and of their savings, of their dwelling houses and subsidiary household economy, their household furniture and utensils and articles of personal use and convenience, as well as the right of inheritance of personal property of citizens, is protected by law.' Such constitution is available at www.departments.bucknell.edu/russian/const/1936toc.html.

3.5.2 *The three prongs of the taking of property clause*

Following the inviolability definition of private property, the *1982 Constitution of China* established three constraints on the governmental taking of private property. According to the *Constitution*, the taking activities include expropriation and requisition. Definitions of expropriation and requisition are not included in the *Constitution* or other legal documents. Generally, the term 'expropriation' is defined as the taking of property ownership by the state. The state, after the expropriation, becomes the new owner of the private property that was taken. The term 'requisition' is defined as the compulsory taking of the use rights of private property for a certain period; during the requisition period,the private owner maintains nominal ownership, and after the requisition, the requisitioned property can be returned to the private owner. Thus, expropriation refers to the taking of total ownership of private property, and requisition refers to the taking of the material components of private property rights for a certain period. They are both governmental infringement on the rights of private owners.

Generally, there are three constraints against the taking of private property: public use or purpose, just compensation and due process. Before the *2004 Amendment*, the constitutional restraints on the government's taking of private property were fragmented. Only one sentence in the third paragraph of art. 10 in the pre-2004 Chinese constitution stipulated that 'the state may, in the public interest, requisition land for its use in accordance with the law'. This provision is definitely insufficient to guard private property from unjust infringement by governmental activities. First, only 'requisition' is stipulated as an action government may take. Expropriation is not included in the *Constitution*. Second, what may be taken is limited to land rather than all private property or property rights. Third, no compensation constraint is established by the *Constitution*, which is the largest defect of this clause.

Notably, the lack of constitutional stipulations regarding property other than land does not preclude the government from requisitioning other property; in addition, that expropriation is not included in the *Constitution* does not preclude the government from expropriating property. In reality, the government's requisitioning of property other than land and the government's expropriation of private property have been frequent since the adoption of the *1982 Constitution of China*. An accurate interpretation is that the *1982 Constitution of China*, before the *2004 Amendment*, offered protection at a constitutional level, although mostly on paper, for the requisition of land only. According to laws and regulations, governments can take other property. Including expropriation, requisition and all private property in the *Constitution*'s taking of property clauses in the *2004 Amendment* indicates that the scope of the constitutional protection of private property is nearly complete in writing, although not sufficiently strong in practice.

Although the *2004 Amendment* stipulates compensation, a large defect in the contextual description remains. The amendment does not clarify the standard or basic principle of compensation. For example, in the *U.S. Constitution*, compensation must be 'just compensation'.[113] Japan's constitution adopts the just compensation standard as well.[114] *German Basic Law* requires that 'compensation shall be determined by establishing an equitable balance between the public interest and the interests of those affected'.[115]

That there is no clear constitutional standard or definition of compensation in China's current constitution does not mean that the government can decide the compensation amount at will and enforce its expropriation or requisition without any restraint. In addition to the public interest requirement, the *Constitution* requires that the decision and enforcement of both the taking of property and compensation shall be 'in accordance with law'.[116] In the suggestions regarding the revision of the *Constitution* submitted by the CPC, the suggestion concerning private property is: 'The State may, in the public interest, expropriate or requisition private property for its use and in accordance with law, make compensation for the private property expropriated or requisitioned' [emphasis added by the author].[117]

However, in the finalised version of the *2004 Amendment*, this suggestion was revised to the following description: 'The State may, in the public interest and in accordance with law, expropriate or requisition private property for its use and make compensation for the private property expropriated or requisitioned' [emphasis added by the author].[118]

According to the party's suggestion, the requirement 'in accordance with law' restricts compensation decisions only. The implication appears

113 The *Fifth Amendment* to the *U.S. Constitution*.

114 *Constitution of Japan*, art. 29. Its third paragraph stipulates that '[p]rivate property may be taken for public use upon just compensation therefore'.

115 *German Basic Law*, art. 14(3).

116 *1982 Constitution of China*, arts. 10(3), 13(3).

117 *Guanyu Xiugai Xianfa Bufen Neirong de Jianyi* [*Suggestions on Revising Partial Contents of the Constitution*].

118 *1982 Constitution of China*, art. 13(3).

to be that the expropriation decision may be made without considering any appropriate legal procedures. The final revision, which imposes the 'in accordance with law' requirement before taking property and compensation, appears to be minor but is actually quite significant. Nevertheless, the lack of clear and restrictive constitutional standards of compensation may allow legislators at national or local levels reckless discretion power in stipulating compensation standards.

In the United States, due process of law is required by the *U.S. Constitution* to restrict the government's taking of property.[119] Due process, without uniform authoritative explanation, is generally analysed from both substantive and procedural points of view. Due process is a legal principle rooted in the common law system with complex jurisprudent understanding and constitutional analysis. China's 'in accordance with law' requirement is to some extent similar to the due process principle in imposing legal restrictions on the government's taking of property. However, what is vastly different is the extent or strength of the restrictions. In the United States, the due process principle can be used as a constitutional principle to review the validity and reasonability of every instance in which the government appropriates or takes property, including the appropriate legislation and enforcement procedures. In China, however, it is nearly always constitutional for the government to take property and make compensation decisions based on some law or legal document. The reasonability of standards and procedures in the pertinent laws and regulations are barely restricted by the 'in accordance with law' principle. In other words, the 'in accordance with law' principle imposes only procedural requirements on the government's decision processes, and compared with the due process doctrine in the United States, its restriction on governmental taking of property is too limited.

The largest worry arising from the Chinese *Constitution*'s role in restricting government power to seize private property is that all of these restraints may be explained within the framework of the fundamental socialist economic system. Because private property and individual economy make up only one component of the socialist economic system (with public property as the dominant component), the protection of private property and the explanation of public interest and compensation can be influenced by such a public property economic system. The scope of public interest purposes may be improperly enlarged. The compensation may be decided too narrowly, considering the service role of private property

[119] The *Fifth Amendment* to the *U.S. Constitution.*

in social development. The procedural requirements derived from the 'in accordance with law' principle, which are unreasonable in their contents and nature, may be explained as being constitutional by considering the needs of a rapidly developing economy. Generally, the incorporation of the private property clause into the socialist economic system creates a danger that the protection of private property may be seriously and unreasonably limited.

3.6 Evolution in the era of globalisation: the inherent change of social forces

To understand the historical development path of the constitutional clauses concerning private property in China, especially in the stage after opening and reform, explicating the link between constitutional reform and the globalisation process can enhance understanding of the dynamic change in the related social forces and that change's influence on the constitutional and legal reform of private property.

3.6.1 Globalisation, localisation and institutional reform

The most usual perspective from which to observe globalisation is economic. Globalisation is defined as the removal of trade barriers and the integration of national economies by economists.[120] There is also the historical analysis of economic globalisation.[121] The debate focuses on two facets of globalisation, prosperity linked to voluntary participation and impoverishment based on malignant coercion.[122]

From a broader perspective, globalisation can be regarded as a process, a system, a force or an age that comprises 'technological, economic, political, and cultural dimensions that interconnect individuals, firms, and governments across national borders'.[123] In addition to the economic

[120] For a discussion of globalisation from an economic perspective, see Fischer, 'Globalization'; Stiglitz, *Whither Socialism*.

[121] See generally Rothschild, 'Globalization'; Williamson and Lindert, 'Does Globalization'.

[122] Milanovic noted that globalisation, in addition to its possible benign effect of facilitating economic prosperity 'based on voluntary exchanges and free circulation of people, capital, goods and ideas', has the malignant feature of being 'based on coercion and brute force' both in the past and today. See Milanovic, 'The Two Faces', 668.

[123] Dierks, *Introduction to Globalization*, p. 17.

effect, cultural, social and institutional changes can also be relevant to this analysis.[124]

The effect of globalisation on a country can be understood comprehensively as a type of institutional change. An emerging dominant approach to study the overall changes in the law, ethics, organisation, economy and politics of a country is called 'new institutional analysis'. Campbell's book first used this new approach to identify and resolve the problems concerning institutional changes in the phenomenon of globalisation. He examined three main problems: (1) the institutional change resulting from globalisation, (2) the mechanism responding to the change, and (3) how 'ideas' rather than self-interest affect institutional change.[125] The United Nations – Research Institute of Social Development (UNRISD) research report observes that globalisation reinforces the drive for market deregulation and privatisation, and the shifts in rules, policy and ideology in turn leads to changes in power relations among social groups and in the effectiveness of established institutions.[126]

Robertson defined the ongoing globalisation as 'the interpenetration of the universalization of particularization and the particularization of universalism'.[127] A new term, 'glocalization', describes the blending of globalisation factors and local contents. Thus, based on this view, globalisation can be regarded as an interdependent process comprising two twin processes, macro-localisation and micro-globalisation. The former is the globalisation of the local, and the latter is the localisation of globality.[128] This argument is also asserted by the World Bank's reports: globalisation and localisation are two factors that simultaneously transform and shape a country or region's development.[129]

3.6.2 *Chinese legal reform after WTO access*

The process to join the WTO is frustratingly slow for many transitional countries, including China.[130] China has been endeavouring to integrate

124 See generally Appadurai, *Modernity at Large*; Campbell, *Institutional Change*.
125 Campbell, *Institutional Change*, pp. 1–30. See also Campbell and Pedersen (eds.), *The Rise*.
126 Wolfe, 'Social Integration'. 127 Robertson, *Globalization*, p. 100.
128 Khondker, 'Globalization Theory'. See also Khondker, 'Glocalization as Globalization', 4.
129 World Bank, *World Development*, p. 2. More penetratingly, Giddens regards globalisation as the 'reason for the revival of local cultural identities in different parts of the world'. See Giddens, *Runaway World*, p. 31.
130 China began efforts to integrate into the global trade system in 1986 when applying to resume GATT (the early form of WTO) membership, but did not succeed before GATT

itself into the world trading system since its openness to the Western world began in the early 1980s. In late 2001, China joined the WTO, which was regarded as a landmark of China stepping into a new globalisation era. For China, the effects of its WTO accession are diverse, with political, economic and legal implications.

Generally, Chinese legal reform is analysed with regard to the necessary revision of Chinese laws to comply with WTO requirements.[131] Analysing globalisation and its influence, Peerenboom notes that the Chinese legal system is moving forward from 'rule by law' to 'rule of law'. The role of economic globalisation in pushing China's political liberalisation and legal progress is clear.[132] However, Gallagher argues that although China is rapidly integrating into the global economy and has been successful in economic development, its openness and reform resulted in a strengthened state, a weakened civil society and a delay in political liberalisation. Gallagher notes that in the progress of China's globalisation, the communist party's staying power was strengthened and political liberalisation delayed.[133] In regard to localisation, Lubman's research examines China's legal reform before its accession to the WTO and emphasises the influence of historical, cultural and institutional contexts.[134] Cultural analysis especially attracts researchers' attention. Day's research focuses on legal thought and culture and their effects on legal reform.[135] Potter's perspective is much broader and more comprehensive. He analysed the driving forces that change the Chinese legal system, considering both globalisation and local cultures.[136] The term 'selective adaptation' describes how foreign ideas are assimilated into local conditions, analysing perception, complementarity and legitimacy.[137]

was replaced by the WTO in 1995. Then China applied to the WTO and finally became a WTO member in 2001. Russia, another giant transitional economy, applied for its GATT membership in 1993 and became a WTO member eighteen years later. For a brief review of Russia's past efforts in applying for GATT and WTO membership, see Aslund, 'Russia's'. For an analysis of the complicated issues concerning China's access to the WTO, see Anderson, 'On the Complexities'.

131 See generally Kong, *China*; Clark, 'China's Legal System'.

132 Peerenboom, *China's Long March*, chap. 10.

133 Gallagher, *Contagious Capitalism*, p. 6.

134 Lubman, *Bird in a Cage*. 135 Day, *Legal Reform*. 136 Potter, *The Chinese*.

137 Potter used this three-element framework in analysing China's selective adaptation feature in its economic regulation reform as a response to the influence of globalisation. Such adaptation results in the mixture of foreign borrowing and local retaining, which are decided to a great extent by power relations. Perception is the understanding of the contents, origins, implications and purposes of foreign and local norms. Complementarity refers to a circumstance in which the apparently conflicting foreign and local norms combine to result in a new effect. Complementarity decides 'the capacity to combine

3.6.3 *Property law reform in China: a gradual, selective and tedious reform*

Previous reform in property law in China followed a gradual path suggested by Stiglitz, rather than the 'shock therapy' adopted by Russia.[138] According to Stiglitz, the case of China shows that the simultaneous creation of new businesses and institutions is equally or more important than changing or reforming old businesses and institutions. He noted that China instituted successful market reform without privatisation.[139] A review of Chinese property law reform shows that such reform has been approaching economic reform slowly. The analysis of the interaction between globalisation and local conditions can explain why the process has been slow.

The drafting work of a specific property law in China was initiated in 1998. Two teams, one led by Wang Liming at Renmin University and the other led by Liang Huixing at the Chinese Academy of Social Sciences, submitted two versions of the law to the NPC. Liang's version reflects more influence from Western legislation and suggests abolishing references to the state and collectives as property owners.[140] Wang's version reflects the traces of local collectivism and state priority.[141] The draft promulgated by the NPC in 2005 maintained the public and collective characters of the ultimate ownership of land, which was finally written into the *Property Law* enacted in 2007. The *2004 Amendment* did not change the fundamental property right structure of land and major natural resources, and according to the *1982 Constitution of China*, the 2007 *Property Law* cannot make any substantial changes regarding state and collective ownership.

Although slow, the evolution from 'public' to 'private' is clearly the path that Chinese property law reform has taken. The *2004 Amendment*, although problematic, can be acclaimed as a milestone in the stronger protection of private property rights. However, this does not mean that private property is equal to public property because the 'sanctity' of public property continues to be emphasised and government maintains the power to take private property for public use, which may remain unlimited. The refusal to accept the concept of 'sanctity' for private property

local and foreign regulatory norms in ways that address globally derived challenges while remaining true to established local values'. Legitimacy analyses 'the extent to which members of local communities support the purposes and consequences of selective adaptation'. See Potter, 'Globalization', 120–1. See also Potter, 'Legal Reform', 478.

138 Stiglitz, *Whither Socialism*, pp. 264–5.
139 Ibid., p. 262.
140 Liang, 'Zhongguo Wuquan'.
141 Wang, 'Wuquan Fa'. See also Wang, *Wuquan Fa*.

shows that the influence of local conditions remains dominant. Moreover, the opinion that the protection of private property is contrary to the principles of socialism in the *Constitution* has developed into a strong force opposing the stronger protection of private property.[142] On the localisation side, however, a strong social force supporting private property protection has emerged rather abruptly in recent years. This is demonstrated most obviously in cases concerning the demolition and relocation of houses, which is discussed in the later sections of this book. This social force from citizens, showing their desire for stronger protection of private property, is also advocated by the globalisation tendency. In the next sections of this chapter, this growing local force (which requests strong protection of private property), combined with globalisation and other local forces, is considered in the context of transitional economic reform to analyse the evolution of the constitutional protection of private property in China.

3.6.4 Reform in transitional economies: gradual reform compared with shock therapy

China's reform, which began in 1978, is considered a gradual approach, which is usually compared with the 'shock therapy' approach adopted by Russia and some Eastern Europe countries such as Poland, Slovenia, Czech Republic and Estonia.[143] The shock therapy approach is based on political reform that features Western-style democracy and economic reform that features privatisation. In China, however, gradual reform neither changed the fundamental political system led by the CPC, nor adopted radical privatisation reform.

Lipton and Sachs are the leading scholars who have been advocating the shock therapy reform approach since the early 1990s. The reform leaders in Eastern Europe called their 1989 revolution a 'return to Europe', and the post-revolution reform was clearly intended to build Western European-style political and economic institutions, namely 'multiparty parliamentary democracies and market economies with large private sectors'.[144] Such reform was deemed 'rapid and comprehensive' with three main

142 Gong, 'Yibu Weibei'.
143 The term 'shock therapy' originated in Poland's radical reform plan, which was initiated on 1 January 1990. Czech Republic and Bulgaria followed Poland's therapy approach in 1991; Russia, Albania and Estonia followed in 1992; and Latvia followed in 1993. See Marangos, 'The Political Economy', 41.
144 Lipton and Sachs, 'Creating', 75.

steps: (1) the ending of excess demand, (2) the creation of market competition, and (3) privatisation.[145] Lipton and Sachs suggest that Poland's privatisation of state firms had to be rapid to 'assure efficient resource use in the future' and to 'prevent the collapse of the stabilization itself in the medium term'.[146] This radical reform disregards existing social contexts and assumes that the pre-reform institutions have little positive significance in facilitating reform and should not be considered seriously when a reform scheme is designed. Privatisation should be rapid and transparent in selling or transferring state enterprises to private sectors without overly considering the existing ownership claims of workers.[147]

The former Soviet Union collapsed in 1991. Soon the Russian government introduced shock therapy or 'big bang reform' to replace the old Soviet institutions with Western-style institutions as soon as possible.[148] During the rest of the 1990s, the shocked Russia performed even worse in economic growth than previously. In 1998, Russia's GDP was only a little more than half (57 per cent) of Russia's average annual GDP in the 1990s.[149] After 2000, under Putin's leadership, Russia entered into a fast-development period with an average GDP growth rate of up to 6.8 per cent.[150] In China, however, in the more than thirty years since 1978, the economy has been increasing at a high annual GDP growth rate of up to 9.8 per cent.[151]

Observing the economic performance thus far, China's gradualist approach is clearly more successful than Russia's shock therapy, and China has the best economic output of all transitional economies.[152] Generally, the economic research shows that a gradualist approach creates better performance than shock therapy.[153] It is even more interesting to compare the economic performance of countries that adopt shock therapy reform. One finding is that Vietnam performed better than Eastern European countries, which – especially the Central European countries – then performed better than the former Soviet Union countries. In addition to

[145] Ibid., 99–101. [146] Ibid., 127.

[147] Ibid., 128. For a specific and detailed discussion of privatisation, see Lipton and Sachs, 'Privatization in Eastern Europe'. For the potential risks and possible methods of rapid privatisation, see Sachs, 'Accelerating Privatization'.

[148] See generally Pomfret, *Constructing*.

[149] These data are from World Bank. See Wang, 'Thirty Years', 53 [150] Ibid.

[151] Between 1978 and 2007, the per capita GDP increased from USD 220 to USD 2,500. Ibid.

[152] For an overall cross-discipline comparative analysis that integrates politics, economics, history, culture, administration, reform process and international relations, see Bucknall, 'Why China', 1023–37.

[153] Popov, 'Shock Therapy', 7–8.

the importance of macroeconomic stabilisation in influencing economic performance, Popov argued that institutional capacity is an important factor that was disregarded by some transitional countries with bad performance. China and Vietnam, although they adopted a gradual approach and 'big bang' reform, respectively, both retain a strong authoritarian regime. Central European countries, represented by Poland, demonstrated better performance than Russia and have a democratic system that is efficient in enforcing laws, executing policies and protecting property.[154] One main reason why Russia and other former Soviet Union countries performed poorly in the first ten years after the reform is that their newly established democratic regimes were so weak that 'they lack strong institutions and the ability to enforce law and order'.[155] This argument can be certified by Russia's booming economic performance in the second ten years after the shock therapy during which Putin's government demonstrated an obvious authoritarian feature. Nevertheless, China continues to move ahead at a speed that other transitional economies cannot match in the short term.

However, this is not the end of the story. What will happen in the future? Will China's gradualist reform go on to be successful for a long time? The 'big bang' countries generally experience three stages of development: the shock period, the recovery period and the fast-development period. In the earliest stages of shock, the sudden upside-down reform of fundamental political and economic institutions results in a mismatch between economic growth and the political and legal systems. The shocked, unstable society and political institutions inevitably influence economic growth negatively. This type of pain may last a long and intolerable time. In the recovery period, the shock pain decreases, and the political and legal systems are more adaptive to the economy than before. Consequently, the economic downturn ends, and an upturn begins at medium speed. After the adjustment and adaptation end, the economy may grow at a much faster pace. However, for gradualist countries such as China, the development stages are in a type of reverse order with the sequence of fast-development stage, adjustment stage and shock stage. In the first

[154] Ibid., 2–4, 27–8.

[155] Ibid., 3. Explaining why Russia performed poorly after the adoption of the shock therapy scheme, Sachs argued, '[d]espite the uproar in recent years about "shock therapy" in Russia, knowledgeable observers understand that it simply never occurred, an obvious point when one compares Russia's disorganized and partial stabilization efforts with the decisive actions in the Czech Republic, Estonia, or Poland'. See Sachs, 'Why Russia', p. 53.

stage, the moderate reform towards market economy liberates people's long-term oppressed creative passion and leads to high-speed economic growth. With the economy moving forward, in the second stage, more reforms leading to political democracy and stronger protection of individual rights are demanded, and the state must make adjustments to match economic growth with individual need. In this stage, the adjustment is nevertheless made without stepping over the fire line, which is the fundamental feature of social and economic systems and political authority. At the point at which the deeper reforms of politics and law cannot match the further development of the economy and the increased requests for constitutional and legal rights, the shock stage may arrive; and the shocks that result from the resistance to outdated political and legal systems may lead to economic depression. Russia is currently in the recovery stage and moving towards the fast-development stage; however, China is on the way from the first stage to the second. For Russia, the problem is how to end the recovery stage and enter the fast-development stage as quickly as possible; for China, the problem is how to delay the coming of the third shock stage or how to be well prepared before the third stage arrives.

3.6.5 *Globalisation and the dynamic evolution of social forces*

Globalisation and localisation together form the context of China's private property reform. In the era of globalisation, the external forces from the globalisation side and the internal forces from the localisation side interact with one another, and both affect social reform in China. In this section, the social forces that influence property law reform in China are analysed and distinguished from the respective globalisation and localisation sides. Then the interactions among the forces and their influence on Chinese property law reform are analysed.

Economic growth has certainly been the primary and most important work of China's government since 1978. High-speed growth with an annual GDP growth higher than 8 per cent has been the focus of governments at both the national and local levels every year.

In the early years of openness and reform, China was in urgent need of capital. To stimulate economic growth, the absorption of foreign direct investment (FDI) was given high-level attention and support and became one of the most important jobs of local governments. The importation of

FDI into China has been a gradual process. In 1979, the *Law on Chinese-Foreign Joint Ventures* was adopted to allow foreign investors to establish their businesses in China in the form of joint ventures.[156] In 1986, foreigners were allowed to establish enterprises with entirely foreign investment after the enactment of the *Law on Wholly Foreign-Owned Enterprises.*[157] And then, in 1988, FDI could be invested in the form of a cooperative joint venture after the enactment of the *Law on Chinese-Foreign Cooperative Joint Ventures.*[158] Foreign investors were also given lots of policy preferences and support by governments that domestic enterprises could not enjoy. The most stimulating policy is taxation preference. An example is the most important taxation, 'income taxation'. Before 2008, FDI enterprises could enjoy a well-known 'Exemption-Two-Reduction-Three' preference, also called tax holidays. According to this policy, the manufacture-oriented enterprises with FDI were given an income tax exemption for the first two years and a half reduction for the following three years.[159]

This taxation preference was stopped at the end of 2007. Since 1 January 2008, the income tax rate for foreign investment enterprises and domestic enterprises has been uniform.[160]

[156] *Zhongwai Hezi Jingying Qiye Fa* [*Law on Chinese-Foreign Joint Ventures*], enacted by the Second Session of the Fifth NPC on 1 July 1979, amended for the first time by the Third Session of the Seventh NPC on 4 April 1990 and amended for the second time by the Fourth Session of the Ninth NPC on 15 March 2001. The Chinese text is available at www.gov.cn/banshi/2005–08/31/content_69775.htm. The English text is available at www.china.org.cn/english/features/investment/36752.htm.

[157] *Waizi Qiye Fa* [*Law on Wholly Foreign-Owned Enterprises*], enacted by the Fourth Session of the Sixth NPC on 12 April 1986 and amended by the Eighteenth Meeting of the Standing Committee of the Ninth NPC on 31 October 2000, available at www.gov.cn/banshi/2005–08/31/content_69774.htm.

[158] *Zhongwai Hezuo Jingying Qiye Fa* [*Law on Chinese-Foreign Cooperative Joint Ventures*], enacted by the First Session of the Seventh NPC on 13 April 1988 and amended by the Eighteenth Meeting of the Standing Committee of the Ninth NPC on 31 October 2000, available at www.gov.cn/banshi/2005–08/31/content_69772.htm. Such a law is also called *Law on Chinese-Foreign Contractual Joint Ventures.*

[159] *Waishang Touzi Qiye he Waiguo Qiye Suodeshui Fa* [*Income Tax Law for Enterprises with Foreign Investment and Foreign Enterprises*], art. 8. This law was enacted by the Fourth Session of the Seventh NPC on 9 April 1991 and its Chinese text is available at www.gov.cn/banshi/2005–07/12/content_14047.htm. For China's income tax change before 2008, see generally Li, 'Tax Incentive'.

[160] *Qiye Suodeshui Fa* [*Income Tax Law for Enterprises*], art. 4. This law was enacted by the Fifth Session of the Tenth NPC on 16 March 2007 and enforced on 1 January 2008. Its Chinese text is available at http://www.gov.cn/flfg/2007–03/19/content_554243.htm. According to this law, the income tax rate for both local and FDI enterprises is unified to be 25 per cent.

In addition to tax preferences, the support of local governments in land use is another factor that attracts FDI. The taxation incentive policy portfolio had been featured as being location-specific, and the expansion of the coverage scope of taxation preferences had been gradual before 2008. In the beginning, tax preferences were given mainly in four Special Economic Zones.[161] In 1984, the preference policies were expanded to cover fourteen coastal (seaside) municipalities; in 1985 they were again expanded to 'coastal economic open regions' in the Yangzte River Delta and the Pearl River Delta, and then even more areas. Specific zones such as Export Processing Zones (EPZ), Development Zones, High Science and Technology Zones, and Tax Free Zones have been actively established by local governments to attract FDI. With the expansion of tax incentive policy coverage, local governments began to compete in attracting FDI by building specific zones in which tax preferences, land use rights and other infrastructure conveniences were offered. The fast development of tax preference areas led to the large-scale expropriation of collectively owned farmland and privately owned houses with land use rights.

In the movement of land expropriation stimulated by FDI attraction, we can identify four social forces represented by four categories of participants: local governments, foreign investors, local rent-seeking groups and individual land right holders.

Local governments have strong motivations to expropriate land. The task of rapidly increasing the GDP has been pushing local governments to develop specific areas with policy preferences to attract FDI. However, this is not the only influential factor to explain local governments' passion for expropriating land. Increasing local revenue by collecting and selling land is another motivating factor that can be identified in the complicated urbanisation process.

Foreign investors as a social power have a twofold influence on private property protection. On the one hand, their strong demand for land use stimulates local governments to take land and land rights from collectives and individuals. On the other hand, foreign investors, as a component of China's globalisation process, are also new private property owners entering China. Many of them are from the countries with fundamental private property systems and became the leading advocates for requesting stronger protection of private property. Standing with investors are their countries of origin, which also facilitate the protection of their citizens'

[161] These special economic zones are Shenzhen, Shantou, Xiamen and Zhuhai.

safety in investing overseas, especially in less developed countries that are generally weak at protecting private property.[162]

Local interest groups mainly include local domestic enterprises. They form the interest alliance with local government officials by rent-seeking activities. With government support, local interest groups can acquire land from the collectives and individuals at low prices. These groups also function as active participants in the urbanisation process. Their influence on private property is mainly negative. Although local interest groups are the holders of property and demand identical protection for their properties as foreign investors enjoy, as unethical and illegal rent-seeking actors, they rely on their close relations with governments rather than on advocating legal reform to actively maintain their property interests. Another interest group in the taking of farmland comprises agents representing collective organisations which are farmland owners. These agents may facilitate the selling of collective lands to obtain unjust personal interest.

Seekers of individual rights include farmers holding farmland use rights and citizens having house ownership and the use rights of urban land. These groups uniformly form the social force promoting stronger protection of private property rights. Compared with foreign investors, the private rights of these groups are more often disregarded by governments. However, with the new openness, their awareness of their rights and their request for private property protection are becoming stronger and stronger with the importing of Western property ideas and the accumulation of property.[163]

Another government function linked to economic growth in globalisation is urbanisation. The aim of urbanisation is, in the globalised era,

[162] In addition to the unilateral advocation of the protection of their investors, the capital-exporting countries have been active in securing their outward investments by making bilateral agreements and multilateral conventions concerning the support and protection of overseas investments. See Miller, 'Protection of Private Foreign Investment', 371–8. The United States has been warning that when alien-owned property is expropriated, adequate and timely compensation must be paid; otherwise, the lack of respect for private property would destroy the investment environment and reduce the amount of needed capital for the economic development of developing countries. See Akinsanya, 'International Protection', 60.

[163] The term 'Right Consciousness' is generally defined as '[t]he general awareness of rights to be claimed or asserted against others, particularly the government'. See Wasby, 'History', p. 398. A survey of 534 respondents and conducted between February and June of 2002 shows that approximately 80 per cent of the respondents agree that the *Constitution* should offer private property holders the protection that is equal to that of public property. See Han and Wang, 'Zhongguo Gongmin', 114.

to transform agriculture-based China to industrialised China. Although from 1949 to 1965, the urban population increased as the result of the massive industrialisation starting in 1966, the ten-year Cultural Revolution that implemented a rustication policy held back the progress of urbanisation. After 1978, urbanisation began to accelerate at an astonishing speed. In the early stages of urbanisation after 1978, employment opportunities created by the inflow of FDI fostered the rapid increase of the urban population. Soon after, the rural-urban migration was driven by the state's industrialisation policies.[164]

City expansion as one component of the urbanisation movement accompanies the explosion of the urban population. The urbanisation of suburbs and rural areas that are adjacent to cities swallows the original farmland on a large-scale. After urbanisation, the collective ownership and individual farmer's leasing rights to farmland no longer exist. A large portion of the farmland was taken by local governments for non-agricultural uses, including the establishment of industrial enterprises and development zones. Farmers, after losing their farmland, can enjoy only individual ownership over their houses, which are attached to this land, but with limited land use rights. The compensation available to them for the loss of their land is often insufficient to maintain their standard of living.

City transformation, also called urban renewal or urban redevelopment, is another component of urbanisation. Urban renewal concerns the replanning and redevelopment of urban land. It includes but is not limited to the relocation of businesses, the clearance of slums, the construction of infrastructure, the protection of the environment and the building of public facilities. It often concerns the large-scale demolition and removal of individual houses and the taking of land use rights. In China, the purpose of urban renewal is not always of a public nature. In some situations, the purpose may arguably be, for example, to develop a commercial zone or an industrial zone.

One reason that local governments are strongly motivated to expropriate land and develop urbanisation projects is because this can help to make local officials' achievements appear successful and thus can be helpful in their promotion. Another reason is that the taking of land

164 Justin Lin, the Chief Economist of the World Bank, commented that, '[a]s more people move to urban areas, not just in China, but elsewhere in Asia and Africa, the focus of development activities must be twofold, ... [r]ural development, which remains critical in agriculture-based economies, and rapid urban industrial development, which is and will be the principal source of growth for the national economy.' See World Bank, 'China's Rapid'.

Table 3.1 *Social forces and their influence on private property protection*

Globalisation/Localisation	Social forces	Influence
Globalisation Side (G1)	International society for the rule of law	Positive
Globalisation Side (G2)	FDI demanding need for more land	Negative
Globalisation Side (G3)	FDI investors calling for more protection	Positive
Localisation Side (L1)	CPC's reform of market and democracy	Positive
Localisation Side (L2)	Development of local interest groups	Negative
Localisation Side (L3)	Citizens' request for private property protection	Positive
Localisation Side (L4)	Urbanisation by local governments	Negative

by removing houses can help to increase local revenues. Local interest groups, by bribing government officials or utilising other rent-seeking measures, either legal or illegal, often push governments to take land for non-public purposes or to take more land than is actually required for the proposed project. The combination of a government with the power of eminent domain and interest groups who have access to capital in many situations leads to the unjust deprivation of individual citizens' property rights.

A popular perception is that globalisation encourages the process of rule of law in China.[165] The real situation is more complicated. Using the government's taking of private property as a typical case, the forces for and against the protection of private property can be observed on both the globalisation and localisation sides. A more detailed combination of social forces that may influence the protection of private property in China is outlined in Table 3.1.

The interactive relation among the previously mentioned social forces will decide the evolution of private property protection in China. During the twenty years after China's openness and reform began in 1979, G2 and

[165] The 2005 China Research Report issued by the Japan Centre for Economic Research (JCER) asserts: 'The speed of reform and market opening has accelerated, and China's market environment has improved thanks to the progress made towards the establishment of the rule of law.' See JCER, *China' s Market*, pp. 17–18.

L2 forces were much stronger than the aggregation of the other four positive forces, which were not strong in the early stages of China's opening and reform. Consequently, the protection of private property at that time was weak. Entering the twenty-first century in the second adjustment stage of gradual reform, the four positive forces became stronger and stronger, which ultimately led to the *2004 Amendment* to the *1982 Constitution of China* as a sign of the positive forces' victory. Perhaps the most important reform of the *1982 Constitution of China* and driven by both global and local forces, the *2004 Amendment* formally declares the constitutional protection of private property, which led to additional property law reform. What will the next stage or shock stage bring? Will reform move towards offering individuals fundamentally stronger protection of private property? The answer is unclear. The social forces G3 and L3, pushed by foreign and domestic individuals, continue to become stronger in calling for greater protection. Simultaneously, G2 and L2 forces, although not stronger than before, nevertheless exert a powerful influence. As for the G1 force, international pressure for more democracy and stronger protection of human rights and private property will be strengthened. For L1, however, the reform led by the CPC (eventhough it will not retreat) may falter or stop progressing because the deepening reform may shake the CPC's leadership status or the fundamentals of the socialist system. For example, the reform leading to the separation of power as a precondition of judicial independence and privatisation reform, which touches the dominant status of the public property system, cannot be accepted by the CPC now or in the foreseeable future. At this time, the L1 force, which is reluctant to pursue the much deeper reforms requested by the forces of G3 and L3, would transform from a positive force to a negative force, hindering the reform of the property system or would at least be weak in playing its positive role. In the second stage, the L4 force is strong in negatively influencing private property protection because of local governments' strong motivation to stimulate growth and acquire revenue. However, the L4 force is limited to some extent by the strong resistance of G3 + L3 and also by the L1, which now defers more to the requests of L3 than before. Thus, at the end of the second stage and the beginning of the third shock stage, the interactive conflict between L3 + G3 and L1 + L4 will decide the future reform path.

Currently and in the ensuing years, the conflict between L4 and L3 will be the first problem to be resolved in the reform of the taking of land and private property protection. Both the central government and

Table 3.2 *The dynamic role of different social forces*

Social forces	Early stage	Adjustment stage	Shock stage
G1	Not Strong	Strong	Very Strong
G2	Very Strong	Strong	Strong?
G3	Not Strong	Strong	Very Strong
L1	Not Strong	Strong	Strong?
L2	Very Strong	Strong	Strong
L3	Not Strong	Strong	Very Strong
L4	Very Strong	Strong	Strong?

the CPC authority, represented by L1, must balance the conflict between L4 and L3 and also address the conflict between the maintenance of its leadership and the socialist system and the request for stronger private property protection and more democracy. For L1, as the reform initiated by the CPC, the exceedingly strong bottom line is the leadership of the party in the political system and the dominant role of public property in the property system, both serving as the foundation of a socialist country. Thus, the question is how much space is left for further reform regarding the constitutional protection of private property without shaking the current basic political system?

The assumptions that are predictable and feasible in the near future are outlined as follows:

> Without changing the public ownership of land and other main production means through privatisation, the relevant reform can be extended to offer individuals more property rights or bundles of rights – for example, to loosen the restrictions on use rights, to enlarge the scope of use rights or to prolong the period of land use rights.

Even without the adoption of a Western-style democratic system, the relevant reforms can strengthen the central government's supervision of local governments' decisions to take private property; judicial independence can also be strengthened within the limited scope of the reviews of local governments' decisions to take private property.

Without easily and feasibly altering the tight link between the central government and interest groups at the national or central levels, much stronger restrictions can be imposed on local rent-seeking groups to sever the interest link between them and local governments.

3.6.6 *Case study: violent taking and bloody resistance*

The weak protection of private property at both the constitutional and legislative levels increasingly leads to more cases in which the property rights holders either were forced to move by violence or had to use violent means or even sacrifice themselves to defend against the invasion of government power. These cases are called 'Bloody Removal' or 'Violent Taking'. Because there are no fair and strong legal restrictions, interest groups with government support initiated a series of bloody removal tragedies in recent years. The most representative cases attracting countrywide attention include the violent removal incident in Jiahe (the *Jiahe* incident) in 2004; the firing case in Maiqili of Shanghai (the *Maiqili* case) in 2005; the coolest *nail house* (*zui niu dingzihu*) incident in Chongqing in 2007; the violent conflict case concerning Couple Pan in Shanghai (the *Couple Pan* case) in 2008; and the suicide incident concerning Tang Fuzhen in Sichuan (the *Tang Fuzhen* incident) in 2009. The *Jiahe* incident and the *Maiqili* case are analysed in this section to unravel the conflict of interest in expropriation, mainly the conflict between the union of local governments and local interest groups on one side and individual rights holders on the other.

3.6.6.1 The *Maiqili* case

Maiqili is a residential area located in the Xuhui District of Shanghai. In 2001, Maiqili was planned by the Xuhui District's government as an urban renewal project (*jiucheng gaizao*), which was approved by the Shanghai Municipal Bureau of Real Estate Administration. On 7 February 2002, Urban Development (*chengkai jituan*), a company owned by Xuhui's government,[166] won the development rights through a competitive bidding process over Maiqili for 265 million Chinese *yuan*. This was the

[166] Urban Development was established in 1996 with investment from the Xuhui District State-owned Assets Supervision and Administration Commission and is a state owned enterprise. The information is from Urban Development's official website, available at www.udcn.com/corporation/ymgl_zjck.asp?id=183.

first time that land was sold in the Xuhui District through competitive bidding.[167]

According to the relevant Shanghai government policy of that time, the government must encourage the winner of a renewal project to arrange for the reinstatement (*huiqian)* of the households that are relocated outside of the renewal area by reducing or exempting the land transfer fee (*tudi churang jin*), which should be paid by the winning company. The Xuhui District government decided to reduce the land transfer fee paid by Urban Development by 30 per cent, which amounted to a reduction of 79.5 million *yuan*. Soon after, however, Urban Development announced that the use purpose of the Maiqili land had been changed from that of a renewal project to land saving or land reserve (*tudi chubei*) and that this adjustment was approved by the Xuhui District government. Urban Development then refused to bear the reinstatement obligation because the use purpose of the area was no longer that of renewal. The compensation resolution was changed from instatement to the exchange of estate or cash compensation. Continuing to insist on reinstatement as compensation, many residents in the Maiqili area refused to move, and after 2003, several violent tactics were used by the removal company's staff to force holdout residents to move.[168] At approximately 1:30 AM on 9 January 2005, two employees from the removal company set fire to a holdout house and a couple older than 70 years died in the fire. The fire and death shocked the public. Two employees were ordered by the vice general manager of the removal company to set the house on fire to frighten the residents. The removal company was a subsidiary attached to the project developer, Urban Development.[169]

The Xuhui District government's role in this case should be noted. The government's planning committee changed the nature of the Maqili project from that of renewal to that of land saving on 23 November 2001 (November 23 Approval), approximately three months before Urban Development bid on Maiqili. Although the use purpose of the land was changed on 7 February 2002, Maiqili was nonetheless offered for

[167] See the news release from the website of Urban Development, available at en.udcn.com/corporation/ymgl_zjck.asp?id=185.

[168] To force holdout residents to move, the removal company's staff cut the electricity cable, released the coal gas, smashed windows, filled the locks and threw the cat body into the residents' kitchen. See Fu, 'Shanghai Maiqili', A17–18.

[169] The vice general manager and one staff member who set the fire were imposed death sentences with two-year reprieves by court. Another staff member who assisted in setting the fire was sentenced to life imprisonment (*wuqi tuxing*).

bidding as a land renewal project. Urban Development won the project and the land transfer fee it was charged was reduced by 30 per cent. Urban Development subsequently used the November 23 Approval to replace reinstatement compensation with cash compensation or the exchange of estates. At only 4,500 *yuan* per square metre plus a 20 per cent premium as a subsidy, the compensation price offered by Urban Development was low. This compensation standard was much lower than housing prices in the area. The price per square metre in a nearby residence area was 30,000 to 60,000 *yuan*, approximately eight to thirteen times the compensation price offered by Urban Development. As for the exchange of estates, the estate offered as compensation was located in a suburb of Shanghai, very far from downtown where Maiqili is located. Moreover, a change in the use purpose or nature of a large-scale project such as that of Maiqili must be approved by the Shanghai municipal government rather than by the lower-level district government. Thus, the approval of the change in the use purpose of the Maiqili project was illegal and thus voidable. In one word, the Xuhui District government's approval of the change in Maiqili's land use purpose was illegal.

This case involves three participants: the local government (the Xuhui government); the local rent-seeking company (Urban Development and its removal company), which is closely linked to the local government; and individual citizens, whose home ownership was compulsorily taken. Local governments, using public power both legally and illegally through illegal approaches and unjust procedures, helped local rent-seeking companies to take peoples' landed property rights in exchange for unjust compensation. As the winning bidder, Urban Development was afforded a significant reduction in the land transfer fee it was obliged to pay. In addition, it was (illegally) allowed by the local government to replace expensive reinstatement compensation with cheaper compensation. This case illustrates how a local government will act in concert with a local interest group to usurp individual private property.

3.6.6.2 The *Jiahe* incident

Unlike the Xuhui government, which stood behind some local interest groups, the local government in Jiahe County, located in Hunan Province, publicly aided a developer to remove holdout residents. In July 2003, the Jiahe County government initiated a commercial real estate project to remove more than 1,100 households with more than 7,000 residents. Many residents in this planned area refused to relocate owing to low compensation.

On 7 August 2003, the Jiahe government issued a notice requiring all staff working in government agencies, state-owned enterprises and public service units (*shiye danwei*) whose relatives lived in the removal area to help the government to persuade their relatives to relocate in a timely manner. The requirement is titled '4-responsibility' (*sibao*), which means every staff member should be responsible for four affairs concerning removal.[170] The staff who could not finish the 4-responsibility job would be given '2-suspension' (*liangting*), in which both job and salary would be suspended, as a liability. A more serious liability was job dismissal or a job transfer to an outlying location.

Li Xiaochun and her sister were both teachers in public schools, which are service units, and their husbands both worked for government agencies. These two couples were required by the Jiahe government to persuade their relative (Li Xiaochun's father), who lived in the removal area, to move quickly. However, Xiaochun's father refused to sign a removal contract. On 28 September 2003, these two sisters' jobs were suspended for one month by the local bureau of education, which is in charge of the public schools for which they worked. To avoid affecting their husbands' government positions, the two sisters divorced their husbands. The following April, Li Xiaochun and her sister were ordered by the local bureau of education to work in an outlying town because they could not persuade their father to move within the required period.[171]

On 21 April 2004, the county government officers, with the help of more than 200 officers from the county court, demolished Li Huiming's house because he refused to move. Li and his wife stood on the roof to defend their house but were arrested for illegally hindering government activities (*fanghai gongwu*).[172] After having their story reported in the media, particularly by CCTV, which is one of the most influential media outlets in China, the *Jiahe* incident was investigated by the Ministry of Construction and the Hunan provincial government. The final conclusion reached in June 2004 was that the removal procedure and enforcement decision were illegal.[173]

[170] Such affairs include the timely evaluation of compensation, the timely signature of a compensation agreement, timely vacancy from expropriated houses and resettlement assistance. See Jiahe County Government's 'No. [2003] 136 Document'.

[171] Luo, 'Chaiqian Yinfa'. [172] Luo, 'Hunan Jiahe'.

[173] Such a conclusion was reached by the Routine Meeting of State Council presided by Prime Minister Wen Jiabao on 4 June 2004. For a brief summary of the investigation findings in English, see Feng, 'Power, Rights and Interests', pp. 80–1. It is argued that the government's behaviour in the *Jiahe* incident reflects the influence of China's long-term

The *2004 Amendment* on private property protection was adopted during the *Jiahe* incident. However, it seems to have had little power in halting the infringement of individuals' private property by local governments. After the initiation of the *2004 Amendment*, in many cases, victims held the constitution in their hands to bring attention to the constitutional principle. However, it seems that the constitutional clauses cannot help them to defend the strong destructive power of local governments and interest groups. There is still an important question: How does one explain the constitutional principles and apply them to strengthen the protection of private property within China's context, a developing market economy with a Socialist nature?

tradition of powerful, all-encompassing authority. The Jiahe government's actions 'are no different from those of autocracies throughout history or of the centralized government of the planned economy era'. See Wang, 'From the Rule', p. 45. A poster put up by the government for threatening residents in holdout houses demonstrated the arrogance of unbridled power. It said: 'Anybody who dares to impede Jiahe's development even for a while will be impeded for all his life.'

4

The symbolised public interest

Public interest or other similar doctrine is the first and, possibly, the weakest threshold among all constitutional restraints for sheltering private property from government power. In democratic countries, both propertarian and democratic systems respect the significance of private property as a key foundation of society and recognise that private property must serve the public, community or social interest. Although theoretical controversy exists, the practical application relating to the protection of private property in both systems is not fundamentally different.

4.1 The United States: public use

The United States represents the propertarian system. This is reflected by the incorporation of 'public use' into the constitution as a limit on the governmental exercise of eminent domain power. Among various terms used to illustrate social or public limits on property, the term 'public use' may be the strictest in restricting government taking. This term can be read justifiably as access to, occupation by and use by the public. However, other relevant terms, such as 'public good', 'public interest', 'public purpose' or 'common good', imply that the direct or indirect link between government taking and public interest or purpose may legalise expropriation or taking activities and thus afford greater discretion.

The restricted explanation based on use by the public is narrow, and the explanation focusing on purpose or interest is broad. The narrow view strengthens the actual use or the right or opportunity to use the condemned property by the public.[1] The broad view considers the benefit or advantage brought to the public, as Nichols states:

[1] Nichols, Nichols on Eminent Domain, §7.2 [2].

> '[P]ublic use' means 'public advantage,' and that anything which tends to enlarge the resources, increase the industrial energies, and promote the productive power of any considerable number of the inhabitants of a section of the state (or which leads to the growth of towns and the creation of new resources for the employment of capital and labor), manifestly contributes to the general welfare and prosperity of the whole community constitutes a public use.[2]

After the *Fifth Amendment* to the *U.S. Constitution* was implemented, explaining 'public' became a contentious issue. Over time, both broad and narrow views have enjoyed dominance. In the courts, the definition of public use has continuously changed over time, so much so that contradictory decisions were handed down by individual courts on a state-by-state basis.

This was largely the case until the federal courts intervened in the government taking cases at the end of the nineteenth century. At the time, the state governments were taking land mainly to build mills, roads, railroads and irrigation facilities. In many states in the nineteenth century, the *Mills Act* allowed a lower riparian owner to build a dam to acquire power for a mill.[3] In the early years, mills served by such dams were generally grist mills, which were required to be open to the public for grinding corn. Later, however, the service scope was enlarged to include other types of mills, such as cotton, saw, paper and manufacturing mills. In some cases, the mills were only or mainly used by their owners. The courts that adopted the broad view often supported the states' statutes concerning mills even if some mills were used by private bodies.[4] These courts strengthened the benefit or advantage brought by the mills to the public. However, for the courts employing the narrow view, the mills statutes could not gain support if they allowed for mills that were not open to the public.[5]

The Federal Supreme Court began reviewing the state cases under the taking clause in 1896 when it decided the case of *Missouri Pacific Ry. Co.* v. *Nebraska*.[6] In this case, the Supreme Court held that the taking of private property by a state for private use violated the *Fourteenth Amendment*. However, the court did not explain what the public use should be. In another early case, *Mt Vernon-Woodberry Cotton Duck*

[2] Ibid. [3] Twenty-nine states had enacted this kind of act by 1884.

[4] See, for example, *Scudder* v. *Trenton Delaware Falls Co.*, 1 N. J. Eq. 694 (1832).

[5] See, for example, *Sadler* v. *Langham*, 34 Ala. 311, 333 (1859); *Ryerson* v. *Brown*, 35 Mich. 333, 338 (1877).

[6] *Missouri Pacific Ry. Co.* v. *Nebraska*, 164 U.S. 403 (1896).

Company v. *Alabama Interstate Power*, decided in 1916, the Supreme Court expressed a clear preference for the broad view in explaining public use. In this case, a power company sought to take private land, water and water rights to manufacture, supply and sell water-produced power to the public. The Supreme Court, in upholding this taking, ruled in its decision that '[t]he inadequacy of use by the general public as a universal test is established.'[7] Justice Holms, delivering the court opinions, explained why the use-by-public approach was not adequate:

> In the organic relations of modern society it may sometimes be hard to draw the line that is supposed to limit the authority of the legislature to exercise or delegate the power of eminent domain. But to gather the streams from waste and to draw from them energy, labor without brains, and so to save mankind from toil that it can be spared, is to supply what, next to intellect, is the very foundation of all our achievements and all our welfare. If that purpose is not public, we should be at a loss to say what is.[8]

The evolution of the U.S. Supreme Court's attitude to the definition of public use in the twentieth century can be generalised as progress towards the adoption of the broad view.[9] As Sprankling commented, the 'public use' test in the United States shifted to the 'public purpose' test.[10] Two landmark cases were particularly important in forging this shift.

The first is the 1954 case of *Berman* v. *Parker*.[11] After Congress's adoption of the *District of Columbia Redevelopment Act of 1945*, the District of Columbia Redevelopment Land Agency (the Agency) – a commission of five members – was established to acquire and assemble, by eminent domain and otherwise, real property for the purpose of redeveloping blighted territory in Washington, DC and preventing, reducing and eliminating blighting factors or causes of blight.[12] To execute a redevelopment plan for a slum area, the agency used eminent domain power to take private property, a department store. However, the condemnee argued

[7] *Mt Vernon-Woodberry Cotton Duck Company* v. *Alabama Interstate Power*, 240 U.S. 30 (1916).

[8] Ibid. In a 1921 case, the Supreme Court ruled that 'what in its immediate aspect [is] only a private transaction may... be raised by its class or character to a public affair.' See *Block* v. *Hirsh*, 256 U.S. 135, 155 (1921). In a 1923 case, the court ruled that 'It is not essential that the entire community, nor even any considerable portion,... directly enjoy or participate in any improvement in order [for it] to constitute a public use.' *Rindge Co.* v. *Los Angeles*, 262 U.S. 700, 707 (1923).

[9] For a review of court rulings concerning public use in and before 1930s, see Nichols, 'The Meaning'.

[10] Sprankling, *Understanding Property*, p. 8.

[11] *Berman* v. *Parker*, 348 U.S. 26 (1954).

[12] *District of Columbia Redevelopment Act of 1945*, secs. 4, 5(a).

that his property was commercial rather than residential, that the store was not a slum house, and that the developer was a private agency rather than a public agency and that the redevelopment of his property was not for public use. Support the third point, the condemnee emphasised that the private identity of the developer rendered the project 'a taking from one businessman for the benefit of another businessman'.[13] However, all of these arguments were rebuffed by the court with an 8–0 vote based on the following arguments.

First, the court decided that the slum clearance fell within the legislature's authority, which is normally called police power. The court decided that it should be the legislature, not the judiciary – which works as 'the main guardian of the public needs to be served by social legislation' – that defines the police power allocated to the government. Second, eminent domain power is necessary for government to realise its purpose of police power. Justice Douglas wrote for the court: 'Once the object is within the authority of Congress, the right to realize it through the exercise of eminent domain is clear. For the power of eminent domain is merely the means to the end.'[14] Third, to deny the argument concerning the private nature of the developer, the court decided that '[t]he public end may be as well or better served through an agency of private enterprise than through a department of government.'[15] Once public purpose has been established, it is up to the legislature to decide on the approach or means that be used to achieve its purpose. The private body as a developer can be a feasible means to achieving the public purpose.

The second landmark case is *Hawaii Housing Authority* v. *Midkiff* in 1984, which solidified the public-purpose-approach of the constitutional 'public use' limit.[16] In this case, the state of Hawaii enacted an act called the *Hawaii Housing Land Reform Act* in 1967, which concerns condemning a landlord's land to transfer ownership to the tenants. On some of the Hawaiian Islands, land was concentrated in a few owners' hands, and residents were having difficulty buying simple fee titles. According to this act, tenants or lessees living on single-family residential lots within tracts at least five acres in size are entitled to ask the government to condemn the property on which they live. The condemnees argued that the use of eminent domain power was unconstitutional because it entailed taking A's private property to transfer it to B for B's private use and benefit.

[13] 348 U.S. 26, 33 (1954). [14] Ibid. [15] Ibid., at 33–4.

[16] *Hawaii Housing Authority* v. *Midkiff*, 467 U.S. 229 (1984).

The Court of Appeals for the Ninth Circuit accepted this argument,[17] but the Supreme Court overturned it with an 8–0 vote, citing a number of factors.

First, the Supreme Court denied the necessity of the government's possession or use of the condemned property. The condemnee argued that in the case of *Berman* v. *Parker*, the government possessed the taken land temporarily. However, in this case, the government did not possess and use the condemned land. This argument gained the appellate court's support but was not accepted by the Supreme Court. In writing her decision, Justice O'Connor confirmed the court's position in understanding public use based on the purpose-approach rather than its literal requirement. There was no need for the government to possess or use the taken property to legitimate the taking, and 'it is only the taking's purpose, and not its mechanics, that must pass scrutiny under the Public Use Clause'.[18] The Supreme Court concluded that the appellate court's interpretation of the *Berman* Case as requiring actual government possession was a 'much narrower proposition'.[19]

Second, the Supreme Court reaffirmed its judicial deference standard developed in the *Berman* Case. Justice O'Conner wrote, '[j]udicial deference is required because, in our system of government, legislatures are better able to assess what public purposes should be advanced by an exercise of the taking power. State legislatures are as capable as Congress of making such determinations within their respective spheres of authority.'[20] The state of Hawaii passed laws to reduce the perceived social and economic evils of land concentration or oligopoly, and declared that doing so fell within the government's police power, and that this purpose was public and rational. The Supreme Court did not require the actual achievement of such a public purpose. It is sufficient for the legislature to satisfy the constitutional requirement of public use by showing that the legislation is rationally related to a conceivable public purpose. Or in other words, the court requires only that 'the Legislature rationally could have believed that the [Act] would promote its objective'.[21]

The *Midkiff* Case thoroughly and clearly signified the Supreme Court's break with the literal use-by-public approach. Additionally, the court's deferential attitude in reviewing the governmental taking legislation or decisions has led to the state governments' great discretionary power and

[17] 702 F.2d 788 (1983).
[18] 467 U.S. 229, 244 (1984). [19] Ibid., at 243. [20] Ibid., at 244.
[21] *Western & Southern Life Ins. Co.* v. *State Bd. of Equalization*, 451 U.S. 648, 671–2(1981).

thus in the broad or even overbroad definition of public purpose. As Sullivan commented:

> *Midkiff* dispels any doubts remaining after *Berman*. It appears that as long as the public use is conceived by the legislature and the purpose is not impossible, the court will endorse a compensated taking even if the actual transfer of property is between private individuals. The court ruling signals its adoption of the broad interpretation that the public use means 'public advantage'.[22]

The Supreme Court did not stop its march towards a broader definition of public purpose after the *Midkiff* Case. In 2005, its decision in the case of *Kelo* v. *City of New London* intrigued nationwide debate around an important question: What should be the parameters of public purpose? In this case, the Supreme Court upheld the City of New London's decision in using eminent domain to take Susette Kelo's private house for economic development, namely to assemble land to convince the pharmaceutical giant Pfizer to establish its headquarters in the city.[23] This time, however, the Supreme Court's decision elicited overwhelming criticism. A core question concerning this case is: Does economic development qualify as public purpose? Analysis of this issue is particularly inspiring and important to developing countries, such as India and China, where governments play a central role in facilitating economic growth.

4.2 Germany: public good test

The *German Basic Law* requires that '[e]xpropriation shall only be permissible for the public good.'[24] The phrase 'public good' has two functions in the German constitution. One function serves as the constitutional limit on government expropriation to protect private property. The other function limits private property by stating that private property must serve the public good.[25] In combining these two functions, the term 'public good' establishes the border between government power and private property.

In Germany, the understanding of public good is based on a broad view – the purpose perspective. It is still possible to satisfy the public good requirement even if government expropriation benefits a private body. As with the U.S. Supreme Court's position in the *Berman* and

22 Sullivan, 'Eminent Domain', pp. 163–4.

23 There are eight other petitioners in this case. See *Kelo* v. *City of New London*, 545 U.S. 469 (2005).

24 *German Basic Law*, art. 14(3).

25 Ibid., art. 14(2).

Midkiff decisions, the German judges held that public purpose can be achieved not only by public bodies but also by private or public-private bodies. What matters is the purpose itself, not the means. Additionally, the benefit to private parties itself does not necessarily lead to a no-public-good decision.[26] In the *Boxberg* case, the FCC expressed its opinion that expropriation does not necessarily violate the public good requirement because it benefits a third private body. In a case concerning land expropriation for a private school, the private nature of the school does not lead to its disqualification as a public good. Instead, the court decided that establishing a private school would benefit society and that its purpose was thus public.[27] The exclusion of public ownership or possession requirements from public good analysis is also seen in federal legislation. The *Federal Building Code* (*Baugesetzbuch*, or *BauGB*),[28] the most important legislation concerning land expropriation, does not exclude private bodies from the compulsory taking of land, and private persons can apply for compulsory purchase under limited statutory conditions.

The government must have statutory power in its execution of expropriation. This requirement is similar to the analysis of police power in the United States. In the case of *Dürkheimer Gondelbahn*, the FCC denied a local expropriation because the local authority had no power in the concerned expropriation. Apparently, the statutory power requirement is the legality limit on government authority and has no relevance to public good analysis. However, governments are the agents of public power designed to serve the public interest. Public purpose cannot be identified in the law in the case of an absence of due power in expropriation. This case concerned the land expropriation for building and managing a cable car that would link the city with a nearby natural area. The court decided that the legislation cited by the local authority authorised the installation and maintenance of a public transportation system, but it did not authorise the expropriation.[29] A list of the public purposes of expropriation can be found in statutory documents, such as *BauGB*. Section 85 of *BauGB* stipulates that the expropriation may only take place under this Code in order:

1. to use a plot, or to prepare a plot for use in accordance with the designations contained in the binding land-use plan,

[26] BVerfG 74, 264 (*Boxberg*, 1987). [27] BVerfG 18.02.1999 – 1 BvR 1367/88.

[28] The Federal Building Code (*BauGB*) is available at www.iuscomp.org/gla/statutes/BauGB.htm.

[29] BVerfGE 56, 249 (*Dürkheimer Gondelbahn*, 1981).

2. in the case of land which is not developed or only developed to a very low level and is not within the area covered by the binding land-use plan but lies within a built-up area, to use this land or to supply it for a use to for infill development in accordance with regulations under building law,
3. to procure plots for compensation in the form of land,
4. to replace rights taken away by expropriation with other rights,
5. to make plots available for development where an owner has not met an obligation under Section 176 para. 1 or 2, or
6. to preserve a building structure situated within the area covered by a preservation statute on one of the grounds contained in Section 172 paras. 3 to 5.

The strictest requirement concerning public good or purpose is the application of the proportionality principle in analysing the necessity of expropriation in achieving the public purpose. Unlike the U.S. courts' deference attitude to government power, the courts in Germany are more active and much stricter in reviewing the relevance of necessity between expropriation and public good. Applying the German approach, the relevance must first be direct. That is, the public good must be the direct result of the expropriation project. In *Boxberg*, two local governments assembled land through expropriation for a motor company (Mercedes Benz) to build its testing grounds. The local authorities argued that this project, by benefiting a private company, can facilitate employment and improve the local economy. However, the FCC decided that the argued general economic good, including job creation and economic improvement, is solely an indirect public good and thus cannot satisfy the constitutional public good requirement. Second, expropriation must be necessary to the achievement of public good. In *Dürkheimer Gondelbahn*, the FCC expressed a clear position in requiring public necessity for expropriation. In this case, the building of and operation of a cable car was performed to create convenient access to a recreational area, which is not a necessary public service offered by government.[30] Second, public good must outweigh the private interest if they coexist in a given case. Although a private body is permitted to accept a public duty to involve itself in an expropriation project and earn profits or benefits, the public good must be predominant. A compulsory purchase whose

[30] Ibid.

benefit is predominantly or completely private, or whose public and private interests are similar, is not allowed under the public good test.[31]

To guarantee the use of expropriated property for the public interest in Germany, the expropriatee has the right to ask for the return of his expropriated property if it is determined that it is not being used for the assigned public purpose. This is called re-expropriation or expropriation-restitution (*Rückenteignung*).

4.3 The anatomy of the public interest doctrine

4.3.1 Government power: eminent domain versus others

A common feature of the industrialisation and urbanisation processes is the rapid expansion of governments' public power.

In the United States, police power is used to describe the government power originating from the sovereignty. According to Chief Justice Taney, police powers are 'nothing more or less than the powers of government inherent in every sovereignty to the extent of its dominion'.[32] These powers are generally used to promote and maintain public health, security, morals and the general welfare.[33] Thus, police power is regarded as a necessary limit on individual freedom and rights, which endows the government with its inherent function.

The definition of police power is elastic. In a broad sense, it can include every type of sovereign power. In this sense, eminent domain is one police power or government power. In fact, very often, the powers of taxation and eminent domain are not excluded from police powers in court decisions. As for the powers influencing property, we can identify three main powers: regulation power, eminent domain power and taxation power. In a narrow sense, as well as to distinguish taking power from other governmental powers, police power is often limited to regulation or regulatory powers in court decisions.[34]

Regulatory powers refer to the powers that limit or regulate private property without taking it. Regulatory powers are typically reflected in

[31] BVerfG 74, 264 (*Boxberg*, 1987).

[32] *Thurlow* v. *The Commonwealth of Massachusetts, etc.*, 46 U.S. 504, 583 (1847).

[33] See the definition in *Encyclopedia Britannica*, which is available at www.britannica.com/EBchecked/topic/467323/police-power.

[34] In the United States, the scope of police power as a regulatory power has been expanding. As Paul commented, police power expanded from the one 'affecting three public concerns – health, safety and, morals' to the one '[including] the catch-all component of general welfare'. See Paul, *Property Rights*, p. 103.

legislation concerning such areas as housing, building, zoning, rent control, public nuisances and subdivision regulation. The influence of regulation on the value of property can be positive or negative. If the regulation substantially infringes on the landowner's interest, it is regarded as regulatory taking and falls into the domain of the taking clause of the *Fifth Amendment*. Regulatory taking was first recognised in *Pennsylvania Coal Co.* v. *Mahon* in 1922, in which the U.S. Supreme Court ruled against a state act that forbade the mining of anthracite coal using a method that caused the subsidence of any structure used as a human habitation.[35] According to the court decision, this act's prohibition of mining infringed on an integral part of the coal owner's property rights-the right to mine itself. Thus, '[t]o make it commercially impracticable to mine certain coal has very nearly the same effect for constitutional purposes as appropriating or destroying it'.[36] Justice Holms, delivering the decision, wrote: 'The general rule at least is that while property may be regulated to a certain extent, if regulation goes too far it will be recognized as a taking.'[37] Additionally, the *Pennsylvania Coal* caseexpresses the Supreme Court's preference for the term 'police power' in a narrow sense for the purpose of distinguishing it from eminent domain. This case developed the well-known 'diminution-of-value' test to draw the line between taking as eminent domain power and regulation as police power. When considering whether the limits of police power have been exceeded, it is necessary to consider 'the extent of the resulting diminution in value'.[38] Justice Brandeis, in his dissenting opinions, noted that the majority decision seems to be based on an assumption of 'average reciprocity of advantage', a rule used in the justification of some police power.[39] If the average reciprocity of advantage cannot be found between the property owner restricted by the regulation and the rest of the community, the concerned police power is not justified and must thus fall within the scope of regulatory taking, for which just compensation must be given.

The 'non-noxious use' test was used to distinguish police power from eminent domain power in the 1887 case of *Mugler* v. *Kansas*.[40] In this case, brewery owners challenged a Kansas law prohibiting the manufacture or sale of liquor in the state on the premise that such acts diminished

[35] *Pennsylvania Coal Co.* v. *Mahon*, 260 U.S. 393 (1922).

[36] Ibid., at 414. [37] Ibid., at 415.

[38] The boundary set by diminution of value test is neither certain nor clear. In a later case, the court supported a state act similar to the one in *Pennsylvania Coal*. See, *Keystone Bituminous Coal Association* v. *DeBenedictis*, 480 U.S. 470 (1987).

[39] 260 U.S. 393, 422 (1922). [40] *Mugler* v. *Kansas*, 123 U.S. 623 (1887).

the value of their property without the compensation stipulated by the constitution. Despite their arguments, the court ruled:

> The power which the states have of prohibiting such use by individuals of their property, as will be prejudicial to the health, the morals, or the safety of the public, is not, and, consistently with the existence and safety of organized society, cannot be, burdened with the condition that the state must compensate such individual owners for pecuniary losses they may sustain, by reason of their not being permitted, by a noxious use of their property, to inflict injury upon the community. The exercise of the police power by the destruction of property which is itself a public nuisance, or the prohibition of its use in a particular way, whereby its value becomes depreciated, is very different from taking property for public use, or from depriving a person of his property without due process of law.[41]

The noxious use test can also be called the 'harm/benefit' test, which articulates the difference between eminent domain and police power as follows: Eminent domain and the expropriation of private property are meant to benefit the public, but police power is meant to prohibit a private owner's noxious use of his individual property, which may harm his neighbourhood.[42] However, the clear boundary set by this test was blurred in the 1921 case of *Block* v. *Hirsh*,[43] in which the court upheld a state act restricting the non-noxious use of private property. The act at issue concerned the rent control of a landlord's houses. The majority decision was that this control fell within valid police power because it was only temporary, and the controlled rent level was reasonable. The approach developed in this case is called 'reasonableness balancing', which implies the allowance of and tolerance towards sacrificing a small degree of private interest to the public. Additionally, reasonableness balancing enlarges the scope of the use of police power in interfering with private property without compensation, stepping over the line drawn by the noxious use test. In essence, this approach means that the court, even in non-noxious cases,

[41] Ibid., at 669.

[42] Oswald, 'Property Rights', 552. In addition, Freund comments:

> Under the police power, rights of property are impaired not because they become useful or necessary to the public, or because some public advantage can be gained by disregarding them, but because their free exercise is believed to be detrimental to public interests; it may be said that the state takes property by eminent domain because it is useful to the public, and under the police power because it is harmful or as Justice Bradley put it, because 'the property itself is the cause of public detriment'.

See Freund, *The Police Power*, pp. 546–7.

[43] *Block* v. *Hirsh*, 256 U.S. 135 (1923).

will still weigh 'the magnitude of the burden to the individual against the benefit to the public interest'.[44] If the statute at issue does not go too far, it is still appropriate use of no-compensation police power.[45] Based on this approach, *Pennsylvania Coal* developed the 'average reciprocity of advantage' analysis the following year, which is still, in essence, a balance between the individual interest and the public interest represented by police power.[46] If government restriction substantially harms a private owner's interest, the statute at issue may depart from the safe scope of police power and will be regarded as taking, which requires just compensation.

Further development after the *Pennsylvania Coal* case as to the distinction between regulatory taking and police power was not made until 1978, when *Penn Central Transportation* v. *New York City* offered the 'Bundle of Rights' analysis, which is still on the track of reasonableness balancing.[47] In this case, Grand Central Station's terminal was listed as a historical landmark, according to local landmark law, and its owner was obliged to maintain the station's historical structure. They were also required to report to the authority in charge before any alteration was made. The majority decision denied the owners' requirement for just compensation and regarded the government regulation as still being the exercise of police power. According to this decision, the regulation of landmark law over the station terminal does not deprive the owner of his or her rights and interests in the property. Obviously, this analysis framework focuses on whether government regulation deprives any substantial right or interest from the bundle of property rights. This can be summarised with a paragraph of this decision:

> [T]he New York City law does not interfere in any way with the present uses of the Terminal. Its designation as a landmark not only permits but contemplates that appellants may continue to use the property precisely as it has been used for the past 65 years: as a railroad terminal containing office space and concessions. So the law does not interfere with what must be regarded as Penn Central's primary expectation concerning the use of the parcel. More importantly, on this record, we must regard the New York

44 Hippler, 'Reexamining 100 Years', 672.

45 The decision says that, '[t]he only matter that seems to us open to debate is whether the statute goes too far. For just as there comes a point at which the police power ceases and leaves only that of eminent domain, it may be conceded that regulations of the present sort pressed to a certain height might amount to a taking without due process of law.' 256 U.S. 135, 156 (1923).

46 In fact, Holms used this approach in another, earlier case in the same year. See *Jackman* v. *Rosenbaum Co.*, 260 U.S. 22 (1922).

47 *Penn Central Transportation* v. *New York City*, 438 U.S. 104 (1978).

> City law as permitting Penn Central not only to profit from the Terminal but also to obtain a 'reasonable return' on its investment.[48]

In Germany, the FCC has denied the recognition of regulatory takings as the expropriations defined by the *German Basic Law*. The regulation activities which can be deemed as regulatory takings in the United States are not the expropriations defined by the *German Basic Law* and thus are not subject to constitutional compensation in Germany.[49] This does not mean, however, that such regulations can be enforced over private rights without constitutional restraint. First, the regulations, which limit the owner's use of his or her property so severely that the substance of ownership is negatively influenced, can be declared to violate art. 14(1) and thus be unconstitutional. Second, equalisation measures may be available. Because such regulations are not the actual expropriations stipulated by the legislature, the compensation stipulated by art. 14(3) is not available. However, some equalisation measure in monetary or non-monetary form should be awarded. Otherwise, the concerned regulation is still unconstitutional. In 1952, the civil and administrative courts in Germany began awarding compensation to property owners who suffered 'unusual sacrifice' owing to regulation activity that is legally authorised. Such compensation is not based on the constitution. Instead, it was developed from the equalisation theory under tort law.[50] In the 1999 *Denkmalschutz* (*Monument Protection*) case, an owner was prohibited from demolishing his old villa, which was designated a historical landmark under the state's law concerning the protection of monuments. For a long time, the owner had failed to find a buyer. The cost of maintenance was expensive. In this case, the FCC clarified two issues: the difference in constitutional application between expropriation and regulation, and the distinction between expropriatory compensation and equalisation or regulatory compensation. In regard to the first issue, although art. 14(3) of the *German Basic Law* is applied to expropriation only, the court can still cite art. 14(1) to declare the excessive regulations unconstitutional. Because the regulation burden on the owner was so heavy that his ownership had essentially been lost, such regulation violated art. 14(1) and was thus unconstitutional.

48 Ibid., at 136.

49 Alexander, *The Global Debate*, pp. 116–17. In a case decided in 1981, the FCC clearly ruled that the compensation stipulated by art. 14(3) of the *German Basic Law* was available only for the actual expropriations. See BVerfGE 58, 300 (*Naßauskiesung* [*Groundwater*] Case, 1981).

50 Ibid., Alexander, pp. 117–18.

In regard to the second issue, although the compensation in art. 14(3) is applied to actual expropriation only, the regulated owner can be remedied through some equalisation measure. In essence, equalisation is similar to expropriatory compensation because they are both compensation designed to mitigate the owner's loss caused by regulation. The main difference between the articles is that equalisation can be awarded by the courts without legislative authorisation, which is a must for the awarding of compensation according to art. 14(3).[51]

4.3.2 *Comparing three government powers*

It is argued that there is no clear and fundamental difference among the three main government powers. They are all inherent and indispensable powers endowed to governments for exercising their functions. They are all, as declared, for public use or public interest. As for property affairs, they all influence private property. As Bell and Parchomovsky commented, '[i]t is difficult to identify a characteristic of eminent domain that warrants treating differently this power from among all government economic powers.'[52] It is possible for three powers to influence private property to produce the equivalent results.[53] The exercise of regulation power can result in the substantial deprivation of an owner's property rights, as can physical taking. Taxation power can also be imposed on private property to make its value shrink or even disappear, similar to regulatory or physical taking (classical eminent domain).[54]

Nonetheless, the three government powers that influence property differ greatly. First, their normal functions vary. Taxing power aims to collect fiscal or government revenue by imposing taxes. The purpose of police power is to restrict the noxious use of private property or realise public interest without substantially harming the property owner's bundle of rights. However, the power of eminent domain is exercised to change the ownership of property (physical taking) or – under the regulatory taking situation – to heavily limit an owner's rights so much that the effect is similar to that of physical taking. The regulation that produces results similar to that of eminent domain is categorised in the governance of taking clause and the exercise of regulatory taking shows clearly the court's solid position in distinguishing between police power and eminent

[51] Ibid., pp. 119–21. See also BVerfGE 100, 226 (*Denkmalschutz*, 1999).

[52] Bell and Parchomovsky, 'The Uselessness', 1426. [53] Ibid. [54] Ibid., 1432.

domain power. Unlike regulatory taking, we find no term, such as 'taxation taking' or 'regulatory taxation', to describe the situation under which taxation is imposed to diminish the value of property similarly to regulatory taking. However, within the appropriate and normal scope of its function, compared to taking, the extent of taxation power's influence on the property is insignificant. Second, the use of eminent domain power is discriminatory. However, for police power and taxation power, they are more non-discriminatory or much less discriminatory. Eminent domain is often used to target one or a group of property holders, but the other two powers are used to regulate citizens universally without prejudice.[55] Third, reciprocity exists under the appropriate use of police and taxation power. Namely, the persons regulated or taxed by government can also have the opportunity to enjoy the benefits brought by such powers. Under eminent domain, however, the persons whose property is taken enjoy unproportionate, few or no reciprocal benefits. Some specific condemnees sacrifice their property to benefit other community members who do not need to sacrifice their property rights. Fourth, the exercise of eminent domain may be accomplished by private bodies. However, the other two powers must be exercised by government. Thus, property redistribution among private bodies is possible when eminent domain powers are used.

Although the uniform goal of the three powers is declared to be for public interest, their influence or harm on private property and their means to their end differ. Compared to police and taxation powers, and considering their substantial influence, discriminatory and non-reciprocity features, and private involvement, eminent domain or taking power is the most dangerous in changing the redistribution of private properties and is thus subject to the strict restraints in the constitution. This is why many countries stipulate in the constitution restrictions specifically on taking or expropriation. Moreover, for the analysis on public purpose or interest, the difference among the three powers are interesting in two aspects. First, the power of eminent domain, as the most dangerous and discriminatory power in interfering with individual property, should be governed most strictly among the three powers. Thus, the analysis of public purpose will be more discrete than that concerning the other two powers. Second,

[55] Discrimination or prejudice in the use of police and taxation power still exist to some extent. For example, the taxation applied to the rich is often higher than that applied to the poor. That is a result-perspective. Nonetheless, the prejudice in the result is still much slighter than that under eminent domain. As for the intention or motivation side, the use of appropriate police and taxation power is generally non-discriminatory.

eminent domain should be the final power to realise public purpose or the function of governments. It will be used only when other government powers cannot achieve the proposed public purpose.[56] In other words, the use of eminent domain must be strictly for public interest and cannot be substituted by the other two powers. This leads to a discussion of the proportionality principle. Additionally, considering the different functions of the three powers, as discussed in the next section, the judicial deference standard in defining public purpose is inappropriate, particularly in countries with statutory legal systems, such as China.

4.3.3 *Authorised by law and judicial deference*

Unlike in the United States where eminent domain power originates in common law, governmental expropriation must be legally authorised in Germany. Article 14(3) of *German Basic Law* requires that expropriation 'may only be ordered by or pursuant to a law that determines the nature and extent of compensation'.[57] This constitutional stipulation has two implications. First, expropriation must be done according to the law, or the expropriation power must be found in the law. Second, the laws concerning expropriation must include stipulations concerning the nature and extent of compensation. Otherwise, expropriation is invalid and cannot be initiated.

The statutes concerning expropriation can be found in many laws in Germany at both the federal and state (*Länder* or *Bundesland*) levels. In fact, the contents or structure of expropriation laws do not significantly differ. Because expropriation mainly concerns land or land rights, the laws covering expropriation are mostly about building, planning, zoning, slum clearance and so on. The most important law concerning expropriation is *BauGB*, which includes thirty-eight specific articles (secs. 85 to 122) on expropriation. Such articles comprise part 5 of chapter 1 and are categorised into three subdivisions which are 'Legal Requirements for Expropriation', 'Compensation' and 'Expropriation Procedure'. The purpose of expropriation is described in the first section under the first subdivision in Part 5. In essence, in subdivision 1, the purpose and other legal requirements form the scope of the government's expropriation power.

[56] Article 87(1) of *BauGB* stipulates, '[e]xpropriation is only admissible in individual cases where this is required for the general good and the purpose to be served by expropriation cannot reasonably be achieved by any other means.'

[57] *German Basic Law*, art. 14(3).

The compensation stipulations in subdivision 2 are the remedies offered to the expropriatee, and subdivision 3 describes procedure requirements.

The purposes identified by *BauGB* are concrete. They are the origins of government expropriation power in the area stipulated by this code. The *BauGB* requires that expropriation 'may only take place' for the purpose identified by the law.[58] If the purpose of government expropriation cannot be found in any valid law, expropriation will be overturned by the court.

Similar to the United States, the German courts also defer to legislatures or statutory power in defining public purpose. Few courts question the public purposes identified in laws. This means that when a public purpose is identified by a law, the court usually does not question the purpose. Instead, the court reviews whether the exact purpose of expropriation corresponds to the legislated purpose. In *Boxberg*, it was decided that the mentioned purpose did not correspond to the urban planning measures defined in sec. 85 of *BauGB*. However, the court mentioned that legislators can pass specific laws for the proposed expropriation purpose, although they did not use this right.[59] This, in addition to indirectly strengthening the 'authority by law' doctrine, shows the court's preference for deferring to the identification of public purposes made by the legislature.

In *Berman*, the taking concerned a slum clearance project. Discussing whether the slum clearance is a type of public purpose, the decision used a paragraph to ascertain the importance of improving housing conditions for the public, such as reducing disease, crime and immorality, reducing residents' life burdens and maintaining their dignity.[60] However, this does not mean that the judge prefers reviewing whether the nature of a legislated project is that of public use or substantially examining the legislated content. In the cited paragraph as follows, the decision explained why the U.S. Supreme Court noted that the role of the judiciary in determining whether power is exercised for a public purpose is an 'extremely narrow one':[61]

> We deal, in other words, with what traditionally has been known as the police power. An attempt to define its reach or trace its outer limits is fruitless, for each case must turn on its own facts. The definition is essentially the product of legislative determinations addressed to the purposes of government, purposes neither abstractly nor historically capable of complete definition. Subject to specific constitutional limitations, when the legislature has spoken, the public interest has been declared in terms well-nigh conclusive. In such cases the legislature, not the judiciary, is the main

[58] *BauGB*, sec. 85. [59] BVerfG 74, 264 (*Boxberg*, 1987).
[60] 348 U.S. 26, 32–3 (1954). [61] Ibid., at 32.

> guardian of the public needs to be served by social legislation, whether it be Congress legislating concerning the District of Columbia . . . or the States legislating concerning local affairs. . . . This principle admits of no exception merely because the power of eminent domain is involved.[62]

To put the specific constitutional limitations aside, judicial deference is not justified in achieving the constitutional goal of private property protection. Eminent domain, among the three government powers, is the power subject to the strictest review. The first issue to be reviewed is public purpose, on which the court should have played a more active role. To take the German and U.S. constitutions as examples, there is no specific stipulation about public interest or similar terms as to the other two powers. Only eminent domain power is expressly imposed with public purpose limits. This reasonably implies that the constitutional review of the public purpose inherent in the other two powers may be a slight review – namely, a review focusing on the procedural appropriateness with judicial deference as the benchmark. As for eminent domain, the review of public purpose must be substantial enough to probe into the justification of the laws concerning public purpose.

4.3.4 *Proportionality principle*

Essentially, expropriation concerns conflict between the public interest and individual rights. When the expropriation power used by government infringes on the constitutional right to private property, public purpose needs to be compared with individual rights to determine whether the public interest is important enough that it should be realised at the expense of individual property. In Germany, the proportionality principle is used to make this comparison.

There is no text stipulation about proportionality in the *German Basic Law*. In fact, proportionality is a constitutional principle developed by

[62] Ibid. Also, in another paragraph, the court rules:

> We do not sit to determine whether a particular housing project is or is not desirable. The concept of the public welfare is broad and inclusive. . . . The values it represents are spiritual as well as physical, aesthetic as well as monetary. It is within the power of the legislature to determine that the community should be beautiful as well as healthy, spacious as well as clean, well-balanced as well as carefully patrolled. In the present case, the Congress and its authorized agencies have made determinations that take into account a wide variety of values. It is not for us to reappraise them. If those who govern the District of Columbia decide that the Nation's Capital should be beautiful as well as sanitary, there is nothing in the Fifth Amendment that stands in the way.

Ibid., at 33.

the courts. In the beginning, the principle of proportionality originated from administrative law with the aim of prohibiting the government from intervening too broadly. After World War II, the proportionality principle was held by the courts as a constitutional principle requiring proportionality between government means and its end.[63] Structurally, proportionality entails a '2-step and 3-test' analysis. The final goal is to determine whether the public interest overwhelms individual constitutional rights, including property.

The first step entails analysing whether any individual rights are infringed by government power. The second step entails analysing whether the means used by public authority are appropriate and whether the infringement is proportional.[64] In the second step, three tests are used to weigh proportionality. The first test is called 'suitability' and is used to analyse whether the means used by the government – for example, expropriation – are suitable for achieving the intended public end. The second test is called 'necessity' and is used to analyse whether government means are necessary for realising public ends. In other words, to decide whether there are other, less restrictive government means that infringe less on individual rights and that could be used for the intended public end. As we described earlier, under expropriation, eminent domain power is the final power to be used for public purpose. The third test is called 'proportionality in the strict sense' and is used to compare the loss resulting from the infringement of individual rights and the public interest realised by government measures. That is, individual loss should be proportional to the public interest.

Although these three tests are not integrated into a proportionality principle structure in the United States, similar doctrines can be found. Three doctrines are applied to achieve results similar to those of the proportionality principle. The 'less restrictive alternative' doctrine requires government, through laws or otherwise, to adopt the least restrictive alternative to achieve its goal when its measures infringe individual rights. In essence, this is an alternative expression of the necessity test.[65] The 'rational relevance' doctrine is used to establish the rational linkage between means and ends, which is what the suitability test does. In *Midkiff*, the purpose of eminent domain is to resolve the oligopoly problem

[63] Baer, 'Equality', 261–4. [64] Engel, 'The History', 6–7.

[65] Article 1 of the *U.S. Constitution* stipulates: 'The Congress shall have Power – To make all Laws which shall be necessary and proper for carrying into Execution the foregoing Powers, and all other Powers vested by this Constitution in the Government of the United States, or in any Department or Officer thereof.' See also Struve, 'The Less'.

concerning local land. After confirming that the use of eminent domain as the means is rationally related to public ends by arguing that '[t]his is a comprehensive and rational approach to identifying and correcting market failure', the Supreme Court decided that 'where the exercise of the eminent domain power is rationally related to a conceivable public purpose, the Court has never held a compensated taking to be proscribed by the Public Use Clause'.[66] It must be again noted that the judicial review of rational relevance is not strict because it does not analyse whether the results of using eminent domain are satisfactory. The court observes only whether '[l]egislature rationally could have believed that the [Act] would promote its objective'.[67] Influenced by a judicial deference test, the court made a less strict examination of the link between means and ends. As noted in *Berman*, '[o]nce the object is within the authority of Congress, the means by which it will be attained is also for Congress to determine'.[68] As for proportionality in a strict sense, in the United States, a similar doctrine is called the 'balancing of interests'. As Aleinikoff defines it, '[t]he metaphor of balancing refers to theories of constitutional interpretation that are based on the identification, valuation, and comparison of competing interests'.[69] Unlike the development of proportionality principle in Germany, which has its origins in public law and aims to protect individual rights from the undue harm of public power, the doctrine of balancing was developed in the United States to restrict the over-protection of individual rights. Thus, the historical origin of the two doctrines differs. As Porat and Cohen-Eliya commented, 'unlike proportionality which was a way to guarantee that rights were not unnecessarily harmed, balancing was a way to ensure that rights were not protected unnecessarily by balancing them against public interests'.[70]

In the German cases concerning expropriation, courts use structural tests, including the proportionality principle, to conduct more comprehensive and thus stricter analyses. In addition to evaluating the suitability and necessity of the used means, expropriation would not be upheld by a court unless it was persuaded that the public interest weighs substantially more than individual property. In practice in the United States, however, the Supreme Court tends to focus mainly on the analysis of rationality. In both *Berman* and *Mikdiff*, the court seldom mentioned necessity tests, less restrictive alternatives and the balance between individual property and the public interest.

[66] 467 U.S. 229, 241–2 (1981). [67] Ibid., at 242. See also 451 U.S. 648, 671–2 (1981).
[68] 348 U.S. 26, 33 (1954). [69] Aleinikoff, 'Constitutional Law', 945.
[70] Cohen-Eliya and Porat, 'American Balancing', 284.

Additionally, the proportionality principle leads to the justification of expropriation-restitution. When a government expropriates land, the amount of land expropriated shall be necessary and proportional to the end that such an expropriation project is expected to achieve. This implies that unnecessary parcels of land, which are taken for public use, shall be returned to their owners, and that if the land expropriated is not used for the proposed purpose or is not used in the assigned time, the original owner has the right to ask for its return.

4.3.5 *The categorisation of public purposes*

4.3.5.1 The practice of legislation

In addition to mentioning the term concerning public purpose in the constitutions, the identification and illustration of public purpose can be found in the laws concerned, mainly the laws concerning expropriation or the compulsory purchase of land. The methods used to define public purpose differ among counties.

The first method is the generalisation method. It can be called definition or simple illustration, which is to define the term 'public purpose' in simple words. Although a brief definition is given, the abstract or general words used still leave great flexibility in illustration. The typical example is Canada's *Expropriation Act.* It says, '[a]ny interest in land, . . . in the opinion of the Minister, is required by the Crown for a public work or other public purpose may be expropriated by the Crown in accordance with the provisions of this Part.'[71] The act explains public purpose as public works. In France, the *Civil Code* defines public interest as 'direct public engineering construction and construction indirectly meeting public interests, and for the need of government's macro control'.[72]

The second method is the enumeration method. The enumeration can be positive or negative. Positive enumeration identifies concrete purposes with public nature, which can be used to justify expropriation, but the negative enumeration specifically excludes those situations which cannot be regarded as the public purpose or interest. Japan's *Land Expropriation Law* lists the examples of public purposes simply. It states that land can be expropriated 'in order to set up various social public undertakings, such as roads, parks, dikes, and harbor construction etc.'[73] The list can also be

[71] *Expropriation Act*, sec. 4(1). This act is available at laws.justice.gc.ca/eng/acts/E-21/.
[72] ADB (Asian Development Bank), 'People's Republic of China', 7. [73] Ibid.

detailed(for example, India's *Land Acquisition Act* [*1894 LAA*] lists eight types of public purpose).[74]

The relevant legislation can also combine both positive and negative listings. A typical example can be found in the legislation of the state of Minnesota in the United States. The legislation first enumerates the permitted situations for public use or public purpose, which are: '(1) the possession, occupation, ownership, and enjoyment of the land by the general public, or by public agencies; (2) the creation or functioning of a public service corporation; or (3) mitigation of a blighted area, remediation of an environmentally contaminated area, reduction of abandoned property, or removal of a public nuisance'.

Following this, the legislation excludes some examples that cannot be regarded as public use by stating the following: 'The public benefits of economic development, including an increase in tax base, tax revenues, employment, or general economic health, do not by themselves constitute a public use or public purpose.'[75]

In some legislation, the combination of both generalisation and enumeration is used. In Taiwan, art. 208 of *Land Law* provides that expropriation is allowed for the need of setting up 'public undertakings' (*gonggong shiye*) and lists the exact situations of public undertakings:

[74] The sec. 3(f) of the *1894 LAA* provides several public purposes: '(i) the provision of village-sites, or the extension, planned development or improvement of existing village-sites; (ii) the provision of land for town or rural planning; (iii) the provision of land for planned development of land from public funds in pursuance of any scheme or policy of Government and subsequent disposal thereof in whole or in part by lease, assignment or outright sale with the object of securing further development as planned; (iv) the provision of land for a corporation owned or controlled by the state; (v) the provision of land for residential purposes to the poor or landless or to persons residing in areas affected by natural calamities, or to persons displaced or affected by reason of the implementation of any scheme undertaken by Government, any local authority or a corporation owned or controlled by the state; (vi) the provision of land for carrying out any educational, housing, health or slum clearance scheme sponsored by Government or by any authority established by Government for carrying out any such scheme, or with the prior approval of the appropriate Government, by a local authority, or a society registered under the Societies Registration Act, 1860 (21 of 1860), or under any corresponding law for the time being in force in a state, or a co-operative society within the meaning of any law relating to co-operative societies for the time being in force in any State; (vii) the provision of land for any other scheme of development sponsored by Government or with the prior approval of the appropriate Government, by a local authority; (viii) the provision of any premises or building for locating a public office, but does not include acquisition of land for companies'. The *1894 LAA* is available at dolr.nic.in/hyperlink/acq.htm.

[75] Minnesota Statutes 2007, subd.11.117.025, available at www.revisor.mn.gov/bin/getpub.php?type=s&num=117.025.

'installations of national defense; communication enterprises; public utility enterprises; water conservancy enterprises; public health; government office buildings, office buildings of local self-governing bodies and other public buildings; educational, academic, and philanthropic undertakings; enterprises operated by the State; other undertakings sponsored by the Government in the public interest'.[76]

The scope of public purpose differs among countries. This reflects the existence of differences in defining the scope of government power in different countries with various social contexts. Even in one country, in different periods, the variance of the scope of government power often leads to a change in the domain of public purpose. Generally, in developing or transitional countries with urgent economic needs or social reform tasks, the scope of public purpose concerning land expropriation is broader than that in developed countries with stable legal systems and mature markets. In India, the land expropriation for economic development – that is, the development of EPZ – is allowed as a public purpose justifying expropriation. Indeed, in many countries, 'land expropriation has become a means for governments to exercise macroeconomic control'.[77] In the United States, however, economic development as public purpose is still a controversial issue. Although the *Kelo* decision allowed economic development as a public purpose for taking land, it was widely criticised by both scholars and legal practitioners. Not long after this decision, several states passed legislation specifically excluding economic development from the list of public purposes.

4.3.5.2 Positioning public purpose

There are four factors used to identify public nature and locate the controversial extent of an expropriation project: purpose, ownership, operation and access. Purpose, or interest, refers to the end of the concerned project; ownership and operation refer to the means or approaches to the end; and access refers to the result or benefit produced by the concerned project. The project with a public nature in all of these factors is the least controversial and always falls into the scope of the most traditional and typical public purposes. A project, if owned and operated by a public agency, with public interest as the purpose and with access to or use by the public, is seldom challenged for its matching with public use or the equivalent

[76] The *Land Act* was promulgated on 30 June 1930, amended for the first time on 31 October 2001 and amended for the second time on 14 June 2006. The English text is available at www.land.moi.gov.tw/enhtml/fileclick.asp?onid=505.

[77] ADB, 'People's Republic of China', 7.

Table 4.1 *The categorisation of public purposes*

Least Controversial	Physical Infrastructure/Public Utilities/Slum Clearance/Urban Planning (owned and operated by government body) Public in purpose, ownership, operation and access
Less Controversial	Physical Infrastructure/Public Utilities/Slum Clearance/Urban Planning (owned and operated by private body or public-private body) Public in purpose and access Operation is subject to government regulation.
Most Controversial	Projects for Economic and Commercial Development (owned and operated by private body) Public in Purpose/Benefit (still questionable) No government regulation

test. Such a project also satisfies the narrow sense definition of public use. An example is the expropriation of land for establishing a public school. The less controversial projects include those with clear public interest as purpose and result (or public access) but also private agencies' involvement, such as assembling land for a private school or a slum clearance project developed by a fully or partially private company. Government regulation is often required to control the operation of private activities meant to meet public ends. The most controversial project is found in a situation in which, although public purpose and public benefit can be identified to some extent, the involvement is mainly private. The most typical example is an economic development project in which the public interest as purpose is arguable, the public benefit is indirect and the expropriated land is owned and used by private bodies. For a generalisation of the categorisation of three positioning scopes, see Table 4.1.

4.4 Public interest in the Chinese context

4.4.1 Public interest test in the constitution

The *1954 Constitution of China* existed for a short period when China transformed from a new democracy state to a socialist state. Because the individual ownership of urban and rural land was allowed at that time, the corresponding stipulation about expropriation for the public interest could also be found in the *1954 Constitution of China*. In this constitution, the phrase 'private property', which was believed to be capitalistic, was not used to denote land, other production means and living materials. Citizens' ownership was mainly restricted to 'legal income, savings, houses and various living materials.'[78] The term 'private property' was used in a clause concerning inheritance only. This clause provides that '[t]he state protects according to law the right of citizens to inherit private property'.[79]

The objects of expropriation were limited to 'urban and rural land and other production means'.[80] During the transition to a socialist state, private property, although allowed by the constitution, was largely limited and could not enjoy the same treatment as that of public property. This is reflected in the constitutional provisions concerning public interest. The term 'public interest' can be found in three articles. Article 10 states the protection of 'the right of capitalists to own means of production and other capital' in its first paragraph. The third paragraph of this article declares that '[t]he State prohibits capitalists from engaging in any unlawful activities which injure the public interest, disturb the social-economic order, or undermine the economic plan of the State'. This paragraph parallels public interest with social-economic order and national economic plans to show that in this constitution, public interest is linked closely with the development of socialist society. The second article concerning public interest is art. 13, which is a taking clause stipulating that for the needs of the public interest, the state may 'requisition by purchase, take over for use or nationalize both urban and rural land as well as other means of production on the conditions provided by law'. However, this article does not mention the requirement of compensation. This also shows the unequal status between public interest and private property. Private property can only exist within the scope that does not hinder socialist development and the public interest, which is in the form of social development and economic planning and, if for the need of public interest, private property should be taken without compensation or with insufficient compensation for developing the planned social and economic projects. The third article dealing with public interest is art. 14, which provides that '[t]he state prohibits the use of private property by any person to the detriment of the public interest.' In fact, art. 14 repeats

[78] *1954 Constitution of China*, art. 11. [79] Ibid., art. 12. [80] Ibid., art. 13.

the legislative intention or the purpose of the third paragraph of art. 10. It strengthens the stipulation that the public interest represented by the socialist government shall be over private property and private property shall be subordinate to the needs of the public interest. Compared with this constitution, however, constitutions in Western countries usually use public interest as a limit on government, and the taking clause attempts to balance the protection of private property and the needs of the public interest.[81]

Because the socialist reconstruction was nearly completed by 1956, this constitution became useless soon after its creation. In the 1975 and 1978 constitutions, the term 'public interest' was removed from the stipulation concerning expropriation. In fact, after the socialist reconstruction, China became a socialist society with the key feature of public ownership of main production means, including land. Individuals' property rights were limited to some living materials only. Thus, both constitutions stipulate that only the state can requisition by purchase, take over for use, or nationalise land or other means of production.[82] At that time, land and other production materials were owned mainly by all of the people or collective organisations. Through expropriation or nationalisation, the collectively owned property was taken to the ownership of all of the people, represented by the government. Because taking activities mainly concerned two properties of a public nature, there is no longer a need to mention public interest as a purpose. With the disappearance of public interest, the term 'private property' linked with inheritance was deleted from the 1975 and 1978 constitutions.

The *1982 Constitution of China* reintroduced the term 'public interest'. Article 10 in the original version of such constitution provided that the state could requisition land for the needs of the public interest. This change was made to keep the pace of post-1978 reform, which allowed the private holding of use rights of land. Additionally, the individuals' property scope was no longer limited to living materials. In addition to legal income, savings and houses, the *1982 Constitution of China* added 'other legal

[81] In Western countries, the state takes private property only in a limited number of situations, such as by taxation or the confiscation of the profits of crime. The government can also impose restrictions over private property when the use of property causes hardship to third parties. To take property for the public interest or purpose is also allowed, but the public purposes are explained in the narrow sense, such as for health, security and so on.

[82] *1975 Constitution of China*, art. 6; *1978 Constitution of China*, art. 6. In the *1975 Constitution of China*, the target of expropriation is land and other production means. However, in the *1978 Constitution of China*, this target is revised to land only.

property' for individual holding. This gave birth to the possibility of holding private rights of land.[83]

With the gradual progress towards a market economy, the status of private economic sectors in the economic system has risen since 1982. This was reflected in the 1988, 1993, 1999 and 2004 constitutional amendments. Generally speaking, the status of private economy was changed from 'supplementary' in the earliest version of the *1982 Constitution of China* to 'important' in the *1999 Amendment*. In addition to stipulating the protection of the private economy in the *1982 Constitution of China*, the *2004 Amendment* supplemented the description of the state's encouragement, support and leading of the private economy. With the change in the status of the private economy, the scope of privately owned property rights had been enlarged since 1982, although such property rights are always limited to non-ownership rights of land. In the *2004 Amendment*, the revisions around the protection of private property were considered a milestone. The term 'private property' was no longer limited to the inheritance clause. It was used to include both living and production materials. In the previous versions of the constitutions implemented prior to 2004, the term 'ownership' instead of 'property' was used to distinguish the public ownership of production materials and the individual ownership of living materials. In this amendment, however, the phrase 'ownership of living materials', which had been used for a long time, was substituted with the term 'private property'. In fact, the use of the term 'ownership' created a barrier in identifying the legal status of privately owned partial rights of land and other production materials, which are owned by the state or collectives. This substitution helps to clarify the constitutional status and legal nature of privately owned things or rights. Moreover, the use of the word 'property' may allow more space for the future reform of the property system.

4.4.2 *Public interest test in other laws*

During the planned economy period in China, before it opened to the outside world and began implementing reforms, property was taken to facilitate national construction (*guojia jianshe*). In the *Measures on Requisition of Land for National Construction* (*1953 Construction Measures*) enacted in 1953, art. 2 stipulates that national construction includes 'national

83 *1982 Constitution of China* (the original version), art. 10.

defense projects, factories and mineral production, railway, communications, water conservancy, municipal construction and other economic and cultural constructions'. In 1958, this definition was revised to include 'the projects concerning factories and mineral production, railway, communications, water conservancy and national defense, and the constructions concerning culture, education, hygiene and municipality and other constructions'.[84] The scope of national construction was enlarged through this 1958 revision. Through the revision, nearly all of the government's construction projects could justify the taking of land.

The first law enacted after 1978 to incorporate public interest terms was the *Law on Chinese-Foreign Joint Ventures*, enacted by the NPC in 1979. Article 2(3) of this law stipulates that: 'The state shall not nationalize or take over joint ventures; under special circumstances and according to the needs of social public interests, the State may requisite joint ventures according to legal procedures with due compensation.'

This paragraph was the earliest legal provision in China to set a basic framework about property condemnation following the practice of Western countries. The same stipulation was introduced into another law concerning FDI in 1986.[85]

As for land taking, the *1953 Construction Measures* was substituted by the *Regulation on Requisition of Land for National Construction* (*1982 Construction Regulation*) in 1982.[86] The purpose of land taking was defined by art. 2 of this regulation to be 'for the economic, cultural and national defense constructions and the constructions of social public affairs'. This regulation did not change the purposes of land taking defined by the *1953 Construction Measures*. In 1986, the *LAL* specifically and clearly established the 'public interest' as the purpose for land taking. Article 2(3) of the *LAL* stipulates that the state may requisition the

[84] *Guojia Jianshe Zhengyong Tudi Banfa* [*Measures on Requisition of Land for National Construction*], promulgated by the State Council (*zhengwu yuan*) on 5 December 1953 and revised on 18 October 1957. The revised document was approved by the Ninetieth Meeting of the Standing Committee of the First NPC on 6 January 1958. The Chinese text is available at news.xinhuanet.com/ziliao/2005–01/06/content_2423639.htm.

[85] *Law on Wholly Foreign-Owned Enterprises*, art. 5.

[86] *Guojia Jianshe Zhengyong Tudi Tiaoli* [*Regulation on Requisition of Land for National Construction*], approved in principle (*yuanze tongguo*) by the Twenty-third Meeting of the Standing Committee of the Fifth NPC on 4 May 1982 and promulgated by the State Council on 14 May 1982. The Chinese text is available at www.npc.gov.cn/wxzl/gongbao/2000–12/07/content_5009542.htm.

collectively owned land for the public interest according to the law. However, there is no definition of or listing about what the public purpose should be.[87] The *LAL* stipulates the expropriation of rural land only. For land in urban areas, the objects of expropriation encompass only houses and land use right because the owner of urban land is the state rather than individuals. In 1994, the *LUREA* stipulated that the land use right acquired by units or individuals can be retracted by the state for the public interest before its contract term expires.[88] As for the expropriation of urban houses, the concerned 1991 and 2001 regulations do not mention public purpose or similar terms.[89]

After the *2004 Amendment*, the *Property Law*, which reflects the *2004 Amendment*'s constitutional value in strengthening the protection of private property, was enacted by the NPC in 2007. Its art. 42 expressly requires that the taking of land and houses shall be for the public interest. No further explanation was given for this term. In fact, the requirement for clarifying the scope of the public interest was strengthened after the *2004 Amendment* to the *1982 Constitution of China*, and this finally led to the clarification of the public interest in a new regulation concerning the expropriation of urban houses (*2011 Expropriation Regulation*). This regulation was enacted by the State Council to replace the previous *2001 Demolition Regulation*, which conflicted with the *2004 Amendment* to the *1982 Constitution of China*.[90] The *2001 Demolition Regulation* does not include public interest limits on the taking of houses.

In the *2011 Expropriation Regulation*, the generalisation and positive enumeration methods are combined to define the public interest. First, the public interest is explained as being 'for the need of safeguarding national security and facilitating the national economic and social development

[87] After 1986, the *LAL* was revised in 1988, 1998 and 2004. However, no revision or supplementation was made as to the term 'public interest'.

[88] *LUREA*, art. 19.

[89] The 1991 regulation is *Chengshi Fangwu Chaiqian Guanli Tiaoli* [*Regulation on the Management of the Demolition and Removal of Urban Houses (1991 Demolition Regulation)*], enacted by the State Council on 18 January 1991. The Chinese text is available at house.focus.cn/news/1991–06–01/4326.html. The 2001 regulation (*2001 Demolition Regulation*) is the revision of the *1991 Demolition Regulation* and was enacted on 6 June 2001. The Chinese text is available at www.gov.cn/gongbao/content/2001/content_60912.htm.

[90] *Guoyou Tudi shang Fangwu Zhengshou yu Buchang Tiaoli* [*Regulation on the Expropriation and Compensation Concerning the Houses Built on the State Owned Land*], enacted by the State Council on 21 January 2011, available at www.gov.cn/zwgk/2011–01/21/content_1790111.htm.

and other public interest'. Following this generalised stipulation are the situations concerning public interest listed in art. 8. The public interest situations enumerated in this regulation include:

i. the need of national defence and diplomacy;
ii. the need of infrastructure construction projects concerning energy, communication and water conservancy and etc., the execution of which is organised by the government;
iii. the need of public utilities which include the science and technology, education, culture, sports, protection of environment and resources, prevention and reduction of disasters, protection of cultural relics, social welfare and municipal administration, and, the execution of which is organised by the government;
iv. the need of constructing the affordable 'comfortable housing projects' the execution of which is organised by the government;
v. the need of the renewal and reconstruction of the old city areas where the dangerous residential buildings concentrate and the infrastructure facilities are obsolete, the execution of which is organised by the government according the law concerning the urban and rural planning;
vi. the need of other public interest stipulated by the Laws or Administrative Regulations.

4.4.3 *The perception of the public interest test in the era of globalisation*

The evolution of the test of the public interest in China's legal system can be generalised into two arguments: one is the evolution from state interest to public interest, and the other is the progress from symbolic declaration to actual implementation.

Although the public interest is mentioned in the *1954 Constitution of China*, during the planned economy period before 1978, it more represented the significance of the public economy and the socialist construction considering the overall context where such a constitution existed. As a limit to land taking, the public interest doctrine did not play any role in practice. The national construction as the purpose of land taking concerned nearly all areas, including the economy, manufacturing, health, education, projects, safety, urban development and national defence, which were all controlled by the state. Some scholars use 'state interest' to include all of these needs.[91] The term 'state interest' is, in essence, an all-inclusive term, of which the public interest is only a part. In a socialist country, the state, represented by a totalitarian communist government, is defined as being a public power authority, which represents all individuals and social organisations.[92] The interest competition among individuals in the market is eliminated because all persons must contribute to and serve a common purpose, which is the illusionary symbolic state interest. The supremacy of state interest means an extreme limit on individual rights and interests.

With China's transition towards a market economy, individual rights began to erode the original uniform and all-inclusive state interest, and dissembled it into three parts: fiscal interest, public interest and individual rights. Fiscal interest refers to the fiscal revenue used to support the operation of government agencies and other public expenditure. Public interest refers to the common good or welfare that is realised through the public function of governments. However, the fiscal interest is collected through the exercise of taxation power and shall be excluded from the public interest. The government, representing the state, is no longer the original supreme authority that disregarded individual rights in the name of state interest and began taking on the role of representative of the public interest, which derives from the collective authorisation of individuals and works as the limit on individuals' rights.

After the disintegration of state interest, China introduced the term 'public interest' into its laws. In the beginning, the public interest as the limit to the governmental taking of property was applied to the properties owned by FDI enterprises as early as 1979. The public interest term had not been introduced into the laws concerning local parties until 1986, when the *LAL* stipulated the public interest requirement as the purpose of land expropriation. However, for the *LAL* and later laws, including the *2004 Amendment*, which were enacted prior to 2011, the public interest doctrine described in them was symbolic only and did not play a role in actively and effectively restricting government expropriation activities. In China, the objects of expropriation are mainly the land in rural areas and the houses in urban areas. For land expropriation in rural areas, the term 'public interest' in the *LAL* and other applicable laws is neither defined nor enumerated, and merely serves as a beautiful and meaningless decoration. In practice, if the government makes a decision concerning land expropriation, few challenges citing the public

[91] Wang and Li, *Xinzhongguo Tudi*, pp. 47–59. [92] Ibid., 47.

interest can be made to overrule such decisions. The government can refer any direct and indirect interest linked to society and the public to public interest. In other words, the government's decision itself served as the decisive conclusion concerning the public interest during the time when there was no upper-level constitutional restraint of government measures. For the expropriation of urban houses, the corresponding regulations prior to 2011 were not limited by the public interest. In practice, the expropriation of houses could be enforced for both the public and non-public interest. Even the companies that developed projects mainly for the private interest could apply for expropriation licenses from the government.

Significant progress towards allowing the public interest doctrine to play an effective role in limiting government expropriation to protect individual property was made in 2011 when a new regulation concerning the expropriation of urban houses was promulgated. This novel regulation clearly clarified public interest situations, which helped to produce actual restrictions on the government expropriation of houses. Moreover, according to this new regulation, the expropriation of urban houses for non-public purposes is no longer permitted. The birth of this 2011 regulation can be viewed as a victory of social forces favouring the protection of individual rights over opposing forces.

In the early years of opening, China was in urgent need of FDI to drive economic growth. The legal protection of FDI investors' property and interests was a key element for attracting foreign investment. During this period, the domestic economy was composed mainly of state and collective bodies, and the individual or private economies that had just appeared could not influence governmental decisions and legislation. In society, the popularity of thoughts and ideas favouring individual property and rights was still lacking. However, the FDI-driven economy representing the dominant influence of FDI as a social power inevitably led to disparate treatment as to property right protection between FDI holders and local parties. This also reasonably explained why the overall legal protection framework (with all three components of 'according to law', 'public purpose' and 'compensation') on property expropriation was reflected in the law concerning FDI enterprises first.

Driven by FDI and export-oriented policies, China began to accelerate its domestic economic expansion with industrialisation and urbanisation as the main features. For both industrialisation and urbanisation, the need and demand for land also expanded. Local governments could acquire the needed land through two main approaches: taking collectively owned land in rural areas and taking back land use rights by expropriating houses in urban areas. During the 1980s and 1990s when China experienced rapid industrialisation and urbanisation, large amounts of rural land and urban houses were taken. Meanwhile, for land taking, the public interest limits stipulated by the *LAL* did not restrict the governments' expropriation decisions because of their abstractness. Even worse, for the expropriation of urban houses, there were no stipulations concerning the public interest in the relevant regulations. In essence, within this period, two strong social forces combined to push forward the birth of legislation favouring them. The first of these social forces was the government's strong motivation in pursuing rapid economic growth and increasing fiscal revenue. The second force was rent-seeking parties seeking to acquire additional land.

During the same period, however, the number of properties controlled by individuals increased and the public's desire for protection of individual rights became stronger. The accumulated social force requesting strong protection of property finally facilitated the incorporation of a private property clause into the constitution in 2004. One issue concerned why the *1982 Constitution of China*, with its doctrine of the public interest, could not play any role in restricting the government's expropriation of land and houses between 1982 and 2004. There are two reasons for this. First, in 1982 and for some years later, with socialist public ownership as the dominant ideology, for both the government and citizens, the public interest was still understood as the same or similar expression of state interest. Second, the forces favouring individual property rights were so weak that they failed to influence the constitution towards limiting lower-level laws and governmental decisions.

However, the *2004 Amendment*, which contained a public interest clause, was expected to play a role with strong support from the social forces favouring private property protection. Entering the twenty-first century, the protection of private property and other individual rights has become a popular notion in China, which doubtless created great pressure on governments at both the central and local levels. However, governments were still reluctant to implement the *2004 Amendment* to revise their laws and regulations and to restrain their expropriation powers because the social forces pursuing GDP growth and fiscal revenue, and seeking rents through land acquisition, were still strong. The freezing balance between favouring forces and opposing forces led to several years in which the *2004 Amendment* could not be used to change the expropriation rules that conflicted with the constitution. As expected, this meant that the revised constitution could not help the individuals whose land and houses were unduly taken. Thus, an increasing number of individuals chose violent conflict or even sacrificed themselves to fight against local governments and rent-seeking bodies because the constitution and laws were nearly useless in helping them to defeat the violent and even bloody expropriation process.

After the adoption of the *2004 Amendment* and the 2007 *Property Law*, the number of violent incidents increased. After the adoption of the *2004 Amendment*, the outdated 2001 regulation, which conflicted with both the constitution and the *Property Law*, was still enforced by government agencies and developers as a means of seizing private property until this regulation was discarded in 2011.

4.4.4 *The birth of the* 2011 Expropriation Regulation*: response to the angry public*

Although the 2007 case of *Nail House* is not the most violent, it is the most famous. It concerned a reconstruction project in an old area of Chongqing city. Wu Ping, the owner of a house located in an area containing approximately 280 families, refused to move because she was not satisfied with the compensation. According to Jiang Ping, the leading scholar in civil law in China, Wu Ping did not believe that the property development project benefitted the public interest.[93] Wu Ping resisted for approximately two years and meanwhile, the developer cut off the water and electricity to and dug a 10 metre-deep pit around her house. This formed an astonishing but magnificent scene: a two-storey brick house standing alone on a mound with deep evacuation around it, similar to a small island in the sea. The local court required the owners to move out of the house prior to 22 March 2007. Otherwise, the house would be demolished. After learning this, Ping and her husband returned to their house with water and food to declare that they would not follow the court order to move. They mounted a national flag and a slogan poster on the roof. On the poster was written the constitutional principle that '[t]he citizen's legal property is inviolable'. Ping, holding the constitution book in her hand, stood before reporters to declare her constitutional right.

[93] Ewing, 'The Coolest'.

This soon caught the attention of the national and international media. Additionally, the Chinese public overwhelmingly supported the Wu Ping couple. According to an investigation conducted by www.qq.com, a leading website in China, the Nail House owners had won the support of more than 80 per cent of the respondents.[94] This house was called 'the coolest nail house in the history' (*shishang zuiniu dingzi hu*).[95] 'Nail' is used as an analogy for 'holdout.'

The story ended with a new negotiated agreement. Perhaps it was the public's involvement that precluded a potentially violent conflict from erupting and allowed the Nail House owners to initiate new negotiations with such a strong developer and the government. However, what is more important for the progress of China's property protection is that, after this case, the discussion of how to revise the *2001 Demolition Regulation* to make it consistent with the *Constitution* and the *Property Law* began to ferment.

On 14 May 2008, Zhang Jian, a citizen in Benxi City of Liaoning Province, killed an employee of a developer company when this employee forcibly entered his house and beat him as a means of inducing him and his family to move out. Zhang stabbed the employee with a knife.[96] On 12 June, Pan Rong and her husband threw the lighted petro bottles to defend the invasion of compulsory demolition, and they were arrested for illegally hindering the execution of a government decision.[97] On 13 November 2009, in Chengdu of Sichuan Province, Tang Fuzhen, standing on the roof of her building as a demolition crew approached, poured gasoline over herself, set herself on fire, and jumped off of the roof. Sixteen days later, she died while in the hospital.[98] This self-immolation incident shocked the country and incited nationwide anger towards violent demolition and unconstitutional regulation. Reacting to the Tang Fuzhen tragedy, five well-known law professors from Peking University, one of China's top universities, jointly submitted a proposal letter to the NPC requiring a constitutional review of the *2001 Demolition Regulation*

94 Ibid. 95 See the news collection for this case at news.sohu.com/s2007/dingzihu.

96 On 4 September of the following year, the local court (Benxi Municipality Intermediate People's Court) ruled that Zhang Jian's activity constituted excessive defence, and he was given three years in jail with a five-year reprieve. After this ruling, Zhang was released from jail. In the court decision, the developer was accused of illegally invading Zhang's house. Zhang's defence is characterised as defending his individual rights from being infringed upon.

97 Huang and Zhao, 'Pan Rong'. 98 Tang, 'Citizens Express'.

on 7 December.[99] An officer working in the NPC responded that the State Council, the enforcing body of the regulation at issue, had begun to revise the outdated regulation. One week later, five professors were invited by the State Council to join a discussion on the revision of the regulation.

On 29 January 2010, the State Council's Legal Office promulgated the draft of the new regulation titled, '*Regulation on the Expropriation and Compensation Concerning the Houses Built on the State Owned Land*', to collect public comments and opinions. By the end of the thirteen-day collection period, the State Council had received opinions submitted online from 13,320 respondents.[100] The most salient of the submitted comments was the assertion that demolition or expropriation for non-public purposes should be removed from the draft.[101] On 15 December, the Legal Office promulgated the second draft for comment. It is rare to invite public opinion twice in the process of drafting a law or regulation.[102]

On 19 January 2011, the new *2011 Expropriation Regulation* was passed by the State Council and enforced on the same day. The clause concerning expropriation for non-public interest was not included in the new regulation. Moreover, the new regulation enumerated the situations of public interest for the first time in China.

Tracing the entire process of revising the old regulation to create a new, constitutional regulation, we find that progress was made by pressuring non-official channels and informal, unorganised public opinion. The regulation was pushed neither by the government's respect for the constitution nor by the formal constitutional review mechanism. Moreover, the revision was not meant to be consistent with the *2004 Amendment* until public complaint mounted to the point that ignoring the public's wishes would have endangered the CPC's governing ability.

99 The advocating professors were Shen Kui, Wang Xixin, Chen Duanhong, Qian Mingxing and Jiang Ming-an. Their proposal letter is available at news.sina.com.cn/c/2009–12–10/115019231469.shtml.

100 Yang, 'Xin Chaiqian'.

101 Demolition for non-public purposes is listed as art. 40 in the first draft of the proposed new regulation. Professor Shen Kui, one of such five proposing professors, submitted eight opinions on this draft and the first opinion is the deletion of such art. 40.

102 During the first comment period, 65,601 responses were collected. During the second comment period, 37,898 responses were collected. See Xinhua, 'Guowuyuan'.

The new regulation was drafted and enacted by the State Council, an administrative agency with law-making power in China.[103] The following questions arise: Must an additional constitutional review of the justification of such a regulation be conducted because the regulation, with public interest stipulations, was enacted by a government agency in charge of expropriation affairs? To concentrate on the public interest side, 'is the scope of public interest defined by the State Council constitutional?'

The new regulation governs the expropriation of urban houses only. No revisions to the *LAL* were made, no new rules were made to define and clarify the public interest instituted for the expropriation of rural land. In fact, without the threshold limit of public interest, the violation of farmers' land rights is no less serious than that of urban residents' rights. When would the revision to enumerate and limit the scope of public interest as to the expropriation of rural land be made? Would it be made only after a series of bloody conflicts similar to the ones that occurred during the house demolitions?

4.4.5 *Public interest in the* 2011 Expropriation Regulation

The new regulation defines public interest as national security, economic development and social development. It is still a broad definition because it includes economic development. In developing and transitional countries, as a leading governmental function, broad economic intervention is usually a necessary part of government power. In the decision concerning the enactment of the *2011 Expropriation Regulation*, the State Council states that the new regulation must consider both the needs of industrialisation and urbanisation, and the protection of individual interests.[104]

[103] According to the chaps. 2 through 4 of China's *Law on Legislation*, there are five main sources of law in a broad sense contained in legal documents: the Laws enacted by the NPC or NPCSC; the Administrative Regulation enacted by the State Council, the highest central administrative government in China; the Local Regulation enacted by the local congresses or governments with legislation power; and the Departmental (Ministerial) Regulation enacted by the ministries and commissions under the State Council. See *Lifa Fa* [*Law on Legislation*], enacted by the Third Session of the Ninth NPC on 15 March 2000 and amended by the Third Session of the Twelfth NPC on 15 March 2015. The Chinese text of this law is available at news.qq.com/a/20150318/054673_all.htm. See generally Paler, 'China's Legislation Law', 301–18.

[104] In its decision, the State Council mentioned that the draft of the new regulation should consider both the needs of industrialisation and urbanisation, and the

This shows that economic development that facilitates industrialisation and urbanisation is still a necessary component of the public interest. An unlimited number of projects can be included under the purpose of economic development. The projects concerned could be owned and operated by the state, owned by the state and operated by SOEs or private companies, or owned by companies with mixed public-private ownership.

In the list of public interest situations, the first three, which concern the need of national defence and diplomacy, the need of the infrastructure organised and enforced by government, the need of the public affairs and utilities organised and enforced by government, are the least controversial. The fourth public interest situation, which concerns affordable housing projects, offers basic houses to poor people, which is regarded as a governmental responsibility. A main concern as to these purposes is that many of the projects initiated under these purposes are developed by non-public companies under government control. It is necessary to use the proportionality principle to identify whether the public interest is the main interest in these projects and whether the public interest concerned is so important that it should be over private property. Unfortunately, however, there is no provision concerning the proportionality principle or the balancing of interests. In reality, public interest is often used by the government and development agencies to achieve non-public interests, such as fiscal or private interest. Lacking the limit of proportionality as a constitutional review standard, we may see the occurrence of a large number of expropriation projects that lack a public interest component, and result in excessive injury to private property and significant losses to fiscal taxation. Descriptions of the two most typical situations resulting from over-broad expropriation follow.

First, local governments excessively expropriate land for the so called city image or local prestige. For instance, a county with a population of only 200,000 persons built an 80 metre-wide central avenue. It was claimed by the local government that such an avenue would be the widest road in the province.[105] On the surface, the addition of a city avenue augments the public infrastructure, and it should be defined as public interest or public purpose. In reality, however, government officials often

interests of house owners. This decision shows that the scope of the public interest should not be narrowed so much that it hinders the pace of industrialisation and urbanisation, or social and economic development. This decision is available at news.163.com/11/0119/15/6QP8ODS000014JB5.html.

[105] Pan, *Chengshihua Jincheng*, p. 55.

build roads to augment their achievements, and such construction simply creates the reputation of a wasteful city.

Second, expropriation is made in the name of public purpose to mainly serve private interests. In 2001, a public university acquired a parcel of land of 1,270 *mu* at a low price of 20,000 Chinese *yuan* per *mu* in the name of enlarging the campus and building teacher dormitories. Later, 981 *mu* of land was transferred to another company with a price of 400,000 *yuan* per *mu* by a company attached to this university. By selling land, the company under the university had made a large profit.[106]

The sixth situation of public interest encompassed by the new regulation concerns the renewal or reconstruction of old city areas. The reconstruction of old city areas began in the 1980s and aimed to renew old and blighted buildings. It is a complex project encompassing social and economic, and public and private interests. Such reconstruction also concerns environmental protection and the maintenance of historical sites. It is usually planned by local governments and is enforced by both governments and developers. In China, urban reconstruction has been criticised for offering opportunities to some companies for developing high-profit real estate projects. Other motivations for urban reconstruction projects include local fiscal revenue, city image and prestige, and local officers' performance and achievement. As projects that usually concern the expropriation of private property, urban reconstruction projects should operate as follows. First, local government should consider the necessity of urban reconstruction mainly based on the consideration of the public interest, which shall be for improving living conditions, facilitating hygienic situations and beautifying the environment. Second, the government should use the proportionality principle to determine the least restrictive method of expropriation and the most limited scope of property expropriation. Third, the government should select participating companies through bidding or negotiation and guarantee that the public interest encompassed by the reconstruction project is distinctive and sufficient enough to allow for the involvement of a private company for its private interest. However, in reality, reconstruction projects often do not start with public purpose in mind. Developers, for their private interests and through rent-seeking activities, persuade government officers to make expropriation decisions in the name of reconstruction, or the government officers in charge initiate such projects for their own achievement, or acquire their own illegal interest or for augmenting local

[106] Ibid., p. 60.

revenue. The collusion or conspiracy between local government officers and rent-seeking companies for the purpose of securing their own interests often leads to an excessive amount of land acquired for reconstruction projects in many places.[107]

In the first draft of the new regulation, the public interest situation concerning urban reconstruction is defined as 'the rebuilding of the blighted houses for improving the citizen's living conditions, the enforcement of which is organized by the government'. To restrict the local governments' excessive use of this purpose to the expropriation of houses, the draft further stipulates a procedural restriction that is mainly for guaranteeing individual interest. An expropriation should not be made unless more than 90 per cent of the owners of the expropriated houses agree.[108] This 90 per cent threshold is regarded as a procedural restraint reflecting public interest, but the developers and local governments objected to it because it restricts the power of local governments to decide the relevant project and increases the costs to developer companies in acquiring land and enforcing projects. In the second draft, this 90 per cent threshold was deleted and the phrases 'the rebuilding of blighted houses' and 'for improving living conditions' were omitted, and a new expression that is less restrictive was added.[109] The new wording concerning city reconstruction is: 'The need of the renewal and reconstruction of the old city areas where the dangerous residential buildings concentrate and the infrastructure facilities are obsolete, the execution of which is organized by the government according to the law concerning the urban and rural planning.'

This revision loosens the first draft's strict and narrow scope of public interest. On the one hand, the improvement of living conditions as the purpose of rebuilding blighted houses limits a government's efforts in pursuing economic objectives. On the other hand, it limits the relevant projects to the rebuilding of blighted houses. In the second draft, the use of the phrase 'reconstruction of old city areas' means that governments can develop a complex project, including the rebuilding of blighted houses and other activities, that could extend beyond the improvement of living conditions. This change is what local governments and their interest groups want. In the second draft, there are two limits on the reconstruction

107 Professor Ma Huaide, a law scholar, pointed out that most city reconstruction projects are for commercial interests rather than the public interest. See Du and Ren, 'Lifa Taolun'.

108 See art. 13 in the first draft of the *2011 Expropriation Regulation.*

109 This revision, made in the second draft, finally became art. 8 (5) of the *2011 Expropriation Regulation.*

of old city areas. The first limit is that a project must be based on the laws of urban and rural planning. The second limit is that a project must be performed in areas with a concentration of dangerous houses and outdated infrastructural facilities. The final official version of the new regulation maintains the expression 'reconstruction of old city areas'. The 90 per cent threshold in the first draft objected to by local governments and developers was finally replaced with a less restrictive limit stipulating that there must be a concentration of dangerous houses and outdated infrastructural facilities in the reconstructed area. Thus, the final version of the new regulation is a result of balancing the interest conflict among house owners, developers and local governments. The relevant provision, which was more favourable to property owners during the draft provision's draft phase, was revised to be more favourable for local governments.

The final listed public interest is very flexible. It provides 'the need of public interest which is stipulated by the Laws and Administrative Regulations'.[110] This public purpose has two implications. The first is that the public purposes stipulated in other laws could be the public purpose for expropriating houses, and the current list in the new regulation is not an exhaustive one. The NPC, NPCSC and State Council can make new provisions to enlarge the scope of the public interest in the future. Another public interest implication is that only the public purposes stipulated by the Laws (enacted by the NPC or NPCSC) and Administrative Regulations (enacted by the State Council) can be used to justify expropriation decisions. Local laws and departmental regulations are excluded from being the legal sources that define the public interest. Although this provision restricts local governments' law-making authority concerning the situations of public interest, it leaves to the central government (the State Council) the discretion of supplementing any new public purpose in the future.[111]

Another defect of the public interest clause in the new regulation is that it lacks the negative enumeration that excludes some specific situations from the public interest. It was suggested that at least commercial interests should be expressly excluded, but this was not performed in the new regulation.[112]

[110] Ibid., art. 8(6).

[111] In the first draft, there is a subclause that allows 'the public interest situation stipulated by the State Council'. This was identified by scholars as being vague and serving to enlarge the identification scope of public interest. In the second and final versions, this subclause was removed. See Du and Ren, 'Lifa Taolun'.

[112] Ibid.

4.5 Economic development as public purpose

For many countries, including both developed and developing countries, a leading controversial issue is whether the economic development aimed at increasing job opportunities and taxation should encompass public use or public purpose to justify the exercise of eminent domain power. The U.S. Supreme Court's 2005 decision in *Kelo* v. *City of New London* led to nationwide discussion of this issue. Additionally, in developing countries, such as China and India, the exercise of government power in taking land and houses for economic growth has been a battlefield of interest conflicts.

4.5.1 *The United States: before and after* Kelo

4.5.1.1 Before *Kelo*

Before *Kelo*, there had been no decisions from the Supreme Court concerning whether economic development can satisfy public purpose or public use requirements. However, two eminent domain cases tried by the Michigan Supreme Court reflected the courts' vibrant attitude towards the justification of economic development as a public use and were preludes to the coming debate around the *Kelo* case.

The arguments supporting economic development as a public use were made in *Poletown Neighborhood Council* v. *City of Detroit* in 1981. The plaintiffs' land was acquired and transferred to General Motors for the construction of an assembly plant. In its decision, the Supreme Court identified the central issue in the case as follows: 'Can a municipality use the power of eminent domain granted to it by the Economic Development Corporations Act . . . to condemn property for transfer to a private corporation to build a plant to promote industry and commerce, thereby adding jobs and taxes to the economic base of the municipality and state?'[113] The state court wrote that this issue was of 'paramount importance' to the future welfare of the state and its residents.

The decision in the *Poletown* case followed the judicial deference attitude found in the 1954 *Berman* case, although the purposes for condemning land differed between the cases. Even if government power is used for economic development, which is far beyond traditional public use, such as the removal of blighted houses identified in the *Berman*, the court still ruled that the legislature's decision about public use should

[113] *Poletown Neighborhood Council* v. *City of Detroit*, 410 Mich. 616 (1981).

be respected. Citing the *Berman* decision, the Michigan Supreme Court wrote, '[w]hen a legislature speaks, the public interest has been declared in terms well-nigh conclusive'. Thus, in this case, the court still insisted on its limited role in reviewing the legislature's decision and, according to the precedents made by the same state court, a review is conducted only to determine whether the legislature's decision is 'palpable and manifestly arbitrary and incorrect.'[114]

The court then examined the necessity of using eminent domain power. The concerned city municipality submitted evidence to prove the severity of its economic conditions, how important it was for the city to revitalise local industry, how the proposed new plant project could help to boost economic growth and why the plaintiffs' land was necessary for the proposed plant site. Because private interest was involved in the case, the court compared private benefit with general economic benefit as public purpose to conclude that the public benefit was 'a clear and significant one', and sufficient to satisfy the requirement of public use for the taking of land. From this decision, we can generalise three steps for reviewing public use made by the court: conducting a limited judicial review of the legislature's decision, reviewing the necessity of the use of eminent domain power and comparing public and private benefit. These reviews are more procedural than substantive. Moreover, in this case, the court showed a preference for democratic-communitarian features. Citing the precedent decisions, the court declared: 'When there is such public need, "(t)he abstract right (of an individual) to make use of his own property in his own way is compelled to yield to the general comfort and protection of community, and to a proper regard to relative rights in others".'[115]

There were two dissenting judges in the case. Although he agreed with the judicial deference attitude to the legislature, Justice Fitzgerald insisted that '(the) determination (about) whether a taking is for a public or a private use is ultimately a judicial question'. Thus, even if an eminent domain action is authorised by the legislature, the court must still review whether such authorisation is lawful or constitutional. Justice Fitzgerald proposed a higher level of judicial review of eminent domain cases. As with the majority decision, his dissenting opinions compared public benefit with General Motors' private benefit. However, he concluded that public benefit was not the main purpose of the proposed project. Unlike slum

[114] *Gregory Marina, Inc.* v. *Detroit*, 378 Mich. 364, 396, 144 N.W.2d 503 (1966).

[115] 410 Mich. 616 (1981). See also, *People ex rel. Detroit & Howell R. Co.* v. *Salem Twp. Board*, 20 Mich. 452, 480–1(1870).

clearance projects, where the main purpose is to ensure public health and welfare, and where the private developer's interests can be achieved incidentally, in this case, public benefits, such as job opportunities and taxation, are incidental to the realisation of private benefit. 'It is only through the acquisition and use of the property by General Motors that the "public purpose" of promoting employment can be achieved.' The public benefit is incidental to the private use only and thus does not constitute a public purpose for justifying condemnation.[116]

Another dissenter, Justice Ryan, distinguished taxation power from eminent domain power. According to his argument, the 'public' for one power is not necessarily the 'public' for another power. Compared to taxation, which also concerns the taking of property, eminent domain is 'far more intrusive.' A distinction that is fully justified is that '[a]s a general proposition then, in the realm of aid to private corporations, "public purpose" (taxation) has been construed less restrictively than "public use" (eminent domain)'. The involvement of private agencies does not necessarily invalidate the public purpose of proposed expropriation, but three common elements must exist to justify the use of eminent domain power involving private interests. The first element is 'Public Necessity of the Extreme Sort Otherwise Impracticable'. Expropriation involving private corporations is an extreme exception to public use examples and to justify public necessity, the indispensability of collective action is required. The expropriation of land must be limited to the use of land by companies producing public interest, and can only be available through the government's coordination. The second element is 'Continuing Accountability to the Public', which means that to some extent, government control must work as a condition for the use of eminent domain power. The third element concerns the choosing of land: 'Facts of Independent Public Significance'. The decision to take a specific parcel of land must be made using the criteria related to the public interest rather than to the private corporation's interests.[117] In essence, Justice Ryan wrote that necessary restrictive conditions must be imposed on the eminent domain measures concerning the transfer of land between private parties.

In 2004, however, the Michigan State Supreme Court overruled the *Poletown* decision in *County of Wayne* v. *Hathcock*.[118] Similar to *Poletown*, individual property was condemned in *County of Wayne* for economic development purposes, such as the establishment of a business and

[116] 410 Mich. 616 (1981). [117] Ibid.

[118] *County of Wayne* v. *Hathcock*, 684 N.W. 2d 765 (Mich. 2004).

technology park. The court, using the aforementioned three elements enumerated by Justice Ryan in *Poletown*, decided that eminent domain could not satisfy the constitutional requirement for public use. For the first element, the court did not agree that the land needed for the proposed park should only be assembled through collective government action. If eminent domain is necessary in this project, then many similar commercial projects throughout the country could request government taking. For the second element, the proposed park project lacked the 'public oversight' or other 'formal mechanisms' necessary to ensure that the running of the park would continue to contribute to public benefit. For the final element, unlike the slum clearance, 'there are no facts of independent public significance (such as the need to promote health and safety) that might justify the condemnation of defendants' lands'.[119]

4.5.1.2 *Kelo* case

Although it is a decision made by a state court, the *Hathcock* decision seemed to start a new period with more limited tolerance of eminent domain and thus stronger protection of private property. However, this glimmer was soon overshadowed by the opposite position presented by the U.S. Supreme Court in *Kelo*.

The issue presented in *Kelo* is essentially the same as that presented in *Hathcock*. To revitalise an economically distressed area, the city of New London decided to assemble the petitioners' land and to transfer it to Pfizer (a pharmaceutical company) to build its facilities. Through the development of such facilities, the New London government expected to achieve several public purposes: 'creating jobs', 'generating tax revenue', 'helping to build momentum for the revitalization of downtown New London', '[making] the City more attractive' and '[creating] leisure and recreational opportunities on the waterfront and in the park'.[120] The majority decided in favour of the city using the traditional arguments concerning public use found in the precedent-setting cases, such as *Mikdiff* and *Berman*.

First, the decision stipulated that the broad view for explaining public use would be adopted. The narrow 'use-by-public' view endorsed by many state courts in the mid-nineteenth century 'steadily eroded over time'. As for the reasons for abandoning the narrow view, the decision stated that the narrow view was 'difficult to administer' and so impractical that it could not cope with the 'diverse and always evolving needs of society'.[121]

[119] Ibid. [120] 545 U.S. 469 (2005). [121] Ibid.

Second, the majority decision was characterised by an attitude of judicial deference in the determination of public purpose. Considering the existence of various social needs in different places and changes in such social needs over time, the decision stipulated that legislatures would be given 'broad latitude in determining what public needs justify the use of the takings power.' Correspondingly, the 'rigid formulas and intrusive scrutiny' would be avoided.[122]

Third, the promotion of economic development is affirmed as 'traditional and long accepted function of government.' Moreover, '[t]here is . . . no principled way of distinguishing economic development from the other public purposes that we have recognized.' Economic development is included in the court's 'traditionally broad understanding of public purpose'.[123]

Finally, the court refused to examine the actual effect of the proposed project. This derives from the attitude of slight or narrow review based on the judicial deference doctrine. The court refused to second-guess both the efficacy of the proposed plan and 'the City's determinations as to what lands it needs to acquire in order to effectuate the project.' The judicial review focused mainly on the legitimacy of motivation and procedure. The purpose of the proposed project was legitimate because it was 'carefully considered', and there was no evidence showing that an illegitimate purpose existed in the instant case.[124] As a result, the land at issue was taken mainly for general economic benefit as a public purpose rather than to benefit a specific person or group of persons.

There are two dissenting opinions in this case. The first dissention was given by Justice O'Connor. After strengthening the function of public purpose to limit the scope of eminent domain power and the necessity of judicial review to control the possible arbitrary decisions of political branches in dividing public-private boundaries, Justice O'Connor identified three types of takings that satisfy a public use test. The first type concerned the transfer of private property to 'public ownership', 'such as for a road, a hospital, or a military base.' The second type included takings to 'transfer private property to private parties, often common carriers, who make the property available for the public's use – such as with a railroad, a public utility, or a stadium'. The third type reflected the examples in *Berman* and *Mikdiff*. 'In certain circumstances and to meet certain exigencies, takings that serve a public purpose also satisfy the *Constitution* even if the property is destined for subsequent private use.' The first

[122] Ibid. [123] Ibid. [124] Ibid.

two types of takings are 'relatively straightforward and uncontroversial' because they meet the narrow view of the public use test, and the third type is necessary for loosening the narrow view's 'too constricting and impractical ways' in defining the public use scope but it is only for 'certain exigencies'.

Justice O'Connor then distinguished this case from *Berman* and *Mikdiff*. In those two precedent-setting cases, the improvement of slum areas and the breaking of land oligopolies were performed for public purpose. In both cases, the pre-condemnation use of the taken property harmed society 'in *Berman* through blight resulting from extreme poverty and in *Midkiff* through oligopoly resulting from extreme wealth'. 'Thus a public purpose was realized when the harmful use was eliminated.'[125] Justice O'Connor concluded that the majority decision inappropriately expanded the scope of public use because the economic benefit generated from the proposed project could be found to some extent in any legal use of private property. Another argument concerns the practical difficulty of isolating private benefit from public benefit. The cases concerning economic development are always decided for the purpose of finding both public and private benefits that merge and reinforce one another.[126] Moreover, even if this difficulty in practical isolation could be resolved, the taking for economic development is 'theoretically flawed' because it departs from the constitutional spirit of using public use tests to limit the government interference in private property. Finally, Justice O'Conner warned that the majority decision would lead to biased treatment of citizens: 'The beneficiaries are likely to be those citizens with disproportionate influence and power in the political process, including large corporations and development firms. As for the victims, the government now has license to transfer property from those with fewer resources to those with more.'[127]

Justice Clarence Thomas's dissenting opinions were based on his literal understanding of the public use test in the constitution. For him, '[t]he most natural reading of the [Takings] Clause is that it allows the government to take property only if the government owns, or the public has

[125] The cited dissent opinions of Justice O'Connor are available at supreme.justia.com/cases/federal/us/545/469/dissent.html.

[126] Justice O'Connor noted that, '[t]he trouble with economic development takings is that private benefit and incidental public benefit are, by definition, merged and mutually reinforcing. In this case, for example, any boon for Pfizer or the plan's developer is difficult to disaggregate from the promised public gains in taxes and jobs.' Ibid.

[127] Ibid.

a legal right to use, the property, as opposed to taking it for any public purpose or necessity whatsoever'. Thus, the majority decision does not 'nod' to the original meaning of the public use test or void the public use clause.[128]

The reaction to *Kelo* was 'swift, strong, and negative'.[129] The *Kelo* decision was widely criticised by both libertarians and communitarians.[130] For the libertarians who strongly support a propertarian system, they were opposed to the broad construction of public interest made by the *Kelo* decision. Even the communitarians who object to excessive and undue protection of private property thought that the Supreme Court 'went too far in the other direction'.[131] Gary Becker, one eminent economist, commented on *Kelo* from a cost-benefit perspective. According to Becker, the sparse and infrequent use of eminent domain can be tolerated, but the regular use would produce harm that outweighed its benefits.[132] As to the political side, many politicians proposed laws limiting the use of eminent domain power for economic development.[133]

Within one year of *Kelo*, forty-seven states had begun reviewing their eminent domain legislation.[134] Many states have passed laws prohibiting the government from taking land for economic development purposes.[135]

4.5.2 The Indian context

4.5.2.1 Wide scope of public purpose in laws passed prior to 2014

In India, the main constitutional clauses (arts. 19(1)(f), 31) for protecting private property were deleted from the constitution through the *Forty-Fourth Amendment* implemented in 1978. The only clause concerning property protection left in the constitution is art. 300-A, which states that '[n]o person shall be deprived of his property save by authority of law'. This stipulation affords private property weak constitutional protection

[128] The cited dissent opinions of Justice Thomas are available at supreme.justia.com/cases/federal/us/545/469/dissent2.html.

[129] Jacobs and Bassett, 'All Sound', 4.

[130] Bell and Parchomovsky, 'The Uselessness', 1413, 1423–5.

[131] Ibid., 1424.

[132] Ibid., 1425.

[133] Ibid., 1425–6.

[134] Gilroy, 'Kelo'. See also Keating, 'Stopping Kelo'.

[135] It was stated that, '[f]orty-three states including Oregon, with one pending passage in Virginia this session, adopted legislation prohibiting government from using eminent domain to achieve a private purpose or to convey property acquired by eminent domain to a private owner.' See Richter, 'State Based'.

because if one person's property is taken according to the law, there would be no further constitutional review of the law concerned. The expropriation made by government through legislation or otherwise is rarely challenged at the constitutional level.

Prior to 2004, the main law concerning expropriation in India had been the *1894 LAA*. The scope of public purpose stipulated in sec. 3(f) of the *1894 LAA* is wide. In addition to the traditional public purposes, such as village development, urban planning, health, education, slum clearance, residential arrangement for the poor and public office, there are three purposes that can widely enlarge the scope of government taking power. The first purpose is that the government can acquire land for planned development and that acquired land can be saved for subsequent disposal. However, the definition of future planned development is so vague that it may be widely inclusive. The second purpose is that the land can be acquired for a corporation owned or controlled by the state. State ownership or the controlling feature itself is regarded as a public purpose, but the purpose of those corporations in taking land is not defined or limited. The third purpose is to take land for any development scheme sponsored or approved by the government. There is no further limit or specification of the scope of such schemes. The economic development projects approved by the government can be included here.[136] Moreover, according to the *1894 LAA*, land acquisition can be made for a company if the company can prove:

1. that the purpose of the acquisition is to obtain land for the erection of dwelling houses for workmen employed by the Company or for the provision of amenities directly connected therewith, or
2. that such acquisition is needed for the construction of some building or work for a Company which is engaged or is taking steps for engaging itself in any industry or work which is for a public purpose, or
3. that such acquisition is needed for the construction of some work, and that such work is likely to prove useful to the public.[137]

As to the last two purposes justifying land acquisition initiated by a company, the terms 'public purpose' or 'useful to the public' afford great flexibility because any direct or indirect benefit generated by construction can be linked to them.

The projects initiated or permitted by the government may be projects characterised as public service or use, such as roads, airports, dams, green

[136] *1894 LAA*, sec. 3(f)(iii), (iv) and (vii).

[137] Ibid., sec. 40(1)(a)–(b).

land or other public facilities. They may also include economic development projects, such as a Special Economic Zone (SEZ). In India, a rapidly developing large country, the wide scope of infrastructure construction and economic projects has led to the rapid loss of individual land, particularly the taking of farmers' or tribal persons' land. A report dated on 3 May 2007 declares that '[a]vailable reports indicate that more than 21 million people are internally displaced due to development projects in India'. Additionally, 'more than 50 per cent of the development induced displaced are tribal peoples.'[138]

Accompanying the rapid expansion of land acquisition without effective public purpose restrictions, the interest conflicts that are enhanced by unsatisfactory compensation have resulted in protests and violent resistance throughout India.[139]

4.5.2.2 Protests in Singur and Nandigram

The Singur incident concerns the West Bengal government's acquisition of 997 acres of fertile agricultural land in Singur. The acquired land was transferred to Tata Motors to establish a car manufacturing plant called the Nano project.

Soon after taking power in May 2006, the then ruling Left Front (LF) government under the leadership of the Communist Party of India (Maoist, CPI (M)) initiated a land acquisition plan for industrialisation. On 26 May, when representatives from Tata visited the proposed land, angry local peasants gathered to protest and resist Tata's entry. Soon after this protest, the Singur peasants formed an organisation called the 'Save Agricultural Land Committee'. Supported and led by the opposition party, Trinamool Congress Party (TCP), the Singur farmers initiated a series of organised protests, including a demonstration parade in front of the government's office.[140]

The proposed land acquisition was legally questioned for its purpose. Does this acquisition satisfy the public purpose required by the *1894 LAA* since the acquired land was transferred to a private business? However, this argument only weakly attacked the government's decision because

[138] Internal Displacement Monitoring Centre, 'India', 12.

[139] For accounts of protests or resistances against the land-grabbing exercise for economic development, see a news article titled, 'The Ugly Side of Land Acquisition in India', available at business.rediff.com/slide-show/2010/may/31/slide-show-1-ugly-side-of-land-acquisition-in-india.htm. For a detailed description of land conflicts and their origins, see Chakravorty, 'The Price of Land'.

[140] Banerjee, 'Land Acquisition', 4718–19.

the public purpose set by the *1894 LAA* is wide enough to accommodate this project. The *1894 LAA* states that after the government makes a declaration according to the *1894 LAA*, '[t]he said declaration shall be conclusive evidence that the land is needed for a public purpose or for a company.'[141] Although this acquisition had been resisted by the peasants' movement since it began, its legality was finally determined by both the High Court and the Supreme Court. The land acquisition in Singur began with the issuance of notices in July 2006. Compensation was made in late September. The acquisition process was decided by the courts to be consistent with the *1894 LAA*. The Calcutta High Court decided that 'no colourable exercise of power' was found concerning the acquisition decision and the land acquisition in Singur 'was made for the public purpose of employment generation and socio-economic development of the area'.[142] In essence, the court did not challenge the public nature of the proposed project.

However, disregarding the court decisions, the agitated farmers continued their protest. On 3 October 2008, after twenty-two months of construction on the plant, Tata decided to move its project off the disputed land owing to the unstable political environment.[143]

The Singur protest did not slow the ruling Communist Party government's steps in pushing forward its land acquisition. Another acquisition plan concerning a larger piece of land of approximately 10,000 acres in Nandigram was enforced by the government using harsh measures. The land was expropriated for an SEZ developed by an Indonesia Group called Salim. Similar to the land acquisition in Singur, this acquisition was resisted broadly and agitatedly by farmers. On 14 March 2007, more than 3,000 policemen marched into the Nandigram area. During the conflict with thousands of local villagers, including women and children, the police fired at and killed at least fourteen people.[144]

The Nandigram violence shocked the nation and the state government was widely attacked. Even the governor of West Bengal, Gopal Krishna Gandhi, criticised the CPI (M) government by speaking of his 'cold horror' concerning the accident.[145] However, the violence continued in Nandigram. In May 2008, additional violent conflicts occurred between local resisters and CPI (M) supporters.

The violence shook the stable ruling status of the LF and CPI (M). The people's anger was reflected in their votes. CPI (M) lost several seats

[141] *1894 LAA*, sec. 6(3). [142] Out Legal Reporter, 'Public Purpose'.
[143] Gupta, 'An Overview', 8. [144] Our Bureau, 'Red-hand Buddha'. [145] Ibid.

in the 2008 and 2009 elections.[146] In 2001, TCP and its alliance won a landslide victory in the state assembly election – TCP won 184 of the 294 seats and its two allied parties won 43 seats. The ruling party CPI (M) won only sixty-two seats. This election was a failure for CPI (M) because it was the first time that it had won less than two-thirds of all seats in the past thirty-four years. On 20 May 2011, TCP leader Mamata Banerjee was sworn in as the chief minister of West Bengal. This signified the end of more than thirty years of ruling by CPI (M), which was called 'the world's longest-serving democratically-elected communist government'.[147]

Incidents in Singur and Nandigram precipitated questions to those in *Kelo*: Where should the boundary between public interest and private property be placed? Obviously, economic development can be used to accommodate many land takings for private use. In both *Poletown* and *Kelo*, in which land expropriation for economic development was upheld, the emphasised economic distress implies that economic development is limited to revitalisation only. Moreover, most state legislatures have kept economic development outside public use or purpose. Thus, land taking in the name of economic development in the United States is infrequent and subject to strict constitutional and legislative limits. In India, without the constitutional review and restrictive legislative clarification, the purpose of economic development had been explained by the government before 2014, when the new law was promulgated, to include many projects with an obvious private nature, such as plants, hotels and resorts. These private projects are linked to public purpose because they can produce more job opportunities and taxation. Explanations that are too wide cause public purpose to lose its function in guarding ex ante the interference of government in the domain of private property.

The interest conflict hidden behind economic development projects is far more complicated than it appears on the surface. In both the Singur and Nandigram incidents, the projects concerned also received support from some people. Not all farmers objected to land acquisition. Particularly after Tata moved out, there were strong requirements for its return. A strong voice was particularly audible from those who had lost farmland and had already spent compensation money. The revival of the Tata project meant jobs and a better future for the protestors.[148] Thus, an embarrassing situation resulted from the faulty legal control of land acquisition. The land has been transferred from one private owner to another, but

[146] In 2008, CPI (M) lost its zila parishad elections in Nandigram and Singur.
[147] de Chowdhuri, 'Rising Star'. [148] Banerjee, 'Singur Votes'.

the expected public benefit justifying the acquisition has not materialised.

Soon after its election victory, the new TCP government pushed the adoption of the *Land Rehabilitation and Development Act* to take back the land given to Tata. Tata battled this act in the High Court, which ruled on 29 September 2011 that the act was constitutional and valid.[149] The High Court required Tata to remove its factory equipment and other belongings from the site. Tata, however, may request compensation. Both sides can appeal to a higher court. In fact, both Tata and the West Bengal government have moved forward in the legal process.

Tata was blamed in the *Land Rehabilitation and Development Act* for not fulfilling its responsibilities in operating the project and in turn, failing to generate the expected job openings. Tata argued that it had invested nearly 1,800 crore in project construction and that the frequent unrest, threats and violence led to the discontinuation of the project.

The case between old government and farmers and the case between new government and Tata both show the necessity of constitutional restraint in balancing interest conflicts and reducing the instability of government land taking policies. Particularly in a country with complicated interest conflicts and dynamic social change, the constitutional restriction on the frequent changing of land acquisition laws that change with changes in government may help to ensure stable property ownership and property rights.

4.5.2.3 The legislature's response to the protests

The unfairness and injustice concerning land acquisition in India produced frequent and violent nationwide protests, always violent protests, which have led to reforms in the legislature in recent years concerning land acquisition.

The first reform was the adjustment of SEZ policy. In April 2008, two months after the Nandigram violence, the Empowered Group of Ministers (EGoM) responsible for approving SEZ set a 5,000-hectare ceiling over the size of the SEZ.

The *Land Acquisition (Amendment) Bill* was introduced in 2007, and aimed to revise and amend the *1894 LAA*. The most distinguishable revision concerns limits on the scope of public purpose. The scope is limited to include traditional public projects, such as national defence

[149] Pandey, 'Mamata wins'.

and infrastructure construction. As to the projects concerning economic development, which request land acquisition for companies, in addition to the showing of general economic interest generated, they cannot be approved unless 70 per cent of the needed land has already been purchased. This 70 per cent threshold is designed to frustrate the motivation of private developers to acquire land through government acquisition. Naturally, this bill was resisted by local governments and big companies.

Another suggested reform of the land acquisition was represented by the introduction of the *Rehabilitation and Resettlement Bill* in the lower house (*Lok Sabha*) of the Indian parliament in December 2007. This bill is based on a *National Resettlement and Rehabilitation Policy* approved by the cabinet in October 2007 as an active response to nationwide opposition to land acquisition for SEZ or other economic purposes. Its main purpose is 'to provide for the rehabilitation and resettlement of persons affected by the acquisition of land for projects of public purpose or involuntary displacement due to any other reason'.[150] It stipulates the minimum benefit to the displaced families. For large-scale displacement, this bill stipulates that a social impact assessment shall be performed.

In September 2011, a more comprehensive bill called *Land Acquisition, Rehabilitation and Resettlement Bill* (*2011 LARR Bill*) was introduced in *Lok Sabha*. This bill integrates the aforementioned 2007 bills and was drafted to replace the widely criticised *1894 LAA*.[151] The dominant feature of this bill is that it shortens the scope of public purpose stipulated by the *1894 LAA*.

The *2011 LARR Bill* enumerates seven lists of situations of public purpose. The first five lists (subclauses i–v) are the least controversial and cover several issues: national safety and defence; public projects, such as railways, highways, ports, power and irrigation; the provision of land for people affected by a project; planned development or the improvement of village or urban sites; the provision of land for residential purposes for the weaker section; the provision of land for government-administered educational, agricultural, health and research schemes or institutions, and the provision of land to house the poor, landless, displaced or

150 *The Rehabilitation and Resettlement Bill* is available at www.indlaw.com/display.aspx?3849.

151 *The Land Acquisition, Rehabilitation and Resettlement Bill* is available at www.kbjnl.com/sites/default/files/pdf/LAQ-RR-Bill-2011-LokSabha.pdf.

individuals affected by a project. The sixth and seventh lists (subclauses vi and vii) cover three issues that are more controversial in constituting public purpose: the provision of land in the public interest for use by the appropriate government for purposes other than those covered under the aforementioned first five subclauses where the benefits largely accrue to the general public, the provision of land in the public interest for public-private partnership projects for the production of public goods or the provision of public services, and the provision of land in the public interest for private companies for the production of public goods or the provision of public services.

Compared to the *1894 LAA*, the scope of public purpose in the *2011 LARR Bill* is much narrower. The three previously mentioned purposes, which augment government power, are omitted from this bill. Land acquisition involving private companies is expressly limited to producing public goods or offering public services. The public purpose beyond the first five lists is allowed, but it must be for government use and the benefits must 'largely' accrue to the public. Nevertheless, this clause gives the government some flexibility and discretionary power. Moreover, the public purposes listed in subclauses v and vi are imposed with an 80 per cent limit. The consent of at least 80 per cent of the people affected by a project must be obtained through a prior informed process.[152]

The *2011 LARR Bill* finally completed its legislative procedure in September 2013. On 29 August 2013, the *LARR* was passed by *Lok Sabha.* The upper house passed it on 3 September 2013 and the president assented to it on 26 September. Starting on 1 January 2014, the new act, called *Right to Fair Compensation and Transparency in Land Acquisition, Rehabilitation and Resettlement Act* (*2013 LARR Act*) came into force and replaced the *1894 LAA*, which had been in effect for 120 years.[153]

As for the provision concerning public purpose, the *2013 LARR Act* reserved most of the provisions in the *2011 LARR Bill* regarding public purpose. Sec. 2 (1) of the *2013 LARR Act* list the following six situations of public purpose: (1) the projects vital to national security or defence; (2) infrastructure projects; (3) the projects for project affected families; (4) the projects for housing of lower income groups; (5) the projects for planned development or the improvement in rural or urban areas or

[152] Ibid., clauses 2–3.

[153] Gazette of India, No. 2839, 19 December 2013. The *2013 LARR Act* is available at www.sngpartners.in/files/right-tofair-compensation.pdf.

the provision of land for residential purposes for the weaker sections in rural and urban areas; and (6) the projects for residential purposes to the persons who are poor or landless, reside in areas affected by natural calamities or are displaced or affected by reason of the implementation of any scheme undertaken by the Government, any local authority or a corporation owned or controlled by the state.

Some revisions were made before the bill was passed. The *2013 LARR Act* lists six types of infrastructural projects of a public nature: the activities or items listed in the notification of the Government of India in the Department of Economic Affairs (Infrastructure Section) number 13/6/2009-INF, dated 27 March 2012, excluding private hospitals, private educational institutions and private hotels; agro-processing, supply of inputs to agriculture, warehousing, cold storage facilities, marketing infrastructure for agriculture and allied activities; industrial corridors, mining activities, national investment and manufacturing zones; water harvesting and water conservation structures, sanitation; educational and research schemes or institutions administered and aided by government; sports, heath care, tourism, and transportation of space programme. Other infrastructure projects are allowed as public purpose only if they are notified by the Central Government and must be after tabling of such notification in the parliament.[154] For the projects involving private companies, 80 per cent consent requirement is still required. However, for the projects involving public-private partnership, the 80 per cent requirement stipulated in the *2011 LARR Bill* was reduced to 70 per cent in the *2013 LARR Act.*[155] The flexible clause, which confers authority to the government to decide other public purpose situations other than the ones listed, was removed. This further narrows the government's power in applying public purpose.[156]

4.5.3 *In the context of China*

4.5.3.1 Enclosure movement in China

Over the course of more than thirty years of opening and reform, the CPC government has focused on economic growth pushed by industrialisation

[154] Ibid., sec. 2(1). [155] Ibid., sec. 2(2).

[156] The government still keeps some discretionary power, which is the decision of other infrastructure projects not listed by the *2013 LARR Act.*

and urbanisation in an effort to industrialise and urbanise agricultural areas. To ensure rapid development, the governments at both central and local levels frequently used their compulsory taking power to change the ownership and rights structure of land.

The term 'enclosure movement' is used to describe the origin and motivation of the UK's early industrialisation process. During industrialisation, common land was enclosed and privately owned, which forced many farmers who had lost land to move to the cities to find employment. In China, scholars borrow this term to describe the progress in which farmers are forced to give up their land or land rights because of the industrialisation or urbanisation projects initiated, implemented or supported by the government.

The most obvious indicator to describe the impact of enclosure is the reduction in the amount of arable land. Through analysis of the data concerning the change of arable land from 1979 to 2008, three apex periods of enclosure, when the amount of arable land rapidly shrank, can be identified.[157] Additionally, all of these periods match China's most rapid periods of industrialisation and urbanisation.

The first apex enclosure period was from 1984 to 1986. At this stage, industrialisation mainly encompassed the establishment of township and village enterprises, and urbanisation was reflected in the change of villages to non-agricultural parts of towns (townisation). The HRS, which began in 1978, motivated farmers to cultivate and increase farming efficiency, creating a glut of spare farm labourers (redundancy). Local governments encouraged the township and village enterprises to develop and absorb the redundant farmers. Moreover, governments at the town level actively enlarged the scope of the township area for urbanisation. The aggregate amount of reduced land during the five years prior to 1984 was only 16,440,000.8 *mu*.[158]

The second apex enclosure period was from 1992 to 1994. To follow the experience of the early opened coastline cities in attracting FDI and pushing forward industrialisation, a greater number of cities established special economic zones called development zones, science and technology zones, export process zones, and so forth. By March 1993, more than 6,000 development zones at the county level and higher were established and occupied approximately 15,000 square kilometres of land, 80 per cent of which was arable land.[159]

[157] Cha, 'Xin Quandi', 15–21. [158] Ibid., 15. [159] Ibid., 19.

The third apex enclosure period was from 1999 to 2006. During this stage, in addition to continuing the establishment of developing zones, the rise of the real estate industry became the main feature of urbanisation. The largest reduction in arable land occurred in 2003 when more than 38,060,000.1 *mu* of arable land was transferred from agricultural use to urban use.[160]

In 2008, the global financial crisis facilitated the fourth apex of the enclosure movement. To help China through the crisis, the central government spent 4 trillion *yuan* on construction projects.[161] Local governments followed the central government and invested more. The expanded demand of land for project construction resulted in the nationwide acquisition of collectively owned farmland and privately owned urban land use rights. The interest conflicts between property holders on the one side and governments linked with developer on the other reached an apex.[162]

What should be noted is that the most recent enclosure occurred after the incorporation of public interest principles into the constitution. However, the weak constitutional protection must defer to the strong demand of economic growth against the backdrop of global crisis. In the name of overcoming financial crisis, various industrialisation and urbanisation projects throughout the country have been aggressively developed, and the public interest doctrine in the constitution plays little role in restricting the unlimited expansion of the governments' taking power.

4.5.3.2 Case of *Gushi*

Gushi County is located in the southeastern region of Henan Province. Before 2004, it was a national level poor county (*guojia ji pinkun xian*), one of the poorest regions in Henan. To facilitate the county's development, Gushi County was planned as one of the future five regional centres by the Henan Provincial Government on 25 March 2004. Gushi County Government was given the authority in economic and social management that should have been enjoyed by a municipality, a higher administration level than county.[163] One month later, Guo Yongchang became the new leader of Gushi County when he was appointed as Secretary of the Gushi

[160] Ibid., 16. For a general overview of the enclosure movement in China in the 1990s, see He, 'The Land-Enclosure'.

[161] Xinhua, 'China's 4 Trillion'.

[162] Yu, Shi and Zuo, 'Zhongguo Disibo'.

[163] Li and Wang, 'Gushi Xianwei'.

County Committee of the CPC. Soon, Guo Yongchang pushed his large-scale urbanisation movement. In 2004, the local urbanisation level was 33.1 per cent. One year later, the government plan called for an increase in the urbanisation level to 35 per cent. By 2010, the urbanisation level should reach 45 per cent.[164] However, the urbanisation strategy did not begin within Guo Yongchang's term. In 1996, the local government of Gushi initiated an urbanisation strategy that used urbanisation to hasten economic growth. Local government leaders found that there was no mid-level city in the vast area around Gushi and thus decided to develop Gushi to be a leading city governing the nearby area.[165] According to Zhou Wei, the leader at the time, the main source of the money for urban construction was selling investors the rights to use land owned or expropriated by the local government. For example in 2002, the local government sold for business development the use right of a parcel of land where the local CPC committee was located. In 2001, the local government expropriated the land use right of an outdated residential area and then sold it to a developer company.[166] However, for the new leader Guo Yongchang, the speed of urbanisation before his term was so slow that he decided to start 'great leap' urbanisation. In addition to the redevelopment of old urban areas through the removal and demolition of houses there, the more radical measures would urbanise nearby farmland. In Guo Yongchang's opinion, the reduction of farmland and farmers was necessary to achieve high-speed economic growth.[167]

The speed of urbanisation under Guo Yongchang's leadership was astonishing. Within only one year after he became leader of Gushi County, the demolition and removal measures comprised approximately 250 thousand square metres of land, and the urban construction projects occupied approximately 400 thousand square metres of land.[168] Incongruously, that same year, the Central Government issued a special notice requiring strict control of the removal and demolition of houses.[169] To address the conflict between the rapid removal and demolition of houses in Gushi and

[164] The data is from Gushi County's *Shiyiwu Guihua* [*The Eleventh Five-Year Plan*].

[165] Yu, Shi and Zuo, 'Zhongguo Disibo'. [166] Ibid.

[167] Ibid. [168] Chen and Zhang, 'Guojia Ji'.

[169] *Guanyu Kongzhi Chengzhen Fangwu Chaiqian Guimo Yange Chaiqian Guanli de Tongzhi* [*Notice on Controlling the Size of Demolition and Removal of Urban Houses and Strengthening the Management of Demolition and Removal*], promulgated by the General Office of the State Council on 6 June 2004, available at www.gov.cn/zwgk/2005–08/15/content_22905.htm.

the Central Government's strict requirements, Guo said that the speedy and large-scale expropriation was allowed for economic development, the primary target of both the state and the party.

The most outstanding leap in urbanisation made by Guo's government was the development of two new urban areas. To realise this plan, the large-scale expropriation of suburban farmland was initiated. More than 20,000 *mu* of farmland was taken for the expansion of Gushi city.[170] Most of the expropriated land was transferred to a private real estate developer for building apartments or houses.

In 1996, the urban area in Gushi was only 6.15 square kilometres. By 2003, the urban area was 22.6 square kilometres. Guo's government pushed the urban size to 37 square kilometres by 2009.[171] The urbanisation achievement made by the Gushi government received high appreciation from the provincial government, and Gushi was planned as one of the areas supported by the provincial government in Henan.[172]

The transferring price of the expropriated land was accused of being too low. For farmers, the compensation price for the acquired land was usually approximately 15,000 *yuan* per *mu*. But the sale price offered to a private developer is approximately 50,000 *yuan* per *mu*. The market value of the concerned land was 300,000 *yuan* per *mu* at that time, a price six times the price offered to developers. Guo responded that the government increased the value of land, not the farmers. Moreover, he said that private developers also played an important role in increasing the value of land.[173] His words imply that private developers deserve a cheap price for the use of government land because they contribute to economic development.

The 'great leap' in Gushi led by Guo Yongchang was once acclaimed by local newspapers and upper level provincial government as the Gushi Miracle (*gushi qiji*), a model sample for urbanisation. But this miracle died in 2008 when Guo was ordered to leave Gushi to take a new position. In 2009, he was arrested for committing economic crimes.

The expropriation of land in Gushi is not an economic miracle. Instead, it represents the popular bubble-like urbanisation movement which has been happening all around China. The motivations for fast urbanisation are various. First, the central government encourages urbanisation as one of the most important approaches to facilitate economic growth and

170 Shi, 'Buyuan Ku-ao'.
171 Yu, Shi and Zuo, 'Zhongguo Disibo'. 172 Ibid. 173 Shi, 'Buyuan Ku-ao'.

achieve the modernisation of China. In Gushi, the upper level provincial government allowed and even appreciated Guo's urbanisation progress. As a result of Gushi's urbanisation achievement, Gushi County Government was raised to a higher administration level: 'the county under the province's direct leadership' (*shengguanxian*). Second, local governments in China use urbanisation to increase their fiscal revenue. A local government can gain a large amount of revenue through the collection of land sale profits, which is the difference between expropriation cost and land sale price. Third, local government officials push urbanisation for individual promotion or illegal income. Guo was arrested for accepting bribery. Two other officials in charge of land affairs were arrested or investigated too.[174] Fourth, some rent-seeking companies illegally collude with local governments to acquire land use rights at a very low cost.

In the name of urbanisation and economic development, local government officials and private developers pursue their interests and form a tight link at the expense of individual rights. The miserable results produced by the so-called miracle of rapid urbanisation ultimately fall on the shoulders of locals who have lost their land. On land expropriated by the Gushi government, most of the planned projects were not developed as expected. Only eight buildings were completed or under construction as of May 2010 in a development zone occupying 2,600 *mu* land. Forty buildings should have been completed by that time. In two new areas of urban expansion, more than two-thirds of newly built apartments were vacant, and lots of land remained undeveloped.[175] Considering that private developers did not have sufficient capital to finish the planned projects, the local government terminated its cooperation with private developers and took back the vacant land at the end of 2008. The crazy expropriation of farmland in the past five years left lots of fertile farmland unused, and the local government does not know how to develop the wasted land.

The large-scale expropriation made by the Gushi government under the leadership of Guo had been resisted by local farmers. However, most of the resisters gave in because of the government's tough measures. In September 2004, approximately 50 *mu* of land in Dapeng Village was expropriated by the government. Seven villagers who advocated resistance were detained, and the villagers were forced to sell their land. The purpose

[174] One of these two officials committed suicide soon after the investigation.
[175] Zuo, 'Huangcheng Gushi'.

of expropriation was to build a factory for stimulating economic growth. However, the expropriated land remains vacant since the compulsory expropriation.[176]

4.5.3.3 The constitutionality of the land reserve system

Land reserve originated in the mid-1990s when a test was made in Shanghai and Hangzhou.[177] The initial scope of land reserve was limited mainly to the need for urban renewal and the reuse of wasted state-owned land. Soon, it became a system for local governments to control the local land supply. The governments at the county and municipality levels established land reserve centres through which state-owned land is reserved, managed and supplied. Before 2007, no uniform law governed the land reserve system, and local governments made their own policies.

In China, the state is the owner of urban land. If individuals and companies need land for construction, they may apply for or buy land use rights from the government. The use of land by individuals and companies is subject to the law. If land holders leave their land unused for a long time, do not use their land according to the assigned use or otherwise illegally use the land, the concerned government would take back the land. The land taken back is saved in a land reserve centre or other authority with the same responsibility. Local governments can allocate or resell the saved land to new users. In essence, the land reserve system is a channel through which a local government operates the leasing and control of land use rights. But retaking illegally used land is not the only source for land reserve. Another main source of land reserve is government expropriation through eminent domain power.[178]

The sale of land through the land reserve system brought in huge revenue to local governments. In 2009, the revenue from the sale of land was 45.8 per cent of the total fiscal revenue of Beijing. For many local governments, the revenue from the sale of land was typically more than

[176] Yin and Cheng, 'Gushi Xian'.

[177] In August 1996, Shanghai established the first land reserve centre in China.

[178] Take Weihai City's policy about land reserve as an example. According to its local policy, local government can take back the leased or allocated land use right for the purposes of public interest, the implementation of urban plan or the renewal of old city area. Moreover, the city government can expropriate farmland for the need of urban construction. The expropriated land is saved into land reserve for the future use which is planned. See *Weihaishi Tudi Chubei Banfa* [*Weihai City Measures on Land Reserve*], art. 5. This document was enacted by Weihai Municipal Government on 17 May 2000 and is vailable at china.findlaw.cn/fangdichan/fdcfg/tudifagui/tudizcfg/98006.html.

60 per cent of local total revenue.[179] Local governments gain revenue so they reserve more and more land. Reserved land is enlarged mainly through either the expropriation of farmland or urban land use rights. Although there was no public interest requirement in the constitution before 2004, both the 1986 *LAL* and the 1994 *LUREA* stipulate that the expropriation of farmland and unexpired urban land use rights shall be for the purpose of the public interest. However, 'public interest' can be defined so widely that it can include any social and economic measure local governments think necessary. For example, Weihai City broadly defines public interest. In addition to the general public interest, Weihai City policy also mentions the need for urban construction, urban planning and the renewal of old areas. Moreover, the policy stipulates 'other need[s]' the government deems necessary as a purpose for land reserve. Usually, a general plan or hasty decision made by the government is sufficient to satisfy a general public purpose.

On 19 November 2007, a specific nation-level document entitled, '*Administration Measures on Land Reserve*' (*2007 Reserve Measures*), was promulgated. Its art. 2 provides that several types of land can be reserved: (1) the land taken back by government according to law; (2) the land purchased by government; (3) the land acquired by government through the exercise of its priority right in purchasing; (4) the land expropriated and approved for transfer to non-agriculture use; and (5) other land acquired according to law.[180]

Although the *2007 Reserve Measures* aims to unify land reserve policy around the country, it does not restrict the scope of land reserve by narrowing the definition of public interest. The *2007 Reserve Measures* stipulates that expropriated farmland can be transferred to the ownership of the state and reserved in a land reserve centre for future construction use.

On 26 April 2010, Mr. Zhang Xingkui, a lawyer in Beijing, submitted a proposal to the NPC requesting a review of the constitutionality of the land reserve system and the *2007 Reserve Measures*.[181] In his proposal, Zhang

[179] Yang, '2009 Nian'. See also Sun, *Zhengdi Jiufen*, p. 126.

[180] *Tudi Chubei Guanli Banfa* [*Administration Measures on Land Reserve*], promulgated by the Ministry of Land and Resources (MLR), the Ministry of Public Finance and People Bank jointly on 19 November 2007, available at www.gov.cn/gzdt/2007–12/04/content_824212.htm.

[181] Zhang Xingkui's proposal is available at www.world-china.org/newsdetail.asp?newsid=3082.

Xingkui noted that some purposes of land expropriation for reserve are against the public interest doctrine in the constitution. For example, after the expropriated land is reserved, it is often used for building commercial apartments or developing of real estate. These purposes should not fall under the scope of public interest. Moreover, land is often expropriated in the name of land reserve without a clear or specific purpose. If there is no precise purpose for the expropriation of land, the expropriation for reserve is against the public interest requirement in the constitution. However, if the specific purpose for expropriation is clear, there is no need for a land reserve system because the expropriated land can be used at once for the assigned purpose without being in the reserve system for days.

Expropriating and reserving land for real estate development has been a popular practice all around China since the 1990s. By the end of 2007, more than 80 per cent of expropriated farm land was used for real estate development and other commercial construction.[182] Of course, local governments can argue that expropriation for real estate development stimulates local economic growth and thus, is for the public interest. But this argument is far from the normal and reasonable understanding of public interest. If this argument stands, local government would be able to expropriate land or land rights for nearly any purpose which is directly or indirectly linked with the social or common good. Thus, land reserve can hide any direct relation between real estate development and expropriation. Land can be expropriated in the name of land reserve for unspecified future urban development and saved as state-owned land in the reserve system. Then, after a period of time, a local government sells the saved land for construction use upon some developer's request.

The first argument for supporting the land reserve system is that it is consistent with the *LAL* and is necessary for land administration based on the current structure of land rights stipulated by the current constitution of China. The *1982 Constitution of China* stipulates two separations relating to land and land rights: the separation between the urban and rural land markets, and the separation between land use rights and land ownership.[183]

First, rural land is strictly separated from urban land. Rural land is mostly owned by collective organisations and urban land is owned by the state. Second, land use rights can be transferred according to law. In rural

[182] Zhao, 'Tudi Falv'.

[183] *1982 Constitution of China*, art. 10.

areas, land use rights can be transferred to farmers through a land leasing contract. In urban areas, local governments can allocate or sell land use rights to companies and other units for construction.

The *LAL* is the main law for governing land rights. To follow the constitution, this law requires individuals who lawfully acquire land use rights to use these rights within the approved use.[184] Land is divided into three categories according to its use: land for farming, land for construction and unused land. Land for farming is mainly composed of collectively owned land in rural areas and refers to land used for agricultural purposes. Land for construction refers to land on which constructions are built. The construction use covers a number of uses: urban and rural housing; public facilities; industries and mining; facilities for energy, traffic, communication, water conservancy and tourism; and military installations. Land other than farming land and construction land is unused land.

Thus, rural and urban land differs greatly in use. Article 43 of the *LAL* stipulates that state-owned urban land is for construction and collectively owned rural land is mainly for agriculture. Rural land cannot be used for construction except building township enterprises, rural residences and local public facilities. Any unit or individual who needs land for construction shall apply for the use of the land owned by the state. Article 43 also defines land owned by the state as land originally owned by the state and expropriated rural land originally owned by collectives.

Some argue that the land reserve system is necessary to realise the land supply requirement stipulated by art. 43 of the *LAL*. Local governments need to expropriate collectively owned land and transfer it to state ownership through the land reserve system before this land is used for construction.

Before the *2004 Amendment*, art. 43 and art. 2 of the *LAL* conflicted; art. 2 stipulates that the state can expropriate the collectively owned land for public interest. After the *2004 Amendment*'s incorporation of the public interest requirement into the constitution, the constitutionality of art. 43 became an issue. The current constitution requires that land can only be expropriated for the public interest. However according to art. 43, government can expropriate rural land for any individual or unit's construction need that might stray from the public interest. The second argument for supporting a land reserve system is that the operation of a land reserve system itself is for the public interest.[185] Hou Fuzhi,

[184] *LAL*, art. 4. [185] Chen, 'Tudi Chubei'.

the official in the land administration department, has argued that the operation of a land reserve system guarantees everyone's land use interest for a number of reasons. First, a land reserve system prohibits the loss of land value through a central supply of construction land. Second, a land reserve system facilitates the stable development of a real estate market through the macroeconomic governmental control of land use. Third, a land reserve system increases the efficient use of land through a fast supply of reserved land. Fourth, a land reserve system strengthens the local government's investment and finance capacity to renew the old city, which improves quality of life.[186]

In fact, the land reserve system forms the government's monopoly in controlling and supplying land. Hou's arguments represent the popular opinions for supporting land reserve and imply that the best or most efficient use of land should be through the government's central control. However, this theoretical foundation is doubtful because it contradicts the basic theorem of a market economy. If the land use decided by the government was the best for society, the public interest doctrine as the constitutional restraint on government power would be nothing. Because of the broad definition of public interest, land reserve and expropriation have led to the government's rapid large-scale devastation of farmland. A county in eastern China, for example, established a land reserve centre in 1999. Among all the reserved land in the county, expropriated land occupies 74.2 per cent. In a city in western China, 92.2 per cent of land reserved between 2003 and 2004 is from expropriated land that was collectively owned before expropriation.[187] Moreover, the monopolised land supply negatively influences the development of a market economy. Land reserve restricts the free flow of land use rights and drives up the price of houses. As the monopolised supplier, the land reserve centre controls the quantity of land supply to push up the auction price, and this drives up house prices.

4.5.4 *Comparative analysis*

Eminent domain, mainly in the form of land expropriation, reflects the conflict between government power and fundamental private rights. The public use or public interest doctrine is the limit on government power and divides public domain from the private zone. This limit on

[186] Ibid. [187] Jiang and Liu, 'Tudi Jiemi'.

government power can be legislative, for example, the practice after the de-constitutionalisation of property in India. The limit on government power can also be constitutional, for example, the experience in the United States. Constitutional public use doctrine can impose a supreme limit over lower level government decisions. Thus, legislation that defines public interest should be reviewed under the constitutional public interest doctrine. As the judicial deference standard used in the U.S. Supreme Court shows, the standard of constitutional review is not substantive; instead, it focuses on the justness of the government's motivation and the procedure in making the public use legislation. Nevertheless, the debate around the *Kelo* decision reflects the demand for a substantive review when eminent domain is used for economic development, which is far from the traditional meaning of public use. Although the Supreme Court's majority decision in *Kelo* did not require substantive review of economic development, many states exclude economic development from the definitions of public use that justify eminent domain. On the one hand, this exclusion shows wide objection to the use of eminent domain for economic development in society. On the other hand, excluding economic development from the definition of public use shows how democracy and the separation of powers can restrict the power of eminent domain in the absence of effective constitutional restraints.

After property as a fundamental right was removed from the constitution in 1978, the public interest limit on land expropriation is at only the legislative level in India. The removal of the constitutional protection of property can be explained as a response to the urgent need of government to hold more flexible power to push forward land reform and economic growth. Unlike the United States, the legislative limits of public purpose had been playing an inactive role in restricting the use of land expropriated by the government for a long time before 2014, because in a developing country, such as India, which has economic growth as one of the most important government responsibilities, land expropriation in the name of economic growth is easily approved by the government. The *1894 LAA* allows a broad scope of public purposes including economic development. In 1991, India started to make significant economic reforms. Learning from China, India started in 2006 to enforce the SEZ law, an important measure for enlarging industrialisation. The loose restraint of public purpose led to a quick expansion of government power in acquiring land for establishing SEZs. The fast development of SEZs led to serious conflict between land-loss farmers and the government. After the Singur protest and Nandigram violence, India's government started to slow down the pace of urbanising and industrialising agricultural areas. The size of land used by an SEZ was required to be limited, and some draft bills restricting the scope of public interest and increasing compensation to farmers losing their land were submitted to the legislative authority. A substantial result of the legislative reform strengthening the protection of land is the *2013 LARR Act*.

China's economic reform after 1978 accompanied the governmental taking of collective land and individual land rights for industrialisation and urbanisation projects. With broader openness and globalisation, awareness of property protection increased and led to more and more resistance to greedy taking of land by local governments and developers. The public interest limit was incorporated into the *LAL* in 1986 and then the *LUREA* in 1994. In 2004, the public interest limit was entrenched in the constitution. The historical treatment of public interest in the laws and constitution is different between India and China. For India, the public interest doctrine was established both legislatively and constitutionally but later was left in the legislative laws only. In China after 1978, the public interest doctrine did not originally exist in either laws or the constitution. The public interest doctrinewas later entrenched in the laws and the constitution sequentially. The difference in the evolution between the two countries may be traced back to differences in the original property system. India originated from a private-property-based colony country with the protection of property in both laws and the constitution. However, after India's independence, to push land reform smoothly, the property protection at the constitutional level was removed. Communist China originated from a public-property-based country with an extremely weak legal recognition of private property. When China transitioned from a planned economy towards a market economy starting in 1978, the legal protection offered to private property holders started to gradually increase in the gradual reform process of China.

Although the doctrine of public interest is now entrenched in China's laws and constitution, its role in limiting the government taking power is still weak or nearly nonexistent. In other words, the public interest principle in the constitution is more of a significant leap on paper than in practice. There are two reasons for explaining such a vacant role. The first reason is that there is no detailed explanation or definition of public interest from legislatures or courts; the absence of clarification leads to its extremely limited effect in influencing legislatures, and the term 'public interest' is seldom used in court. The other reason is that even if public interest were clarified, it would be defined so broadly that it could include economic development or another economic purpose. A broad definition of public interest would not effectively limit government power. Compared with India where public purpose is not in the constitution, China offers less protection to property holders even though public interest is defined in its constitution. Without a democratic mechanism, the government of China has more concentrated power than India to enforce a policy of economic stimulation. In India, laws concerning expropriation are passed by congresses or legislatures. In China, however, the central and local administrative governments have the same power as legislatures to make enforceable legal documents. For example, the regulation concerning the expropriation of urban houses is enacted by the State Council. Although the State Council's regulations shall be subject to the constitution and the laws of the upper level congress, the State Council's stipulations about public interest are nearly free of any constitutional or legislative restraint because there is no clear definition of public interest found in the upper level documents. Thus, inside the political system, the expropriation power of the Chinese administrative government must be exercised through self-discipline. Although there is no constitutional review of public purpose in India, its administrative government is restrained by social forces and the separation of legislative and judicial powers.

The weak restraint on government power has resulted in much broader land expropriation in China than in India. In India, the government's expropriation of land for economic development mainly focuses on the SEZ projects that are planned, approved and supervised by governments. However, in China, expropriation of land occurs for projects that are directly, indirectly, mainly or partially linked with economic growth. A non-inclusive list of such projects include: development zones or other zones for economic growth, university towns, urban renewal areas, financial zones, new city areas, commercial centres or shopping streets and real estate development. Some projects are condemned as being mainly for private interest, especially nationwide real estate development for the purposes of land expropriation. The largest expropriation was made through the land reserve system after the mid-1990s. Land reserved for future urbanisation or industrialisation has become a nearly all-inclusive purpose for the expropriation of land. More seriously, unlike the usual post-project practice in the United States or India, expropriation with the purpose of land reserve is a pre-project practice in China. Usually, land expropriation should be a project-target process, meaning that expropriation should not occur until the project is carefully demonstrated and identified as being for a public purpose. But the expropriation for land reserve is often made when there is no detailed and demonstrated project. The fact that most expropriated and reserved farm land is offered to real estate developers exhibits how weak the private property rights of citizens are when confronted by the government's taking power. Urbanisation, industrialisation and economic growth are only superficial purposes. Often, the real purpose behind government expropriation is to increase fiscal revenue and the private interests of developers and government officials; this is far from what a constitutional public purpose should be.

Both India and China are standing at the crossroads of private property protection. Government will not and cannot move forward with more aggressive steps to expropriate private property because the people have shown strong intolerance of ruthless and untamed expropriations. Will the government retreat? If yes, to what extent? To what extent should the scope of public purpose be narrowed?

In India, the main enforced limit is the ceiling of land used for SEZ. The proposed reform bill, the *2011 LARR Bill*, reflects the government's positive attitude in restricting expropriations by clarifying the strictly limited scope of public purpose. Although not excluding economic development expressively, the public purpose stipulated in the *2013 LARR Act* imposes more restrictive requirements on projects which are beyond the traditional public purpose or include a private entity's involvement. The proposed 80 per cent or 70 per cent limit will make the exercise of governmental expropriation power more difficult where private involvement is concerned; the proposed limit will also strengthen individual property rights. It is expected that the *2013 LARR Act* will greatly restrict the frequency of governmental expropriation.

In China, the prospective reform limiting the public purpose of expropriation is less optimistic. After a series of violent and bloody incidents of resistance, the State Council revised its old regulation on the expropriation of urban houses. The enumeration of public interest in the new regulation does not exclude the reconstruction of old urban areas, the most controversial purpose for house expropriation because it is the only purpose in the enumeration beyond the traditional public purposes. The public nature of reconstruction projects is questioned because these projects are always linked with economic development and the involvement of private developers. In the first draft of the *2011 Expropriation Regulation*, there was a 90 per cent consent limit on reconstruction projects, but this provision was deleted because it would definitely increase the difficulty for governments and developers to enforce reconstruction projects. There is also a clause in the enumeration which leaves government wide discretion to add to the list of public purposes through the enactment of future laws and administrative regulations. Thus, any progress in narrowing public purpose in this new regulation is minimal. There is no reform yet to the expropriation of farm land, which is much more serious in invading property than the expropriation of urban houses. Tracing the historical development of the public interest doctrine in legislatures and judicial practice, and considering the dynamic conflict of social forces behind the public interest doctrine, a realistic prediction can be made: the economic development and urbanisation will not be excluded from the scope of public interest for a long time. Thus, what practical and feasible reform could strengthen the protection of private property in China?

4.6 Reforming the public interest doctrine in China

4.6.1 A gradual approach for narrowing the public interest scope

It is naive to suggest the exclusion of economic development from the scope of public interest. Even the United States, renowned for its protection of property rights, cannot totally erase economic development from the domain of public use, nor can China, a country without separation of powers and with the pressing needs of a developing economy.

The ADB suggests that China should make a gradual reform as to the scope of public interest. According to an ADB report, the ideal reform plan is to define public interest as 'public facilities and public welfare undertakings that do not aim to profit, but serve the public, and have benefits shared by the society'.[188] This definition is consistent with the narrowest approach of defining public interest, and economic development projects are beyond this definition. But, this definition is not practical for China currently and long term. Even in the United States, the *Kelo* decision allows economic development as a public use. Some states still do not expressly exclude economic development from the domain of public use. Even the ADB thinks this narrow definition is only a 'long-term objective'

[188] ADB, 'People's Republic of China', 8.

for China.[189] The ADB suggests that China should narrow public interest gradually, and a transition period should be allowed. In the transition period towards the final goal, land used for construction of organic towns shall be left out of land expropriation.[190] In fact, nearly all projects targeting economic development concern urbanisation or industrialisation. This transitional reform plan is designed to narrow the scope of urban construction projects executed through land expropriation and to include those projects excluding organic township construction only.

Organic township construction is part of urbanisation. Whether the organic town construction shall be excluded from the scope of land expropriation is beyond legal analysis. However, why is the construction of organic towns not allowed for land expropriation but other types of urbanisation are still allowed in the transition period? The resolution of this issue is not easy and needs interdisciplinary analysis combining economic, political and ecological perspectives. It can be strongly argued that township construction is as important as other urban construction. Thus, this reform plan might not occur in the near future. The remaining question is this: can any practical reform be suggested before the urbanisation projects are reduced by law and policy?

4.6.2 Reform suggestions from legal perspective

Reform in the legal arena concerns not what projects should be kept and what should be excluded, but to set limits on the economic development projects frequently used as the public purpose justifying land expropriation. Compared to the suggestion about removing some important part from the scope of urbanisation, a return to the fundamental goal of the constitutional public interest doctrine is more significant. The government's expropriation power should serve the public and not the private interests, which include the unjust re-allocation of private property and the official's individual interest.

First, expropriation projects should be divided into two categories: projects without private involvement and projects with private involvement. Here, private involvement should be understood as the involvement by a company, an individual or any other non-governmental involvement, including the involvement by SOEs, which operate independently for profit. As a country transitioning from a planned economy to a market economy that still keeps a public property system, huge numbers of SOEs

[189] Ibid., 11. [190] Ibid., 8.

can be found in China. In China, most SOEs are not similar to public corporations in Western countries. These public corporations are usually established to take some public responsibility, such as the offering of a public service that should have been born by government.[191] They are not for-profit, or their profit margin is very narrow. In addition, SOEs are subject to strict government regulation.

A project with whole or partial private involvement should be subject to a stricter examination than a project without private involvement. This proportionality principle can be introduced as a review standard. The public interest or benefit generated by the concerned projects must be greater than the private interest brought to the non-governmental entities that operate such projects. In other words, the private benefit can only be incidental to the public interest. If the private interest is so significant that it overwhelms the public interest, the concerned project must be excluded from the scope of public purpose and the land required for expropriation must be refused. The project developer then must rely on some non-expropriation channel for their land, for example, to buy land use rights in the market or through the government auction.

The public benefit generated from the proposed project must be subject to independent and careful analysis; it usually includes job opportunities, economic survival and the increase of taxation or revenue. 'Independency' requires that an analysis be made by an independent authority uninfluenced by either the government officials in charge of the project or the private developers. 'Carefulness' means that such report shall consider all necessary parts of the project, and the evidence supporting the conclusions should be sufficient and persuasive.

The Necessity Test also should be applied. Subject to this test, the proposed expropriation must be necessary to achieve the public benefit. In other words, the expropriation of property must be the final approach used for such project. If the project can be realised through an alternative to expropriation, expropriation shall not be used. If the alternative approach cannot satisfy every need, partial expropriation may be used to supplement the remaining need. When a project requires the expropriation of land, the exhaustion of other alternatives for acquiring land must be proved. Other non-expropriation alternatives include the acquirement of construction land through the market or government auction, the allocation of state-owned construction land, or the offering of unused land.

[191] Ibid., 7.

Then, the Sequence Test is proposed. After the necessity for expropriation is proved, land expropriation shall be made in a sequential order. Fertile, arable land shall be the last consideration for expropriation; because there is so little of this land, it has been near the bottom line of food safety in China. In fact, the *LAL* states that arable land should be protected significantly.[192] Local governments are required by the *LAL* to maintain the current amount of arable land. If upon approval some parcel of arable land is transferred for a construction use, the developer should be responsible for cultivating the same amount of new arable land as the transferred land. If this developer cannot cultivate the new arable land, it should pay the government a cultivation fee, which is used specifically for the cultivation of new arable land.[193] Basic agricultural land, which concerns the whole nation's food security, shall not be less than 80 per cent of all arable land and shall be subject to the strict control of local governments.[194] In addition, the *LAL* requires that for construction uses, the unused land should always be considered before cultivated land, and land with bad quality is expropriated before land of good quality.[195] This provision is the sequence requirement. To generalise the sequence test, farm land must be categorised into several groups, which are ranked in sequential order according to the significance of the land to food security and community interest. The expropriation of land shall be made from the land in the upper position of this sequence, with less significance given to land in the lower position. Land from the lower level land shall not be considered for expropriation unless land from the upper level land is unavailable or inappropriate for the proposed use. The land that is categorised at the lowest level of this sequence shall be strictly protected from the invasion of expropriation. The land at the lower level can be set as a safety zone in which it is prohibited from being taken for any project with private involvement. The sequence test is mainly for the public interest, which is considered to be more important than a wholly or partially public interest generated by the proposed expropriation project. Nevertheless, the enforcement of the sequence test can help to control the scope of economic development and play a role in reducing the invasion of the expropriation power into the domain of private property rights.

A Minimum Percentage Consent threshold can be introduced as another limit. For projects with private involvement, consent from a

[192] *LAL*, arts. 31 and 34.
[193] Ibid., art. 31. This is called the preservation system of arable land.
[194] Ibid., art. 34. [195] Ibid., art. 36.

minimum percentage of people influenced by such projects should be required before land expropriation. The 90 per cent limit suggested for the transformation of dangerous and outdated houses is so high that local governments and developers strongly resist it. A lesser percentage could be a balance point accepted by both individual right holders and their opposing social forces. The minimum percentage can be relatively low in the beginning and can be raised to a higher level as society progresses. The consent threshold might not be uniform for all projects with private involvement. The percentage for an expropriation project with private involvement should be higher than a project with only partial private involvement.

4.6.3 *Reforming the land reserve system*

The current land reserve system leaves public interest doctrine in a nearly meaningless situation. If the land reserve system remains outside the aforementioned tests and encroaches on public interest, the current law and the suggested reform measures cannot hold back the expansion of land expropriation.

The aim of reform is to remove the pre-project land expropriation from the land reserve system. If the land reserve is allowed as public purpose without any strict limit, it will largely depreciate the effect of the suggested reform measures which aim to tame the expansion of expropriation power. A better reform of the current legislation is to expressly exclude land reserve, urban planning or any other similar general and abstract terminology from the scope of public purpose.

The strongest resistance to the reform of the land reserve system is from local governments which are backed by local rent-seeking groups. At the governmental level, the motivation for maintaining pre-project land reserve for land expropriation originates from the current local fiscal system. In 1994, the 'the system of tax-sharing' (*fenshuizhi*) substituted the past 'system of tax-responsibility (tax-contract)' (*caizheng baogan*).[196] The system of tax-responsibility was introduced as a trial in 1980 in Guangdong Province. According to this system, local governments and

[196] *Yusuan Fa* [*Budgetary Law*], enacted by the Second Session of the Eighth NPC on 22 March 1994. The Chinese text of this law is available at www.npc.gov.cn/wxzl/gongbao/2000–12/05/content_5004614.htm. Such change of policy was first made at the Third Plenum of the Fourteenth Central Committee of the CPC in November 1993 and then was written into the 1994 *Budgetary Law* the next year. See Lin, 'Land Development', 20.

the central government negotiated and agreed on a lump-sum revenue amount remitted to the central government by local governments. The revenue above this remittance number was attributed to local governments. Under this system, the local government was strongly motivated to increase the local revenue because the surplus amount can be kept completely by local governments. With years passing by and economic growth moving fast, this system created great disadvantage to the central government. The responsibility agreement set the fixed amount of remittance atfive years. Within the agreed five years, the baseline amount of remittance was fixed, but the revenue increased very fast each year. This system of tax-responsibility led to a situation in which the central government could not share the surplus resulting from the rapid increase in revenue within the contract period. The 1994 tax-sharing system used a share percentage to substitute the fixed remittance amount. The central government takes a percentage of each year's local revenue. This new system increased the central government's share of local revenues while decreasing the local governments' share. Thus local governments started to seek new resources for increasing their revenue, and the sale of land use rights for construction (land conveyance) became the first option. With the exhaustion of urban land controlled by local governments, new sources of land were sought for increasing local fiscal revenue. There are mainly two approaches to acquire new land for government's ownership: (1) to obtain land use rights back through expropriation, and (2) to transfer collectively owned farmland to state ownership through expropriation.[197] The introduction of the land reserve hastened the pace of land expropriation with little public interest limitation.[198] The phenomenon that local governments increase revenue through land conveyance is called the 'local land finance' (*tudi caizheng*).

[197] Through expropriating rural land and converting it for construction use, local governments in China can acquire the 'expropriation surplus', which is the difference between the value of land for limited pre-expropriation agricultural use and that for much wider post-expropriation commercial use. In reality, because the existing compensation formula does not even reflect the full value of land's agricultural use and the officers tend to use the low end of such formula when decide compensation, the real surplus acquired by governments is much larger that the aforementioned one. See Washburn, 'Regular Takings', 84, 87–8.

[198] In Guandong, the revenue from land conveyance achieved 57 per cent of the local extra-budgetary revenue in 1999. In 2003, the land conveyance revenue reached 53.96 per cent of the local extra-budgetary revenue nationwide. In many municipalities and towns with rapid economic growth, this percentage even reaches as high as 80 per cent. See Lin, 'Land Development', 21.

Revenue-motivation for expropriation is closely linked to performance-motivation. GDP growth is the evaluation standard, and economic performance has been a heavy burden on both local governments and their officials. Urbanisation and industrialisation can always stimulate growth or GDP much faster than agricultural development. Among construction projects, real estate development has been used by local governments as the most important way to stimulate economic growth. In fact, most land that was expropriated in the name of urban renewal or industrialisation was finally offered to private developers to build commercial apartments. This performance-motivation is further strengthened by private developers' seeking rent. To acquire land to pursue high profits, private developers frequently bribe officials to help them to take land quickly and cheaply. After the land is acquired, many private developers do not start the approved construction projects. Developers saved a great deal of land and created a shortage in the land and housing supply to push up the prices of land and houses. Activity by private developers that raises house and land prices stimulates more demand of land for construction. Local governments are motivated to expropriate more land to meet this demand and to chase new revenue.

Thus, two obstacles that lead to the strong local resistance to the reform of the land reserve and expropriation system are the revenue-sharing system and the GDP-oriented performance evaluation over local governments. To reform and overcome these two obstacles is a tough job that cannot be finished in the short term. But in recent years, suggestions from scholars for reforming the taxation-sharing system have started to accumulate. Some measures taken by the central government have shown a reconsideration of the current land reserve system. In 2009, the MLR issued an emergency notice about the collection of necessary information of land reserve. The ministry declared in the notice that it would comprehensively investigate the land reserve system to improve regulation of the system.[199]

Currently in China, the land reserve system has pushed former property holders to the edge. On one side of this edge, individual property holders have no space to retreat and serious social resistance and violent unrests

[199] *Guanyu Kaizhan Tudi Chubei Zhidu Jianshe he Yunxing Qingkuang Diaocha de Jinji Tongzhi* [*Emergent Notice on the Investigation of the Construction and Operation of Land Reserve System*], promulgated by the MLR on 4 September 2009. The Chinese text of this document is available at www.shanxigov.cn/n16/n2382/n18501/n18822/n20214/9317821.html.

would be more widespread if the expropriation power moved forward unchecked. On the other side, governments hesitate between retreat and no retreat. Considering the difficulty in the short term in reforming the policies concerning local governments' revenue and performance motivations, the substantial reform restricting land expropriation by narrowing the scope of public interest and abolishing land reserve for land expropriation is not expected. There is another issue about the constitutional protection of private property. Even if the public interest doctrine plays little role in restricting the expropriation power, the property holders' interests would still be guaranteed if the compensation for their property was sufficient and just. So is the compensation to the former property holders just and reasonable in China?

5

Unjust compensation

Following public interest, compensation is the second threshold designed for the protection of property by the constitution. If the public interest used to justify expropriation stands, the next issue is to decide the amount of compensation. Compensation is used to make whole individuals whose properties were sacrificed for the public good. Compensation has two implications for the protection of private property. One implication is to correct the possible unfairness brought by a compulsory taking. Another implication is to restrain the government's taking power which might be loosened by the broadly explained doctrine of public interest if the paid compensation is sufficiently large.

5.1 To compensate: why and what?

Compensation is required based on the rationale that a person who sacrifices his property for the benefit of his community deserves reimbursement. To illustrate this argument in more detail, two key elements must be identified. The first element is the 'sacrifice-benefit' test, which means the property owner has done nothing wrong and has sacrificed his property for the benefit of others in the community. The second element is the equality or equal sharing principle. One person's loss or sacrifice shall be borne in the form of compensation by the whole society equally.[1] The equality function of compensation is to facilitate the fairness or fair treatment to all members in society. John Fee points out that compensation aims at protecting individuals from being singled out to bear the costs for public good.[2] The equality function also implies the offering of protection to minorities who are forced to surrender their property by a government which represents the majority. Like public purpose, compensation aims at balancing the conflict between private property and public interest.[3] On

[1] Cheng, 'The Rationale', 298. [2] Fee, 'Reforming', p. 132.
[3] Durham, 'Efficient Just Compensation', 1277.

the one hand, it helps to ease the injustice of the expropriation power in harming private property and thus, offers protection to private property. On the other hand, it facilitates the accomplishment of the government's common good through compensation of the taken property.

From this balancing view of compensation, the appropriateness of the compensation quantum is a key issue. An insufficient compensation both hurts the property owners' interest and encourages the government's misuse of its eminent domain power. If compensation is excessive, it may satisfy the property owner, but it discourages government projects that benefit the public. Epstein deems just compensation as the prices for government initiatives. Think of taking as a market. In this market, the price of compensation can alter the government's demand for land taking. The too-high price of compensation facilitates the government's abandoning of worthwhile public projects and the too-low price fastens the government's pace in the excessive taking of the land which should be better in its owner's hand.[4] Another problem of excessive compensation is that it can result in the reduction of political resist to the expropriation project which is not an unproblematic public one.[5]

How should the balance be set in the constitution and expropriation laws? Compensation is required by constitutions in many countries, although the exact use of the term varies between countries. The following are typical compensation terms found in constitutions: 'just compensation' (United States, Japan and South Korea), 'appropriate compensation' (German *Weimar Constitution*), 'equitable compensation' (*German Basic Law*), 'just and equitable compensation' (South Africa) and 'compensation' (Italy and China). The difference in the use of terms reflects differences in exact compensation standards.

What should be compensated? The scope of compensation also differs among countries, and starts from a simple question: what does the property owner or holder lose? Compensation is designed to compensate a property owner's loss caused by the exercise of eminent domain power and thus, defer the government's motivation in taking property. However, the social obligation of property and the achievement of public interest should limit unreasonable enlargement of compensation available to the owner.

There are three categories of loss caused by or attributed to eminent domain. The first category is property loss or the loss of the property's market value. In the case of real estate, this loss includes the land and

[4] Epstein, *Supreme Neglect*, pp. 89–90. [5] Garnett, 'The Neglected', 142–3.

its attachments. The second category is the loss of the subjective value of property, which is specifically attributed to the property owner only. It is the loss of the value the owner himself endows or projects in his property.[6] It concerns the loss of social ties with the local community, the historical or memorial significance of property to the owner, the owner's personal enjoyment with the surrounding environment and so on. The subjective value lost in expropriation is not usually reflected by the market value of the property because it is specifically linked with the owner himself. The third category concerns the consequential damage or other property losses caused by expropriation. It is distinguished by the loss of objective market value because it is the loss of property beyond the expropriated property itself. It also differs from the loss of subjective value because it is usually economic in nature and can be calculated in a monetary form. This category includes, but is not limited to the following: losses concerning the business operation in the expropriated real estate, for instance, the loss of good will or expected profit; the costs concerning moving and resettlement; losses in unproductive investment – for example, the loss of harvests in farmland and the loss of decoration cost used for a starting shop; the costs concerning the dealing of expropriation affairs – for example, the expenditure concerning lawyers, valuation, land surveying and property registration; in the case of partial taking, the losses of the remaining parcel's value caused by expropriation; and finally, the transaction costs of changing jobs. For the farmers losing land by expropriation, the transaction cost for their job change is huge if no suitable land is offered as a substitute for their lost land. They have to spend time and money on searching and training for a new job.

In most countries, the compensation based on the objective market value is supported. The controversy occurs on the compensation's coverage of the loss of subjective value and the consequential loss. As a representative country, the United States mainly compensates the market value of property, although under some exceptional cases, a limited scope of consequential damage is considered also by courts. Although the *German Basic Law* does not mention market value, in practice, the expropriation laws in Germany usually include both market value and

[6] Wyman generalised the subjective loss as, '[t]hese include losses due to an owner's sentimental attachments to the property or community in which it is located, and idiosyncratic tastes that have no market value. Intangible losses also include losses owners suffer from being deprived of the autonomous choice of keeping or selling their property.' See Wyman, 'The Measure', 255.

consequential losses. In India, the coverage of compensation is much broader and includes market value, damages and a solatium reflecting the involuntary nature of displacement.

5.2 The United States: fair market value as the test for just compensation

The *Fifth Amendment* stipulates that 'nor shall private property be taken for public use, without just compensation'.[7] The compensation for taking property is required to be 'just'. There is no more explanation of what 'just compensation' means in the constitution.[8] In the practice of the U.S. Supreme Court, there are two cases that play the most important role in formulating the judicial articulation of just compensation.

In the case of *Monongahela Navigation Co.* v. *United States*, decided in 1893, Monongahela Navigation Company's lock and dam number seven and its appurtenances were compulsorily purchased by the government. The issue under debate is not the appropriateness of the government's condemnation power but the amount of compensation. In the majority decision, Justice Brewer illustrated the meaning of 'just compensation' stipulated by the *Fifth Amendment*. He distinguished 'the damages by way of compensation' with 'punitive or exemplary damages' and noted that compensation should be 'the equivalent for the injury done'. The latter damages (punitive or exemplary ones) were punishment in nature and should not be supported in an expropriation case. The adjective 'just' used before 'compensation' is to make the significance of compensation 'emphatic'. He said in the ruling: "There can, in view of the combination of those two words, be no doubt that the compensation must be a full and perfect equivalent for the property taken; and this just compensation, it will be noticed, is for the property, and not to the owner.'[9]

[7] In the colonial period before the birth of the constitution, there had been no just compensation required for government taking. The main reason explained by Treanor is that most taken lands at that time were undeveloped and with few value. See Treanor, 'The Origins', 694.

[8] The doctrine 'just compensation', also called 'just terms compensation', exists in the UK and most commonwealth countries. Different from the market value definition in the United States, just compensation is defined as the value to the owner which includes market value and other losses to the owner in the UK and Australia. See Chan, 'Land Acquisition', 144, 148.

[9] *Monongahela Navigation Co.* v. *United States*, 148 U.S. 312, 326 (1893).

According to this decision, just compensation shall be decided fairly to cover the value of property taken by government. This equivalency test became the foundation on which the latter fair market value test was developed. In the case of *L. Vogelstein & Co., Inc.* v. *United States*, the market value of the property at the time of taking was decided to be the measure of compensation.[10] In the case of *Olson* v. *United States*, the court ruled that 'equivalent is the fairly decided market value of the property at the time of the taking contemporaneously paid in money'.[11]

Thus, just compensation is explained by the U.S. Supreme Court as the market value of the taken property at only the time of the taking. The owner's past investment, interest or benefit is not considered because '[t]he public may not by any means confiscate the benefits, or be required to bear the burden, of the owner's bargain'.[12] The purpose of the adoption of the fair market value as compensation test is to put the property owner 'in as good a position pecuniarily as if his property had not been taken'.[13] The court emphasised that what shall be safeguarded by the constitution is 'the property rather than the cost of it'.[14]

When deciding the market value of the taken property, 'all elements of value that inhere in the property' shall be considered. The key consideration in deciding the market value is the 'highest and most profitable use' of the property. This use should be the current use or the use which is likely needed 'in the reasonably near future' only if the need in the near future influences the property's market value.[15] Even if the most profitable use of the taken property has to be decided in combination with other property, it can be considered to the extent that the combination is 'reasonably sufficient to affect market value'.[16] In calculating market value, the preferred method is the 'willing buyer-willing seller' approach or comparable sale method, which means 'what a willing buyer would pay in cash to a willing seller' at the time of taking.[17]

The Supreme Court's understanding of just compensation is based on property-target rather than owner-target. As a result, the compensation derived is value-target rather than loss-target. In the *Monongahela* case, judges in fact expressed inconsistent analysis around the nature of compensation. The compensation was first described to be for the 'injury' which reflects in essence the attitude of owner-target implying that compensation should be equivalent to the property owner's loss.

[10] *L. Vogelstein & Co., Inc.* v. *United States*, 262 U.S. 337, 340 (1923).
[11] *Olson* v. *United States*, 292 U.S. 246, 255 (1934). [12] Ibid.
[13] Ibid. [14] Ibid. [15] Ibid., at 255. [16] Ibid., at 256.
[17] *United States* v. *564.54 Acres of Land*, 441 U.S. 506, 511 (1979).

However, just compensation was clearly noted as being for the property rather than the owner. The currently enforced fair market value test for just compensation established by the U.S. Supreme Court is obviously away from owner-target or loss-target.

The fair market value test has been criticised for its insufficiency in compensating the property-loss individuals.[18] The criticism is that it does not reflect the requirement of the 'just' nature of compensation. Generally, opposing opinions are based on the owner's position or are loss-oriented. The criticism is that compensation should cover the injury or loss the taking brings to the concerned owner. The compensation based on market value is often less than the injury sustained by an owner. Epstein distinguishes the property's 'use value' with its 'exchange value'. The use value corresponds to the injury to some owner because it is 'the distinctive subjective value an owner attaches to holding and using property'.[19] The exchange value corresponds to the market value of property and is expected by the owner to be realised through market exchange. What makes use value exceed the exchange value is usually for reasons of 'convenience and sentiment'.[20]

The shared purpose of both use value and market value is to restore through the offering of compensation to the property owner when his situation is destroyed by the government's compulsory taking. The difference between use value and market value exists only in to what extent the property owner recovers. Should the purpose of compensation be to leave a property owner objectively or subjectively indifferent to taking? The market value test does not bring full compensation to owners. All value concerning the property can be categorised into two types. One is its market value, which is transferable, and the other value is the owners' subjective value or special value which is specifically adaptable to the owner and thus, nontransferable.[21] After the *Kelo* decision, there have been

[18] In the movie *Up* produced by Disney, Carl and Ellie decorated their house together. After their marriage, they had lived in their house for many years and finally, Carl held Ellie's hand as she passed away in theirs house. Carl refused a developer's offer which was far more than market price. For him, the value of his house cannot be compensated by any market value.

[19] Epstein, *Supreme Neglect*, p. 91.

[20] Ibid. For the criticism targeting the insufficiency of market value test, see Fegan, 'Just Compensation', 286–7.

[21] Justice Marshall said:

> Although the market-value standard is a useful and generally sufficient tool for ascertaining the compensation required to make the owner whole, the Court has acknowledged that such an award does not necessarily compensate for all values an owner may derive from his property. Thus, we have held that fair market value does not include

critics proposing the increasing of compensation to rein in the expansion of eminent domain power in the name of economic development because the public interest itself cannot play such a role.[22] However, to replace market value with use value or the owner's injury also has been questioned for a long time.

The first argument against the compensation to subjective value is the practical difficulty in applying for it. A property owner's self-valuation or subjective value cannot be used as the test because it is possible he will exaggerate the property value. But it is hard to find a fair rule in deciding use value or all value for the property owner from the perspective of an outsider. In the case of *United States* v. *564.54 Acres of Land*, Justice Marshall refused the subjective value test because there are 'serious practical difficulties in assessing the worth an individual places on particular property at a given time'.[23] Compared with the subjective value, the market value test is 'a relatively objective working rule'.[24]

The second argument from the Supreme Court is based on social obligation theory. The uncompensated part of property value is regarded as a necessary burden that a citizen should bear. In the case of *Kimball Laundry Co.* v. *United States*, Justice Frankfurter illustrated this social obligation argument:

> The value of property springs from subjective needs and attitudes; its value to the owner may therefore differ widely from its value to the taker. Most things, however, have a general demand which gives them a value transferable from one owner to another. As opposed to such personal and variant standards as value to the particular owner whose property has been taken, this transferable value has an external validity which makes it a fair measure of public obligation to compensate the loss incurred by an owner as a result of the taking of his property for public use. In view, however, of the liability of all property to condemnation for the common good, loss to the owner of nontransferable values deriving from his unique need for property or idiosyncratic attachment to it, like loss due to an exercise of the police power, is properly treated as part of the burden of common citizenship.[25]

However, in equalising the loss derived from the police power, or non-taking regulations, to the loss derived from taking, this argument is less persuasive. Taking power is more discriminating than other government

> the special value of property to the owner arising from its adaptability to his particular use.

See 441 U.S. 506, 511 (1979).

[22] Wyman, 'The Measure', 242–3. [23] 441 U.S. 506, 511 (1979). [24] Ibid.

[25] *Kimball Laundry Co.* v. *United States*, 338 U.S. 1, 5 (1949).

powers because it targets specific persons. The loss from non-taking power is distributed among unspecified citizens more equally and fairly, but the loss from taking must be borne by specific persons. This unequal distribution means that the loss or cost borne by takees is above average if sufficient compensation is not available. Without full compensation, the obligation imposed on takees is more than that on others, and this inequality leads to unfair treatment among citizens.

5.3 Germany: the linking clause and equitable balance

In Germany, the constitutional stipulation regarding compensation is found in art. 14(3) of the *German Basic Law*. The relevant provisions have two distinctive features.

First, the constitutional requirement of compensation is expressly stipulated by the *German Basic Law* as a premise to an enforceable expropriation. It is required by the *German Basic Law* that '[i]t (expropriation) may only be ordered by or pursuant to a law that determines the nature and extent of compensation'. This clause is known as the *Junctim-Klausel*, or linking-clause provision. According to this clause, the relevant law must stipulate the nature and the extent of compensation before an expropriation is initiated. This clause is helpful in strengthening the protection of private property by requiring the inclusion of the necessary contents of compensation in the relevant legislation in advance and thus restricting the scope of expropriation allowed by the constitution.[26] Moreover, the clause protects the public from bearing an unforeseen expropriation cost or burden.[27]

However, in theory, this clause might make inverse expropriation or constructive expropriation unconstitutional because no prior legislation regarding compensation contents can be found for such expropriation. In a case decided by the FCC in 1981, the compensation awarded for the regulations with the effect of expropriation was questioned because no relevant legislative stipulations were found.[28] In this case, the owner of a gravel pit was refused a permit to extract the subsurface water under his land, which he had been extracting for decades. The *Water Resources Law* according to which the refusal was issued does not stipulate compensation for this type of water regulation and was argued against by the plaintiff as unconstitutional. The FCC finally supported the

[26] BVerfGE 24, 367 (*Deichordnung*, 1968). [27] Mostert, 'German Law'.

[28] BVerfGE 58, 300 (*Naßauskiesung*, 1981). See also Mostert, 'German Law'.

constitutionality of the relevant law, and this decision was criticised for discarding the constitutional restrictions on regulatory measures.[29] If the prohibition of water extraction constitutes expropriation, the *Water Resources Law*, which does not stipulate compensation, shall be invalid. The Constitutional Court denied the water right's property status and concluded that the *Water Resources Law*'s prohibition is not bound by the *Junctim-Klausel*, and thus no compensation is required by the constitution.[30] After this case was transferred to the civil court, compensation was awarded to the plaintiff. However, this compensation decision was based on non-constitutional law.[31]

Second, the *German Basic Law* provides an 'equitable balance' doctrine for determining compensation and states that compensation 'shall be determined by establishing an equitable balance between the public interest and the interests of those affected'.[32] The issue that remains for the courts is how to explain this equitable balance approach. Is there any difference between such an approach and the just compensation principle in the United States?

Regarding the constitutional stipulations that concern property, the *German Basic Law* follows the previous *Weimar Constitution* to a certain extent. Both documents mention the social obligation of private property. The *Weimar Constitution* stipulates that '[p]roperty obliges.' 'Its use shall simultaneously be service for the common best.'[33] The *German Basic Law* includes a similar stipulation, which states that '[p]roperty entails obligations'. In addition, '[i]ts use shall also serve the public good.'[34] Reflecting this socially obligatory nature of property, the standard for compensation in the *Weimar Constitution* is 'appropriate compensation',[35] which had been viewed as expressing the same meaning as that of equitable compensation required by the *German Basic Law* before the late 1960s. However, the two constitutions also differ. Regarding property, the *German Basic Law* offers better protection than the *Weimar Constitution*. For example, regarding the compensation issue, the *Weimar Constitution* allows the

[29] Alexander, 'Property', 755–65.

[30] The court decided that the land ownership in the constitutional meaning does not entail the subsurface water because water resource should be more public nature. Ibid.

[31] Ibid.

[32] In addition, the constitution stipulates the availability of judicial remedy to compensation disputes. Article 14 (3) of *German Basic Law* provides that: 'In case of dispute concerning the amount of compensation, recourse may be had to the ordinary courts.'

[33] *Weimar Constitution*, art. 153(3).

[34] *German Basic Law*, art. 14(2).

[35] *Weimar Constitution*, art. 153(2).

exclusion of appropriate compensation by the legislature.[36] However, the *German Basic Law* does not authorise this flexible power to change the constitutional compensation standard to the legislature.

The equation of equitable compensation and appropriate compensation might result in the compensation for property being lower than the property's market value. The German constitution allows substantial discretion in determining the exact amount of compensation to legislators. Although market value is often used as the basis of compensation measurement, an adjustment that might produce an amount lower than the market value is allowed by the approach of equitable balance. This explanation was clearly expressed by the FCC in the 1968 case *Deichordnung*, in which the court ruled that the constitution does not require that only market value approach be used and that the legislature could make laws to determine a compensation that might be less than market value.[37] That is, in the eyes of the FCC, market value or full compensation can be adjusted for the sake of balance.

The FCC's explanation of equitable compensation has been questioned, particularly after the 1968 *Deichordnung* case. Regardless of this constitutional explanation, the high courts continued to insist that compensation should reflect market value or be a full compensation that left the property-losing owner in the same circumstances he or she would have known had there been no expropriation.

The legislation that concerns expropriation under the constitution tends to use market value as a basic standard in combination with equitable consideration to calculate compensation. The *BauGB* stipulates compensation in subdivision 2. Compensation is awarded to cover the concerned owner's loss with respect to forfeited property rights and other loss. The calculation of the compensation for a loss that concerns property rights is based on the 'current market value'. The time for the assessment is the date when the expropriation authority makes its expropriation decision.[38] In addition to the loss of the primary property right, other losses of an incidental nature can be compensated. Such other losses primarily include: the loss suffered by the affected owner relating to his or her livelihood, profession or task; the decrease in value of the remaining part of his or her property in a case of partial expropriation; and moving expenses. When determining these incidental losses, the assessment shall

[36] Article 153(2) of *Weimar Constitution* provides that: 'It has to be executed with appropriate compensation, unless specified otherwise by Reich law.'

[37] BVerfGE 24, 367 (*Deichordnung*, 1968).

[38] *BauGB*, sec. 95(1).

be based on providing 'due weighting to the respective interests of the public and of the parties concerned'.[39]

Regarding the constitutional stipulations that concern expropriatory compensation, it can be concluded that: (1) the linking clause in the *German Basic Law* requires the inclusion of compensation and its nature and content in the legislation on expropriation; (2) the *German Basic Law* allows the legislature to determine the exact nature, content and measurement of such compensation in the concerned legislation; and (3) the *German Basic Law* requires that such expropriatory compensation should reflect an equitable balance.

5.4 India: compensation without constitutional restraint

5.4.1 *The war between the judiciary and the legislature*

Like the fate of the public interest principle in the developmental history of the constitution, in India since the constitution's promulgation in 1949, the function of the constitutional stipulation concerning compensation in limiting governmental expropriation weakened and finally ended with the legislature's victory over the judiciary.

The original structure of property protection in the constitution was nearly comprehensive. Property was stipulated a fundamental right in art. 19(1)(f). The public purpose and compensation requirement for expropriation or other deprivation of property was stipulated by art. 31(2), which provides the following:

> No property, movable or immovable, including any interest in, or in any company owning, any commercial or industrial undertaking, shall be taken possession of or acquired for public purposes under law authorising the taking of such possession acquisition, unless the law provides for compensation for the property taken possession of or acquired and either fixes the amount of the compensation, or specifies the principles on which, and the manner in which, the compensation is to be determined and given.

In this provision, compensation and public purpose serve as limits on or prerequisites to the government's expropriation of private property. The relevant stipulation resembles the *Junctim-Klausel* of the *German Basic Law*. A law concerning expropriation that does not provide compensation or the principles for or manner of determining such compensation is invalid.

[39] Ibid., sec. 96(1).

Two issues relevant to art. 31(2) precipitated the debate between judicial and legislature authority. The first issue was the relationship between art. 31(2) and its previous clause, art. 31(1). Article 31(1) provides that '[n]o person shall be deprived of his property save by authority of law.' The Supreme Court in India explained that both clauses concerned the same subject: the acquisition of property.[40] This explanation implies that both clauses shall be read sequentially as a whole in the following manner: any deprivation of property, including but not limited to expropriation or acquisition, shall not be made by the state save according to laws that provide public purpose and compensation. However, this explanation was objected to by legislature. A main concern of the legislature was that this explanation was so broad that it included 'any curtailment of a right to property'.[41] According to such an explanation, even a purely regulatory legal provision, which curtails the property right but does not constitute the acquisition or expropriation of property or a property right, is required to include compensation. Otherwise, this provision is invalid.

The second issue is the explanation of the word 'compensation'. The compensation in art. 31(2), although it was not defined by 'just' or a similar term, was explained by the Supreme Court as a just or full one. However, the legislature side argued that art. 31(2) left the determination of the principles, manner and amount of compensation to the legislature's discretion. The case of *The State of West Bengal* v. *Mrs. Bela Banerjee and Others*, which was decided in 1953,[42] is a benchmark ruling that illuminates the origin of this controversial issue and eventually resulted in the *Fourth Amendment*. The *Fourth Amendment* was used by the legislature to reject the Supreme Court's explanation of the two issues explained earlier.

In the *Banerjee* case, the *West Bengal Land Development and Planning Act 1948* (*1948 Act*), which stipulated that the amount of compensation not exceed the market value of the land on 31 December 1946, was judged by the Supreme Court to violate art. 31(2) and thus to be unconstitutional. The Attorney General, who represented the government, argued that 'compensation' as used in art. 31(2) did not imply a full and fair

40 *State of West Bengal* v. *Mrs Bella Benerjee*, 1954 SCR 558; *W. B.* v. *Subodh Gopal*, 1954 SCR 587; *State of Madras* v. *Namasivaya Mudaliar*, 1964 6 SCR 35.

41 See *Statement of Objects and Reasons Appended to the Constitution (Fourth Amendment) Bill* (1954). The text of this document is available at indiacode.nic.in/coiweb/amend/amend4.htm.

42 1954 SCR 558.

monetary equivalent and could be interpreted to mean 'what the legislature might think was a proper indemnity for the loss sustained by the owner'.[43] Furthermore, it was argued that art. 31(2) authorised the legislature full discretion in determining the scope of compensation. If 'compensation' in art. 31(2) was explained as a full equivalent compensation which can be used to limit the legislature's promulgation of the concerned law, it would render nugatory the legislature's constitutional authority to determine the principles and manner of compensation.[44]

The Supreme Court disagreed. It decided that although the legislature was granted the authority to determine the principles that concern the compensation amount, 'such principles must ensure that what is determined as payable must be compensation, that is, a just equivalent of what the owner has been deprived of'.[45] In essence, the Supreme Court's explanation limited the scope of the legislature's authority to determine compensation to satisfaction with the requirement of a just equivalent. The court went on to explain why the *1948 Act* at issue was inappropriate. This debatable act established a compensation ceiling that reflected the market value of land on a certain anterior date (31 December 1946), without considering the date when the land acquisition decision was made. Therefore, even if a parcel was acquired many years after this date, when the market value of land might be much higher because of the country's rapid industrialisation, the 1946 ceiling would still be used as the compensation standard. Thus, the Supreme Court ruled that 'the fixing of the market value on 31 December 1946, as the ceiling on compensation, without reference to the value of the land at the time of the acquisition is arbitrary and cannot be regarded as due compliance in letter and spirit with the requirement of art. 31 (2).'[46]

The legislature quickly responded to this decision. In 1954, the year after the *Banerjee* decision, the *Fourth Amendment* was proposed; and in 1955, this new amendment came into force. This amendment conferred on the legislature nearly complete discretion in determining compensation.

The amendment rejected the Supreme Court's position in its explanation of art. 31(1) and art. 31(2). It inserted art. 31(2)(A) into the constitution, which states: 'Where a law does not provide for the transfer of the ownership or right to possession of any property to the state or to a corporation owned or controlled by the state, it shall not be deemed to provide for the compulsory acquisition or requisitioning of property, notwithstanding that it deprives any person of his property.'

[43] Ibid., at 562. [44] Ibid. [45] Ibid., at 563. [46] Ibid., at 564.

Moreover, the amendment replaced the words 'taken possession of or acquired' in art. 31(2) with the terms 'compulsorily acquired or requisitioned'. This replacement phrase together with the language inserted into art. 31(2)(A) represents a clear classification of two types of property deprivation. One type is compulsory acquisition and requisition requiring the compensation defined by art. 31(2)(A) and governed by art. 31(2). The other type is the deprivation of a property right without the transfer of ownership or the right to possession to the state, which is governed only by art. 31(1), and which does not stipulate public purpose and the compensation requirement.[47] This revision's objective is to 'distinguish it (acquisition or requisition) from cases where the operation of regulatory or prohibitory laws of the state results in "deprivation of property"'.[48]

Another addition to art. 31(2) that was included in this amendment aimed at the overall exclusion of the judicial check on legislature's laws concerning compensation: 'no such law shall be called in question in any court on the ground that the compensation provided by that law is not adequate'.[49] By making the adequacy of compensation extrajudicial, this new provision sought to grant the legislature an arbitrary power to determine any standard or amount of compensation even if that standard or amount departed from the just equivalent of a property's market value. In fact, there was a division of opinions regarding this amendment. The government stated that the amendment was in accord with the Drafting Committee's intention. However, this statement was refuted by B.R. Ambedkar, who was a member of the upper house (*Rajya Sabha*) of parliament. Ambedkar said that this amendment was not drafted by the Committee.[50]

Without being blocked by the *Fourth Amendment*, the Supreme Court continues in its insistent efforts to protect the constitutional compensation limit because the word 'compensation' still existed in the constitution and judges could interpret it in the manner they considered to be appropriate. In the 1965 case *Vajravelu Mudaliar* v. *Special Deputy Collector*,

47 Rao, 'Property Rights'.

48 *See Statement of Objects and Reasons Appended to the Constitution (Fourth Amendment) Bill* (1954).

49 Ibid.

50 Ambedkear thought this amendment was so ugly that he did not like to look at. At that time, he also introduced three opinions on compensation to the congress. One supported the market value standard. The second proposed no compensation, and the third safeguarded the *zamindari*-abolition legislation. See Shourie, 'The Manu'.

Madras & ANR.,[51] the Supreme Court upheld its 'just equivalent' definition of compensation, which was previously argued in the 1954 *Banerjee* case.[52] The court did not believe that the continued adoption of this definition conflicted with the *Fourth Amendment*, which provides that the adequacy of compensation is not justiciable. To determine compensation, there may be several feasible modes or principles, each of which results in a different value or price. The court cannot stipulate that the law should have adopted one rather than another of these modes or principles 'for this would relate only to the question of adequacy'.[53] In the view of the Supreme Court, the legislature should not make arbitrary decisions regarding the calculation of compensation without any constitutional restraint. The principles or valuation methods stipulated by a law shall continue to aim at the just equivalent of property value, namely, just compensation as described by the Supreme Court. The Supreme Court does not question which among several reasonable approaches is most suitable to the achievement of the final end because the matter concerns the adequacy of compensation, which should not be questioned by the court according to the *Fourth Amendment*.

However, in the case of *State of Gujarat* v. *Shri Shantilal Mangaldas & ORS*, which was decided in 1969,[54] the Supreme Court ruled that according to the *Fourth Amendment*, '[the] compensation fixed or determined on principles specified by the Legislature cannot be permitted to be challenged on the somewhat indefinite plea that it is not a just or fair equivalent.'[55] However, this ruling does not mean that the court says nothing with respect to offering a constitutional guarantee of compensation. The principles of compensation established by laws can still be challenged on the ground that 'they are irrelevant to the determination of compensation'.[56]

In its decision regarding the 1970 case *Rustom Cavasjee Cooper* v. *Union of India* (the *Bank Nationalisation* case),[57] the Supreme Court strengthened its position that compensation was a basic guarantee of the constitution that provided a right to compensation to the expropriated owners – that is, 'an equivalent in money of the property compulsorily acquired'.[58] The court noted that '[t]he Constitution guarantees that the expropriated owner must be given the value of his property, i.e., what may be

[51] 1965 SCR (1) 614. [52] Ibid., at 625–6. [53] Ibid., at 627.
[54] *State of Gujarat* v. *Shri Shantilal Mangaldas & ORS*, 1969 (3) SCR 341.
[55] Ibid., at 365. [56] Ibid.
[57] *Rustom Cavasjee Cooper* v. *Union of India*, 1970 SCR (3) 530. [58] Ibid., at 607.

regarded reasonably as compensation for loss of the property and that such compensation should not be illusory and not reached by the application of irrelevant principles.'[59] The Supreme Court's attitude seemed to integrate different approaches in the two previously mentioned decisions. The Supreme Court ruled that the different lines of thought in the two cases finally 'converge in the ultimate result' and supported the view that the principles of compensation determination established by law shall be relevant to and appropriate in the determination of compensation.[60]

The Supreme Court's solid position in upholding the just equivalent standard and the strict judicial review of legislation upset the parliament and soon the *Twenty-Fifth Amendment* was enacted with an aim of removing the word 'compensation' from the constitution. This amendment replaced the word 'compensation' in art. 31(2) with 'amount'. 'Compensation' was omitted to remove '[the] difficulties placed in the way of giving effect to the Directive Principles of State Policy', which resulted from the judicial interpretation illustrated by the 1970 *Bank Nationalisation* case.[61]

Article 31 (together with art. 19(5)) was finally omitted by the *Forty-Fourth Amendment* in 1978. All constitutional restraints on expropriation were removed, and the compensation issue was placed fully within the scope of the legislature's discretion.

5.4.2 *Compensation package in legislation prior to 2014*

Prior to 2014, the *1894 LAA* (as amended) was the chief law among all of the central and local laws concerning expropriation. It provides 'the market value + others' package as compensation. Specifically, the compensation formula is as follows:[62]

$$\text{Market Value} + \text{Damages} + \text{Solatium} + \text{Interest}$$

There is no stipulation regarding the methods used to calculate market value in the *1894 LAA*. In the court's practice, the primary method used is 'comparable sale'. If this method is inapplicable, two methods (the 'capitalisation of income' and the 'expert assessment') can serve as

[59] Ibid., at 608. [60] Ibid., at 538.

[61] See *Statement of Objects and Reasons appended to the Constitution (Twenty-fifth Amendment) Bill* (1971), available at indiacode.nic.in/coiweb/amend/amend25.htm.

[62] The ADB report separates moving expenses from damages and lists them independently. See ADB, 'Compensation and Valuation', 37.

supplementary alternatives.[63] Sec. 24 of the *1894 LAA* requires that the following matters should be considered when determining market value: (1) the degree of urgency which has led to the acquisition; (2) any disinclination of the person interested to part with the land acquired; (3) any damage sustained by him which, if caused by a private person, would not render such person liable to a suit; (4) any damage which is likely to be caused to the acquired land, after the date of the publication of the declaration (under sec. 6); (5) any increase to the value of the land acquired likely to accrue from the use to which it will be put when acquired; (6) any increase to the value of the other land of the person interested likely to accrue from the use to which the land acquired will be put; (7) any outlay or improvements made to the land acquired without the sanction of the Collector after the publication under sec. 4(1);[64] and (8) any increase to the value of the land on account of its being put to any use which is against law or public policy.

The damages incurred by acquisition include the following: (1) loss of standing crops and trees; (2) the owners' damage by reason of serving the acquired land to his other land; (3) the loss arisen from the acquisition's affection of other property or his earnings; (4) the reasonable expenses incidental to the place change; and (5) the diminution of the profits of the land between the time of the publication of the declaration (under sec. 6)and the time of the Collector's taking possession of the land.[65]

Considering the compulsory nature of such acquisition or the involuntary nature of owner relocation, a solatium is provided.[66] The amount of the solatium is a certain percentage (the solatium rate) of the computed market value. After the 1984 amendment to the *1894 LAA*, the solatium rate was increased from 15 per cent to 30 per cent.[67] The solatium can be deemed the compensation to the person who is injured in emotion or convenience by involuntary acquisition. The introduction of solatium enlarges the scope of compensation from exchange value to user value. The solatium does not appear in all legislation concerning acquisition. For

[63] Ibid., at 39–42.

[64] The Collector refers to the Collector of a district, and includes a Deputy Commissioner and any officer specially appointed by the appropriate Government to perform the functions of a Collector. See *1894 LAA*, sec. 3(c).

[65] Ibid., sec. 23(1). [66] Ibid., sec. 23(2).

[67] Sec. 23(2) provides that: 'In addition to the market value of the land as above provided, the Court shall in every case award a sum of [thirty per centum] on such market value, in consideration of the compulsory nature of the acquisition.' Ibid.

example, the *National Highway Act* (*NHA*) does not include the provision of solatium.[68]

'Interest' refers to the amount determined by the court, which is calculated at a rate of 12 per cent per annum on the market value of the acquired land for a period between the date of the publication of the notification (under sec. 4(1)) and the date of the award by the Collector or the date of taking possession of the acquired land, whichever is earlier. In addition, if the court awards an amount that exceeds the amount determined by the Collector, the concerned person shall be paid the interest on such excess at a rate of 9 per cent per annum from the date on which the Collector took possession of the land to the date of payment of such excess into Court.[69]

The compensation package stipulated by the *1894 LAA* is the world's foremost in its expansiveness and comprehensiveness. The package includes consideration for property loss and damages or injury to the person interested. In addition to compensation for the expressly listed damages, a fixed rate solatium is awarded as compensation for the emotional distress incurred by involuntary relocation. The scope of damages is described by the ADB as 'more generous' than counterpart provisions in most developing and developed countries.[70] However, the impressiveness of the *1894 LAA*'s legislative stipulations does not naturally result in the conclusion that the compensation is unquestionably sufficient in practice. In India, the compensation for land acquisition was often criticised as insufficient. The market value calculated based on market information is often lower than the actual market price. One reason for this difference is that the sale price is often understated to avoid the high rate of transaction taxation.[71] Another reason is that government officers in charge tend to decide compensation conservatively because they are afraid of being investigated by anti-corruption agency if they decide a high number of

[68] However, in practice, a solatium is included in the compensation pack for an acquisition that occurs under the *NHA*. This practice is explained as occurring 'out of "habit" from applying the *LAA*'s compensation provisions.' See ADB, 'Compensation and Valuation', 37, 39.

[69] *1894 LAA*, sec. 28.

[70] ADB, 'Compensation and Valuation', 38.

[71] Ibid., 39. In India, the transaction taxation is known as stamp duty, the rate of which varies across states in a range from 10 per cent to 14.5 per cent. The stamp duty is 13 per cent in Delhi, 14.5 per cent in Uttar Pradesh and 12.5 per cent in Haryana. In addition, income taxation, heavy rates of municipal taxes on usable property, regulations and rent controls on land and used property also result in distortion. See Morris and Pandey, 'Towards Reform', 2084.

compensation to land owners.[72] Moreover, the ADB has noted critically one important problem that contributes to insufficient market value: the increased value of the acquired land caused by development projects is not considered in the compensation. The compensation for damages was often not fulfilled in practice because of the affected individuals were unaware of their legal rights. The interest required by the *1894 LAA* was not always paid.[73]

5.5 China

5.5.1 'Compensation' in the constitutions

Before the *2004 Amendment*, there had been no constitutionally required compensation. The *1954 Constitution of China* provided a public interest requirement but no compensation. The 1975 and 1978 constitutions eliminated the public interest requirement and compensation for expropriation. The *1982 Constitution of China* enacted during the early period of China's opening and reform years resumed the *1954 Constitution of China*'s public interest requirement but did not include compensation until the *2004 Amendment*. In 2004, through the amendment, the compensation requirement was incorporated into the *1982 Constitution of China*.

With respect to the governance years of the *1982 Constitution of China*, the acceptance of compensation test occurred twenty-two years later than the acceptance of the public interest requirement. Was this delay an intentional arrangement or an unintentional omission? Consider the background of the era when the constitution was drafted in 1982. At that time, only three years had passed since the declaration of China's openness and reform policy. Socialist and public property systems remained dominant in the nation's political system. During the early years, the reform was of experimental nature and occurred step by step, or gradually. From early 1980s until today, the gradually increasing reform related to the economy and the property system has been accompanied by the gradually strengthened protection of private property. In the earliest version of the *1982 Constitution of China*, the individual's economy was defined only as

[72] Mahalingam and Vyas, 'Comparative Evaluation', 101.
[73] ADB, 'Compensation and Valuation', 38.

supplementary to the public economy.[74] Correspondingly, the protection offered to individual property or private property by the constitution was limited. If public interest and compensation could not be included in the constitution at the same time but had to be incorporated in a sequential order, which came first and which followed? In 1982, the result was that only public interest was entrenched in the constitution in the form of the limit on land expropriation.

First, compared with the doctrine of public interest, compensation can offer more substantial protection to property holders in China. The scope of public interest can be interpreted so large that it imposes very few limits on expropriation. In a developing country like China, public interest can be interpreted to include a substantial number of projects, which may be publicly or privately developed. That is, a loose interpretation of public interest can enable the government to easily avoid the constitutional limit. However, compensation involves a highly quantified requirement, which is less easily avoided if its standard or test is stipulated clearly.

Second, compensation means substantial payment which is used to cover the losses of property or property right owners. In the early years of reform, when the shortage of capital was a significant problem, the incorporation of compensation into the constitution could have been a cause for concern that the constitutional requirement for compensation would be too strict and hinder the pace of national modernisation because the high compensation would increase the government's expropriation cost.

Third, compared with public interest, the compensation requirement reflects more respect for individualism and private property. Public interest is used as a premise for the compulsory relinquishment of private property. Although public interest can function as a limit on the governmental power to expropriate, it has strong implication of social obligation for property-owning individuals. In fact, as a remedy required to be paid to the expropriated individual, compensation reflects the spirit of respecting individual or private ownership rights. In the early years around 1982, socialism with features of public property and a planned economy continued to dominate mainstream ideology in society. Although the individual economy and the corresponding private property or property right were

[74] In his report submitted to the NPC, Peng Zhen, then the deputy director of Committee on the Revision of Constitution, stated that: 'Individual economy occupies only a small part of the whole national economy. Its existence hinders neither the status of the Socialist public property system as the foundation of our country's economic system nor the development of the public property system.' See Peng, 'Guanyu Zhonghua'.

allowed to a small extent at that time, the drafters of the *1982 Constitution of China* were reluctant to adding more limits, such as compensation, which expressly supports individualism and private property. Obviously, public interest is more compatible with socialism and public property than compensation because it implies that individual rights shall be subordinate to the public interest or, in more expansive political interpretation, the national interest or state interest.[75]

During the early 1980s, the limited protection of private property in the *1982 Constitution of China* corresponded to the limited scope of the individual economy and the limited recognition of private property. In addition to the absence of compensation, the limited protection of private property was also reflected by the limited scope of private property. The term 'private property' was only used to refer to the right to inherit and was not used to refer to all of the property and rights held by individuals. The protection was aimed at the citizen's ownership of property. However, 'ownership' is too limited to include all of the rights connected with property.

The later 1988, 1993 and 1999 amendments did not include the compensation requirement. After the *1993 Amendment*, scholars started to call on legislators to consider the incorporation of compensation into the constitution.[76] The constitutional incorporation of compensation did not arrive until the status of the private economy was raised to a sufficiently high status. In the *1988 Amendment*, the private economy was constitutionally recognised. The term 'private economy' is distinguished from 'individual economy' primarily by the use of employees. 'Individual economy' refers to an individual or household operation with primarily self-labour and a limited number of employees, who are defined as 'helpers'. However, the private economy expands to include operations using employed staff. For a long time, 'eight employees' had been used as the standard in distinguishing an individual economy from a private economy.[77] If the number of employees is more than eight, the business operation was called private economy.[78] Compared with an individual

[75] In his report, Peng Zhen stated: 'China is a Socialist country. The national and social interest is fundamentally consistent with individual interest.' Ibid.

[76] Wang, 'Xinzhongguo Xianfa'.

[77] Gan, 'Xinzhongguo Xianfa', 152.

[78] The individual businesses reflecting individual economy are called 'individual industrial and commercial household' (*geti gongshanghu*) and the private businesses for private economy are called 'privately run enterprises' (*siying qiye*) which are defined as the enterprises owned privately and with more than eight employees. See Young, 'Wealth but not Security', 116.

economy, a private economy was described by socialist scholars as an economy in which there are more possibilities to exploit others because of the existence of employment. Thus, the term 'private economy' was entrenched in the constitution later than the term 'individual economy'. Another significance of this distinction is that the private economy with employment demands more productive materials, for example, land or land rights. In the earliest version of the *1982 Constitution of China*, only the individual economy was incorporated, and correspondingly, the individual's property right was primarily limited to necessities for living. The recognition of the private economy established the foundation for the enlargement of private property's scope in the later constitutional amendments. In the *1993 Amendment*, the term 'market economy' was used in place of 'planned economy'. In the *1999 Amendment*, non-public economy, including the private and the individual economy, was raised to the status of 'important component'. Finally, based on more recent efforts to raise the non-public economy's constitutional status and in response to the increasing number of requests by individuals for property protection, the limited protection of property in the *1982 Constitution of China* was finally amended to encompass a more comprehensive framework.[79] In the *2004 Amendment*, the term 'private property' was used to include productive means and living necessities and both ownership and non-owner rights.[80] The most obvious improvement, which implies a change in the original subordinate status of private property, is the incorporation of a compensation requirement. However, in this amendment, 'compensation' is not defined and a clarifying adjective, such as 'just' or 'adequate', does not accompany the word 'compensation'. This compensation requirement is a symbol that clearly reflects the status of private property in the constitution, which has been raised higher than before but remains a work in progress with respect to the final objective of just and full protection.

In precise language, the term 'market economy' added to the *1982 Constitution of China* in 1993 refers to a socialist market economy. When the amendment was introduced in 2004, the property system was still dominated by public property. Although the status of the non-public economy was raised to that of an important economic factor, it remained

[79] Wang, 'Guanyu Zhonghua'.

[80] According to Wang Zhaoguo, then the vice chairman of the NPCSC, the use of the term 'private property' can make the object of constitutional protection include productive means and living necessities. In addition, the term 'property right' is defined more accurately and comprehensively than the original 'ownership'. Ibid.

less important than the public economy. Correspondingly, the improvement of property clauses could not raise the level of private property protection to full protection or the level enjoyed by public property. This impossibility is reflected by two aspects of the amendment. One is the unequal description of inviolability in relation to different properties. Public property is stipulated as 'sacred and inviolable'. However, private property is only 'inviolable' not 'sacred'. The other aspect is the omission of 'just' or 'full' before the word 'compensation'. Full compensation implies that individual interest should be treated as not less important than public interest. The absence of 'full' or 'just' before 'compensation' seems to place individual property or interest on a level that is subordinate to the public, social or national interests. Thus, a compensation less than the full value of the expropriated property is allowed by this undefined compensation requirement.

The undefined compensation requirement leaves to the legislature substantial flexibility in stipulating the exact compensation standards or principles. In fact, various stipulations concerning compensation were present in legal documents prior to 2004. Thus, no revision is required to make such documents consistent with the undefined constitutional compensation requirement until the uniform definition or explanation of a constitutional compensation requirement is provided.

5.5.2 'Compensation' in the laws

5.5.2.1 Compensation in land expropriation

The earliest stipulation concerning compensation appeared in the 1950 *Regulation on Reforming Suburban Land* (*1950 RRSL*) after the foundation of the New China.[81] Article 14 of this regulation stipulated that for expropriated farmland, the compensation shall be an 'appropriate price' or 'the exchange with the same amount of nationally owned land'. This article also stipulated the resettlement of farmers who lost land and the 'fair and reasonable' compensation of the loss that considered the owner's investment in the land and other loss.[82] There is no definition or explanation of 'appropriate price' in the regulation.

81 *Chengshi Jiaoqu Tudi Gaige Tiaoli* [*Regulation on Reforming Suburban Land*], promulgated by the State Council (*zhengwu yuan*) on 21 November 1950. Its Chinese text is available at news.xinhuanet.com/ziliao/2004–12/13/content_2328565.htm.

82 Ibid., art. 13.

The *1953 Construction Measures* categorised the farmers affected by land expropriation in two groups. Expropriated farmland owners shall be paid 'a compensation fee for the requisitioned land' or offered some substitutable land.[83] In addition, compensation shall be paid to cover the loss of properties attached to the requisitioned land and the loss of crops. The compensation fee for the expropriated land equals the gross production results for the most recent 3 to 5 years. The compensation for the attached properties shall be 'fair and reasonable'.[84] If the compensation is the supply of a parcel of substitutable land (exchange of estate), the fee used to assist the displaced farmer's removal shall be paid. For farmers who cultivate state-owned land, the compensation shall be an appropriate subsidy based on the consideration of 'the living conditions of such farmers'.[85] Moreover, the measure provides the resettlement of the farmers who have lost land, which primarily takes the form of an offer of new employment.[86]

For the expropriation of urban land, compensation was decided according to the fair and reasonable price of the houses and other properties attached to the expropriated land. Generally, the compensation was paid for the affected house. However, the loss of the land underneath such a house was not compensated. Nevertheless, if such land was owned by another person than the owner of the expropriated house, the owner of the concerned land was compensated according to his or her living conditions.[87]

In the version revised in 1958 (*1958 Construction Measures*), the standard of compensation was reduced from the gross production results of 3 to 5 years to the gross production results of the last 2 to 4 years. What is most noticeable concerning compensation is the addition of a new article (art. 9), which concerns the no-compensation situation. According to this article, when a parcel of collectively owned land is requisitioned, there is no need to offer compensation if the meeting of the collective's members or their representatives determines that the concerned land requisition does not affect the lives of the collective's members.[88] Generally, this revision that appeared in the *1958 Construction Measures* substantially decreases the compensation available to farmers who have lost land stipulated by the *1953 Construction Measures*.

The decrease in compensation in the *1958 Construction Measures* can be linked to a change in the social background. In 1953, farmland was

[83] *1953 Construction Measures*, art. 8. [84] Ibid.
[85] Ibid., art. 9. [86] Ibid., art. 13. [87] Ibid., art. 17. [88] Ibid., art. 9.

primarily owned by farmers. After several years of socialist reconstruction, nearly all farmland was unified and owned by collective organisations until 1958. Thus, in the *1958 Construction Measures*, the compensation for the requisitioned land was stipulated to be provided to collectives rather than farmers. Because the living situation of farmers had improved substantially after the introduction of agricultural cooperatives, the original compensation standards in the *1953 Construction Measures* were thought to be relatively high.[89] Thus, the revision that decreased compensation linked the compensation with the living standard of farmers rather than the value of the expropriated land or land rights. The reason for the stipulation of no compensation was individuals were increasingly expressing their support for national reconstruction and voluntarily relinquished their rights to compensation.[90]

In the *1982 Construction Regulation*, the compensation package that covers the expropriated farmland includes compensation for the concerned land, a resettlement fee, compensation for properties attached to the land and compensation for the growing crops. This regulation set the standard for calculating the compensation and resettlement fees for arable land (including vegetable-growing land). The establishment of the exact standards of the compensation and resettlement fees for non-arable farmland is left to the provincial governments. The compensation standard for arable land is 3 to 6 times the average annual land output. Regarding the resettlement fee, the standard is 2 to 3 times the average annual output per capita with a cap of 10 times the average annual output per *mu* (10-times ceiling). If the compensation that is calculated based on these standards cannot maintain the original production and living standards of the affected individuals, on the approval of the provincial government, the resettlement fee can be increased within an upper limit, which is that the total compensation and resettlement fee shall not exceed a number that is 20 times the average annual output of the expropriated land (20-times ceiling).[91] In addition, this regulation stipulates that the relevant unit is responsible for organising and assisting in the resettlement.[92]

Compared with the *1958 Construction Measures*, the compensation standard of the *1982 Construction Regulation* was significantly

[89] This explanation was given by Tao Xijin, then the Deputy Secretary-general of the State Council. See Tao, 'Guanyu Guojia'.

[90] Ibid. [91] *1982 Construction Regulation*, arts. 9–10. [92] Ibid., art. 12.

higher. In addition to the raising of compensation standard for land, a resettlement fee was added to the compensation package. The no-compensation stipulations in the *1958 Construction Measures* were removed.

In 1986, the *LAL* was enacted. Its stipulations concerning compensation, arts. 28 and 29, were borrowed from the *1982 Construction Regulation.*

In the 1998 amendment to the *LAL*, the compensation package was substantially increased. In art. 47, the compensation standard for land was increased from '3 to 6 times' to '6 to 10 times', and the resettlement fee standard was increased from '2 to 3 times' to '4 to 6 times'. The basis of calculation remained the average annual output of the expropriated land within the most recent three years. The 10-times ceiling of the resettlement fee was increased to 15 times, and the 20-times ceiling of the total compensation was raised to 30 times.

For land expropriated for the purpose of constructing large- and medium-scale water conservancy and hydropower projects, a specific regulation was applied. In 1991,[93] the compensation standard for such projects was 3 to 4 times the average annual output, and the resettlement fee was 2 to 3 times the annual output per capita. However, if the expropriation of land was for the construction of large-scale flood-control, irrigation or drainage projects, the compensation standard could be decreased.[94] Thus, the compensation and resettlement standard under this regulation is less than the counterpart standard under the *LAL*. Although the 1998 amendment to the *LAL* increased the compensation and resettlement standard, this regulation was not revised until 2006, when the standard of the compensation and resettlement package was changed to '16 times the average annual output', which is stipulated by art. 22 of the new regulation.[95]

[93] *Dazhongxing Shuili Shuidian Gongcheng Jianshe Zhengdi Buchang he Yimin Anzhi Tiaoli* [*Regulation on Compensation for Land Expropriation and Migrant Resettlement Concerning Large- and Medium-Scale Water Conservancy and Hydropower Projects*], promulgated by the State Council on 15 February 1991. The Chinese text is available at www.law110.com/law/guowuyuan/2123.htm.

[94] Ibid., art. 5.

[95] *Dazhongxing Shuili Shuidian Gongcheng Jianshe Zhengdi Buchang he Yimin Anzhi Tiaoli* [*Regulation on Compensation for Land Expropriation and Migrant Resettlement Concerning Large- and Medium-Scale Water Conservancy and Hydropower Projects*], promulgated by the State Council on 7 July 2006. The Chinese text is available at www.gov.cn/flfg/2006–08/13/content_367585.htm.

5.5.2.2 Compensation for expropriated houses

The *1991 Demolition Regulation* stipulates compensation for expropriated urban houses and their attachments. This regulation stipulates that the houses that are demolished shall be compensated, and, the cost of temporary building within the approved period shall be offset with 'appropriate compensation'.[96] The regulation implies that the compensation provided to the owner of a permanent house shall be more than the appropriate compensation provided to the owner of a temporary building.

There are three compensation forms: the exchange of estate, monetary compensation and the combination of the first two forms, or mixed compensation. In monetary compensation, the calculation standard is the replacement price, which is based on the building cost of a house.[97] In the exchange of estate, the price discrepancy between the substitute house and the demolished house is decided by the provincial government.[98] Regarding the compensation for the attachments of the concerned house, this compensation should be 'appropriate'.[99] If the expropriated house is not for residential use, the economic loss that arises from the suspension of manufacture and operation caused by the expropriation should be covered by 'appropriate compensation'.[100]

In addition, this regulation offered compensation to the users of the expropriated house. They shall be offered houses for accommodation in the resettlement or transitional period. If the users arrange for their residence by themselves, a fee for temporary resettlement shall be offered. In addition, compensation for the relocation shall be paid.

This regulation has many defects in arranging for compensation and resettlement. First, it uses the replacement price as a standard to calculate monetary compensation and to determine the price difference between the exchanged estates. The replacement price is based on the construction and decoration cost, which is lower than the market price of the expropriated house. Second, according to their use purposes, the houses are categorised and the owners receive discriminative treatment in compensation. If the concerned house is for non-public-interest use, which is generally the status of an individual residence, the compensation for the house's attachments is only appropriate compensation, which is often less than the real value of the attachments or less than their replacement cost. However, for houses originally for public-interest use, the houses

[96] *1991 Demolition Regulation*, art. 19. [97] Ibid., art. 20.
[98] Ibid., art. 23. [99] Ibid., art. 21. [100] Ibid., art. 34.

and their attachments received compensation based on replacement price. Third, 'appropriate compensation' for the suspension of manufacture and business operation might be insufficient. Fourth, there is no stipulation regarding the time based on which the replacement price is calculated. Another defect is that the compensation is not paid by the government but by the unit in charge of demolition and removal, which is usually a construction unit or the developer of the relevant project.[101] As noted in the previous chapter on public interest, there was no public interest requirement regarding the expropriation of urban houses before 2011. The expropriation could be made for either public or private purposes. Even if the expropriation was for public purpose, the construction of the concerned project on the original site of the expropriated house was authorised to be managed by a construction unit or the developer. After receiving the government's demolition and removal approval, the construction units or developer were in charge of compensation payment and the execution of removal. This approach was widely criticised because the compensation should have been paid and the removal performed by the relevant government authorities.

In 2001, the 1991 regulation was revised for the 2001 version (*2001 Demolition Regulation*). The stipulations regarding compensation were revised to correct certain defects, primarily including the three defects described in the previous paragraph. The replacement price standard was replaced with a new standard, which is known as the market evaluation price. The amount of cash compensation and the price discrepancy with respect to the exchange of estates shall be determined based on the evaluation price, which is calculated in consideration of the location, use purpose, space size and other factors of the expropriated house.[102] This revision represents substantial progress towards basing the calculation of compensation on the market value standard. However, the approach is still not a fair test of market value. The appropriate compensation for the attachments of an expropriated house with non-public-interest use was changed to cash compensation. This method implies that the compensation for such attachments shall be based on market price rather than an appropriate amount, which may be much lower than the market value.[103] The owners of houses can request a relocation fee and resettlement remedy fee according to this revised regulation.[104]

[101] Ibid., arts. 3, 19. [102] *2001 Demolition Regulation*, art. 24.
[103] Ibid., art. 25. [104] Ibid., art. 31.

On 19 January 2011, the new *2011 Expropriation Regulation* was enacted to replace the *2001 Demolition Regulation*. The new regulation was revised to respond to the 2004 constitutional amendment. In the new regulation's title, the term 'demolition and removal' of the old regulations was discarded. The new title uses the term 'expropriation and compensation', which is consistent with the constitutional description. Regarding the public interest requirement, the new regulation defines public interest and omits the expropriation for a non-public interest, which was included in the 1991 and 2001 regulations. Moreover, some significant improvements were made with respect to compensation. One highly progressive revision was to stipulate the government as the payer of compensation.[105] The compensation standard for the value of the expropriated house is expressed as being 'not lower than the comparable market price of the house at the time when the expropriation is publicly announced'.[106] The time of valuation is clarified, and this stipulation clearly adopts the comparable market price as the valuation method. In addition to the value of the house, in the new regulation, the scope of compensation covers the relocation cost, temporary resettlement and the loss for the suspension of manufacture and business operation, which were also covered by the 2001 regulation. However, improvements were made. The appropriate compensation standard for the suspension of manufacture and operation was omitted. The new stipulation concerning the compensation for the suspension includes the consideration of the revenue before the expropriation, the length of the suspension period and other relevant factors.[107] Such factors are directly linked to the actual loss caused by the suspension.

5.5.3 *Disparate treatment between the two expropriations*

The compensation for expropriated land (rural property) substantially differs from compensation for expropriated houses (urban property). The basic method used to determine compensation for farmland was the capitalisation of income. However, for expropriated houses, the basic test for compensation evolved from the replacement price, to the evaluation price and then to the current comparable market price. Like the evolution of public interest doctrine, the reform of the compensation standard for expropriated farmland lags far behind the reform concerning the

[105] Ibid., art. 17. [106] Ibid., art. 19. [107] *2011 Expropriation Regulation*, art. 23.

expropriation of urban houses. There are two reasons for this reform gap between farmland and urban house expropriation.

5.5.3.1 First reason: the practicality of the valuation method

The first reason for the reform gap concerns the practicality of the valuation method. One premise for the use of the market value method is that there is a mature exchange market that can offer transaction information sufficient to serve as the basis of price valuation. For urban houses, a mature transaction market has been established; however, an effective transaction market for farmland and its land rights is lacking.

The development of the market for urban houses commenced in 1990, when the land use right was allowed to be transferred using a legal document titled '*Provisional Regulation on Land Use Right Conveyance and Transfer in Municipalities and Towns*', which was enacted by the State Council. According to chapters 2 and 3 of this regulation, the use right of the state-owned urban land can be separated from its ownership and offered to some unit or to individual users. The land use right in the hands of units and individuals can be transferred in the market. Thus, there are three levels of market for land use rights and the ownership of houses or buildings. The first level market is between local governments and the units or individuals in need of land for construction. In this level of market, construction units or companies can acquire the land use rights that are offered by government. The second level of market is for the transfer of land use rights among units or individuals, and in this market, the privately owned land use rights can be exchanged. After construction, the constructed buildings or houses can be transferred in the third level of the market.

In 1991, when the *Demolition Regulation* was enacted, the transaction market for land use rights and constructed buildings (houses) remained in an embryonic stage and could not offer comparable sale information sufficient for calculating the market value of the expropriated houses. Thus, in the 1991 regulation, a replacement price that used the construction cost as the calculation basis was employed as a substitute for the comparable market method. In 2001, when the relevant market had been developed for more than ten years, the *2001 Demolition Regulation* used the evaluation price to substitute replacement price. 'Evaluation' was defined by the Ministry of Construction as the market price of the expropriated house in art. 3 of a document titled '*Guidance Opinions on the Valuation of the Demolished and Removed Urban House*', which was promulgated in 2003.[108] However, the evaluation price is not the same as the market value test.

In practice, three elements are used as references when the market price of the expropriated houses is determined: the transaction price of a comparable house, the market price promulgated by local governments and the circumstances of the demolished house.[109] In fact, this three-element valuation method can result in a final compensation price that is lower than the market value of the expropriated house. The reason is that the latter two elements were often used to establish a price that is much lower than the actual market price of the expropriated house. In practice, the price promulgated by local governments was most often used as the basis of valuation. To take Shanxi Province as an example, the authorised appraiser is required to use the guidance price promulgated by government as the basis of determining the evaluation price.[110] In Zhejiang Province, the baseline price promulgated by government was required to be used as the calculation basis with the consideration of other elements, such as the direction in which the house faces, the location and the replacement price.[111] Generally, a local government's reference or guidance price was established and promulgated once annually.[112] Thus, such a price cannot reflect the real market value of a house. First, it is not a current or instant market price because it is established once per year. Considering the rapid development of the real-estate market in China, the market price of houses might vary over a wide range within several months. Second, the urban area is divided into parts whose valuations are based on different reference prices. All of the houses located within the same division enjoy the same or a similar reference price. This coarse

[108] *Chengshi Fangwu Chaiqian Gujia Zhidao Yijian* [*Guidance Opinions on the Valuation of the Demolished and Removed Urban House*], enacted by the Ministry of Construction on 1 December 2003. The Chinese text is available at www.gov.cn/gongbao/content/2004/content_62911.htm.

[109] Ibid., art. 14.

[110] See art. 11 of *Shanxisheng Chengshi Fangwu Chaiqian Jiage Pinggu Banfa* [*Shanxi Province Measures on the Valuation of the Demolished and Removed Urban House*], which was promulgated by Shanxi Provincial Government on 11 December 2004. The Chinese text of this document is available atsn.mof.gov.cn/lanmudaohang/zhengcefagui/200805/t20080524_41017.html.

[111] See arts. 9 and 10 of *Zhejiangsheng Chengshi Fangwu Chaiqian Jiage Pinggu Zanxing Banfa* [*Zhejiang Province Provisional Measures on the Valuation of the Demolished and Removed Urban House*], which was promulgated by Zhejiang Provincial Construction Department on 28 June 2002. The Chinese text is available at www.hangzhou.com.cn/20040101/ca552313.htm.

[112] Ibid., arts. 4, 8.

division of prices conceals the price differences among houses located within the same section. Third, local governments, which are motivated to increase their local fiscal interest through expropriation, tend to establish reference prices that are significantly lower than market value.

The unfair or insufficient compensation that results from the use of the governmental reference price has encountered increasingly greater resistance in many locations. Particularly after the *2004 Amendment*, the demand for sufficient compensation calculated according to real market value became increasingly stronger. Although this amendment does not define compensation and it remains the discretion of the legislature or the government to provide a detailed explanation of the compensation standard, there have been strong statements from citizens that the compensation paid to property owners should be based on normal, popularly accepted compensation that reflects the constitutional value – that is, compensation based on market value. The adoption of the *2004 Amendment* can be described as fomenting the request for much stronger protection of property in society primarily through the inclusion of the public interest limit on the scope of expropriation and the compensation paid to the expropriated.

The request that the 2001 regulation be revised and made consistent with the new constitutional amendment was finally responded to in early 2010, when a draft of a new regulation was publicly promulgated and opinions were invited. A short time later, the *2011 Expropriation Regulation* was enacted.

In the 2011 regulation, the compensation standard is clearly defined as the comparable market price: the 'market price of the comparable house'.[113] The latter two elements used to adjust the market price in the old, three-element combination were eliminated. The currently enforceable valuation standard is purely a market value test. In the *Measures on the Valuation of the Expropriated House on State-owned Land*, which provides detailed rules on the valuation of expropriated houses for appraisers, art. 13 requires that the comparable transaction method should be used for valuation if the transaction record of comparable houses is available.[114]

113 *2011 Expropriation Regulation*, art. 19.

114 *Guoyou Tudi shang Fangwu Zhengshou Pinggu Banfa* [*Measures on the Valuation of the Expropriated House on State-owned Land*], promulgated by Ministry of Housing and Urban-rural Development on 3 June 2011. The Chinese text is available at www.gov.cn/zwgk/2011–06/07/content_1878698.htm.

The market for rural land remains underdeveloped although this market has evolved with the progress of the reform of rural land rights. Individual farmers were immediately awarded the ownership of rural land through a revolutionary land reform after the foundation of New China. However, this individual ownership officially ended in 1956, when the *Model Chart for Advanced Cooperatives of Agricultural Production* was enacted by the NPC.[115] Article 13 of this charter required the farmers to transfer their productive means, including land, to cooperatives for collective ownership. The 1975, 1978 and 1982 constitutions stipulate the collective ownership of rural land. After the reform and openness policy was introduced, land use rights were separated from collective ownership and awarded to farming households through land contracting. The period of land contracting or land tenure was determined to be at least fifteen years by the CPC Central Committee's *No. 1 Central Committee Document* in 1984. Rural land was prohibited from being sold, rented and changed to non-agriculture use by this document. Land use rights were permitted to be transferred to other households for cultivation under exceptional circumstance and on the collective (contractor)'s approval. In essence, the transfer of land use rights was highly restricted at that time. In 1986, the double system that consisted of collective ownership and the household use right was written into the *LAL*. In 1993, the contract period of land use rights was prolonged to thirty years (for arable land) by the CPC Central Committee and the State Council.[116] Additionally, this document stipulates that land use rights can be transferred under two preconditions: the maintenance of the land's original use and the agreement of the contract issuer. At that time, the collective organisations had substantial authority to intervene in the contracted land use rights. The approval had to be available from the collective organisation before the contracted land was transferred. In addition, the contractor or transferor often violated the contract and reacquired or altered the contracted land without the agreement of the contractee or transferee. To maintain the stability of the contracted land use rights within their contract period and protect

[115] *Gaoji Nongye Shengchan Hezuoshe Shifan Zhangcheng* [*Model Chart for Advanced Cooperatives of Agricultural Production*], enacted by the Third Session of the First NPC on 30 June 1956. The Chinese text is available at www.npc.gov.cn/wxzl/wxzl/2000–12/10/content_4304.htm.

[116] *Guanyu Dangqian Nongye he Nongcunjingji Fazhan de Ruogan Zhengce Cuoshi* [*Several Policy Measures about Current Agriculture and Rural Economic Development*], promulgated by the CPC Central Committee and the State Council on 5 January 1993. The Chinese text is available at www.chinalawedu.com/falvfagui/fg22016/12025.shtml.

the interest of farmers from being infringed by collectives, the CPC issued a document in 2001 to prohibit any contractor from interfering with the households' contracted rights by reacquisition, alteration or in other ways.[117] In 2002, the *RLCL* was enacted to systemise the regulation and protection of the use rights of rural land. The contract period of arable land is thirty years. For grassland, the contract period is twenty to fifty years. For woodland, it is thirty to seventy years.[118] The autonomous control of the rights holders of their contracted land was strengthened by this law by prohibiting the collectives, as the contractors, from reclaiming or altering the contracted land. Land use rights were allowed to be transferred through (for example) subcontracting, leasing, exchange and transfer.[119] The contractor's agreement as the premise for transaction was removed by the *RLCL*. However, the transaction was not allowed to change the original agricultural use and the collective ownership of the concerned land.[120]

In 2007, the *Property Law* listed the contracted land right as a type of property use and interest right. This law finally separates the right to use rural land from the land's ownership and makes the rural land use right an independent property right.[121]

The transfer of the contracted land right was allowed in 1993. However, the relevant transaction market remained underdeveloped because of the strict restrictions on transactions imposed by the collective organisations until 2002, when the *RLCL* was enacted. Although the *RLCL* and the *Property Law* clarify the contracted right as an independent property right, transfers did not occur because of the lack of detailed practicable stipulations. In 2005, the Ministry of Agriculture promulgated a document titled '*Measures on Managing the Circulation of the Use Right of the Contracted Rural Land*' to regulate and facilitate the market transactions in connection with contracted land rights.[122] In addition, in recent years, experimental reform measures have been introduced by local governments to facilitate rural land transactions. For example, the Chongqing

[117] *Guanyu Zuohao Nonghu Chengbaodi Shiyongquan Liuzhuan Gongzuo de Tongzhi* [*Notice on Improving the Work Concerning the Transfer of Contracted Rural Land*], enacted by the CPC Central Committee on 30 December 2001. The Chinese text is available at www.qzwb.com/gb/content/2002–11/05/content_655171.htm.

[118] *RLCL*, art. 20. [119] Ibid., art. 32. [120] Ibid., art. 33. [121] *Property Law*, chap. 11.

[122] *Nongcun Tudi Chengbao Jingyingquan Liuzhuan Guanli Banfa* [*Measures on Managing the Circulation of the Use Right of the Contracted Rural Land*], promulgated by the Ministry of Agriculture on 19 January 2005. The Chinese text is available at www.moa.gov.cn/govpublic/NCJJTZ/201006/t20100606_1532776.htm.

government promulgated the *Chongqing Provisional Measures on the Management of Rural Land Exchanges*, which officially inaugurated rural land exchanges on 1 December 2008.[123] On 4 December, the first rural land exchange in China was established to offer a physical market for rural land transaction.

Compared with the market for urban land and houses, today's rural land market is significantly underdeveloped. Transactions that involve contracted land rights are primarily conducted through mutually agreed contracts between individuals. The lack of physical trading location and a central registration system makes it difficult to collect transaction information. The transaction volume is insufficient to provide the needed comparable references that are necessary to determine the value of land or land rights expropriated by the government. According to the Development Research Centre of the State Council, the percentage of the transacted arable land among total arable land was still low in 2007. Among the nine provinces that were investigated, Zhejiang has the highest percentage: 19.8 per cent. In the other provinces, the percentage ranged from 2 to 10 per cent.[124] Zhang Yue-e evaluated the maturation of the rural land market in Chongqing in 2008 and concluded that only one small area near the city's downtown has a mature rural land market and that in most parts of Chongqing the rural land market is still in the developmental stage.[125]

5.5.3.2 Second reason: the property right structure

Another reason why the reform of the compensation for expropriated rural land has lagged behind that for urban houses is the property right structure. For an urban house, its owner enjoys the ownership of the house and the use right of the attached construction land. When expropriation occurs, the house's owner is the primary right holder with respect to receiving compensation. However, expropriated farmland belongs to a collective organisation, and its use right belongs to individual farmers. That is, there are two key interested subjects, who should be compensated for the expropriation. An insufficient compensation must be allocated

[123] *Chongqing Nongcun Tudi Jiaoyisuo Guanli Zanxing Banfa* [*Chongqing Provisional Measures on the Management of Rural Land Exchanges*], promulgated by Chongqing Municipal Government in December 2008. The Chinese text is available at www.gov.cn/gzdt/2008–12/10/content_1173675.htm.

[124] Chongqing, 10.84 per cent; Sichuan, 10 per cent; Hubei, 10 per cent; Heilongjiang, 8.9 per cent; Hunan, 6 per cent; Liaoning, 2 per cent. See Liu, 'Zhongguo de Tudi', 123.

[125] Zhang, 'Chongqingshi Nongcun', 46–8.

between collective organisations and individual households, which further lessens the insufficient compensation to individuals. The land compensation fee, which represents the largest part of the total compensation, is paid to the collective organisation.[126] According to the implementation regulation of the *LAL* (*LAL Regulation*), the compensation for the attachments and the growing young crops is paid to the relevant owners. Regarding a resettlement fee, individual farmers can receive it only when they resettle by themselves. If resettlement is organised by a collective or other organisation, the organiser can claim the resettlement fee.[127]

In the allocation system, the collective organisation plays a role as the direct receiver and decisive allocator of compensation payment. The dominant status of the collective organisation in the allocation of compensation preserves a hierarchy that originated in the planned economy period: farmers as collective members shall be subordinate to collective organisations.

This allocation is unfair to farmers. First, the percentage of compensation allocated to farmers is too low. The literature reveals that a thirty-year land right should represent 75 to 95 per cent of the total land value. Thus, the allocation percentage should correspond to this value percentage.[128] Second, farmers are not the direct receivers of compensation funds. All compensation is paid to the collective organisation for further allocation between the organisation and the farmers. However, as the owner of independent land rights, as ascertained by the *RLCL* and the *Property Law*, farmers should be paid compensation directly. The *RLCL* stipulates that '[t]he Contractee has the right to acquire the corresponding compensation when his land is expropriated, requisitioned or occupied according

126 Of all compensation for expropriated land paid to X village in A province in 2006, the land compensation fee represented 43.2 per cent, the resettlement fee 36.6 per cent and the compensation for attachments and young crops 20.2 per cent. The percentages are calculated based on statistics from Gao Han's research. See Gao, *Jiti Chanquan*, p. 157. According to the research done by Zhu Dongkai and Shi Guoqing, 60 to 70 per cent of all income from the sale of the expropriated land went to relevant governments, 25 to 30 per cent went to villages (collectives) and only 5 to 10 per cent was paid to land-loss farmers. According to Chen Ming's research on the cases of expropriation in some area of Zhenjiang Province, governments acquired 56.97 per cent of total land sale income, developers acquired 37.79 per cent, and, villages and farmers received only 5.24 per cent. See Li, 'Chaiqian Jingjixue', 39.

127 See art. 26 of *Tudi Guanli Fa Shishi Tiaoli* [*Regulation on Implementing Land Administration Law*], which was enacted on 27 December 1998 and amended on 8 January 2011 by the State Council. Its Chinese text is available at www.gov.cn/gongbao/content/2011/content_1860861.htm.

128 Han (ed.), *Zhongguo Nongcun*, p. 74.

to law.'[129] This statement implies that individual farmers have the right to compensation and thus should receive the compensation directly without reallocation by the collective organisation. Third, the compensation fee is paid by construction unit rather than government authority.[130] However, if the expropriation is compulsory, the government should be the payer of compensation.

The insufficiency of the compensation amount and the unfairness in the compensation allocation are worsened by the agent problem. A collective organisation consists of farmers as members with selected or appointed leaders as the agents of all of the members of such organisation. To take the most popular collective organisation 'village' (*cun*) as an example, the agent is a village committee that consists of one director and other committee members elected by the village residents.[131] The moral hazard of agents might result in two problems, which harm the interest of the farmers with respect to compensation. First, agents who are bribed by developers in need of land might accept a lower compensation standard to acquire their own illegal individual interest. Second, agents might misappropriate a part of the compensation fee for their own interest. In addition to the possible individual embezzlement of the compensation fee, the agents have an incentive to obtain as much compensation as possible for their organisation's control and use.[132]

The distribution of the land compensation fee is a controversial issue. For a long time, the unsatisfactory distribution decisions made by collective agents resulted in frequent conflicts between agents and farmers. Generally, the distribution scheme was left to be determined by an autonomous mechanism inside the collective organisation because there is no stipulation regarding the distribution amount or percentage in the *1982 Construction Regulation* or the *LAL*. The judicial interpretation of *RLCL*, which was issued by the Supreme People's Court of China (SPC), stipulates that a collective organisation or its agents can determine how to allocate the compensation payment according to the democratic procedure stipulated by law.[133] However, if the enforceable local regulations

[129] *RLCL*, art. 16. [130] *1982 Construction Regulation*, art. 9.

[131] See art. 6 of *Cunmin Weiyuanhui Zuzhi Fa* [*Organic Law of the Village Committee*], which was enacted by the Fifth Meeting of the Standing Committee of the Ninth NPC on 4 November 1998 and amended by the Seventeenth Meeting of the Standing Committee of the Eleventh NPC on 28 October 2010. The Chinese text of this law is available at www.china.com.cn/policy/txt/2010–10/29/content_21226000.htm.

[132] Han (ed.), *Zhongguo Nongcun*, p. 75.

[133] *Organic Law of the Village Committee*, art. 24.

or rules stipulate allocation methods, such regulations and rules shall be applied. If collective members sue because of the unsatisfactory distribution amount, the court refuses to hear the suit.[134]

In response to the strong request by farmers for reasonable compensation, in its *Decision on Deepening the Reform and Strengthening Land Administration* (*2004 Land Decision*) issued in 2004, the State Council required that compensation and resettlement methods be improved.[135] According to this decision, the purpose of the improvement is to prevent the lives of farmers who lose land from being worsened by expropriation. If the compensation and resettlement fee paid according to the current laws and regulations cannot maintain the original living standards of such farmers, resettlement subsidies should be increased on approval by the provincial governments. If the total compensation reaches the *LAL* ceiling but remains insufficient to maintain the original living standards of the farmers who have lost land, local governments may pay additional subsidies using the income received from the auction of the use rights of state-owned land.

This decision requires that local governments use the original living standard of farmers who lose land as the compensation standard (the no-worse-off standard). For this purpose, the decision authorises local governments to pay compensation that can exceed the maximum ceiling amount stipulated by the current law and regulation. To explain the details of this decision, the MLR issued its *Guidance Opinions on the Improvement of the Compensation and Resettlement Concerning Land Expropriation* (*2004 MLR Guidance*) in the same year.[136] In addition to repeating the original living standard requirement of the *2004 Land Decision*, an additional reform measure requires land management authorities at a provincial level to establish a unified local annual output standard. This standard is based on a consideration of the characteristics and quality of

[134] *Guanyu Shenli sheji Nongcun Tudi Chengbao Jiufen Anjian Shiyong Falv Wenti de Jieshi* [*Interpretation on the Trying of Cases Concerning Rural Land Contracting Law*], passed by the Adjudication Committee (*shenpan weiyuanhui*) of the SPC on 29 March 2005, available at www.legaldaily.com.cn/misc/2005–08/01/content_175847.htm.

[135] See the third part of *Guanyu Shenhua Gaige Yange Tudi Guanli de Jueding* [*Decision on Deepening the Reform and Strengthening Land Administration*], which was promulgated by the State Council on 21 October 2004 and is available at www.gov.cn/zwgk/2005–08/12/content_22138.htm.

[136] *Guanyu Wanshan Zhengdi Buchang Anzhi Zhidu de Zhidao Yijian* [*Guidance Opinions on the Improvement of the Compensation and Resettlement Concerning Land Expropriation*], issued by the MLR on 3 November 2004. Its Chinese text is available at www.mlr.gov.cn/zwgk/flfg/tdglflfg/200506/t20050617_68344.htm.

arable land, the production investment of the farmers, the price of agricultural products and the categorisation of the relevant agricultural land. This approach might represent an initial step in reforming the average annual output standard used for compensation decisions because factors in addition to output are included in the consideration.[137]

As to the allocation of land compensation fees inside collective organisations, the most distinguishable legal improvement was made in 2010 when the *Organic Law of the Village Committee* was amended to require that the allocation and use of compensation fees for expropriated land be decided by the meeting of village members. This revision could restrict organisation agents' misuse of power. Several local governments also introduced some reform measures concerning the allocation issue. The *2004 Land Decision* stipulates that the primary portion of compensation fees should be used for farmers and requires provincial-level governments to enact the detailed measures. Following the *2004 Land Decision*'s requirement, provincial-level governments started to create local allocation measures. For instance, the Shanxi Provincial Government requires that at least 80 per cent of land compensation fees be allocated to individual members.[138]

[137] Similar provisions can be found in local rules. See arts. 8 and 9 of *Jiangsusheng Zhengdi Buchang he Beizhengdi Nongmin Jiben Shenghuo Baozhang Banfa* [*Jiangsu Province Measures on Compensation and Minimum Livelihood Guarantee for the Expropriated Farmers*], which was promulgated by Jiangsu Provincial Government on 31 July 2005 and is available at xfj.nantong.gov.cn/art/2007/12/26/art_7235_161002.html.

[138] See art. 13 of *Shanxisheng Zhengshou Zhengyong Nongmin Jiti Suoyou Tudi Zhengdi Buchangfei Fenpei Shiyong Banfa* [*Shanxi Province Measures on the Allocation and Use of Compensation Fee for the Expropriated and Requisitioned Collective Rural Land*], which was promulgated by Shanxi Provincial Government on 17 October 2005 and is available at www.chinaacc.com/new/63/74/117/2006/1/li9165253143151600210325–0.htm. Other local provisions include: *Henansheng Bangongting guanyu Guifan Nongmin Jiti Suoyou Tudi Zhengdi Buchangfei Fenpei he Shiyong de Yijian* [*Henan Provincial Government General Office Opinions on Regulating the Allocation and Use of Land Compensation Fee for Collective-owned Land*] (2006); *Sichuansheng Nongyeting guanyu Jiaqiang Nongcun Jiti Jingji Zuzhi Buchangfei Jiandu Guanli de Yijian* [*Sichuan Provincial Agricultural Department Opinions on Strengthening the Supervision and Management of Land Compensation Fee of Rural Collective Economic Units*] (2005); *Tianjinshi Nongcun Gongzuo Weiyuanhui guanyu Jiaqiang Nongcun Jiti Jingji Zuzhi Zhengdi Buchangfei Fenpei Shiyong Jiandu Guanli Gongzuo de Yijian* [*Tianjin Municipal Committee of Agriculture Work Opinions on Strengthening the Supervision and Management of Land Compensation Fee of Rural Collective Economic Units*] (2006); *Jilin Sheng Nongye Weiyuanhui guanyu Jiaqiang Nongcun Jiti Jingji Zuzhi Zhengdi Buchangfei Fenpei Guanli de Yijian* [*Jilin Provincial Committee of Agricultural Work Opinions on Strengthening the Management of the Allocation of Land Compensation Fee of Rural Collective Economic Units*] (2009).

5.5.4 *Unconstitutionality issues*

5.5.4.1 Unequal treatment between farmers and urban asset holders

The constitutionality of the current legal stipulations concerning compensation is questioned because they offer unequal treatment among property owners. The compensation for urban properties is based on the market value, but the compensation available to the owners of rural land or rural land rights is calculated using annual output standard, which violates the principle of equality, a basic constitutional principle. The *1982 Constitution of China* stipulates the principle of equality by stating that '[a]ll citizens of the People's Republic of China are equal before the law.'[139] The article concerning equality is the first article in the chapter titled 'The Fundamental Rights and Duties of Citizens' and indicates that Chinese citizens shall be treated equally in both legal rights and obligations.

Although this equality principle was entrenched into the constitution as early as 1954,[140] it has been disregarded in legislation and administration in China. The most notorious example, described as a serious long-term violation of constitutional principle of equality, is the *hukou* system. The term '*hukou*' refers to the household registration record held by Chinese citizens. This system officially started in 1951 when the Ministry of Public Security promulgated the *Provisional Regulation governing Urban Household Registration* (*1951 Hukou Regulation*).[141] This regulation required that households register in a public security agency to obtain a registration record (*hukou*). Furthermore, any changes to the *hukou* must receive approval from and be registered in the public security agency. The *hukou* system was used by the government to control the migration of citizens. When a person moved from one place to another, he was required by this regulation to report to the public security agency, cancel his former *hukou* and apply for a permit of changing residence.[142] The 1949 *Common Programme* and *1954 Constitution of China* both stipulated citizens' freedom of residence and migration.[143] However, what is ironic is that

139 *1982 Constitution of China*, art. 33(2).
140 *1954 Constitution of China*, art. 85.
141 *Chengshi Hukou Guanli Zanxing Tiaoli* [*Provisional Regulation governing Urban Household Registration*], promulgated by the Ministry of Public Security on 16 July 1951. The Chinese text is available at www.chinacourt.org/law/detail/1951/07/id/48.shtml.
142 *1951 Hukou Regulation*, art. 5.
143 *Common Programme*, art. 5; *1954 Constitution of China*, art. 90. See Chen and Seldon, 'The Origins', 646.

this unconstitutional provision stated in its first article that the purpose of its enactment was to protect people's 'freedom of residence and of movement'. In 1958, the NPCSC promulgated the *Regulation on Hukou Registration* (*1958 Hukou Regulation*) to stipulate the *hukou* system for the first time in legislation at the central legislature level.[144] This regulation also applied the *hukou* system to all the people, including both urban and rural residents.[145] In addition to the control of migration, the *hukou* was used to establish people's identities, with which the allocation of benefits was linked. For example, the *hukou* was used by shop assistants in identifying a buyer's right to purchase stipulated rationed goods between 1960 and 1978, when basic consumer goods were in short supply.[146] As the identity of a person, the *hukou* has been linked with various social benefits in China. These benefits include school education, health care and employment. If a person wants to enjoy entitlement benefits in some city, he must have a local *hukou*. For a long time, the *hukou* has been used to control the migration of urban residents from small cities to large cities as well as the migration of farmers from rural areas to urban areas. Although the mobility of people (especially the mobility of rural residents) was loosened following opening and reform, the *hukou* is still linked closely with the local benefits available to local residents. Residents working in the same city with different *hukou*s are treated differently in employment and local entitlement benefits. The social benefits attached to an urban *hukou* are always better than those attached to a rural *hukou*. The *hukou* has been criticised as a system discriminating against the rural population.[147]

Discrimination based on compensation is the derivation of *hukou* discrimination. From the acquisition of rights to the limiting of the transaction of land rights and the protection of land rights in the constitutional and legislative systems, discrimination is linked with the *hukou* identity closely from start to the end. Farmers, as members of rural collectives, can acquire land use rights for the construction of rural residence houses

[144] *Hukou Dengji Tiaoli* [*Regulation on Hukou Registration*], enacted by the Ninety-first Meeting of the Standing Committee of the First NPC on 9 January 1958. The Chinese text is available at news.xinhuanet.com/zhengfu/20010525/589581.htm.

[145] *1958 Hukou Regulation*, art. 2.

[146] Han, 'The Hukou System', 358.

[147] Afridi and Li point out that, '[i]n China, one's *hukou* status determines entitlement to economic resources and opportunities such as education, employment, and social welfare benefits.' This, in turn, establishes one's position in the social hierarchy. *Hukou* status is permanent for most people because rural-to-urban *hukou* conversions are granted only through very limited channels. See Afridi and Li, 'Social Identity', 4.

and for cultivation. Thus, the use right of rural land is a right linked with farmers' identity, which is fixed by their rural *hukou*. If a farmer loses his rural membership or converts his rural *hukou* to an urban *hukou* and gives up his membership in a collective, his rural land use rights must be given up too. Rural land is limited to agricultural use and the building of rural houses and public facilities mainly in rural areas. Such land cannot be transferred to individuals or enterprises directly, and the conversion of its use to urban construction must be achieved through the government. Thus, the land use right that farmers acquire with their rural *hukou* identity is limited in transaction too. Their land use right cannot be transferred for non-agricultural use, and the transaction of land use rights is limited to the land's original use purpose and within the local rural market only.

Like long-term discrimination in social benefits, the level of compensation available to farmers who hold rural *hukou*s is much lower than that available to urban residents whose house and attached land use rights are expropriated. From 1991 to 2011, the compensation standard for the expropriation of urban properties evolved from the original replacement price to a three-element combination (evaluation price) and then to the current comparable market price, which is similar to the fair market value test found in the United States. However, for the expropriation of rural land, the compensation standard has been an annual output test. Although the number that is multiplied by the baseline annual output was raised in 1982 and then in 1998, the compensation remained insufficient for compensating farmers' losses. After the *2004 Amendment*, both the public interest limit and market value test were introduced in the *2011 Expropriation Regulation*. However, for the expropriation of rural land, little improvement in the legislation has been made to strengthen the public interest limit and raise compensation levels following the *2004 Amendment*. The most recent adjustment to the multiplier in the NPC laws occurred in 1998, which means there have been no adjustments to the multiplier in more than seventeen years at the national legislature level, even though economic growth in China has been booming and the *2004 Amendment* entrenched compensation requirements into the constitution.

Even worse, the compensation to farmers whose land is expropriated for the construction of large- and medium-scale water conservancy and hydropower projects is much lower than the normal compensation available to land-loss farmers. The public interest feature of such projects is hardly challenged. Thus, the debate on the expropriation linked to such projects focuses on the compensation side. Unfortunately, the land-loss farmers affected by such projects are offered compensation that is much lower than that given to land-loss farmers affected by other projects.

5.5.4.2 Constitutionality issue concerning the subjects to be compensated

The current laws give farmers secondary status, subordinate to collective organisations. Collective organisations, as the ownership holders, dominate throughout the process of negotiating, deciding on and allocating compensation, which contradicts the recent developments of constitutional stipulations and the concerned laws. The *2004 Amendment* stipulates that any private property that is expropriated shall be compensated. The 2007 *Property Law*, in its first article, states that its purpose is to protect property right according to the constitution. According to the *Property Law*, the contracted land use rights are stipulated as an independent property right. It further stipulates that the holders of the contracted rural land are entitled to compensation according to art. 42(2).[148] According to art. 42, the expropriation of rural land and urban properties shall be for the public interest and be compensated for according to the authority and procedure stipulated by Law.[149] Here, 'Law' in China's legislation system is explained as legal documents passed by the NPC or NPCSC.[150] However, most of the currently enforced regulations or rules governing expropriation are enacted by the State Council and its ministries or local governments. The legality and even constitutionality of such regulations or rules are questioned.

Because the 2007 *Property Law* stipulates land use rights as independent property rights, farmers, as the holders of such property rights, shall be compensated directly. That the independence of land use rights as property is guarded by the constitution means that the right holder shall be given the same treatment as that enjoyed by other property holders, such as the ownership holders of collective rural land. The current regulation, which stipulates collective organisations' dominant position over farmers, treats farmers discriminately and thus violates the constitution's principle of equal treatment, departing from the constitutional spirit in recognising and protecting private properties and property rights.

The right to 'direct compensation' farmers should have been given is further segmented into two parts. The first right is the right of direct involvement in the expropriation process. There are two arguments

[148] *Property Law*, art. 132. [149] Ibid., art. 42. [150] *Law on Legislation*, art. 7.

against this right. Individual members' direct involvement may cause increasing transaction costs for the expropriation process because governments or developers in need of land have to address both collective organisations and the members in such organisations who are affected by expropriation projects. Moreover, the affected farmers are members of the concerned collective organisation. The agents of such an organisation, who are elected by farmers, should have representative power on behalf of all members in dealing with expropriation and compensation affairs. However, both arguments cannot stand. Suppose there is a situation where only one farmer's land is expropriated. This farmer's involvement does not significantly increase transaction costs concerning the collective action problem because he does not have to negotiate with other members. According to the current laws, it is still the collective organisation, as the nominal owner of the affected land, that joins negotiations with the government and developer, receives compensation and decides on allocation. Article 2 of the *Organic Law of the Village Committee* defines the scope of the village committee's responsibilities as follows: the dealing of village public affairs and public facilities, mediation of disputes between villagers, assistance in maintaining social public security and reflection of villagers' opinions to the government. The dealing of land use rights that are private property rights does not fall within this agent organisation's scope of responsibilities. However, the agents can represent the organisation or all members in dealing with compensation concerning the aspect of ownership rights. The Village Committee operates based on autonomous documents that are adopted by the meeting of villagers, such as *Villagers' Charter of Autonomous Governance* and the *Common Agreement of Villagers.*[151] Can agents represent all or some members in dealing with expropriation and compensation affairs if such a charter or agreement passed by villagers' meeting authorises them to do so? Does the expropriation decision belong to public affairs as stipulated by art. 2? The response is definitely no. The land lease or use right is an independent property right with the nature of private property, as established by the 2002 *RLCL* and then strengthened by the *2004 Amendment* and the 2007 *Property Law.* It should not be decided through one majority democratic mechanism, such as villagers' meeting, because the constitutional protection of private property shelters the rights of individual holders of private property from being infringed upon by the democratically represented majority decision, which is a decision made by either the government

[151] *Organic Law of the Village Committee*, art. 27.

representing the majority in the society or an autonomous body such as a village. The *Organic Law of the Village Committee* stipulates that a village's autonomous documents and villager meeting decisions shall not conflict with the *Constitution*, Laws (by the NPC and NPCSC), administrative regulations and national policies, and they shall not infringe on the villager's personal rights, democratic rights and legal property rights.[152] This stipulation further strengthens the notion that a village member's independent legal property rights, including land use right, shall be executed by the right holder himself, independently and without illegal interference from the village collective.

The second right is the right of the 'direct receiver'. As the owner of an independent property right, farmers shall be paid compensation directly by the government under the expropriation situation or by the developer if an agreement concerning compensation is achieved, which means that, as an owner of land or the partial rights of land, a collective organisation can only receive compensation corresponding to its portion of land rights, namely the ownership portion. Project-affected farmers have the right to receive the part of compensation corresponding with their use rights, namely the use right portion. Direct receiver rights can also restrict organisation agents from usurping compensation fees and restrain the agent's moral hazard.

5.5.4.3 The constitutionality and legality of compensation standards

Even if there is no authoritative explanation about the constitutional compensation principle, the constitutional equality principle requires that farmers be treated equally under compensation standards, methods and principles. The current compensation pack to urban residents for their expropriated houses include compensation for the taken houses, compensation for moving and temporary resettlement and compensation for the suspension of business.[153] The compensation to the expropriated house is calculated based on the house's comparable market price and can be made in the form of monetary compensation or the exchange of estate. Basically, the compensation to the owners of urban houses covers property losses and some incidental loss incurred in the expropriation. Although the scope of compensation can still be arguably enlarged, the basic fair market value test, which reflects the constitutional value, is entrenched for the expropriation of urban houses.

[152] Ibid., art. 27(2). [153] *2011 Expropriation Regulation*, art. 17.

A guiding principle for compensation for expropriated rural land is the maintenance of the original living standard or the no-worse-off test. This principle was first stipulated by the *1982 Construction Regulation* in its art. 10 and entrenched in the *LAL* in its art. 29 in 1986. Before the *2004 Land Decision*, the compensation for expropriated rural land was limited by a maximum ceiling of compensation. If the general annual output standard did not allow for farmers to maintain their original living standard, the local governments would increase the resettlement fee under the maximum ceiling, which was 20-times in the *1982 Construction Regulation* and the 1986 *LAL* and adjusted to 30-times in the 1998 amendment to the *LAL*. At this stage, the original living standard was not a primary and practical compensation standard because it was limited by the maximum ceiling. Even if compensation reaching the maximum ceiling was not sufficient in maintaining the farmers' original livelihood, the compensation would not increase. The *2004 Land Decision* allowed local governments to break the limit of the maximum ceiling and strengthen the significance of the original living standard. This breakthrough erected the status of the original living standard as the main compensation standard or principle for land-loss farmers.

However, some questions remain. The *2004 Land Decision* was not an official legal document stipulated by the *Law on Legislation*. Although it is promulgated by the State Council, it is not in the form of Administrative Regulation, and its enactment does not follow the formal legislation procedure required by the *Law on Legislation*.[154] It is more the central government's requirement or guidance to local governments to push forward additional reforms made by local governments. Following the *2004 Land Decision*, the MLR and some provincial governments (not all) promulgated new rules or policies to allow the compensation pack to exceed the maximum 30-times ceiling. However, the *2004 Land Decision* is questioned for its compulsory enforceability in restraining local governments, and the fact is that not all provinces follow this guidance completely. Even now, more than ten years after the decision, some provinces still do not have local policies or rules to execute the *2004 Land Decision*'s requirements. Moreover, the legality of the breakthrough of the compensation ceiling stipulated by the *2004 Land Decision* and some local governments' documents is questioned because such decisions and documents conflict with the upper-level *LAL*, which does not allow breakthrough of the maximum ceiling.

[154] *Law on Legislation*, chap. 3 'Administrative Regulations'.

5.5.4.4 Original living standard versus fair market value

The *2004 Land Decision* uses an original living standard as the basic guiding principle for compensation. According to the official explanation given by the MLR, which is in charge of the management of land resource, 'the fundamental principle of compensation and resettlement is to guarantee that the land-loss farmers' original living level is not lowered after the land taking'.[155] As to the stipulations concerning compensation, the largest difference between the *2004 Land Decision* and the previous provisions is that the *2004 Land Decision* allows breakthrough of the original 30-times ceiling of total compensation for the purpose of maintaining land-loss farmers' living standards.

The 1998 *LAL* stipulates that the calculation standard for compensation for arable land is 6 to 10 times the average annual output within a period of three years prior to expropriation. For the standard of the resettlement fee, it is also in a range of between 4 and 6 times. For compensation for other agricultural land (non-arable land), the standard is stipulated by the provincial governments, referring to the standards for arable land. Thus, local governments are legal if their local standards of compensation fall within the range allowed by the *LAL*. Local governments tend to offer a lower level compensation within the allowable range to peasants.[156] In precise words, many governments are reluctant to adopt the maximum multiplier within the range in their local rules. The standard for non-arable land is lower than that for arable land, which might result in new discrimination between land right holders; in particular, the holders of non-arable land enjoy a multiplier for calculating compensation which is lower than that used for the holders of arable land.

In the province of Shandong, the range of the calculation multiplier for arable land within the urban planning scope is between 8 and 10 times. However, if the arable land is outside the scope of urban planning, the range is reduced to between 6 and 8 times. If the land is non-arable agricultural land, for example, grass- and wood- land, the range is further reduced to between 5 and 6 times of the nearby arable land's average annual output. When the taken land is used for a village's or town's public facilities or public utilities, township enterprises or the farmers' residential needs before expropriation, the range is 5 to 7. For unused land, the compensation standard is only 3 times the nearby arable land's

[155] Xia, 'Jiedu'. [156] Zou and Oskam, 'New Compensation Standard', 112.

average annual output.[157] Although the standard of the resettlement fee for arable land expropriation is stipulated as being 6-times, the highest level allowed by *LAL*, for non-arable collective land, this standard is lowered to 4-times.[158]

In the province of Guangdong, the range of the compensation multiplier for pools used for fish raising (*yutang*) is the highest, between 8 and 12 times. For paddy fields (for growing rice), the range falls to between 8 and 10. For other arable land, the range is 6 to 8; for other non-arable agriculture land, it is 5 to 7. For unused land, the standard shall be 50 per cent of the compensation standard for its nearby arable land. For land with non-agriculture construction, the standard is the same as the standard for nearby other arable land. The range for the resettlement fee is different between arable land and non-arable land. For arable land, the calculation multiplier range for resettlement fee is between 4 and 6. By contrast, for non-arable land, the range is only 3 to 5. The compensation standards are provided in Guangdong's local regulation enforcing *LAL*, which was adopted in 1999.[159] There have been no changes in the latter revisions, including the 2008 revision, which was made after the *2004 Land Decision*.

The popularly used compensation scheme in local legislation sets the range of the multiplier according to the nature of land. Generally, the compensation range for arable land is higher than that for non-arable land. The compensation for cultivated land is higher than that for unused land, which assumes that arable (or cultivated) land is more valuable than non-arable (or uncultivated) land. However, this assumption cannot

[157] Article 25 of *Shandongsheng Shishi Zhonghua Renmin Gongheguo Tudi Guanli Fa Banfa* [*Shandong Province Measures on the Enforcement of Land Administration Law*], which was enacted by the Tenth Meeting of the Standing Committee of the Ninth Shandong Province People's Congress on 22 August 1999 and amended by the Eleventh Meeting of the Standing Committee of the Tenth Shandong Province People's Congress on 25 November 2004. The Chinese text is available at www.mlr.gov.cn/zwgk/flfg/dfflfg/200501/t20050121_64682.htm.

[158] Ibid., art. 26.

[159] Article 30 of *Guangdongsheng Shishi Zhonghua Renmin Gongheguo Tudi Guanli Fa Banfa* [*Guangdong Province Measures on the Enforcement of Land Administration Law*], which was enacted by the Thirteenth Meeting of the Standing Committee of the Ninth Guangdong Province People's Congress on 27 November 1999, amended by the Sixth Meeting of the Standing Committee of the Tenth Guangdong Province People's Congress on 26 September 2003 and amended for the second time by the Seventh Meeting of the Standing Committee of the Eleventh Guangdong Province People's Congress on 28 November 2008. The Chinese text is available at www.gd.xinhuanet.com/zt12/2012–07/30/c_112571371.htm.

stand because land's real value is decided by the market or exchange. For the same reason, some uncultivated land may have greater market value than nearby cultivated land.

The discriminative treatment in compensation to different parcels of land with different use purposes conflicts with the basic constitutional compensation principle of maintaining that the land or property holder's situation is not worsened by expropriation, at least on the objective value of his property. Without questioning the justification of the annual output test, the discriminative arrangement of calculating multipliers leads to unfairness and insufficiency with regard to compensation available to farmers. Suppose there is a parcel of non-arable land with higher output than nearby arable land. According to the aforementioned local stipulations, the compensation multiplier to such non-arable land is much lower than that available to the owner and holder of the arable land with a lower output. Likewise, although unused land and land used for construction use in rural areas have no agricultural output, their value might be higher than that of arable land or other agricultural land. However, according to the current compensation provisions, the compensation standard for them is almost the lowest among all types of rural land. Thus, the setting of the compensation standard (multiplier) according to different use purposes or natures of the concerned land conflicts with the constitutional principle which requires that the compensation should target the value of the specific property.

Local governments' preference in using a lower level multiplier in the range of compensation multipliers allowed by the *LAL* was criticised by an officer from the MLR.[160] Some local governments even delayed the payment of compensation fees to land-loss farmers because they wanted to use the fees to supplement shortages of fiscal sources. The *2004 Land Decision* aimed to raise the compensation available to land-loss peasants by allowing breakthroughs of the 30-times ceiling, but these breakthroughs have been sparsely enforced by local governments. The breakthrough stipulated by the *2004 Land Decision* is an authorisation from the central government, rather than a compulsory requirement or legal obligation imposed on local governments. According to the *2004 Land Decision*, local governments may (rather than 'shall' or 'must') raise compensation above the 30-times ceiling if the compensation calculated based on the *LAL* standards is not sufficient in maintaining the land-loss peasants' original living standards.

[160] Xia, 'Jiedu'.

A reform measure proposed in the *2004 Land Decision* is the unification of the compensation standard. The *2004 Land Decision* required that provincial governments make and promulgate local uniform annual output standards or land section prices (*qupian jiage*) to make compensation for land 'the same land, the same compensation' (*tongdi tongjia*).[161] The following *2004 MLR Guidance* went on to strengthen and push forward the adoption of a uniform annual output and comprehensive and uniform land section price. According to the *2004 MLR Guidance*, local governments, when making such uniform annual output standards, may take the following factors into their account: the type and quality of the expropriated land, the farmers' investment, the price of agricultural products and the levels of the concerned landand so on. A comprehensive multiplier aggregating both the land compensation multiplier and the resettlement fee multiplier shall be made. If the compensation using this comprehensive multiplier is unable to ensure land-loss peasants maintain their original living standard, the multiplier can be lifted to 30-times or higher. As to land section price, it was suggested to local governments only. A land section price means that the price for all land in the same area (land section, *qupian*) should be unified to function as the compensation standard. When making the land section price, the following factors can be considered: the type of land, agricultural output, the location of land, the levels of land, the per capita amount of arable land, the demand and supply of land, the level of local economic development and the minimum-guarantee level of local urban livelihood, among others. Then, in 2005, the MLR issued a notice (*2005 MLR Notice*) to urge local authorities in charge of land resource to push forward the unification of compensation prices and offered guidance on how to calculate the uniform annual output and land section price.[162] In 2010, following the State Council's requirement of strengthening land compensation, MRL issued a notice (*2010 MLR Notice*) that stipulated that the uniform output standard and land section price should be enforced nationwide.[163]

161 It means that the land located in the same section or area should be compensated using the same standard.

162 *Guanyu Kaizhan Zhiding Zhengdi Tongyi Nianchanzhi Biaozhun he Zhengdi Qupian Zonghe Dijia Gongzuo de Tongzhi* [*Notice on the Job Concerning the Making of Uniform Annual Output Standard and Land Section Price for Land Expropriation*], promulgated by the MLR on 23 July 2005. The Chinese text is available at www.mlr.gov.cn/zwgk/zytz/200508/t20050812_69436.htm.

163 *Guanyu Jinyibu Zuohao Zhengdi Guanli Gongzuo de Tongzhi* [*Notice on Further Improving the Administration of the Land Expropriation*], promulgated by the MLR on 26 June 2010.

The reform on the unification of compensation standard classifies all collectively owned land in one municipality to several areas or sections and sets the same compensation standard (uniform annual output or comprehensive section price) for all land within the same area. Although local governments can select either annual output or the comprehensive section price as the compensation standard, the *2004 Land Decision* encouraged the final adoption of a comprehensive price. The Changchun municipal government promulgated its annual output standard in 2008. In 2010, this standard was substituted by a comprehensive land section price.[164]

Although reforms aimed at unification, as an important measure to improve compensation mechanisms and protect peasants' interests, were strengthened by the *2010 MLR Notice*, the insufficiency and unfairness in compensation of both the annual output standard and the comprehensive land section price are still questioned. Take the annual output standard promulgated by the Changchun municipal government in 2008 as an example. This standard categorises all arable land into dry farmland, paddy land and vegetable land. For the first two land types, the uniform annual output standard is applied within the municipality scope, excluding some towns. For vegetable land, the municipality is divided into three areas, and different uniform output standards are applied in different areas. The uniform output set for vegetable land is the highest, and the uniform output for dry land is the lowest. Each annual output standard was calculated based on the output of all arable land within the same applicable area for the previous three years. Thus, this standard does not consider the specific situation of each farmer's land, and compensation based on this uniform standard cannot reflect the real value or output of the expropriated land. Suppose the output of a parcel of land is higher than the average output of all land in the same area. The owner or right holder of this parcel of land would be compensated based on the uniform average

The Chinese text is available at www.mlr.gov.cn/zwgk/zytz/201007/t20100713_154433.htm.

164 *Guanyu Gongbu Changchunshi Shiqu Gengdi Pingjun Nianchanzhi he Zhengdi Buchang Biaozhun de Tongzhi* [*Notice on the Promulgation of Average Annual Output and the Compensation Standard for the Expropriated Arable Land in Changchun Municipality*], promulgated by Changchun Municipal Government on 14 April 2008. The Chinese text is available at china.findlaw.cn/fangdichan/fdcfg/tudifagui/zgtdf/tudifa/68284.html; *Guanyu Gongbu Shishi Changchunshi Shiqu Zhengdi Qupian Zonghe Dijia de Tongzhi* [*Notice on the Promulgation and Execution of Comprehensive Land Section Price for the Expropriated Land Area in Changchun Municipality*], promulgated by Changchun Municipal Government on 19 April 2010. The Chinese text is available at www.cc.jl.gov.cn/wcss/cczf/info/2010–04–19/128/113231.html.

output, which may lead to insufficient compensation. Likewise, two pieces of expropriated land that have the same use purpose but different outputs in the past three years would be given the same compensation standard. In addition, the setting of different uniform outputs for different pieces of arable land still results in the possibility that some specific arable land with a high value falling within the low-output standard scope, would only garner compensation based on the low-output standard imposed by the government.

In 2010, the Changchun Government replaced its annual output standard with comprehensive land section prices. The scope of the municipality is categorised into seven areas. For each area, there is a uniform land section price that acts as the standard for calculating both land compensation fees and resettlement fees. This new stipulation does not categorise collective land according to its nature or type. For land within the same applicable area 'land section' or *qupian*, regardless of its use or nature, the same compensation standard is applied. First, this practice is questioned because of its conflict with the *LAL*. The *LAL* requires that the original use purpose be considered when compensation is calculated.[165] Second, the unification of an average price standard still results in a situation where specific land with a value higher than the average level of all land within the same applicable area or land section is undercompensated.[166]

Another issue is timeliness. The standards made by local governments are not adjusted in a timely manner. For example, the province of Jiangsu did not adjust its standards, which were promulgated in 2004, until 2011.[167] The lag of adjustment further pushes compensation available

[165] Article 47 of the *LAL* provides that compensation is offered according to the original use purpose of the expropriate land.

[166] Some local governments stipulate adjustment or exception to the uniform price. The province of Shandong set uniform prices for applicable areas with adjustment to prime land and unused land. For prime farmland (*jiben nongtian*), the standard is 1.2 times the uniform price; for unused land, the adjustment multiplier is 0.8. Nevertheless, the adjustment still cannot resolve the issue of the insufficient compensation to some specific land. See *Shandongsheng guanyu Shishi Zhengdi Qupian Zonghe Dijia Biaozhun de Tongzhi* [*Shandong Province Notice on Implementing the Standard of Comprehensive Land Section Price in the Area of Expropriated Land*], promulgated by General Office of Shandong Provincial Government on 20 March 2009. Its Chinese text is available at www.jndlr.gov.cn/tabid/62/InfoID/1953/frtid/128/Default.aspx.

[167] *Jiangsusheng Zhengfu Guanyu Tiaozheng Zhengdi Buchang Biaozhun de Tongzhi* [*Jiangsu Provincial Government Notice on the Adjustment of Compensation Standards to the Expropriated Land*], promulgated by Jiangsu Provincial Government on 25 March 2011. The Chinese text is available at www.jiangsu.gov.cn/xxgk/zycq/bcbz/201105/t20110526_600295.html.

to land-loss farmers away from the real land value or sufficient compensation. The *2010 MLR Notice* requires that the uniform standard be adjusted dynamically every two or three years. Similar requirements for adjustment frequency were stipulated in some local rules. For example, in the province of Shandong, it is required that the uniform prices be adjusted every three years.[168] Although this dynamic adjustment requirement shortens local governments' adjustment intervals, it cannot reflect the instant value of the land at the time of expropriation.[169]

The land section price is used as a new standard for enforcing the principle of not being worse off than original livelihood levels. The most fundamental difference between this standard and the traditional annual output standard is the incorporation of many other elements in addition to the output of land. The factors used in deciding land section price include the type, output and location of land; the level of agricultural land; the amount of per capita arable land; the supply and demand of land; the local economic development situation; a minimum guarantee of local urban livelihood; and other factors.[170] There are several methods suggested by the MLR for calculation of the land section price.[171] The first is the annual output multiplier. For this method, the uniform annual output within the past three years in some specific area is calculated first. Next, a multiplier is used with this annual output to obtain the land section price. On its face, the calculation process is the same as that of the original annual output standard. However, the key difference is that when deciding on a multiplier, some non-output factors – such as the local economic development situation and local livelihood levels – need to be considered, which means the multipliers found under the new land section price standard can be higher than those found under the original *LAL* output standard. Moreover, this multiplier can be higher than the 30-times ceiling set by the *LAL*.

[168] Another example is the concerned local stipulation in the Shannxi Province. The adjustment frequency there is 'every 2 to 3 years'. See *Shannxisheng Zhengdi Tongyi Nianchanzhi Biaozhun ji Qupian Zonghe Dijia Pingjun Biaozhun* [*Shannxi Province Uniform Annual Output Standard and Comprehensive Land Section Price*], promulgated by General Office of Shannxi Provincial Government on 13 April 2010. The Chinese text is available at www.shaanxi.gov.cn/0/sxzb/6169.htm.

[169] Chan points out that the price for agricultural products has changed frequently in recent years in China and even in the world. See Chan, 'Recent Reform', 9.

[170] *2005 MLR Notice.*

[171] *Zhengdi Qupian Zonghe Dijia Cesuan Zhidaoxing Yijian* [*Guidance Opinions on the Measurement of Comprehensive Land Section Price in the Expropriated Land Area*], promulgated by the MLR on 23 July 2005. The Chinese text is available at www.mlr.gov.cn/zwgk/zytz/200508/t20050812_69436.htm.

Two other methods suggested by the MLR are comparable measurement and measurement with adjustments based on land price. The former uses past comparable expropriation cases in the comparable areas in recent years as a reference to set the current land section price. The latter uses the price of rural land as the basis for calculation, with adjustments based on other influential factors. For these two methods, correction or adjustment based on relevant influential elements is needed.

Thus, within the same land section or area, compensation based on the land section price is generally higher than that based on uniform annual outputs. Take a city in central China as an example. In this city, the calculated land section price changes from 50,000 to 260,000 *yuan* per *mu*. By contrast, when using the annual output standard with a stipulated multiplier of 18, the calculated compensation changes from 19,000 to 36,000 *yuan* per *mu*. Even if the multiplier is raised to 30, the highest allowed by *LAL*, the compensation changes from 32,000 to only 60,000 *yuan* per *mu*, far lower than that based on the comprehensive land section price.[172]

Compared with the original compensation scheme, with annual output as the main or even the only consideration, land section prices indeed raise the overall compensation to land-loss farmers under most situations. However, for individual farmers, the adoption of this method may not be fair, and the compensation available may be worse than that based on an annual output standard. The land section price may lower the compensation to some individual farmers whose land has higher output or greater value than other farmers' land located in the same section. It also results in unfair treatment for some farmers whose land has high output who are given lower compensation than that based on the original annual output standard because their land is categorised in a section with a low price. One main purpose of unifying the compensation standard is to maintain social stability. The original output standard calculates each piece of the expropriated land based on its output within the past three years. Thus, landowners with land located in the same place may be given different compensation because their respective pieces of land have different outputs. The unification of a compensation standard within a specific area aims to offer the same compensation standard to all land-loss farmers without distinguishing differences in the outputs of their respective land to ease conflicts incurred by uneven treatment in compensation. However,

[172] Zhong and Huang, 'Zhengdi Tongyi', 42. According to the research by Lv, Liu and Long, all land section prices found through several calculation methods are higher than the standard calculated based on annual output only. See Lv, Liu and Long, 'Zhengdi Qupian'.

the problem is that, in aiming to reduce unfairness, unification results in new unfair treatment issue. Although unification resolves the so-called unfairness issue of 'same land different price' (*tongdi butongjia*), it causes a new unfairness issue, 'different land same price' (*butongdi tongjia*). Moreover, unification conflicts with the *LAL*. The *LAL* stipulates that the expropriated land be compensated for based on its annual output. The comprehensive consideration of various factors for the calculation of land section prices conflicts with the *LAL* too because the *LAL* stipulates annual output as the only one element in the calculation of compensation.[173]

Even if we consider the overall compensation within one land section, the use of the land section price may not fundamentally improve the insufficient compensation problem. The most often used method for the land section price is the 'multiplier method', which is a continuation of the original output standard. Although local governments are permitted by the central government to raise the multiplier beyond the *LAL* ceiling based on the local economic situation and livelihood levels, they are reluctant to break the 30-times ceiling in practice. For example, there is no multiplier higher than 30-times in the scheme of land section prices promulgated by the province of Shannxi, which uses the annual output method to set land section prices.[174] Because there is no compulsory requirement or clear standard for the raising the multiplier, local governments can still choose to not or only slightly increase a multiplier.[175]

The current compensation standard based on annual output in China is regarded as being significantly insufficient. Fair market value is the commonly accepted explanation of the constitutional compensation principle. To decide fair market value, the mostly accepted method is the comparable sales approach, which uses the transaction information of comparable land sales as reference in deciding the value of expropriated land. The sales value of land is affected by both current use and future use. It is the best and highest use of the land that determines the sales price. China's *LAL* stipulates that compensation for rural land be decided based only on its original use, which omits the consideration of the future use of land from the calculation of compensation.[176]

173 Fu, 'Tongdi Tongjia'.

174 *Shannxisheng Zhengdi Tongyi Nianchanzhi Biaozhun ji Qupian Zonghe Dijia Pingjun Biaozhun* [*Shannxi Province Uniform Annual Output Standard and Comprehensive Land Section Price*].

175 Li and Shi, 'Zhengdi Qupian', 59–60.

176 For the consideration of reasonable future use, See Sprankling, *Understanding Property Law*, p. 647. For the application of market value method, see ADB, 'Compensation and Valuation', 6–13.

The use of annual output as the method for calculating compensation moves compensation away from the expropriated land's real market value. Even if the land's future use is excluded by the *LAL*, the comparable sale of land use rights with the existing use restriction should be used in the first place in deciding the market price of such land. However, the relevant undeveloped market cannot offer sufficient market information as a reference. Thus, annual output, which is, in essence, an income or capitalisation approach, is used as an alternative. This income or capitalisation approach assumes that the value of a property is determined by the income or benefit the property is expected to produce.[177] There are two steps for using this approach. First, the net income is calculated based on the annual output of land or other income in recent years. Then, the future benefit of the land at issue is transferred to present value using a capitalisation rate. This rate is the basis for deciding the multiplier in practice. Decisions about the rate or multiplier are critical because they affect the amount of compensation to land-loss farmers. In India, the multiplier used for assessing farm land is usually 10.[178] Compared with India's practice, China's use of multipliers from 10 to 16 in deciding the total compensation packs of expropriated arable land does not seem to be low. However, it is difficult for us to conclude that farmers in China enjoy a higher or at least the same compensation standard as farmers in India. There are six reasons.

First, the capitalisation of income method serves as a supplemental substitute to the comparable sales method in India. It is used only when comparable sales data are not available, reliable or sufficient. By contrast, in China, it serves as the only method for valuation stipulated by *LAL*. Even in areas where the market of land use rights offers sufficient comparable sale information, the capitalisation method is still used for valuation.

Second, as Ding commented, the suppressed pricing policy used by the government distorts the market of agricultural goods and results in too-low prices for agricultural products in China. In many developing

[177] Ibid., ADB, 8.

[178] *K. Posayya & ORS.* v. *Special Tahsildar*, 1995 SC 1641. In its decision, the court ruled that a 10-year multiplier is 'suitable'. In another case, it was ruled that 'when the rate of return on investment was 8.25 per cent in the years 1971 and 1972, a person investing his capital in agricultural lands would ordinarily accept 2 per cent to 3 per cent more than what he could obtain from gilt-edged securities or other forms of Safe investment and therefore the proper multiplier to be applied for the purpose of capitalization could not in any event exceeded "ten"'. See *Special Land Acquisition, Davangere* v. *P. Veerabhadarappa and Ors.*, 1984 2 SCC 120. See also *Krishi Utpadan Mandi Samiti* v. *Malik Sartaj Wali Khan and Anr.*, (2001) 10 SCC 660.

countries, the prices of agricultural products are artificially suppressed to subsidise industrial development indirectly. Ding noted that this partially explains why the compensation based on a 200–300 multiplier still cannot satisfy farmers.[179]

Third, there are two rights holders, collective organisations and farmers as individual members, over one parcel of land. The agent problem might result in the undervaluation of compensation. Furthermore, the final compensation is divided between organisation and individual farmers.

Fourth, a solatium is offered to supplement land compensation in India. By contrast, in China, there is no such solatium.

Fifth, for expropriated land used for building large- and medium-scale water conservancy and hydropower projects, art. 51 of the *LAL* excludes the construction of such projects from the application of compensation standards stipulated by art. 47 and authorises the State Council to make the relevant compensation stipulations concerning expropriation for such projects. For a long time, the compensation standard concerning such power and water projects was lower than the *LAL* standard. In 2006, the standard for total compensation (land compensation + resettlement fee) concerning such projects was increased to be 16 times annual output, the same as the maximum level of the 10 to 16 times range stipulated by the revised *LAL* in 1998. According to the 2006 regulation concerning large- and medium-scale water conservancy and hydropower projects, if the 16-times compensation cannot ensure that land-loss farmers maintain their original living standards and consequently needs to be increased, the application for increasing can be submitted to the authority in charge for approval. For compensation to expropriation projects other than water and power projects, the 1998 *LAL* clearly stipulates that compensation can be lifted to a level of no more than 30-times the annual output. The *2004 Land Decision* allows breakthroughs of the 30-times ceiling. However, the stipulations concerning 30-times and its breakthrough are not applied to water and power projects.

Finally, there is no stipulation concerning compensation for partial takings in the *LAL*. If an expropriation concerns only a partial taking of land, such taking might cause a loss in value of the remaining land. Thus, decreases in the value of the remaining land as a result of expropriation need to be covered by compensation. In India, the *1894 LAA* stipulates that losses owing to severance shall be compensated.[180] By contrast, in China,

179 Ding, 'Policy and Praxis', 8.
180 *1894 LAA*, art. 23.

farmers are not entitled to demand compensation for the severance losses incurred by partial taking.

5.6 Reform towards full compensation: India versus China

The purpose of compensation is to leave property-loss owners in a situation that is the same as or similar to that had the expropriation not been made. In other words, all the losses incurred by expropriation should be covered by compensation. The expropriated property is the main loss but does not represent all losses. In addition to property loss, other losses include property owners' subjective value and other damages directly incurred by expropriation. Although subjective value cannot be practically calculated, a solatium can be given as compensation to ease the compulsory nature of expropriation. Compared with the owners of urban property, farmers might lose more or be hurt more from expropriation because in rural areas, land offers not only a residence but also a job, as the land is used to make a living. Land owners in cities mainly lose their property in expropriation. When farmers lose land, they lose both property and the jobs at which they are skilled. The transaction cost of changing from cultivation to other jobs is also a part of farmers' losses in expropriation. This issue is especially pertinent in developing countries such as India and China, where it can be difficult for land-loss farmers to find other farmland for cultivation owing to the scarcity of land and the enormous number of farmers. If land-loss farmers have to find a new job in the city, they will need time to adapt to urban employment.

Now, in China, the compensation for expropriated urban houses and the attached land use right is based on the market value, which is mainly calculated through the use of the comparable sales method. Moving, temporary resettlement and the suspension of business are covered as well. However, there is no solatium to cover the portion of losses concerning subjective value.[181]

[181] A rare example on solatium in China is found in Guangzhou's local policy. Article 25 of *Guangzhoushi Chengshi Fangwu Chaiqian Guanli Banfa* [*Guangzhou Measures on the Demolition and Removal of Urban Houses*] stipulates that an amount equal to 20 per cent of the market price of the expropriated house should be added if such house is located in the historical old downtown area. This document was enacted by the Third Meeting of the Standing Committee of the Twelfth Guangzhou People's Congress on 3 September 2003 and invalidated in 2012 because of its conflict with the State Council's *2011 Expropriation Regulation*. The Chinese text of this document is available at www.lawtime.cn/info/gongcheng/difangfaguizhengce/2010083011782.html.

More controversial reforms have occurred with regard to the compensation to land-loss farmers. The current compensation scheme for expropriated farm land is too insufficient in reflecting land's real market value or covering farmers' losses to ease the frequent social unrest. Even in India, which has a much higher compensation standard for displaced persons, violent protests incurred mainly by farmers have urged the government to reform the current compensation and resettlement pack. The most recent reform initiation is the initiation of the *2011 LARR Bill*, which was put into force in 2014. In China, the revision of the *LAL* was initiated in early 2009. The most difficult revisions concern the scope of expropriation and compensation for farmland.

5.6.1 *India: brave step for proposing the* 2011 LARR Bill *and enacting* 2013 LARR Act

First, this 2011 bill introduced a 'higher-value' approach in deciding market value. According to this bill, the market value of the expropriated land shall be the higher of the following two values: the minimum land value registered for the sales deeds in the area where the land at issue is situated and the comparable sales price. If the previously mentioned minimum value and sales price cannot be decided on because of a lack of registration or insufficiency of comparable sales, the state government shall specify the floor price of the expropriated land based on comparable sales prices in the immediate adjoining areas decided using the 'higher one' approach.[182]

Second, the *2011 LARR Bill* proposed a higher compensation standard for farmers in rural areas. For expropriation in rural areas, the previously mentioned market value shall be multiplied by a factor or multiplier of 2. For an expropriated asset in an urban area, the multiplied factor is only 1.[183]

Another distinctive improvement is raising the solatium to a large extent. The calculation basis number is enlarged from the market value of the land to both the market value and the value of assets attached to land. Moreover, the percentage 'solatium rate' is raised from the original 30 per cent to 100 per cent.[184]

Decisions about the compensation pack can be generalised in four steps: (1) deciding the initial market value of the land at issue using

[182] *2011 LARR Bill*, clause 26. [183] Ibid., clause 26(2) and the First Schedule.
[184] Ibid., clause 29 and the First Schedule.

the higher-one approach; (2) multiplying the concerned factor number by the initial market value to obtain the finalised market value of land; (3) calculating a total compensation by aggregating the land value and the value of attached assets; and (4) aggregating such total compensation and solatium to obtain a finalised compensation amount. The compensation pack proposed by this 2011 bill does not stipulate the compensation specifically for moving expenses, losses due to partial taking, damages to the owner's other property or earnings and the diminution of profits during the expropriation process, which are covered by the *1894 LAA*. In fact, all these damages and other damages incurred by expropriation, with the loss of subjective value, are covered by the raised solatium. In total, the compensation amount set by this 2011 bill is significantly more than that stipulated by the *1894 LAA*. For land expropriation in urban areas, the affected family can receive money 2 times the market value of the land and its attachments. In rural areas, the concerned money compensation is 4 times the market value of land and its attachments.

What is also noted is the offer of developed land. If the expropriation project concerns urbanisation, 20 per cent of the developed land should be offered to project-affected families at a price equal to the costs of acquisition and development. If such an offer is accepted, an equivalent amount will be deducted from the compensation pack.[185]

However, the previously mentioned compensation is not all which is available to the families affected by expropriation. The *2011 LARR Bill* further stipulates the rehabilitation and resettlement pack, which includes the provision of housing units in the case of displacement; land for land; the choice of annuity or employment; a one-year subsistence grant for displaced families; transportation costs; cattle shed/petty shops costs; a one-time grant to artisan, traders and certain others; an offering of fishing right in the case of irrigation or hydel projects; a resettlement allowance; coverage of stamp duty and registration fees; and benefits for scheduled castes and tribes (SC/ST).[186]

Most benefits in the rehabilitation and resettlement pack can be given in the form of cash. If no employment is chosen, a one-time payment of five *lakhs* (1 *lakh* = 100,000) *rupees* or not less than 2,000 *rupees* per month per family for twenty years shall be paid. The subsistence grant is 36,000 *rupees*, and, for the SC/ST, an additional 50,000 *rupees* shall be paid. The transportation cost is 50,000 *rupees*. A minimum of 25,000 *rupees* is offered for the construction of a cattle shed or petty shop. A one-time

[185] Ibid., the Second Schedule. [186] Ibid., the First and Second Schedules.

grant of no less than 25,000 *rupees* is offered to affected artisans, traders and certain others. The resettlement allowance is 50,000 *rupees*.[187]

In addition, the *2011 LARR Bill* stipulates that the Requisitioning Authority should provide infrastructural facilities and basic minimum amenities to ensure that the resettled families can enjoy a reasonable standard of community life in the new village or colony.[188]

Certainly, the total compensation and resettlement arrangements proposed by the *2011 LARR Bill* raise the acquisition costs of land greatly. Developers claimed that this bill increased land costs by 80 per cent.[189] The responses from the business sectors have been heavy criticism because the increased acquisition costs encumber economic growth.[190] However, the social forces favouring land-loss farmers finally won.[191] The *2013 LARR Act* revises very little in the part concerning compensation. One revision regards the 'higher one' approach. The term 'minimum value' was replaced with 'market value'.[192] If the expropriation projects are for private companies or public private partnerships, the consented amount of compensation is compared with the market value registered and comparable sales price.[193] Another revision regards the multiplier. For rural land, the multiplier '2' was replaced with a range 'from 1 to 2' in the *2013 LARR Act*.[194] Decisions about the exact number in the range are based on the distance of the project from an urban area. Thus, compensation to expropriated rural land changed from 2 times market value to 4 times market value.

5.6.2 *China: staggering step for reforming the* LAL

In early 2009, the MLR started its revision work for the *LAL*. It was reported that the revision draft was distributed to specified persons and authorities for comments and had not been submitted to the State Council for further legislation procedures. To respond to the social request for the revision of the *LAL* to improve the protection of farmers' land, in the regular meeting (*changwu huiyi*) of the State Council, which passed the

187 Ibid., the Second Schedule.
188 Ibid., clause 31 and the Third Schedule.
189 Ramnani, 'End of Affordability'.
190 Industry Body Assocham required congress review *2011 LARR Bill* as 'it is heavily loaded in favour of land owners and may not create conducive environment for economic growth.' See *The Times of India*, 'Assocham seeks'.
191 For the stipulations about compensation, see secs. 27–31 and three schedules of *2013 LARR Act*.
192 Ibid., sec. 27(1)(a).
193 Ibid., sec. 27(1)(c).
194 Ibid., the First Schedule.

2011 Expropriation Regulation, prime minister Wen Jiabao expressed that the State Council would fasten the revision of the *LAL* and submit the revised version to the NPC as soon as possible.[195] Research and investigations regarding the revision of the *LAL* were initiated by the Legal Office of State Council in early 2011. It is estimated that the revision of the *LAL* will not be finished quickly because it is only in the early period of a long and tedious legislation process. Moreover, substantial improvements to compensation and resettlement in land expropriation are not optimistically expected.

In China, legislative progress normally follows a party-administration-legislation route. First, the CPC makes instructions or guiding principles as to major reform issues in its decisions. Then, the administrative authority in charge starts an investigation and research to finish the suggested draft of the concerned law or law amendment. Finally, the draft is submitted to the legislature authority for passing. A conservative prediction of reform in land compensation and resettlement can be based on the observance of the recent decision made by the CPC and the opinions of the land administration authority. In October 2008, the CPC Central Committee adopted its *Decision on Major Issues Concerning the Further Reform and Development of Rural Areas* (*2008 CPC Decision*).[196] This decision requires that land compensation be improved. As to the compensation standards, this decision uses the term 'reasonable compensation', rather than full or just compensation. Moreover, this decision requires that the compensation sum be decided according to the 'same land same price' principle and paid to the collectives and farmers fully and in timely manner. As to resettlement, this decision requires that land-loss farmers' employment, housing and social security issues be resolved. Apparently, this decision did not make any substantial breakthrough to push the standard of compensation towards a full or just standard based on the market value of land. The resettlement measures mentioned in the decision are only a repetition of past practices.

The opinions of the land authority can be found in the unpublished revision draft made by the MLR.[197] In this draft, the revision opinions

195 Yang, 'Tudi Guanli Fa'.

196 *Zhonggong Zhongyang guanyu Tuijin Nongcun Gaige Fazhan Ruogan Zhongda Wenti de Jueding* [*The CPC Central Committee's Decision on Major Issues Concerning the Further Reform and Development of Rural Areas*], passed by the Third Plenary Meeting of the Seventeenth CPC Central Committee on 12 October 2008. Its Chinese text is available at www.gov.cn/jrzg/2008–10/19/content_1125094.htm.

197 MLR, *Revision Draft of LAL* (2009), on file with the author.

concerning land compensation and resettlement mainly include the incorporation of some key provisions found in the *2004 Land Decision* and *2004 MLR Guidance*. First, the draft mentions three guiding principles for compensation: (1) land in the same location or area shall be paid the same compensation; (2) compensation shall be fair and reasonable; and (3) the payment of the compensation sum shall be in full and in a timely manner. Second, the compensation standard suggested by this draft is still the comprehensive land section price stipulated by the *2004 MLR Guidance*. Third, on the resettlement side, this draft proposes that a social welfare system be established for land-loss farmers and local government take actions to help land-loss farmers to find new employment.

In a routine meeting held on 28 November 2012, the revision draft of the *LAL* was passed by the State Council. According to the official report, the most important revision regards compensation to land-loss farmers. The draft was then submitted to the NPCSC following the legislation process. According to this draft, there are two main revisions, both of which are about compensation. First, it is suggested that art. 47 of *LAL*, which includes the 30-times ceiling and the limit of original land use, be deleted. Second, it is suggested that government guarantee land-loss farmers' new housing and offer them social insurance (*shehui baozhang*). However, as to the detailed compensation standards, the State Council is authorised to make them.[198]

5.6.3 *Comparative analysis and reform suggestions*

Unequal treatment among property right holders in China is reflected clearly by the arrangement of discriminative compensation. Among the four forms of land property rights, namely state ownership rights, collective ownership rights, rural land use rights and urban use rights, three types of discriminative treatment are identified.

The first is the hierarchical order of the three land rights in rural areas. Clearly, state ownership prevails over collective ownership, which prevails over private land use rights. The collective ownership of rural land is limited in use to agricultural production and rural area construction. In the urbanisation process, governments first transfer collective land to state ownership through expropriation and then sell the land for a fiscal return. In fact, local governments take the largest part of the return from

[198] Lin and Yu, 'Rang Beizhengdi'.

land sales.[199] Between collective organisations and private land right holders, collective organisations, working as independent right claimants, are involved in negotiations with developers and governments and address compensation and payment affairs. Although private land use rights are recognised by the *1982 Constitution of China* and 2007 *Property Law* as independent property rights, the rights holders are not independent claimants in the expropriation process. As to the distribution, the currently enforced *LAL* stipulates that the land compensation fee, which is the larger part of the total compensation payment, goes to collectives; the resettlement fee, the smaller part, is given to farmers. Although some provinces began to require that most parts of land compensation fees be given to farmers following the *2004 Land Decision*, this requirement still conflicts with the *LAL* and is not enforced by many local governments.

The second discriminative treatment is unequal treatment between state ownership and private land use rights in urban areas. Home owners in urban areas enjoy ownership over their houses and the use rights of land attached to their houses. When houses are taken by governments, two rights, house ownership rights and land use rights, are eliminated by the governments. The valuation of houses is based on the comparable sale price of houses. In fact, this price includes payment to both the house and its attached land use rights. In this pricing pack, however, the valuation of land use rights is limited to the use right's original use purpose, which is use as a private residence. Thus, given a situation in which the concerned land use right is reasonably expected to be used for a purpose producing higher value than the existing use purpose, a valuation based on original use does not reflect the real value of the concerned land use right. Like land control in rural areas, local governments control the supply of land for construction, and the land collected through the expropriation of houses is sold by governments for fiscal revenue. As to urban land, governments, representing the state, enjoy ownership qualifications over the land even if the use rights of such land are attached to private houses. Thus, the expropriation of houses in fact resumes the state's full ownership of the land attached to private houses. After the sale of land, governments receive the larger part of the return, which is the interest corresponding with construction purposes, and private owners receive the smaller part, which corresponds with private residence or commercial use.

The third unequal treatment is between urban private right holders and rural private right holders. Urban residents are compensated using the

[199] Gao, *Jiti Chanquan*, 160.

standard of market value, which is based on comparable sales methods and limited in residence use purpose. Land-loss collectives and farmers are compensated using the average annual output method, which is stipulated by the *LAL*. To satisfy the requirements of the no-worse-off principle, this method has been adjusted to reflect the land section price in some provinces following the *2004 Land Decision*. The land section price is still based on the annual output method but considers more factors such as social and economic development and the minimum level of local livelihood. In general, valuations based on land section prices lead to higher valuations than the simple output method. However, there are still two defects. One defect is the issue of timeliness. The unified land section price or annual output standard is promulgated every two or more years; it is not the instant valuation of the concerned land. By contrast, in urban areas, the valuation is based on the instant market price of comparable estates. Another defect is unification. The unified compensation standard is applied to all rights holders of land in the same price section. It is inevitable that some farmers with higher production or better land cultivation are undercompensated under such unification standards. By contrast, in urban areas, rights holders are compensated on an individual basis, and the concerned valuation considers the detailed specific features of the concerned real estate.

The compensation and resettlement pack available to the losers of land and house is much lower than that found in the Western countries, which can be represented by the United States. The compensation based on market price available to urban residents in China is not far from the real estate's real market value, except under some situations in which the reasonably expected change of land use is not calculated into the valuation. In rural areas, compensation based on the unified land section price does not reflect the best and highest use values of land, and the local governments' motivation in chasing high returns from land expropriation leads to their reluctance in raising land section prices actively and reasonably. Compared with India, which is also a leading developing country in the world, compensation standards to private property holders are much lower and more unfair. The current compensation standard in India is mainly based on market values or comparable sales prices. Although distorted information in the market might lead to a valuation lower than the real market value, the solatium, which was adjusted from 30 per cent to 100 per cent, can help to reduce this insufficiency in decision regarding a total compensation pack. In addition, the multiplier, which can reach 2, can help to increase sufficiency in compensation to land-loss farmers.

China and India are both progressing towards urbanisation and industrialisation pushed by globalisation. They share the same difficulties in resolving the issues of how to balance the protection of private property and the government's task of economic growth. In recent years, they have both encountered radical social unrest, caused mainly by farmers whose land was expropriated for urbanisation and industrialisation projects without fair compensation. However, the reform responses to social forces requiring strong protection of private property are different in the two countries. India has been performing more quickly and more actively than China.

As to the proposed reform, India's progress in improving compensation and resettlement, as reflected in the proposed *2011 LARR Bill*, is astonishing. The enacted *2013 LARR Act* changes the *1894 LAA*'s heavy favour for developers and governments with regard to overcompensation towards land owners. This change represents a movement from a past unbalance with unfavourable treatment to land-loss individuals to a new unbalance with unfavourable treatment to the development of public projects. Considering its overly radical pace of reform, the quick conception of the *2013 LARR Act* is questioned. Nevertheless, at least this Act reflects India legislators' attitudes in reforming compensation to protect private property owners better. In the same period, the proposed revision of China's *LAL* is still conservative in the raising of compensation. Particularly as to the compensation issue concerning rural land, the most recent proposal of revision does not make any substantial progress in raising the level of compensation. It is interesting to note that China, with the constitutional stipulations of private property, performs much poorer in compensating private property owners under both the current standards and the expected reform measures than India, which has no constitutionalisation of property.

One explanation is the democratic mechanism issue identified in the previous chapter. Although property is not constitutionalised in India, a democratic mechanism based on separation of power and a direct voting system quickly moves the voices of farmers and other social forces seeking stronger protection of property rights to the ears of congressmen and government officials. In China, which lacks the Western style democratic restraints of government, the pressure formed from social unrest calling on property protection moves to the government at a slower pace. In other words, the response from government is less sensitive and active than that in India.

Another explanation is the feature of the property system in China. India is a country with private ownership as the main and fundamental form of land property. By contrast, the public property form still dominates the property system of land in China. Private rights holders are in the lowest level of the system and are given the weakest protection, reflected by low and unjust compensation. Three property forms of land right are assigned different use purposes, among which the public property form enjoys the use purpose with the highest value. For the construction of urbanisation or industrialisation projects, the demanded land must be state owned. The current property system of land prohibits the direct supply of collective rural land to the demanders in urban construction. The private land use right that is attached to urban houses is prohibited from being sold to construction demanders too. The government, which controls the supply of land for construction purposes, can earn huge returns by compulsorily purchasing rural land or private land use rights in urban areas with low compensation costs and then selling for a monopolised price. The raising of compensation to private rights holders means the reduction of land sale returns in the hands of governments. The motivation to chase high profit produced by the expropriation of land leads to governments' strong resistance in restraining the scope of expropriation and especially raising levels of compensation.

The long-term reform goal is to break the government's monopoly status in supplying construction land and develop a market in which rural land and urban land use rights can be legally transacted between individual sellers and buyers directly and more freely. The governments' original role of working as a land broker should change to the role of working as a regulator. In the direct transaction market, the government can set regulations around the types of land that are allowed for transactions and collect the taxation around transactions. However, this would certainly reduce both the government's revenue and individual officers' opportunities for illegal returns. As a result, such a measure would be resisted especially strongly by local governments for which land revenue has become a main part of local revenue. The leadership party's attitude in forming a transaction market concerning rural land is conservative and discreet. According to the *2008 CPC Decision*, the establishment of a unified market of land and the breaking of the rural-urban separation shall be 'gradual'.[200]

Forming a unified land market can provide sufficient reference information to determine the real market value of land or land rights that are

[200] After the promulgation of this decision, there have been no substantial or exact measures regarding the unified market of land.

expropriated, thereby enhancing private owner compensation. However, forming the land market would be a lengthy process at the expense of government land revenue; thus, a market will not likely be formed in the short term. In fact, a market will not be formed until a new policy substitutes the land revenue policy and resolves local governments' fiscal revenue needs. The next question is what reform measures can be adopted to enhance compensation before the unified market is formed?

For house-loss urban resident compensation, the comparable sales method currently used reflects the value of land use rights attached to houses and is limited to its original use. Although under certain situations, where land use right holders can expect reasonably a new future use that would increase the value of their land rights, valuation is difficult because a market is not available, wherein the owners of a house can directly sell their house and the attached land use rights to constructors. In the current house market, houses and attached land use rights are only transferred among house suppliers and demanders. The land use right market includes the following two levels: in one level, the government is the land supplier, and the developers need land; in the second level, the land use rights are transferred among developers for construction. Both market levels concern the construction-use land right. The problem with using the transaction information in the land use right market for a construction purpose is that the relevant transaction price is not formed between a willing buyer and a willing seller of land use rights attached to a house, and this price is distorted. The second level is derived from the first level. The first level land market for construction is monopolised by the government, and the price formed in this market is distorted by government's monopoly control over the land supply. When the market price for construction land is used as the reference to calculate the market value of a house and its attached land use rights, a significant practical challenge is eliminating the distorted price and unbalanced factors.

Two practical suggestions may improve compensation to house-loss urban residents. One suggestion is upward adjustment using the transaction information in the construction land market after the transaction price in the house market is established if the concerned house owners have a reasonable expectation of a future new use of their land before expropriation. If the adjustment remains difficult, the second suggestion is that a percentage of the solatium is given to the concerned house owners. The solatium percentage can be a range – for example, 10 to 30 per cent; the authority in charge can set a percentage within this range considering the transaction information in the construction land market.

For land-loss farmer compensation, a strong suggestion includes borrowing India's practice and supplementing the compensation with a solatium. Land is the source of livelihood for farmers. When farmers lose land, they lose not only property but a familiar career and their job linked with the land. The percentage of solatium may be determined based on the transaction cost of shifting to a new job. If the land-loss farmers are offered comparable land or a new job with free training and guaranteed work as compensation, a lower percentage of solatium is offered to cover their subjective loss from involuntary displacement. However, if the farmers are offered cash compensation, a higher percentage of solatium shall be offered to cover both the subjective loss and loss from changing jobs. For a better resolution, the government can offer three solatium package options for the farmers: (1) 'offering of substitutable job or land + a lower percentage'; (2) a higher solatium percentage without a substitute job or land; or (3) a medium level solatium percentage and a job or a parcel of land, which can partially substitute for the loss; for instance, a farmer whose original farming job was growing crops is offered land that is appropriate for growing fruit.

The land section price should be changed to a minimum compensation standard, which may only be adjusted upward. If collectives or farmers can offer evidence that their actual output is so high that they should be compensated more than the sum based on the land section price, the adjustment shall be allowed. Considering local governments' motivation to decrease the land section price, the *LAL* shall be revised to increase the multiplier and stipulate the current annual output standard as a compulsory minimum standard. If the land section price is lower than the *LAL* minimum standard, the latter compensation should be applied. However, under this scheme, local governments may tend to base a land section price only on the *LAL*'s minimum standard. To push local governments to raise the land section price standard in a timely manner, the relevant law can compulsorily require that the local land section price be raised as a percentage that corresponds to the growth percentage of the local land revenue every fixed term (for example, every year).

When deciding the appropriate percentage range for the previously mentioned solatium and the *LAL* minimum standard, another necessary consideration is the scope of expropriation. In other words, the proportionality principle should be applied to the scope of the public purpose and the level of compensation. If a public purpose scope that justifies the expropriation is so broad that it includes many urbanisation and industrialisation projects, the percentage of solatium and minimum standard should be higher. There are two rationales for this argument. One rationale is that more compensation should be offered to offset the justice lost in an expropriation with weak restraints on public purpose. Individuals should be compensated more heavily because the scope of property loss should have not been so broad. Raising the compensation can also play the role in restraining expropriation power that the public purpose principle should have played. A second rationale is that governments should share their revenue from a broad expropriation scope with the affected private owners because part of the revenue should have been given to the right holders if the land was transferred through a transaction between the right holders and potential demanders. In addition, the levels of compensation should correspond to the public nature of the expropriation project. If the public nature is not very strong (for example, private companies are involved), a higher level should be stipulated.

The final reform suggestion concerns the relationship between a collective and its members. Individual farmers should be offered an opportunity to directly and independently negotiate compensation with the government. An additional suggestion includes clarifying and writing the distribution percentage for the land compensation fee between farmers and their collective into the future revised *LAL*.

6

Ineffective procedural and institutional mechanisms

Among the three prongs for constitutional protection of private property, the weakest and most easily neglected is procedural restraint. The expropriation procedure is designed to produce and enforce an appropriate expropriation decision that leads to a fair result. In the *U.S. Constitution*, the constitutional procedural requirement is expressed through the term 'due process'. The *German Basic Law* uses a more ambiguous and general expression, wherein it states that expropriation can only be ordered by or pursuant to a law that includes compensation stipulations. China followed the German-style expression by stating that expropriation or requisition shall be 'according to law'. The phrase of 'pursuant to law' or 'according to law' does not only refer to procedural restraint. The law pursuant to expropriation includes both substantive and procedural stipulations.

The expression of 'according to law' requires and authorises that the below-constitution laws stipulate both detailed standards for public purpose and compensation as well as the procedure for ordering expropriation. Regarding what the procedure stipulated by law should include, this type of constitutional expression imposes no limits through its literal reading. Instead, the *U.S. Constitution* places the term 'due' before 'process' as the restraint on the legislative expropriation process. Thus, the illustrative questions remain: What process is due? Alternatively, what detailed constitutional procedural requirements should be imposed on the expropriation procedure? Should the procedure include an authorisation or review mode? What type of institutional mechanism, mainly for constitutional review institutions, should be developed? This chapter responds to these questions.

6.1 The United States: due process

6.1.1 *Due process: its origin and development*

The term 'due process' originated from clause 39 of the *Magna Carta*, which was initially promulgated in 1215. This clause stipulates the following: 'No free man shall be seized or imprisoned, or stripped of his rights or possessions, or outlawed or exiled, or deprived of his standing in any other way, nor will we proceed with force against him, or send others to do so, except by the lawful judgment of his equals or by the law of the land.'[1]

In this original text, the term 'due process' refers to 'law of the land' or 'the lawful judgment of his equals', which is a type of procedural or rule of law restraint on the Monarch's misuse of power in protecting the feudal barons' privilege in certain liberties. In 1354, the phrase 'due process of law' was first used in a legislative document supplementing the *Magna Carta*, which stipulated the following:[2] 'No person of what estate or condition that the person be, shall be put out of land or tenement, nor taken, nor imprisoned, nor disinherited, nor put to death, without being brought in answer by due process of the law.'

The authoritative work that linked the original expression 'the law of the land' with the later term 'due process' was completed by Edward Coke in 1608. In the second part of his treatise '*The Institutes of the Laws of England*', Coke writes that 'for the true sense and exposition of these words . . . where the words, by the law of the Land, are rendered without due process of law'.[3]

For the long-term historical development of 'due process of law', the controversial argument has included an explanation for the term 'due' or the following question: what process is due? 'Process' specifically refers to the procedural arrangement regarding the summons and execution of judgement. More specifically, 'it referred to those writs which summoned parties to appear in court, as well as those by which execution of judgments was carried out'.[4] In using due process during

[1] The document is available at www.fordham.edu/halsall/source/magnacarta.asp/. In a shorter version promulgated later, this clause 39 was renumbered to be clause 29. This shorter version is available at www.archives.gov/exhibits/featured_documents/magna_carta/translation.html.

[2] See *(1354) 28 Edw. 3, c. 3* (UK). In Australia, this document was renamed to *Due Process of Law Act 1354* when it was first republished under the *Legislation Act 2001*. It is available at www.legislation.act.gov.au/a/db_1787/current/rtf/db_1787.rtf.

[3] Coke, *The Second Part*, p. 50.

[4] Jurow, 'Untimely Thoughts', 272.

judicial review, the UK tradition has been positive and defers to the legislature.[5]

In the United States, the due process principle is incorporated into the fifth and fourteenth amendments of the constitution. The *Fifth Amendment* stipulates that '[no person shall] be deprived of life, liberty, or property, without due process of law', and the *Fourteenth Amendment* extends due process limit to the states by requiring that '[no state shall] deprive any person of life, liberty, or property, without due process of law'.

The function of due process clause is procedural due process.[6] The procedure clearly stipulated by the constitution shall be observed when deciding the constitutionality of lower-level legislation. This is the basic guarantee of constitutional procedural due process. However, a more controversial question is whether the constitution should impose more limits on legislation and executive actions beyond the statutory requirements. In developing due process through the U.S. Supreme Court, the scope of this term has expanded from procedure to substance. Beginning in the second half of the nineteenth century and mostly developing in the twentieth century, the term 'substantive due process' has been developed by the Supreme Court through its expansive explanations. The *Dred Scott* v. *Sandford* case decided in 1856 might be the Supreme Court's first application of substantive due process.[7] Through this case and a series of later cases, the Supreme Court established that the due process clause imposes not only a procedural guarantee but also substantive limits on state legislation and government actions that might infringe individual liberties or fundamental rights.[8] In essence, substantive due process embraces more constitutional rights than are clearly enumerated by the constitution. The un-enumerated liberties or rights are mainly inferred by the Supreme Court through its expansive explanation of the constitutional terms or spirit. In general, there are three categories of substantive fundamental liberties or rights that fall under the shelter of due process: the enumerated rights in the *Bill of Rights* (the first eight amendments), the equal protection rights that are part of the *Fourteenth Amendment* and the rights of citizens to be involved in political processes, such as the right to vote, associate and give speeches.

5 Mate, 'The Origins', 217.

6 Alexander, 'The Relationship', 324.

7 Justice Scalia states that this case 'was very possibly the first application of substantive due process in the Supreme Court' in his dissention opinions in *Planned Parenthood of Southeastern PA.* v. *Casey*. See 505 U.S. 833, 998 (1992).

8 *Lochner* v. *New York*, 198 U.S. 45 (1905); *Roe* v. *Wade*, 410 U.S. 113 (1973).

Substantive due process was formed to absorb substantial constitutional values and rights, either enumerated in the constitution or inferred from natural law, into the scope of due process protections. Due process was expanded based on the Supreme Court's expansion of its judicial review power over the legislative and executive powers.

The two sets of review tests based on substantive due process are distinguished as follows. If fundamental rights, such as life, liberty and property, are concerned, strict scrutiny should be used to examine the constitutionality of the relevant legislation and government actions, including whether the procedure is sufficient. However, if the concerned rights are non-fundamental, most typically economic regulations, a basic level of scrutiny (minimal scrutiny) or a rational basis test is applied. The two levels of scrutiny were developed by the famous footnote 4 in the 1938 *United States* v. *Carolene Products Co.* decision. In this case, the court used the rational basis test to examine whether the congressional act that prohibited the shipment of skimmed milk compounded with any fat or oil other than milk fat for resembling milk or cream violates the *Fifth Amendment* through ruling that, 'regulatory legislation affecting ordinary commercial transactions is not to be pronounced unconstitutional unless in the light of the facts made known or generally assumed it is of such a character as to preclude the assumption that it rests upon some rational basis within the knowledge and experience of the legislators'.[9]

In the decision for this case, the court used a rational basis test to uphold economic legislation. In footnote 4 of this decision, Justice Stone suggested that heightened scrutiny (strict scrutiny) should be applied to legislation concerning individuals' fundamental rights or rights under the equal protection clause.[10] Stone's suggestion was applied to the case *Skinner* v. *Oklahoma* four years later. In *Skinner*, Justice Douglas used the heightened scrutiny to strike down Oklahoma's *Habitual Criminal Sterilization Act*, which stipulated that forced sterilisation can be imposed on a

9 *United States* v. *Carolene Products Co*, 304 U.S. 144, 152 (1938). As to a much stricter scrutiny, n. 4 in this decision says: 'There may be narrower scope for operation of the presumption of constitutionality when legislation appears on its face to be within a specific prohibition of the Constitution, such as those of the first ten Amendments, which are deemed equally specific when held to be embraced within the Fourteenth.'

10 According to Ely, *Carolene Products* case separates 'property rights from individual freedom' and applies a lower standard of constitutional review of economic rights. However, this is contrary to the constitution framers' intention, which is '[to assign] a much higher standing to property ownership' than the secondary status assigned by this ruling. See Ely, *The Guardian*, p. 140.

habitual criminal who was convicted of two or more felonies involving moral turpitude. Strict scrutiny was used because the right deprived by the act at issue was fundamental. Justice Stone wrote the following:

> We are dealing here with legislation which involves one of the basic civil rights of man. Marriage and procreation are fundamental to the very existence and survival of the race. The power to sterilize, if exercised, may have subtle, far-reaching and devastating effects.
>
> ... There is no redemption for the individual whom the law touches. Any experiment which the state conducts is to his irreparable injury. He is forever deprived of a basic liberty [emphasis added by author].[11]

If we compare this decision with a prior decision from 1927, which concerned forced sterilization, we can see a trace of the progress in substantive due process over the years. Strictly speaking, these two cases do not concern the same issue; although, both concern forced sterilisation. The 1927 case *Buck* v. *Bell* concerns forced sterilisation of a feeble-minded female rather than a habitual criminal. The Supreme Court used a rational basis test to uphold a lower court's judgement, which stated that 'she may be sexually sterilized without detriment to her general health and that her welfare and that of society will be promoted by her sterilization'.[12] Notably, this case also concerned a fundamental right or basic liberty.[13]

Express use of strict scrutiny originated with a decision concerning racial discrimination in 1944.[14] In the decision, the court ruled that legal restrictions curtailing civil rights for a single racial group were subject to 'the most rigid scrutiny'.[15]

During the Warren Court (1953–69), two-tier scrutiny was fully developed and entrenched in the Supreme Court practice. Using the minimal scrutiny or rational basis test, the court upheld most cases concerning economic legislation. Strict scrutiny was mainly used for cases concerning equal protection or 'suspect classification' cases and cases that affected fundamental rights.[16]

During the Burger Court (1969–86), an intermediate scrutiny between strict and minimal scrutiny was established. It is also referred to as the

[11] *Skinner* v. *Oklahoma*, 316 U.S. 535, 541 (1942).

[12] *Buck* v. *Bell*, 274 U.S. 200, 207 (1927).

[13] Though the *Skimmer* does not overrule *Buck*, it deferred many sterilisation cases.

[14] O' Brien, *Constitutional Law*, p. 1249.

[15] *Toyosaburo Korematsu* v. *Unite States*, 323 U.S. 214, 216 (1944).

[16] For example, during the Warren Court (1953–69), the court actively used the rational basis test to review economic legislation's constitutionality. O' Brien, *Constitutional Law*, p. 1249.

'strict rationality' test or 'exacting scrutiny' and is used to test cases concerning gender discrimination.[17] The review standards for the three scrutiny approaches differ. Their strictness level corresponds with the significance of the concerned right or liberty in the constitution. Strict scrutiny is used to review the cases that concern fundamental or the most important constitutional rights. Invasion or deprivation of individual rights is unconstitutional without a compelling state interest. When intermediate scrutiny is used, the review focuses on the 'substantial relationship between the means and ends of legislation'.[18] However, for the minimal test, it asks only whether the concerned legislation has a rational or reasonable basis.

6.1.2 Private property and due process

The states in the United States have highly diverse state-level legislative expropriation procedures. Hudson categorised state legislation on the expropriation process into three groups: the group that provides a full process, the group that completely abrogates procedural protection and the group that offers intermediate protection or standing.[19] A full process includes both prior personal notice and a pre-condemnation (court) hearing, but the opposite extreme offers neither prior notice nor a prior hearing. The intermediate state statutes either offers some judicial review of eminent domain but defects in prior notice to the takee, or offers prior notice but does not offer the takee a prior hearing opportunity.[20]

The Supreme Court did not clearly and strongly endorse the due process for eminent domain until after 1970s. The Supreme Court's attitude towards due process has evolved from a weak requirement to gradually stronger restraints. In one early decision in 1890, the Supreme Court declared that the takee did not have to be compensated before the government's actual taking.[21] In the decision in *Catlin* v. *United States* in 1945, the Supreme Court held that 'in condemnation proceedings appellate review may be had only upon an order or judgment disposing of the whole case, and adjudicating all rights, including ownership and just compensation, as well as the right to take the property'. This decision required some process or procedure for eminent domain, but it did not clarify the due process or procedure for eminent domain. It did not clarify

[17] Ibid., 1250. [18] Ibid. [19] Hudson, 'Eminent Domain', 1286, 1322–7.
[20] Ibid., 1289.
[21] *Cherokee Nation* v. *Southern Kansas Ry. Co.*, 135 U.S. 641, 658 (1890). See also *Sweet* v. *Rechel*, 159 U.S. 380, 400 (1895).

whether a final court judgement is required before actual government possession. The *Catlin* decision's ambiguity left few restraints for the states in generating their due process legislation based on their own understanding and needs. Moreover, a property holder's appellate rights can be deferred until after the order or judgement has concluded.

Four years later, the Supreme Court made small progress in strengthening the due process requirement through its ruling in the case of *Cohen* v. *Beneficial Industrial Loan Corp.*[22] This decision ruled that certain orders that concern important rights can be appealed even if the entire case has not concluded.[23] This decision clearly states that an appeal process may potentially be initiated before condemnation.

Substantial progress in clarifying and strengthening the constitutional due process restraint of eminent domain began in the 1970s, which was the period of due process revolution.[24] In the case of *Mathews* v. *Eldridge* in 1976,[25] the Supreme Court discussed the tests used to decide the sufficiency of procedural due process; although, it did not support that a prior evidentiary hearing is necessary. In this case, the administrative decision that terminated the respondent's social security benefit was challenged based on the argument that the respondent's right to procedural due process as stipulated by the *Fifth Amendment* was abridged because an evidentiary hearing should have been provided before termination. The district court and appeals court both supported the respondent. Although the Supreme Court reversed the appellate court decision by stating that an evidential hearing was not necessary for due process in this case, it outlined the tests for analysing sufficient due process in a property-deprivation case. Justice Powell delivered the court's opinion, citing previous decisions, and strengthened due process by stating that '[due process] is not a technical conception with a fixed content unrelated to time, place and circumstances.' Instead, '[it] is flexible and calls for such procedural protections as the particular situation demands.'[26] Thus, the constitutional sufficiency of an administrative procedure must

[22] *Cohen* v. *Beneficial Industrial Loan Corp.*, 337 U.S. 541 (1949).

[23] This decision appears to identify 'a small class [of orders] which finally determine claims of right separable from, and collateral to, rights asserted in the action, too important to be denied review and too independent of the cause itself to require that appellate consideration be deferred until the whole case is adjudicated'. Ibid., at 546.

[24] Hudson, 'Eminent Domain', 1299.

[25] *Mathews* v. *Eldridge*, 424 U.S. 319 (1976).

[26] *Cafeteria Workers* v. *McElroy*, 367 U.S. 886 (1961); *Morrissey* v. *Brewer*, 408 U.S. 471, 481 (1972).

be considered based on a balance analysis of 'the governmental and private interests that are affected'.[27] The *Mathews* decision provided three general factors that are required for the due process analysis: (1) the private interest that will be affected by an official action; (2) the risk of an erroneous deprivation of an interest through the procedures used and the probable value, if any, of additional or substitute procedural safeguards; and (3) government's interest, including the function involved as well as fiscal and administrative burdens that the additional or substitute procedural requirements would entail.

Entering the 1980s, the Supreme Court sequentially solidified the due process guarantee of property through its decisions in three cases: *Logan* v. *Zimmerman Brush Co.* in 1982, *United States* v. *James Daniel Good Real Property* in 1993 and *Lingle* v. *Chevron* in 2005.[28] In *Logan*, the court used the logic identified in *Mathews* to analyse the constitutional sufficiency of a procedure concerning deprivation of one person's property interest. The competing interests that are balanced include the importance of the private interest, the length or finality of the deprivation, the likelihood of governmental error and the magnitude of the governmental interests involved. After considering these factors, the court concluded that a post-deprivation hearing would not be adequate to satisfy the constitutional due process requirement.[29] In *Good*, a forfeiture procedure involved the house and land of a person who was charged with promoting harmful drugs and did not include prior notice and adversarial proceeding. The Supreme Court stated this procedure was inconsistent with the *Fifth Amendment* due process requirement. In this case, the court still used the three-factor formula in *Matthews* to analyse whether prior notice and hearing were necessary for due process. By weighing the three factors, the court thought Good's property right over his home was 'a private interest of historic and continuing importance',[30] which outweighs the government's interest and requires an additional proceeding that comprises prior notice and a hearing to reduce the possible unacceptable erroneous risk of an ex-parte seizure as well as protect the owner's important property interest.[31] The Court further strengthened a general rule established through precedent, 'individuals must receive

[27] 424 U.S. 319, 335 (1976). [28] Hudson, 'Eminent Domain', 1304.

[29] *Logan* v. *Zimmerman Brush Co.*, 455 U.S. 422, 433–6 (1982).

[30] *United States* v. *James Daniel Good Real Property*, 510 U.S. 43, 53–4 (1993).

[31] Ibid., at 53–5.

notice and an opportunity to be heard before the Government deprives them of property'.[32] Although this general rule is not absolute, the only exceptions include certain 'extraordinary situations', where the government interest is so important that it justifies postponing the hearing till after the forfeiture.[33]

In 2005, the *Lingle* case clarified the distinction between due process and taking clause cases. This case concerned a rent cap regulation passed by the Hawaii legislature to control retail gas prices. The regulation was challenged by the respondent based on the argument that it unconstitutionally took his property. Using the 'substantially advance[s]' formula, both the district and appeals courts held that the regulation, which constituted a regulatory taking but did not offer compensation, violated both the *Fifth Amendment* and the *Fourteenth Amendment*. The Supreme Court remanded this case to lower court for further proceeding because the 'substantially advance[s]' formula shall not be used as a test for deciding a regulatory taking case.[34]

The 'substantially advance[s]' formula was developed in *Agins* v. *City of Tiburon* in 1980.[35] In this case, certain zoning ordinances, which were challenged for unconstitutional taking, were supported by the Supreme Court through saying that such ordinances 'substantially advance legitimate governmental goals'[36] In *Lingle*, the court held that this formula developed from due process rather than taking precedent.[37] It is a 'means-end test' that examines the substantial relationship between regulating private property and achieving a public end. Following this logic, the Supreme Court distinguished takings and due process claims. Even if compensation is offered to the takee, the takee can still challenge the government's taking decision using a due process claim. In *Lingle*, the court held the following:

> It does not bar government from interfering with property rights, but rather requires compensation 'in the event of otherwise proper interference amounting to a taking.' Conversely, if a government action is found to be impermissible – for instance because it fails to meet the 'public use' requirement or is so arbitrary as to violate due process – that is the end of the inquiry. No amount of compensation can authorize such action.[38]

[32] Ibid., at 48. [33] Ibid., at 53. [34] *Lingle* v. *Chevron*, 544 U.S. 528 (2005).
[35] *Agins* v. *City of Tiburon*, 447 U. S. 255, 260 (1980). [36] Ibid., at 261.
[37] There is no question that the 'substantially advances' formula was derived from due process, not takings, precedent.
[38] 544 U.S. 528, 543 (2005).

The *Lingle* decision clearly affirms that laws or regulations with the effect of taking property must be examined for constitutionality by both the taking clause, which encompasses public use and just compensation, and the due process clause. In addition, it clarifies the remedy for violating due process, which invalidates the government action regardless of compensation.[39]

6.2 Germany and India: authorisation mode

6.2.1 Germany

The *German Basic Law* only requires that expropriation is ordered 'according to law'. The expropriation procedure is stipulated by both federal and local legislation. This constitutional restraint can be referred to as statutory authority, which reflects the fundamental principle that property is an individual's constitutional right and the government can only interfere with this right pursuit to a law drafted and passed by a democratically elected legislature.[40] In essence, this constitutional requirement indirectly reflects due process to a certain extent; although, the constitution does not expressly use the term 'due process' or its alternatives. Currie commented that, 'it represents an early and often neglected aspect of the Due Process Clauses'.[41] The leading legislation on expropriation is *BauGB*, which illustrates a typical expropriation procedure in Germany.

The expropriation authority is the higher administrative authority responsible for administering expropriation affairs.[42] This authority is typically set at the regional level in most states and is independent from the authority that is responsible for the public purpose underlying the expropriation.[43] The entire procedure is composed of a preliminary or preparatory stage and a formal stage.

The preliminary stage is used to prepare for the formal expropriation initiation procedure; it comprises two steps. The first step is the application for expropriation; the application is submitted to the municipality, wherein the proposed land is located, and the municipality then transfers the application and its comments to the expropriation authority within one month.[44] The second step is the preparation for hearing. The authority is required to prepare sufficiently such that the procedure can be

[39] Penalver and Strahilevitz, 'Judicial Takings', 311–12. [40] Currie, 'Lochner Abroad', 340.
[41] Ibid. [42] *BauGB*, sec. 104(1). [43] Voss, 'Appropriate Compensation', p. 59.
[44] *BauGB*, sec. 105.

completed in one session. In addition to providing opportunities to the applicant, owners and affected authorities for presentation, if necessary, opinions from experts or related authorities should be collected.[45]

The formal expropriation procedure is initiated by a hearing. The parties summoned include applicant, land owners, other parties with interest in the proposed land and the municipality. The period of summon shall be one month. Several pieces of information are required in the summons: (1) the identity of the applicant and affected land; (2) the summary of the key issues in the expropriation with a reminder that the full text of the application is available in the authority's office; (3) a request for timely submission of any objection in writing; and (4) advice that a decision would be made with no regard for whether the concerned parties failed to attend the hearing.[46] Public notice about the hearing is required in a customary manner and with the necessary information.[47]

Throughout the procedure, the expropriation authority strives to facilitate an agreement between the related parties. For a partial agreement, the related parties agree on the expropriation purpose but disagree on compensation.[48] Where the parties do not mutually or fully agree, the procedure is completed through an expropriation decision; this decision is a resolution on expropriation, which shall include a reminder of and basic information about a court ruling. Where the expropriation is approved, this resolution shall contain the following information: the persons affected by and the beneficiaries of expropriation; other parties involved; the expropriation purpose and the time period during which the land will be used for the proposed purpose; and the subject of expropriation.[49]

Upon request by the involved parties, the authority can make a preliminary decision on the transfer or encumbrance of the land ownership proposed for expropriation or on any other right alteration caused by expropriation. However, advance payment of the anticipated compensation to the concerned beneficiary shall be ordered.[50] For a partial agreement, such advance payment shall be ordered if allowed by agreement.[51] If an urgent situation demand is based on public welfare, the expropriation authority can resolve to permit the applicant to possess the proposed land before

[45] Ibid., sec. 107(1)(2). [46] Ibid., sec. 108(3). [47] Ibid., sec. 108(5).
[48] Ibid., sec. 111. [49] Ibid., sec. 113(1)(2). [50] Ibid., sec. 112(2).
[51] Ibid., sec. 111.

the procedure is completed. However, this measure requires negotiation during the hearing stage.[52]

6.2.2 *India*

Although India borrowed from other legal systems in producing its laws, including the constitution from its former coloniser, the UK, as with the United States; unlike the United States, it did not include the term 'due process' in its constitution. The omission was deliberate by the framers of the constitution. The due process clause in the draft of the constitution published in 1947 was deleted before the constitution was passed.[53] Mate provided two general factors that influenced the Constituent Assembly in discarding the due process clause. One factor is the influence of then-U.S. Supreme Court Justice Felix Frankfurter, who opposed substantive due process. The constitutional advisor B. N. Rau was so influenced by Felix during his visit to the United States that he pushed the drafting committee to avoid absorbing due process into India's constitution after his return.[54] A second factor is the social background under which the leading Congress party was led by Nehru and included socialist-oriented reform. This influence facilitated incorporation of the social-aspirational directive principles, limits on property rights and removal of due process protection for property.[55] Apparently, removing the due process clause was aimed at strengthening the governing power of parliament and the administration branches to lead social reform through reducing the intervention by judicial power.

The Indian constitution adopts a German-style statutory authority requirement, which states in its art. 21 that '[n]o person shall be deprived of his life or personal liberty except according to procedure established by law.' This article and a second article (art. 19), which stipulates the basic rights to freedom, are considered together under the subtitle 'Right to Freedom'. The right to property was stipulated by art. 19(1)(5) when the constitution was created in 1949. Before the property right was removed from the constitution in 1979 as a basic constitutional liberty right, it was protected by art. 21. In the late 1970s, the Indian Supreme Court began to develop due process jurisprudence through its expansive interpretation.[56] However, the due process perspective developed by the Supreme Court

[52] Ibid., sec. 116. [53] Mate, 'The Origins', 217. [54] Ibid., 221–3.
[55] Ibid., 226. [56] Ibid., 217.

is not applied to property rights after 1979, only the fundamental life and liberty rights are stipulated by art. 21. To summarise, currently both the article with constitutional statutory authority and the judicial due process principle that has developed are not applied to property rights.

Similar to Germany, the expropriation procedure is stipulated by various legislation. Before 2014, the *1894 LAA* was the main and leading legislation concerning expropriation in India.

The *1894 LAA* procedure comprises two phases. The first phase begins with sec. 4(1) Notification and ends when sec. 6 Declaration is realised. The second phase begins with sec. 9 Notice and ends with a sec. 11 Award.

The officer in charge of the land acquisition is the 'Collector', who is appointed as the acquisition officer by the appropriate Government. When a parcel of land in a locality is necessary for a public purpose or a company, the Collector shall publish a preliminary notification under sec. 4(1) of the *1894 LAA* (sec. 4(1) Notification). This notification shall be made public through a three-step procedure: (1) publication in the *Official Gazette*; (2) publication in two daily newspapers circulating in that locality of which at least one shall be in the regional language; and (3) placing a notice that includes the substance of the notification at convenient places in the locality.

After notification, the Collector can arrange for a survey of the target land to examine whether the land is appropriate for the proposed use. If the survey officers must enter a building or enclosed garden or courtyard, they shall obtain the occupiers' consent or provide the occupier with at least seven days of advance notice in writing. If the survey causes damage to the occupier, compensation shall be paid.[57]

Any person interested in the land referred to in the notification has the right to submit their objection in writing to the Collector within thirty days after notification. The Collector shall arrange a hearing for the objectors. If he believes it is necessary, the Collector can inquire further. After the hearing, the Collector must submit a report that includes his comments on the objections to the appropriate Government for approval.[58]

If the appropriate Government approves the Collector's report and decides to acquire the proposed land, a declaration (sec. 6 Declaration) shall be made publicly through the publication approaches used for the sec. 4(1) Notification. After the appropriate Government order, the Collector can cause the acquired land to be marked out unless this step is completed after the sec. 4(1) Notification.[59] The first phase must end

[57] *1894 LAA*, sec. 5. [58] Ibid., sec. 5A(1)–(2). [59] Ibid., sec. 8.

within one year after the sec. 4(1) Notification, otherwise the entire procedure shall begin anew.

The second phase begins with the sec. 9 Notice. Following the Government's decision to approve acquisition, the Collector shall provide public notice at convenient places on or near the land to be taken, declaring the Government's intent to acquire the land and inviting compensation claims for all interests in the target land.[60] Personal notice shall be served to the occupiers or any other persons known or believed to be interested in the land.[61] Next, the Collector shall inquire into the objections (if any) as to the target land measurements and value as well as the respective interests of the persons claiming compensation.[62] For the inquiry, the Collector is empowered to summon and enforce witness attendance and document production.[63]

After inquiring into the claims, the Collector shall make an award (sec. 11 Award), stating the scope of the land to be acquired as well as the compensation and its apportionment among the interested persons.[64] The second phase must be completed within two years after the sec. 6 declaration. In total, the entire acquisition procedure shall be completed within three years.

Any person interested in the target land who refuses the sec. 11 Award may, by submitting a written application to the Collector, require that the matter be referred to the Court by the Collector.[65] However, the court procedure does not prevent the Collector from possessing the targeted land. The Collector can represent the appropriate Government and occupy the expropriated land free from all encumbrances after the sec. 11 Award.[66]

The *1894 LAA* requires that the Collector shall tender full amount of compensation to the persons interested in the land upon the award before taking possession of land. If any interested person refuses the tendered compensation, the Collector can deposit the payment at the court to which the case is referred.[67]

Similar to relevant German legislation, the *1894 LAA* allows an agreement among the interested persons and prior occupation of the land under certain urgent situation. If persons interested in the target land reach an agreement at any stage of the acquisition procedure, the Collector can make an award based on the terms of the agreement.[68]

[60] Ibid., sec. 9(1). [61] Ibid., sec. 9(2)–(4). [62] Ibid., sec. 11(1).
[63] Ibid., sec. 14. [64] Ibid., sec. 11(1). [65] Ibid., sec. 18. [66] Ibid., sec. 16.
[67] Ibid., sec. 31(1)–(2). [68] Ibid., sec. 11(2).

If an unforeseen emergency that requires repairing or maintaining traffic, navigation channel, irrigation, water supply, drainage and electricity, among other considerations, the Collector can immediately possess the land after publishing the sec. 9 Notice. For additional urgent situations, as determined by the appropriate Government, the Collector can possess the land for a public purpose fifteen days after publication of the sec. 9 Notice. Before the urgent occupation, the *1894 LAA* requires that 80 per cent of the total estimated compensation shall be tendered to the persons with interest in the land.[69]

The *1894 LAA* has two phases: the land acquisition decision and the determination of the precise manner of execution, including compensation. The *2013 LARR Act* substantially revised the full procedure to enhance the restrictions on the government and the difficulty and tedium in acquiring the land.

First, the Collector's power was greatly reduced. According to the *1894 LAA*, the Collector could decide what constitutes a public purpose. The *2013 LARR Act* stipulates a detailed Social Impact Assessment (SIA) procedure for determining a public purpose. The Collector cannot execute the additional powers – for example, to decide the compensation, possess the land and initiate urgent acquisition – at his discretion, as under the *1894 LAA*, because the new law stipulates details regarding execution of such powers.[70]

Second, the full decision process was refined to include the SIA and determination of the Rehabilitation and Resettlement Scheme (R&R Scheme). The new land acquisition procedure includes two phases, the pre-notification period and the notification period. In the first period, the appropriate Government must perform an SIA study, mainly to assess the social impact and determine the public purpose.[71] To perform the SIA

[69] Ibid., sec. 17(1)–(3A). If the amount paid exceeds the amount decided by the Collector in his award, the excess may, unless refunded within three months from the date of Collector's award, be recovered as an arrear of land revenue. Ibid., sec. 17(3B).

[70] The *2013 LARR Act* includes the detailed formula that lists what should constitute compensation and how to calculate the compensation amount. *2013 LARR Act*, the First Schedule. The Collector cannot make the possession decision until all the requirements in the law are satisfied. Ibid., sec. 39. The situations under which the Collector can initiate urgent acquisition are limited to two: natural calamities and national defence. For other situations, the acquisition should be approved by Parliament. Ibid., sec. 41(2).

[71] The SIA report should include: assessment as to whether the proposed acquisition serves public purpose; estimation of the affected families and the number of those families likely to be displaced; extent of lands, public and private, houses, settlements and other common properties likely to be affected by the proposed acquisition; whether the extent of land proposed for acquisition is the absolute bare-minimum extent needed for the project;

study, representatives of the interested persons and the relevant authorities should be notified, and a public hearing is required.[72] The SIA report should be published and appraised by a group of experts.[73] In the second period, in addition to the typical procedure, which includes notice, hearing objections and determining of exact scope of the land and compensation, the R&R Scheme must be drafted, reviewed, approved and published.[74]

Third, under the *2013 LARR Act*, the Land Acquisition, Rehabilitation and Resettlement Authority (LARR Authority) must be established. The LARR Authority includes one Presiding Officer who must be an experienced legal practitioner.[75] The LARR Authority is authorised with the same powers vested in a civil court to hear disputes on land acquisition. Thus, proceedings before the LARR Authority are judicial in nature.[76] Any person interested who has not accepted the Collector's award can submit his written application to require a decision by the LARR Authority.[77] If the LARR Authority's award remains unacceptable, the appeal can move to a High Court.[78] The objections mainly include the land measurement, compensation, the person paid, R&R rights and the compensation apportionment. The appropriate Government's decision on the public purpose and SIA report findings shall be final.[79]

6.3 China

In China, the expropriation procedure for urban houses differs from the rural land procedure due, at least partially, to the different real estate right structures between urban and rural areas.

6.3.1 Procedure for expropriating urban houses

6.3.1.1 Pre-2011 procedure

In China, the expropriation procedure before 2011 was established by the *1991 Demolition Regulation*; the subsequently revised version is the *2001 Expropriation Regulation.*

whether land acquisition at an alternate place has been considered and found not feasible; and a study on the social impact of the project, the nature and cost of addressing the impact and the impact of these costs on the overall project costs compared to the benefits of the project. Ibid., sec. 4(3).

72 Ibid., secs. 4(2), 4(5). 73 Ibid., secs. 6–7. 74 Ibid., secs. 17–20.

75 The Presiding Officer is or has been a District Judge or has been a qualified legal practitioner for not less than seven years. Ibid., sec. 54(1).

76 Ibid., secs. 61–2. 77 Ibid., sec. 65(1). 78 Ibid., sec. 74. 79 Ibid., sec. 16.

Both the 1991 and 2001 regulations divide the entire procedure into three stages: the application stage, approval stage and enforcement stage.

The persons that initiate the expropriation procedure are referred to as 'the persons in charge of demolition and removal' (PDR) who need land use rights for construction. Although the PDR may be a unit or an individual according to the *1991 Demolition Regulation*,[80] in practice, nearly all PDRs are units; most PDRs are real estate development companies. The *2001 Demolition Regulation* only limits PDRs as units;[81] they are referred to as PDRs because they are also responsible for demolition and removal after their application is approved.

A PDR's application is submitted to the relevant government authority for approval. The authority is the government agency charged with administering real estate affairs at the county level or higher.[82] The first stage ends when the authority makes a decision and issues a license for demolition and removal to the PDR. The documents required for application and approval include the approval documents from the relevant government as well as the plan and scheme for demolition and removal.[83] The relevant documents required by the *1991 Demolition Regulation* are generally defined as 'the approval documents thc State stipulates' generally, and the *2001 Demolition Regulation* clearly defines the documents as the documents approving construction projects, the construction land planning license and the approval for a use right in state owned land. The *2001 Demolition Regulation* also imposes a new requirement for the application materials, the bank's certificate letter regarding the PDR's saving fund for the proposed compensation and resettlement. The *1991 Demolition Regulation* does not set a time limit for the authority's approval process, and the *2001 Demolition Regulation* requires the review within thirty days from the application.[84]

The second stage begins with publication of the government notice. If the authority decides to issue a demolition and removal license, it shall provide public notice that includes the information concerning the PDR, the scope of demolition and removal and the period for demolition and removal.[85] With the license, the PDR can begin demolition and removal. The PDR must negotiate compensation and resettlement with

80 *1991 Demolition Regulation*, art. 3.

81 *2001 Demolition Regulation*, art. 4.

82 *1991 Demolition Regulation*, art. 6; *2001 Demolition Regulation*, art. 5.

83 *1991 Demolition Regulation*, art. 8; *2001 Demolition Regulation*, art. 7.

84 *2001 Demolition Regulation*, art. 7.

85 *1991 Demolition Regulation*, art. 10; *2001 Demolition Regulation*, art. 8.

the affected persons, who are typically the owners of the target houses or tenants, if the house is leased.[86] If an agreement cannot be reached through negotiation, the compensation and resettlement issue is submitted to the relevant authority or the local government if the authority is affected by the demolition and removal. The 2001 regulation requires that a decision concerning compensation and resettlement made within thirty days after the application.[87]

The PDR must perform the detailed demolition and removal. The PDR can also authorise other units to demolish and remove the target houses, where the unit is qualified. However, the government authority in charge is prohibited from accepting PDR's authorisation.[88]

If the owners of the target houses are not satisfied with the compensation decision, they may sue in court. During the court proceeding, the demolition and removal continue if the PDR has provided compensation or temporary resettlement arrangements to the affected persons.

If the affected persons refuse to move outside the target house during the stipulated period of removal decided by the authority, the local government can prepare a compulsory enforcement order to authorise the relevant authority to compulsorily remove and demolish the target houses. This compulsory order can also be issued by a court upon the authority's application.[89]

6.3.1.2 Post-2011 procedure

In the *2011 Expropriation Regulation*, the expropriation procedural reforms were substantial. Although the *1982 Constitution of China* does not include detailed and clear requirements for the expropriation procedure, in the *2011 Expropriation Regulation*, art. 3 stipulates that the procedure shall follow three principles: 'democratic decision', 'due procedure' and 'transparency of information'.

The *2011 Expropriation Regulation* excludes expropriation for non-public purposes. Thus, the PDRs, which are typically enterprises that develop real estate, cannot initiate or enforce demolition and removal after this regulation. Only the appropriate government authority can initiate and enforce administrative expropriation procedures. Government at the municipality or county level is responsible for expropriation and

86 *1991 Demolition Regulation*, art. 12; *2001 Demolition Regulation*, art. 13.
87 *1991 Demolition Regulation*, art. 14; *2001 Demolition Regulation*, art. 16.
88 *1991 Demolition Regulation*, art. 9; *2001 Demolition Regulation*, art. 10.
89 *1991 Demolition Regulation*, art. 15; *2001 Demolition Regulation*, art. 17.

compensation in its territory. The detailed expropriation is executed by the authority authorised by the appropriate government.[90]

When a house must be expropriated for a public purpose, the authority drafts a project proposal on expropriation and compensation and submits it to the supervising government. After receipt of the project proposal, the appropriate government must organise the relevant departments for discussion and research. Simultaneously, the project is offered to the public for comments. The period for collecting public comments shall last no less than thirty days.[91] If the expropriation is for reconstruction of old city areas and most of the affected persons believe that the project violates the regulation, a meeting of hearing between the affected persons and public representatives is required.[92] Before the expropriation decision, the risk of social unrest shall be evaluated. If the proposed expropriation concerns a large group of persons, the decision must be made through a discussion in an executive meeting of the government.[93]

After an expropriation decision, the appropriate government shall publicise the decision in a timely manner. The publication shall offer information concerning the compensation scheme and a reminder on the opportunity for an appeal. If the affected persons refuse to accept the expropriation decision, they can either apply for administrative reconsideration by a higher level government authority or bring a court suit against the decision.[94]

Based on the project proposal approved by the appropriate government, the authority in charge negotiates the compensation and resettlement details with the affected persons. If the parties cannot agree within the negotiation period stipulated by the expropriation decision, upon the authority's application, the appropriate government decides the compensation details. The compensation decision shall be publicised within the territory in which the expropriation project exists.[95]

If the affected persons do not apply for administrative reconsideration or initiate a court proceeding within the period stipulated by law and refuses to move when the period for moving stipulated by the compensation decision expires, the appropriate government can apply for a compulsory expropriation order from a court.

This regulation requires that compensation is tendered before the house owners move.[96]

[90] *2011 Expropriation Regulation*, art. 4. [91] Ibid., art. 10. [92] Ibid., art. 11.
[93] Ibid., art. 12. [94] Ibid., arts. 13–14. [95] Ibid., art. 26. [96] Ibid., art. 27.

6.3.1.3 Comments

The pre-2011 procedure has been criticised for its extreme unfairness to the private property owners and other concerned right holders. First, the developer companies (PDRs) are responsible for executing the expropriation details, including initiation of the expropriation application, the compensation negotiation with the property owners and enforcing demolition and removal, which should be executed by a government authority with public power. Second, the affected property owners are poorly notified. Under the 1991 and 2001 regulations, the authority does not need to notify the affected persons before it approves a license. The affected persons are not notified with any information about expropriation until the license is approved. They are notified of an expropriation decision to require that they cooperate with the expropriation that follows.[97] Third, the affected individuals have few opportunities for having their voice heard by government before the authority makes its decision and, thus, little involvement in and influence on the authority's decision-making process. Finally, the entire procedure is distinctively led by an administrative body. The compulsory order for taking the target houses can be made and enforced by the executive government without a prior court remedy.

Compared with the old procedure, the currently enforced procedure stipulated by the *2011 Expropriation Regulation* is significant progress. First, the enterprises concerned (project developers) are excluded from expropriation procedure. The procedure mainly involves two sides: the government on behalf of the public interest and the private right owners. Second, the role of the authority was transformed from a decision maker to a decision executor. The expropriation decision is made by the authorised local government. Although this change does not fundamentally alter the administrative decision power, it is helpful for generating more discrete decisions.

Under the old regulations, the authority that could make expropriation and compensation decisions was typically the department in charge of urban construction, which is subordinate to the local government. Two factors might influence the authority's impartiality in decision making.

[97] The old regulations use very arbitrary words to stipulate the affected persons' obligation in cooperating with expropriation affairs, and this expression reflects the then rule makers' indifference to the citizen's private property rights. For instance, art. 5 of the 1991 regulation provides that the persons whose houses are demolished and removed 'must comply with the need of urban construction and move out within the stipulated removal period.' See *1991 Demolition Regulation*, art. 5.

The first factor is its interest in the purpose for expropriation. Urban houses are mostly expropriated for urban renewal, and real estate development fall within the scope of the authority's responsibilities. The second factor is that a government department supervises the real estate developers and construction companies. The tight interest relationship between the authority and business entities might drive the authority to support developing companies that apply for demolition and removal and lead to corruption as well as other rent-seeking activities. Attributing the decision power to a higher level government in the 2011 regulation may facilitate decisions that are based on more comprehensive considerations for the project and its influence on the entire local society. In addition to the opinions of the authority in charge of construction, opinions from the other relevant agencies and the public are also considered by the local government in its decision. Although it is impossible to eliminate the corruption problem, this change may aid in reducing the rent-seeking activities to a certain extent because it enhances the rent-seekers' difficulty in corrupting the decision maker. The government in charge must consider the social stability issue and discuss how expropriation might influence a large number of persons. The decision must be approved in the government's executive meeting (which makes decisions collectively), and the leaders from local government and concerned subordinate department participate.

Third and most distinctively, the information transparency and right holder involvement improved. The expropriation and compensation project draft shall be publicised to collect public opinions, which are rendered by both the affected persons and others in society. The information on the collected opinions and the project proposal revisions based on the public opinions must also be publicised for society. In addition, a meeting to hear opinions is required if the proposed expropriation concerns reconstructing old city areas.

Fourth, the final compulsory taking order can only be awarded and executed by a court. The old regulations endow the local government with a decision power to order compulsory occupation. The administrative government could organise compulsory demolition and removal when the order is issued. However, the 2011 regulation deprives the appropriate government of the power to deciding and executing a final compulsory taking or occupation. Compulsory expropriation shall be enforced on a court decision and through the court's arrangement. This reform was implemented to eliminate the original administrative compulsory taking and establish a judicial procedure.

6.3.2 *Procedure for expropriating rural land*

The expropriation procedure for rural land is stipulated by the *LAL* and supplemented through *LAL Regulation* promulgated by the State Council in 1998 and relevant rules by the MLR, such as the *Measures on Public Notice for Land Requisition* (*2001 MLR Notice Measures*) enacted in 2001[98] and *Provisions on the Hearing for National Land Resources* (*2004 MLR Hearing Provisions*) enacted in January of 2004.[99] Beginning in 2004, certain unsubstantial reform measures were created, mainly through the MLR's efforts.

6.3.2.1 The procedure in the *LAL* and its implementation regulation

The full procedure can be initiated by a unit or individual that needs land for construction.[100] For urban construction needs, the government can also initiate the expropriation procedure. Before the expropriation decision, the government authority in charge must approve the conversion of land use purpose.[101] In China, each parcel of land is assigned with a specific use purpose, and its use cannot be converted without prior approval. In rural areas, most land is for agricultural use, and the remaining land is used for constructing the collective members' houses and building village and township enterprises, as well as public facilities in the relevant village and town territory. For urban construction outside of the village and township territory, the construction unit must apply to use state-owned land.

Approval of the land use conversion is based on the government's plans for the land use, including the annual plan and the overall plan for land utilisation. If the land use is converted from an agricultural use to a construction use, the conversion should be consistent with the relevant urban or village and town planning.[102] Land use conversion is controlled to regulate land and plan land resource distribution, especially to guarantee food safety through controlling a sufficient amount of the cultivated land.

98 *Zhengyong Tudi Gonggao Banfa* [*Measures on Public Notice for Land Requisition*], promulgated by the MLR on 22 October 2001. The Chinese text is available at www.gov.cn/gongbao/content/2002/content_61573.htm.

99 *Guotu Ziyuan Tingzheng Guiding* [*Provisions on the Hearing for National Land Resources*], promulgated by the MLR on 9 January 2004. The Chinese text is available at www.gov.cn/gongbao/content/2004/content_62947.htm.

100 *LAL*, art. 43(1). 101 Ibid., art. 44. 102 *Ibid.*, art. 44(3); *LAL Regulation*, art. 19.

If the concerned construction projects are approved by the State Council or are for road, pipeline or a large infrastructure and approved by the government at a provincial level, the appropriate approval authority for land use conversion is the State Council. If the land use is converted to enforce the overall land utilisation plan and falls within the allowable scope for land use in constructing municipalities, villages or towns, the land use conversion can be approved by the authority that originally approved the overall utilisation plan. For other projects, the approval authority shall be the government at the provincial level.[103]

The approval authorities are the State Council and governments at the provincial level. The State Council is responsible for approving expropriation of the following land: (1) prime farmland; (2) cultivated land (excluding prime farmland) exceeding 35 hectares (ha); and (3) land exceeding 70 ha. The government at the provincial level is charged with approving the land expropriation projects that do not fall within the State Council's approval authority.[104]

Where the approval authorities for land use conversion and expropriation are the same, the concerned procedures can be administered simultaneously.[105]

Typically, the municipality and county governments submit an application to the appropriate authority to approve the land use conversion and expropriation to enforce an urban plan. These governments must prepare three projects (reports, *fang-an*) for approval: the land use purpose conversion project, arable land complementation project and expropriation project.[106] The complementation project arranges to supplement the pool of cultivated land with other lands to substitute for the expropriated cultivated land and maintain the amount of arable land for food security. After approval, the municipality and county governments can begin to supply the expropriated land to the construction units that need the land.

The following is the implementation procedure for an approved land expropriation project, which can be generalised as a 'two-announcement and one-registration system'.[107] The first announcement is the land expropriation project announcement. After the expropriation project is approved, the municipality and county governments shall publicly announce the project within the village or town territory within ten

[103] *LAL*, art. 44. [104] Ibid., art. 45. [105] Ibid.
[106] *LAL Regulation*, art. 20. [107] ADB, 'People's Republic of China', 9 (fn. 8).

days after receiving the approval.[108] The announcement shall include title of the approval government authority, the approval document number, the use purpose, the expropriated land scope and square meters, and the compensation standard. After the announcement, the persons who have ownership or user rights in the target land register their rights for compensation with the local land administration department within the time limit stipulated by the land expropriation announcement.[109]

After registration for compensation, the department charged with land administration must draft a compensation and resettlement project proposal. In generating the project proposal, the land administration must consult other relevant government departments. The project must be fully prepared no later than forty-five days after the land expropriation announcement.[110] The project proposal must be publicly announced to invite opinions from the affected collective organisations and farmers. Based on the collected opinions, the compensation and resettlement projects can be revised.[111] The *LAL* and its implementation regulation do not require a formal hearing. However, beginning in 2001, the MLR requires that a hearing is offered at the affected right holders' request.[112]

Next, the compensation project must be submitted to the appropriate government for approval. After approval, the project implementation begins. If the affected collectives or farmers oppose the compensation standards, the appropriate government should arrange for negotiation. If negation does not yield an agreement, the dispute over the compensation standard can be submitted to the authority that approved the land expropriation for a decision. However, the dispute resolution does not influence implementation of the land expropriation project.[113]

[108] *LAL*, art. 46; *LAL Regulation*, art. 25; *2001 MLR Notice Measures*, art. 4.

[109] *LALRegulation*, art. 25(1)(2).

[110] *2001 MLR Notice Measures*, art. 7.

[111] *LAL Regulation*, art. 25(3); *LAL*, art. 48.

[112] *2001 MLR Notice Measures*, art. 10. The right to a hearing is also stipulated by the *2004 MLR Hearing Provisions* in art. 19, which stipulates the detailed process of organising a hearing. The hearing process is composed of three steps: notice, application and holding a meeting. First, the affected collectives and farmers shall be informed in writing of their right to apply for a hearing before the authority in charge submits an application for approval that concerns expropriation compensation and resettlement or conversion of basic farmland use to a non-agricultural construction (art. 19(1)). Second, the affected persons can submit an application to require a hearing in writing to the authority in charge within five working days after the receipt of the hearing notice (art. 21). Next, the authority holds the hearing. Before the hearing is held, the authority in charge must notify the affected persons and relevant departments in writing about the hearing at least seven working days before the hearing (art. 25).

[113] *LAL Regulation*, art. 25(3).

For compensation and resettlement fee payment, the *LAL* does not require that it is tendered before occupation of the land. The *LAL Regulation* requires that the compensation fee and other relevant fees must be paid within three months after the compensation and resettlement decision.[114] Thus, the relevant government can occupy the expropriated land immediately without advance compensation after the compensation and resettlement decision. If the proposed expropriation is for an urgent situation, such as emergency rescue and disaster relief, the target land can be occupied and used without making the typical announcement and following the approval procedure in advance. The approval and compensation decision can be made within six months after the urgent situation ends. This implies that a land-right holder whose land is expropriated for an urgent situation will be compensated after a much longer time than normal.[115] In practice, cases of delayed payment and usurpation of the compensation and resettlement fee often incur violent resistance.

The *LAL* does not stipulate a judicial review procedure for land expropriation and compensation decisions. The affected collectives and farmers can bring an administrative suit against the government's expropriation and compensation decision under *Administrative Litigation Law*.[116] However, judicial review cannot impede enforcement of the approved expropriation project during the court process. On the other hand, if the affected farmers refuse to deliver the expropriated land to the government after the effective expropriation and compensation decision, the appropriate government can order delivery of the land. If the affected farmers continue to refuse transfer, the land administration authority can request that the court compulsorily enforce the delivery.[117] It is ridiculous that, on one hand, the court accepts and reviews the suit against the government expropriation by the affected farmers, but on the other hand, the court may arrange for compulsory enforcement of the land transfer upon the government's application while it is simultaneously reviewing the expropriation case.

6.3.2.2 Post-2004 reform

In its *2004 Land Decision*, the State Council required an improved expropriation procedure. The main improvement by the decision is to offer the

[114] Ibid., art. 25(4). [115] Ibid., art. 27.

[116] *Xingzheng Susong Fa* [*Administrative Litigation Law*] was enacted by the Second Session of the Seventh NPC on 4 April 1989 and amended by the Eleventh Meeting of the Standing Committee of the Twelfth NPC on 1 November 2014.

[117] *LAL Regulation*, art. 45.

affected collectives and farmers an opportunity for involvement before the first announcement. Before this decision, the affected farmers could not obtain information and voice their opinion before the land expropriation decision. Their involvement and the hearing opportunity only apply to the compensation decision. The *2004 Land Decision* requires three actions to be completed before the land expropriation project is submitted for approval: (1) the affected farmers should be informed of the information relevant to the land expropriation; (2) the survey of the land proposed for expropriation should be affirmed by the affected collectives and farmers; and (3) the land administration authority should hold a hearing if necessary. The documents relevant to this information, affirmation and hearing should be included in the application materials for land expropriation approval.[118]

Following the *2004 Land Decision*, *2004 MLR Guidance* was issued on 3 November 2004. In the third part of the guidance, the MLR stipulates the improvement measures required by the *2004 Land Decision*. The local land administration departments must inform the affected farmers about land expropriation, obtain the farmers' confirmation of the land survey and organise a hearing before they submit the application for land expropriation approval.

The expropriation procedure stipulated by the *LAL* and its implementation regulation is undue because it does not fairly balance government power and private property rights. The government has the advantage, and the affected farmers' due process rights are neglected. The land expropriation decision is made by the government through a one-sided decision procedure without involvement by the affected farmers. The affected farmers are not notified until after the expropriation decision. Even for the compensation and resettlement project, the concerned farmers are only offered an informal right to voice their opinions, but a formal hearing procedure is not required by the *LAL* and its regulation. For the compensation and resettlement project decision, no stipulations concern the initial negotiation for compensation between the government authority in charge and the affected farmers.

The *2001 MLR Notice Measures* made slight progress through stipulating a formal hearing. However, this hearing is not organised until after the expropriation decision. Thus, this hearing is in the post-expropriation-decision stage. Although the local government authority in charge must consider the opinions collected through the hearing, it is not required to consider all of the opinions from the affected persons when it makes its

[118] *2004 Land Decision*, para. 14.

final decision. In fact, the local government, driven by a great motivation in expropriating land to increasing its fiscal revenue, often disregards the reasonable opinions submitted in the hearing and attempts to determine the compensation as soon as possible.

The *2004 Land Decision* and *2004 MLR Guidance* moved the hearing to the pre-expropriation-decision stage. The *2004 Land Decision* requires that a hearing is held before the expropriation decision without clearly stating that the hearing is only for compensation and resettlement. Considering the notification requirement in the prior step from such a decision, it seems that the hearing includes all of the expropriation issues. Based on this decision, the prior notification should offer the affected farmers information on the purpose for the use and the location of the proposed land expropriation, the standard of compensation and resettlement approaches. Following notification, the hearing is arranged to hear the affected persons' opinions on the issues included in the notification. Thus, a reasonable explanation is that the *2004 Land Decision* proposes a hearing that concerns all of the issues relevant to the expropriation decision. The affected farmers should be given an opportunity to opine not only on compensation and resettlement but also on the public purpose for the proposed land use, which is required before an expropriation decision under the *2004 Amendment* to the constitution. Unfortunately, the *2004 MLR Guidance* limits the affected farmers' right to a hearing on compensation and deprives the right holders' opportunity to voice their opinions on the public nature of the proposed expropriation's purpose. This defect yields the following conclusion: the Chinese government believes that its expropriation decisions should not be challenged by the affected collectives and individuals; the affected persons can only argue with government about the compensation they deserve in the hearing meeting.

Additional progress in the expropriation procedure includes the requirement for pre-occupation payment. The *2004 Land Decision* requires all compensation and resettlement fee fully paid before occupation and use of the expropriated land. The expropriated land should not be occupied and used before compensation is paid. However, the *2004 MLR Guidance* does not clarify that compensation is required before the government occupies the expropriated land; it only states that compensation and the resettlement fee shall be paid to the collectives whose land is expropriated within the time limit stipulated by law after the compensation project is approved.[119]

[119] *2004 MLR Guidance*, para. 13.

To respond to increasing anger from affected farmers who were not sufficiently compensated or whose compensation was delayed or usurped, the General Office of the State Council issued an urgent notice (*2010 Urgent Notice*) on 15 May 2010.[120] This notice requires that the compensation fee is timely and fully paid and that the farmers and their houses are not demolished before they are resettled. One month after the *2010 Urgent Notice* was issued, the MLR issued a notice providing that the target land should not be compulsorily condemned before the dissenting affected farmers understand and support the expropriation decision.[121] However, no detailed, practical and powerful measures were offered in the notices to improve the expropriation procedure and enhance its fairness. At the central government level, there is no clear requirement for advance compensation to the affected persons before the target land is occupied. One exception is a local legislation in the Guangdong Province that provides that the unit and individual whose land is expropriated has the right to refuse delivery of their land before the compensation and resettlement fee is paid.[122]

6.3.3 *Comparative analysis and comments*

The expropriation procedure should be designed to achieve three goals. The first goal is to appropriately restrict the exercise of the government's eminent domain power. In other words, the appropriateness of this procedure should be based on the balance between the public interest and private property protection. The second goal is to offer the property-right holders an opportunity to claim their rights. The third goal is to introduce an impartial remedy opportunity into the procedure to resolve the dispute between individual property holders and government authority. Typically, the possible mistakes in using eminent domain power by an expropriation authority are corrected through judicial review or court involvement. To achieve these three goals, the corresponding procedure should include at least six key points: prior preparation, prior notification,

[120] *Guanyu Jinyibu Yange Zhengdi Chaiqian Guanli Gongzuo Qieshi Weihu Qunzhong Hefa Quanyi de Jinji Tongzhi* [*Urgent Notice on the Strict Management of Land Expropriation and the Protection of People's Legal Interests*], promulgated by the General Office of the State Council on 15 May 2010. The Chinese text is available at www.law110.com/law/guowuyuan/law11020062271.html.

[121] *Guanyu Jinyibu Zuohao Zhengdi Guanli Gongzuo de Tongzhi* [*Notice on Further Improving the Management of Land Expropriation*], promulgated by MRL on 26 June 2010. The Chinese text is available at www.mlr.gov.cn/zwgk/zytz/201007/t20100713_154433.htm.

[122] *Guangdongsheng Shishi Zhonghua Renmin Gongheguo Tudi Guanli Fa Banfa* [*Guangdong Province Measures on the Enforcement of Land Administration Law*], art. 32(5).

a prior hearing opportunity, negotiation, advance compensation and the availability of judicial review.

Prior preparation requires that government authority collects full and accurate information on the land or other property, right holders and proposed project before it officially initiates the expropriation procedure. Preparation can include a land survey, project investigation and information collection on property-right holders through a land registration agency or other methods. The purpose for the prior preparation is to facilitate the expropriation authority's cautiousness in initiating expropriation and limit its discretion in making expropriation decisions. It may also enhance efficiency in the latter procedures.

After the expropriation procedure is initiated, the concerned persons and units should be notified with information on the proposed expropriation. The purpose of prior notification is to offer condemnees timely and sufficient information to preparation for the coming negotiation or defence with the government authority.

The hearing is arranged to offer the condemnees an opportunity to claim their rights, object or negotiate compensation; it can aid the expropriation authority in making its expropriation decision reasonably and legally by providing all of the parties with the relevant information. By combining the notification with a hearing, the information transparency might also limit potential misuse of government power.

An opportunity for negotiation should be offered before a compulsory decision for a mutual agreement between the condemnee and condemner and before the private property is taken involuntarily from its holder.

Advance payment of compensation is used to eliminate the occurrence of delay in paying compensation to the condemnees, and it has three justifications: (1) to show the respect to condemnees' property right through the procedure of 'payment first occupation later', (2) to reduce the government officers' possible usurpation of the concerned compensation money, and very important to the condemnees, (3) to fund the condemnees in covering their up-front expenditure concerning and making early preparation for the coming removal.

Finally, judicial review is a final examination on the legality and constitutionality of the administrative authority's expropriation decision.

In democratic countries, these elements are widely recognised as basic and necessary components of a due process for expropriation. According to the U.S. Supreme Court in its decisions after the 1970s, taking a person's private property should be reviewed considering both the takings and due process clauses. The weight of consideration should be on the side of the private property owners because their right to property is stipulated by the constitution. Substantively, private property cannot be taken unless an overwhelming national interest justifies the taking or expropriation. Procedurally, the affected individuals should be given prior notification, hearing opportunities and court review before a final expropriation decision. Although the German constitution authorises the legislature to stipulate the expropriation procedure, the procedure requires careful preparation before the hearing, notification that includes necessary information on the hearing to aid the claimants in their right to prepare for the hearing well, and a negotiation opportunity for an agreement before a compulsory decision. Although India does not currently have a private property clause in its constitution, the land expropriation procedure includes prior preliminary notice, a prior preparatory survey and a hearing opportunity; it also allows for an agreement. In both Germany and India, advance compensation and court appeals are available.

These basic elements are strongly advocated in guidelines or proposals by international organisations, such as the Food and Agriculture Organization of the United Nations (FAO) and World Bank. In its report on compulsory land acquisition, the FAO notes that the expropriation procedure is critical for rendering the exercise of government power 'efficient, fair and legitimate'.[123] The report suggests that the entire expropriation procedure should include seven sequential steps: planning, publicity, valuation and submission of claims, compensation, possession, appeals and restitution. Planning includes preparation through surveying and data collection to select and render a decision on the target land. Planning should be completed before the next step, 'publicity'. For the publicity step, notice and a public meeting (hearing) should be offered. Compensation must be paid before the government physically possesses the land. When dissatisfied rights holders fight the government decision in the court, they should be allowed to challenge the expropriation decision, process and compensation.[124] In addition, the affected owners have the right to ask for the expropriated land if the purpose for its acquisition no longer exists. Negotiation may be concurrent with the compensation decision. The FAO report proposes certain countries' practices that require prior good faith negotiations, which 'can save time and money when they produce solutions which leave the owners and occupants satisfied enough with the outcome and thus unlikely to prolong the process by submitting appeals'.[125]

[123] FAO, 'Compulsory Acquisition', 15. [124] Ibid., 16. [125] Ibid., 26.

Notably, in developing countries, such as India and China, poor property or right owners, most of whom are displaced farmers, may not fully or effectively use procedural opportunities. One reason for this observation is they lack the necessary financial resources to hire professional services, including consultation, valuation and attorney services. A second reason is illiteracy. Poor and undereducated persons may not clearly understand their legal rights and the full information related to the procedural affairs. The third reason is a lack of courage and experience in interacting with government officials. In India, although the right holders affected by expropriation legally have the opportunity to appeal the compensation package, few appeal because they lack the relevant knowledge and fear interacting with officials.[126] Thus, assistance and advocacy from both government and non-government organisations are demanded.[127]

The procedure should be flexible. One typical exception includes urgent situations under which the government can possess private property without a full procedure. Although this flexibility is to avoid jeopardising the public interest by a time-consuming procedure under certain urgent situations, the private property holders should be awarded timely compensation for their sacrifice to society or others. In both Germany and India, the relevant legislation clearly requires that compensation is tendered before the government possesses the private property for urgent reasons.

It is important to look again at China to examine how far its expropriation procedure is from the due process requirements that are derived directly or indirectly from constitutional stipulations or values and are popular in democratic countries.

The expropriation procedure was constructed in an era without constitutional restraints on eminent domain power, which is extremely unfair to property holders. During this time, the expropriation procedure could be initiated by non-government units. To expropriate urban houses, the units, which were often business entities, could even execute detailed functions, which should have been performed by government authorities, such as negotiation with the right holders, demolition of houses and resettlement of displaced persons. If negotiation did not produce an agreement on compensation and resettlement, the business entities with the expropriation license could apply for a compulsory demolition order from the government. Apparently, this arrangement placed individual property holders in a weak position, which was squeezed and pressed

[126] ADB, 'People's Republic of China', 37. [127] FAO, 'Compulsory Acquisition', 49–51.

by both government powers and business giants. The business entities that initiated expropriation, which were typically great business powers, were supported by the government and motivated with a high interest in expropriation and frequently used illegal or violent approaches to remove the property holders. In this procedure, the expropriatees were not given notification and an opportunity to claim their rights until after an expropriation decision. In other words, they only had an opportunity for involvement and to voice their opinion in the second half of the procedure, which was the compensation decision stage. To expropriate urban houses, the right holders were notified after an expropriation license was issued. They did not have information available, nor did they have an opportunity to voice their objection against the developer company that initiated the procedure and the government authority that made the decision during the decision-making portion of the expropriation procedure. They were not given an opportunity for a hearing on the compensation issue. To expropriate rural land, the expropriation decision was made without informing and hearing from the affected farmers. In the second part of the procedure, which considered the compensation issue, the law only required that the authority 'listen to the people's opinions'.[128] An official and formal hearing was not required.

The *2004 Amendment* greatly stimulated and strengthened people's consciousness of their rights. To respond to the society-wide request for effective and fair private property protection based on the newly amended constitution, the expropriation procedure was improved, although the improvement was neither satisfactory nor timely. The expropriation procedure for urban houses was fully improved through enforcement of the new *2011 Expropriation Regulation* seven years after the *2004 Amendment* was enacted. For consistency with the constitution's public interest requirement for expropriation, non-government entities cannot initiate the expropriation procedure. Prior notification and collection of people's opinions are required before the expropriation decision. The relevant government authority must also make certain prior preparations before the expropriation decision. It must ensure that the construction projects underlying the expropriation are consistent with government planning, such as an economic and social development plan and an urban planning. The authority must also evaluate the risk to social stability. Moreover, additional improvement measures worth recognising include compensation before the government possesses houses and compulsory occupation

128 *LAL*, art. 48.

executed by court. However, a large drawback persists: the hearing opportunity is only offered when the expropriation concerns reconstruction of old city areas, and most affected persons express objection during the opinion collection stage. In other words, a hearing is only provided in situations that concern many affected persons. In fact, the inherent purpose underlying this type of hearing is to ease broad social complaints through face-to-face communication in the hearing. Fundamentally, the hearing is not provided to respect each affected individual's right to object and defend their property before government officials through a hearing. This type of hearing is essentially offered for social stability considerations.

The expropriation procedure concerning rural land was improved through certain informal approaches rather than official revision of the *LAL*. The decision by the State Council and the guidance opinions by the MLR do not decide through official law-making procedure, although they bind the lower local governments to a certain extent. The improvements were less progressive than the improvements related to expropriation of urban houses. As illustrated in Chapter 4 of this book, a clear scope of public interest has not been identified for expropriation of rural land after the *2004 Amendment*. Correspondingly, the *LAL* was not revised to clearly eliminate private entity initiation and participation in expropriation. Although the affected farmers are offered a hearing opportunity under both the *2004 Land Decision* and the *2004 MLR Guidance*, their claims are limited to the compensation issue. An additional drawback for the hearing is the notification time. The MLR requires at least seven working days between the notification and hearing. In practice, seven days are not sufficient for the affected farmers to collect information, seek consultation and unify opinions, which are necessary to be well prepared for the hearing. The greatest shortcoming that remains concerns advance compensation issues. Except in the limited circumstances of local legislation, such as in Guangdong, there is no guarantee of pre-taking compensation in the legislation or other legal documents at the country level. In addition, the available judicial remedies for expropriation of urban houses and rural land differ. According to the *2011 Expropriation Regulation*, if the right holders bring a suit challenging the expropriation decision in a court, governmental occupation of the expropriated houses cannot be executed until the final court decision.[129] For expropriating rural houses, the administrative suit brought by the affected farmers against an expropriation authority, which is mainly for compensation disputes, cannot prevent

[129] *2011 Expropriation Regulation*, arts. 14, 28.

implementation of an expropriation decision. The government might argue that a long and tedious court procedure would jeopardise the efficient fulfilment of public interest. However, the legality of occupation prior to a court decision is uncertain or doubtful because the court should make a final decision. The question whether or not the prior government occupation should be permitted must be answered by considering the level of constitutional protection for the private property interest at issue. As a right established by the constitution, private property should be weighted more heavily in procedural guarantees than lower-level rights that are not constitutionally protected. Among the various types of private properties, real estate, including houses and land, should at least be given a judicial remedy opportunity before it is taken by government. Real estate is not fungible, and the unjust harm from compulsory occupation and deprivation cannot be fully repaired by post-ante compensatory cash. For fungible property, a post-occupation court remedy may be allowed.[130]

6.4 Constitutional review

A more critical issue concerning judicial remedy is whether the court can apply the constitution in deciding an expropriation case. If it can, which court has the power, and what is the review procedure? The essence underlying these questions is the court's authority in adjudicating the constitution or justiciability of the constitution. If courts cannot apply the constitution to overrule unconstitutional legislation or governmental actions, the constitution loses its significance for protecting private property and becomes only a beautiful decoration on the paper.

6.4.1 *The modes of constitutional review: European mode versus U.S. mode*

There are two main modes of constitutional review in the world. One is the European mode, which has been adopted by most Western European countries. Second mode is the American mode used by the United States, Canada and India.[131]

The European mode establishes a constitutional court that is independent from both ordinary courts and legislature. It is independently responsible for explaining the constitution and deciding whether statutes and acts conflict with the constitution. Thus, ordinary courts have no

[130] Hudson, 'Eminent Domain', 1314.

[131] Sweet, 'Why Europe', 2769–70.

authority to decide the constitutionality of a statute. If a judge in an ordinary court encounters an issue concerning constitutionality, he must refer the issue to the constitutional court for a response. In addition to this judicial referral, in Germany, there are two other ways of initiating the FCC's constitutional review. One is abstract review, which is usually initiated by political parties to challenge a law for its unconstitutionality. The second way is constitutional compliant, initiated by a citizen who claims that some law or government action infringed his constitutional fundamental rights.[132]

The American mode imposes the authority of constitutional review on any judge. Any judge trying a case can apply the constitution to resolve the constitutionality issue. This judicial power for applying the constitution is based on art. 3 of the *U.S. Constitution*, which stipulates that '[t]he judicial Power shall extend to all Cases, in Law and Equity, arising under this Constitution.' In the famous 1803 case of *Marbury* v. *Madison* that entrenched the courts' judicial power of constitutional review, Justice Marshall declared the following in the court's ruling:

> So, if a law [e.g., a statute or treaty] be in opposition to the Constitution, if both the law and the Constitution apply to a particular case, so that the Court must either decide that case conformably to the law, disregarding the Constitution, or conformably to the Constitution, disregarding the law, the Court must determine which of these conflicting rules governs the case. This is of the very essence of judicial duty. If, then, the Courts are to regard the Constitution, and the Constitution is superior to any ordinary act of the Legislature, the Constitution, and not such ordinary act, must govern the case to which they both apply.[133]

As Sweet comments, the European review mode is 'concentrated', but the American mode is 'diffuse'.[134] This argument is correct in attributing constitutional review authority. Considering specific cases that concern constitutionality, however, the American mode is 'concentrated', and the European mode is 'diffuse' because any judge in the United States can decide both the constitutional and additional issues in one case. However, for the European mode countries, constitutionality and non-constitutionality issues should be considered by the constitutional court and ordinary court, respectively. Thus, the European mode includes abstract review, wherein the constitutional court decides whether certain legislation is constitutional without considering the detailed litigation.

[132] Kommers, 'The Federal Constitutional Court', 474–6.

[133] *Marbury* v. *Madison*, 5 U.S. (1 Cranch) 137 (1803).

[134] Sweet, 'Why Europe', 2770.

In the United States, however, constitutional review is always initiated by a concrete case or controversy. The court must combine constitutional review with the case in a concrete review.[135]

6.4.2 *The scope of constitutional application*

Should constitutional review include only the public relationship, or both public and private relationships? This question concerns the scope of constitutional application. For this issue, an agreeable answer has not been produced. According to traditional public-private division theory, the constitution should only concern the public relationship that involves government activity. The relationship between private parties should be governed by private law, such as civil law. In practice, the United States is the representative government that has adopted this theory, and its constitution only has a vertical effect. In the United States, 'state action' is required as a premise for courts to invoke the *Bill of Rights* to offer constitutional protection to private parties.[136] The constitution unquestionably applies in cases between the government and private party – for example, cases concerning eminent domain. A dispute between private parties (for example, a private party is accused of infringing another private party's constitutional right) must be connected to the government to constitute state action for the application of the constitution.[137]

In contrast to the 'state action' limit in the United States, Ireland allows direct application of the constitution to private disputes. If a person's fundamental constitutional right is infringed, he can be protected by a court through directly invoking the constitutional provisions without regard for whether the infringer is a government authority or private party. The Irish Supreme Court developed direct application of the constitution through two cases.[138] In the 1961 case of *Educational Co. Ltd.* v. *Fitzpatrick*, the Irish Supreme Court ruled that a person's constitutional rights should be protected by courts, and a person's constitutional right results in a duty from other citizens 'to respect that right and not to interfere with it.'[139] In a 1973 case, the Irish Supreme Court clarified that 'the Irish Constitution confers a right of action for breach of constitutionally protected rights against persons other than the state and its officials'.[140]

[135] Ibid., 2770–1. [136] Gardbaum, 'The "Horizontal Effect"', 396.
[137] Ibid., at 395–6. [138] Onufrio, 'The Constitutionalization', 4.
[139] *Educational Co. Ltd.* v. *Fitzpatrick* (No. 2) [1961] IR 345.
[140] Justice Costello's words in the case of *Meskell* v. *CIE* [1973] IR 121.

In Canada and Germany, the constitutions can be indirectly applied to private relationships. Similar to the U.S. practices, the Canadian Supreme Court requires government action for constitutional protection of the fundamental rights stipulated in the *1982 Charter of Fundamental Rights and Freedoms.* However, unlike the United States, Canadian courts can apply constitutional values to develop common law, which is used to resolve private disputes.[141] To generalise, the Canadian Supreme Court distinguishes 'constitutional rights' from 'constitutional value'. For constitutional rights, courts should hold vertical standing to limit application of the constitution to the scope of government action. In fact, this is the clear stipulation of the *Charter* itself. The *Charter* stipulates that it applies to legislative and executive governments at both federal and province levels.[142] For constitutional value, courts have a duty 'to apply and develop the principles of common law in a manner consistent with the fundamental values enshrined in the Constitution'.[143]

Germany clarified its indirect application of the *German Basic Law* to private disputes in the well-known *Lüth* case of 1958. In this case, a film director, whose new film was boycotted by the defendant, applied for an injunction against the boycotting. The regional court granted an injunction, citing a general clause concerning good morals in the *German Civil Code* (*BGB*). However, this decision was overruled by the FCC because the lower court did not interpret and apply the general clause in a manner consistent with constitutional values.[144] From this case, the FCC indirectly applied the constitution in a general manner, as follows. First, the courts must discern the constitutional values or objective order of values inherent in the fundamental rights. Second, the value must influence or radiate to civil norms (for example, general clauses in the civil code). Third, the courts should interpret and apply civil norms such that the norms are consistent with constitutional values.

The *Lüth* decision is a positive response to the influential 'third-party effect of constitutional rights' (*Drittwirkung*) theory, which gained popularity in the early 1950s. Not using the *unmittelbare Drittwirkung*, or the direct approach suggested by certain scholars represented by

141 Gardbaum, 'The "Horizontal Effect"', 398.

142 *Constitution Act* (1982), sec. 32 (1).

143 *Dolphin Delivery*, [1986] 2 S.C.R., 605.

144 Sec. 826 of *German Civil Code* states that '[a] person who, in a manner contrary to public policy [good morals], intentionally inflicts damage on another person is liable to the other person to make compensation for the damage.' This *Code* is available at www.gesetze-im-internet.de/englisch_bgb/. See also Gardbaum, 'The "Horizontal Effect"', 405.

Nipperdey,[145] the FCC finally adopted the *mittelbare Drittwirkung*, or the indirect approach, which is less radical and, thus, easier to accept in Germany, which is a country with a long-term theoretical tradition of public-private division.

After *Lüth*, the FCC solidified its indirect approach through a series of cases. In the 1993 case *Guarantee*, the FCC affirmed that courts have a duty to protect a citizen's fundamental right to private autonomy through the civil code's general clause concerning good morals. In this case, a debtor's daughter signed a guarantee contract for her father's interest with the loaner bank. According to the court, if the imbalance in the bargaining power between the bank, which had the dominant power in the deal, and the daughter with the weaker position was not remedied by the court, the concerned constitutional right to private autonomy would not be protected. The FCC ruled that the duty of the law is 'to reinforce the fundamental right positions of both parties in order to prevent that – for one of the parties – the substitution of private autonomy for duress'.[146]

The path through which the constitution influences private litigation is similar in Germany and Canada. In both countries, the courts must apply constitutional values to interpret or influence private law norms, which are then applied to resolve private litigation. However, the difference between the two countries is that the German court's constitutional duty is broader. The private law provisions governing private disputes that are inconsistent with constitutional fundamental rights shall be invalidated because such fundamental rights 'constitute directly applicable higher law norms'.[147]

Although differences in the detailed institutional design and scope of constitutional review exist, a common practice among Western countries is applying constitutional review through a court system to guarantee that legislation and government actions are constitutional.

6.4.3 *China: the dawn light of judicial review and its death*

Although the institutional design of constitutional review differs, both the European and the American modes offer constitutional protection to the fundamental rights holders through constitutional adjudication. In

[145] Onufrio, 'The Constitutionalization', 4–5.
[146] German Law Journal, 'Federal Constitutional Court'.
[147] Gardbaum, 'The "Horizontal Effect"', 406.

China, however, constitutional adjudication or constitutional justiciability is far from a resolution, which yields weak or absent constitutional protection of private property.

The dawn light of the introduction of the constitution into judicial review occurred in 2001, when the Supreme Court issued a positive response to the lower-level court's inquiry into whether the constitution can be applied in deciding a case. The case is the well-known case *Qi Yuling* v. *Chen Qiaoqi etc.* (*Qi Yuling* case), which is acclaimed as 'the first case of judicial application of the constitution'.[148] In 1990, Qi Yuling (Qi), then a high school student in Shandong Province, was admitted by a college. The defendant Chen Xiaoqi (Chen) used Qi's admission notification (which she took from the high school) and Qi's identity and went to study at college. Three years later, Chen graduated and found a job in a bank. Qi was misled to believe that she failed the national admission examination and lost the opportunity for college education. Owing to their poverty, Qi's parents could not afford to return her to high school for the next year's admission examination. Later, Qi found a job in a factory, which paid a much lower salary than Chen's bank job. In 1999, after discovering the truth, Qi filed a suit in Zaozhuang Municipality Intermediate People's Court (trying court) to claim compensation for infringement of her rights in both her name and education. In addition to Chen, the other defendants included Chen's father, who planned and executed the appropriation of Qi's name and education opportunity, the high school from which Qi's admission notification was transferred to Chen, the college that accepted Chen and the local education commission that was responsible for college admission affairs. In its ruling, the trying court decided in favour of Qi because the defendant infringed her right to her name. However, the right to education was not recognised by the trying court because the right was only a general personality right in China's legal system. In fact, there is not a clear list with this right in the *General Principle of Civil Law* which enumerates civil rights.[149] Qi then appealed to Shandong Province Higher People's Court (appealing court). A core controversy in the appeal proceeding was whether the right to education stipulated by the *Constitution* can be applied to a civil case. Although a right to education is not clearly enumerated in civil law, it is in

[148] Shen, 'Is It the Beginning', 199.

[149] *Minfa Tongze* [*General Principle of Civil Law*], enacted by the Fourth Session of the Sixth NPC on 12 April 1986. The Chinese text is available at www.npc.gov.cn/wxzl/wxzl/2000–12/06/content_4470.htm.

art. 46 of the *Constitution*, which stipulates that 'Citizens of the People's Republic of China have the right as well as the duty to receive education'. The appealing court submitted this issue to the SPC for judicial interpretation. In a brief response, the SPC firmly allowed judicial application of constitutional stipulations as follows:

> After study, we hold, on the basis of the facts in this case, that Chen Xiaoqi and others have violated the fundamental right to receive education enjoyed by Qi Yuling in accordance with the provisions of the Constitution by means of violating rights to a person's name. Because this violation has resulted in actual damages, commensurate civil liability arises. Reply is hereby given.[150]

Upon SPC's response (*2001 SPC Interpretation*), the appealing court ruled in favour of Qi Yuling. It ruled that Qi's right to education, which is a basic right stipulated by the *Constitution*, was infringed, and thus, her loss incurred through violation of her right to education shall be compensated by the respondents.[151]

Although the *Qi Yuling* case was acclaimed by society as China's first case concerning judicial application of the constitution; however, it was not the first instance, as certain scholars argued.[152] The SPC confirmed the lower courts' application of the constitution in 1988, when the SPC responded to an inquiry on whether the constitution could be applied in deciding an employee protection issue submitted by the Tianjin Higher People's Court (*1988 SPC Response*). This case concerned an employee injured at work, who was refused compensation by the employer based on a disclaimer that stated 'no injury incurred during employment is compensated' on the registration form for the job application. In its response, the SPC held that the labour protection offered to employees 'is stipulated expressively by the Constitution and thus a right which should be enjoyed by the employee', and such a disclaimer seriously violates not

150 *Zuigao Renmin Fayuan guanyu yi Qinfan Xingmingquan Shouduan Qinfan Xianfa Baohu de Gongmin Shoujiaoyu de Jiben Quanli Shifou Ying Chengdan Minshi Zeren de Pifu* (*Fashi* 2001 25 *Hao*) [*The SPC's Response to the Inquiry Whether or Not Should A Person Who Infringes Another Person's Constitutional Right to Education through the Infringement of His Right to Name be Imposed Civil Liability* (SPC Judicial Interpretation No. 2001 (25))], promulgated by the SPC on 24 July 2001. The cited interpretation is translated by Liu Yuqing, see Shen, 'Is It the Beginning', 204–5. The full version of this interpretation is available at www.law-lib.com/hzsf/law_detail.asp?id=15994.

151 See the ruling on *Qi Yuling* case by Shandong Province Higher People's Court. The document number of this court decision is '1999 *Lu Min Zhong Zi Di* 258 *Hao*' ['Shandong-Civil-Final 1999 (258)'].

152 Yin, '*Xianfa Sifahua*', 9.

only 'the Constitution and relevant laws' but also 'the Socialist morality' and is thus void.[153]

Before the late 1980s, the SPC's attitude towards constitutional justiciability tended to be negative. In its response to a local higher court issue in 1955, the SPC denied direct application of the constitution to a criminal case by stating that 'the Constitution is not appropriate to be cited as the basis for deciding a crime and the corresponding penalty in a criminal case'.[154] In another response issued in 1986 to a local higher court's inquiry on how to cite law sources in writing court decisions concerning civil and economic disputes (*1986 SPC Response*), the sources of law mentioned by the SPC did not include the *Constitution*.[155] Combining these two documents, one may conclude that the SPC did not allow the direct use of the constitution in both civil and criminal cases before 1988. Notably, however, we cannot conclude that the SPC arbitrarily refused constitutional review from the *1986 SPC Response*. Although the SPC expressly does not permit direct citation of the constitution in its response, it allows negative application of the constitution, which can play a role in constitutional review to a certain extent. Negative or indirect application of the constitution refers to constitutional review of certain directly applied below-constitution statutes and acts. In the *1986 SPC Response*, the SPC stated that the local legislation enacted by local congresses and their standing committees cited in court decisions shall not contradict the *Constitution* and national legislation enacted by the NPC or NPCSC. Based on this response, the court can indirectly and partially apply the constitution. 'Indirectly' means that the courts can use the constitution to invalidate unconstitutional rules or regulations, although the courts cannot cite and apply the constitution directly to a case. 'Partially'

[153] See the SPC's response to Tianjin Higher People's Court, titled '*Zuigao Renmin Fayuan guanyu Gugong Hetong Gongshang Gaibu Fuze Shifou Youxiao de Pifu*' ['*The SPC's Response to the Inquiry about the Enforceability of An Employment Contract Clause Which Exempts the Employer's Liability to the Injured Employee*'], promulgated by the SPC on 14 October 1988. It is available at www.people.com.cn/item/flfgk/gwyfg/1988/113208198802.html.

[154] See the SPC's response to Xinjiang Higher People's Court, titled '*Zuigao Renmin Fayuan guanyu zai Xingshi Panjue zhong Buyi Yuanyin Xianfa zuo Lunzui Kexing Yiju de Fuhan*' ['*The SPC's Response about the Inappropriateness of the Citation of the Constitution Clauses in Criminal Case Rulings*'], promulgated by SPC on 30 July 1955. It is available at www.people.com.cn/item/flfgk/gwyfg/1955/113611195501.html.

[155] See the SPC's response to Jiangsu Higher People's Court, titled '*Zuigao Renmin Fayuan guanyu Renmin Fayuan Zhizuo Falv Wenshu Ruhe Yinyong Falv Guifanxing Wenjian de Pifu*' ['*The SPC's Response about the Citation of Legal Rules in the Writing of Court Documents*'], promulgated on 28 October 1986. It is available at www.people.com.cn/item/flfgk/gwyfg/1986/113901198604.html.

means that the 1986 response did not authorise the courts to review the constitutionality of all non-constitution laws or rules. The regulations enacted by the State Council, and laws enacted by the NPC or NPCSC do not fall within the scope of constitutional review. In general, this 1986 response tends to recognise the partial effect of constitutional review.

Although the *1988 SPC Response* demonstrates that the SPC began to approach constitutional justiciability in a positive manner, it did not garner the nation-wide attention as with the *2001 SPC Interpretation*. After the *Qi Yuling* case, the SPC and its judges began to actively and publicly announce their support for direct application of the constitution in suits. Huang Songyou, who was the SPC judge at the time, explained the significance of allowing constitutional justiciability in reply to a newspaper interview and published article. In an article concerning his comments on the *Qi Yuling* case published in the SPC newspaper, Huang noted why it is important and necessary for courts to directly apply the constitution in their rulings.[156] First, constitutional justiciability is critical for advancing the nation's guiding principle 'ruling the country according to law'. If the courts were not allowed to use constitutional stipulations to resolve significant issues concerning country governance or protect citizens' fundamental rights, the constitution would lose 'the authority it should have had'. He writes: 'Ruling the Country according to Law should be, first, Ruling the Country according to the Constitution'. Second, it is necessary to strengthen the validity of the constitution. Not all of the components of the constitution are reflected in and enforced through laws subject to the constitution. If the constitutional stipulations that cannot be enforced by other laws are not directly applied, the constitution cannot fulfil its role. Third, it is required for court rulings. During China's fast development, many new conflicts and controversies frequently arise that cannot be managed in a timely manner by ordinary non-constitution laws. The constitutional principles' abstractness and generality provide the court judges with great flexibility in applying the constitution to resolve new problems. Thus, direct application of the constitution can help resolve the various disputes. He also highly praised the *Qi Yuling* case's significance and the *2001 SPC Interpretation* for creating a constitutional justiciability precedent. Huang insisted that the *2001 SPC Interpretation*, not the *1988 SPC Response*, should be the ice-breaking precedent for constitutional justiciability in China. In the 1988 response,

[156] Huang, 'Xianfa Sifahua'.

although the SPC mentioned that the *Constitution* can be cited as legal basis to overrule a disclaimer, it is not the only legal source. Even without citing the constitution, the court could also apply the laws concerning labour protection or fundamental morality (public policy) stipulated by the *General Principles of Civil Law* to void a disclaimer. In the *Qi Yuling* case, however, the SPC allowed the lower court to use the constitution as the sole and direct legal source for its decision. In addition, the 1988 response concerned protection of a civil right. However, the *2001 SPC Interpretation* concerned the right to education, which is a citizen's fundamental right as stipulated by the constitution.

The dawn light of the constitutional justiciability was dead before it shined around. On 18 December 2008, the SPC officially announced that the *2001 SPC Interpretation* was no longer enforceable. In fact, this interpretation had not been applied to a case after *Qi Yuling*.[157] In its decision (*2008 SPC Decision*), the SPC asserted that the interpretation was annulled because 'it has been stopped from being applied'.[158] In addition to *2001 SPC Interpretation*, twenty-six interpretations were also annulled on the same day. For another twenty-six interpretations, the bases were clear and included one of the following: (1) the annulled interpretation is substituted with a new interpretation; (2) the annulled interpretation conflicts with the relevant law; or (3) the annulled interpretation does not apply owing to the change in circumstances. However, the basis for the 2001 interpretation annulment is not clear because it does not detail a persuasive basis for the annulment. From the reason given, we know that the interpretation was not enforced before the official announcement in 2008. When did the courts stop applying this interpretation in practice? Why did the courts stop applying this interpretation before it was officially annulled? These inquiries remain unanswered.

Chen speculates that there are at least two possible reasons for annulling the *2001 SPC Interpretation*. One is that the SPC was wrong to apply the constitutional right to receive education in a civil case. A second reason may be that the SPC was wrong to allow constitutional justiciability through its interpretation.[159] The two reasons in Chen's speculation are also the focus of discussions in academic circles. In essence, both

[157] Tong, 'A Comment', 675.

[158] *Zuigao Renmin Fayuan guanyu Feizhi 2007 Niandi Yiqian Fabu de youguan Sifa Jieshi (Diqipi) de Jueding* (*Fashi* 2008 15 *Hao*) [*The SPC Decision on Annulling the Relevant Judicial Interpretations Which Were Enacted Before the End of 2007 (the 7th Annulment)* (SPC Judicial Interpretation No. 2008 (15))], promulgated by SPC on 28 December 2008. It is available at www.npc.gov.cn/npc/xinwen/fztd/sfjs/2008–12/27/content_1465018.htm.

[159] Chen, 'Qi-an Pifu', 11.

reasons refer to one issue: Should the constitutional provisions, including fundamental rights, be applied to private litigation?

Whether it was appropriate to cite the right to receive education has been questioned because the right can be found in the *Education Law*, which was enacted in 1995.[160] This law stipulates that if a person infringes the education receiver's 'legal rights and interest', he should be liable to compensate for the loss from his infringement.[161] Thus, it was not necessary to apply the constitutional provision in the *Qi Yuling* case. However, this notion is questioned by supporters of the *2001 SPC Interpretation*. Similar to the *General Principles of Civil Law* which was enacted in 1986, the *Education Law* does not clearly stipulate an educatee's right to receive education. Whether the 'legal rights' mentioned by the law include the right to receive education has not been decided.[162]

More keen debates among scholars focus on the constitutional justiciability issue or, more precisely, the issue concerning the direct effect of the constitution. In the month following the *2001 SPC Interpretation*, the Law School of Peking University organised a discussion seminar on the interpretation. The participants were divided by either their support of or objection to direct application of the constitution. The supporters' argument was mainly that allowing the direct application will better protect citizens' fundamental rights. The objectors' argument was mainly that the constitution should be limited to the relationship between the government and citizens, which is a type of vertical effect theory.[163] Two leading authorities for constitutional law in China published articles that expressed their opposing opinions on the *2001 SPC Interpretation*. Professor Xiao Weiyun from Peking University commented that the SPC response and court decision concerning *Qi Yuling* case are significant to maintaining the *Constitution*'s dignity, protecting citizens' basic constitutional rights and facilitating the *Constitution*'s application in cases.[164] However, Professor Xu Chongde from Renmin University objected based on the rationale that constitutional justiciability is inconsistent with the fundamental reality of China and its current political system.[165]

Undoubtedly, the SPC's 2001 interpretation appropriated the NPCSC's authority in constitutional review. The NPCSC's attitude towards this interpretation has been neutral or negative. According to a constitutional

160 *Jiaoyu Fa* [*Education Law*], enacted by the Third Session of the Eighth NPC on 18 March 1995. The Chinese text is available at www.gov.cn/banshi/2005-05/25/content_918.htm.

161 Ibid., art. 81. 162 Xiao, 'Xianfa', 4. 163 Cha, 'Qiyuling-an'.

164 Xiao, 'Xianfa', 4. 165 Xu, 'Xianfa', 45.

law scholar: 'There were signs that the Standing Committee of the NPC had noticed the content and purpose of the Reply long before its annulment and had reservations about it.'[166] The NPCSC may have never officially criticised and annulled the interpretation because it did not want to embarrass the SPC.[167]

6.4.4 *China's constitutional review mechanism*

The current Chinese constitution embraces the NPC's supreme status through stipulating that: 'The National People's Congress of the People's Republic of China is the highest organ of state power.' Additionally, the NPCSC is the NPC's 'permanent body'.[168] Artcle 62 of the constitution stipulates that one of the NPC's duties is to 'supervise the enforcement of the *Constitution*'. Artcle 67 of the *1982 Constitution of China* authorises the NPCSC to 'interpret the *Constitution* and supervise its enforcement'. Moreover, the NPCSC has the following power:

1. to annul those administrative regulations, decisions or orders of the State Council that contravene the *Constitution* or other laws;
2. to annul those local regulations or decisions of the organs of state power of provinces, autonomous regions, and municipalities directly under the Central Government that contravene the *Constitution*, other laws or administrative regulations.

The SPC is defined as a national agency that is inferior to and under the leadership of the NPC. Artcle 128 of the *1982 Constitution of China* provides the following: 'The Supreme People's Court is responsible to the National People's Congress and its Standing Committee. Local people's courts at various levels are responsible to the organs of state power which created them.' In addition, the SPC has a power of making judicial interpretation (*sifa jieshi quan*), which is defined as the one to interpret the issues about 'how to specifically (*juti*) apply the law and legal rules in the process of trials'.[169] Such a power is limited to the specific application of

[166] Tong, 'A Comment', 675. [167] Ibid., 676. [168] *1982 Constitution of China*, art. 57.

[169] See art. 32 of *Renmin Fayuan Zuzhi Fa* [*Organic Law of People's Courts*], which was enacted by the Second Session of the Fifth NPC on 5 July 1979, amended for the first time by the Second Meeting of the Standing Committee of the Sixth NPC on 2 September 1983, amended for the second time by the Eighteenth Meeting of the Standing Committee of the Sixth NPC on 2 December 1986 and amended for the third time by the Twenty-fourth Meeting of the Standing Committee of the Tenth NPC on 31 October 2006. The Chinese text is available at www.people.com.cn/item/flfgk/xianfa/x8301.html.

the relevant legal rules in the trial of cases and does not include the power of interpreting the *Constitution* or any Law (*lifa jieshi quan*), which is clearly and particularly awarded to the NPCSC by the *Constitution.* Thus, the NPCSC has an interpretation power which is higher than the SPC's judicial interpretation power.[170]

The NPC appoints the SPC president, and the NPCSC appoints the SPC vice presidents and justices.[171] Thus, according to Xu, where the SPC, which is an inferior agency, overrules legislation passed by its superior agency, the NPC and NPCSC, it opposes the fundamental political system established by the constitution.[172] Thus, the SPC's 1986 response regarding legal citation does not permit courts to avoid citing a law from the NPC and NPCSC, even if the judge believes the concerned is unconstitutional. However, one question raised by the *1986 SPC Response* is why it does not permit a court to avoid citing unconstitutional administrative rules enacted by the State Council, which is not an agency that is superior to the SPC. The answer might include the inherent political background of the government agency design. The State Council is typically led by the CPC leader who has a higher status than the SPC president in the party.

The *1986 SPC Response* permits courts to avoid citing unconstitutional local legislation or ministerial rules. However, this ruling may conflict with the *Law on Legislation* enacted by the NPCSC in 2000. According to the *Law on Legislation*, where the SPC believes that the administrative rules or local legislation are unconstitutional or oppose the laws enacted by the NPC or NPCSC, it may submit a written request to the NPCSC for a review.[173] This law implies that when the lower courts believe local legislation is unconstitutional, they can only refer such legislation to the NPCSC for review through the SPC application.

The constitution does not expressively endow the SPC with the authority to apply the constitution or review a legal document's constitutionality. However, we cannot conclude that the *2001 SPC Interpretation* or constitutional justiciability definitely contravenes the *Constitution.* The *Constitution* establishes the indirect effect of the constitution and empowers the NPC and NPCSC with the corresponding constitutional review authority, but it does not expressively preclude a direct effect from the constitution. Although the SPC was not given express authority to apply the constitution in private litigation, it has general authority as the supreme judicial organ, which could include an authority to apply laws, including the

[170] Killion, 'China's Amended Constitution', 70. [171] Ibid., art. 34.
[172] Xu, 'Xianfa', 45. [173] *Law on Legislation*, art. 99(1).

constitution, at least based on jurisprudence rationale.[174] The *Constitution* requires that '[a]ll State organs, the armed forces, all political parties and public organizations and all enterprises and institutions must abide by the *Constitution* and other laws. All acts in violation of the *Constitution* or other laws must be investigated.'[175] Thus, the SPC can insist it is reasonable that the constitution must be used in litigation to fulfil the requirements of this article, which cannot be effectively enforced solely through the NPCSC review mechanism.

The *2008 SPC Decision* announced that the SPC did not intend to exercise constitutional justiciability. The basis for the SPC's withdrawal may be linked to the change in political system. In essence, the real supremacy in China is the CPC leadership. The party's decisions and preferences in political decisions strongly influence the government authorities' operations.

Kellogg acutely observed the way that politics influenced the birth and death of the *2001 SPC Interpretation*. He links the *2008 SPC Decision* with the SPC's new president and his political departure from what his predecessor did. When the *2001 SPC Interpretation* was generated, the then SPC president Xiao Yang placed his efforts in strengthening 'the role of the courts as neutral adjudicators of disputes.' However, the new president Wang Shengjun required that judges consider the principle of 'Three Supremes' (*sange zhishang*) which are the interest of CPC, people's interest and, the constitutional and legal rules.[176] In fact, Wang developed this principle based on obvious political considerations underlying the communist party's new policy change, which has emphasised social harmony and social stability since 2004. It is not difficult to understand that the reform towards a more impartial and independent court system through enlarging the courts' judicial review power, which was initiated by the *2001 SPC Interpretation*, was not consistent with the CPC's need to maintain social harmony without disrupting the party leadership.

The death of the *2001 SPC Interpretation* eliminated combining the constitutional review mechanism through direct application of the constitution by the SPC and the NPCSC's abstract review. Currently, Chinese constitutional review is limited to the narrow NPCSC abstract review, which is both inactive and ineffective.[177]

[174] Artcle 123 of the *1982 Constitution of China* provides that, '[t]he people's courts of the People's Republic of China are the judicial organs of the State'.

[175] Ibid., art. 5. [176] Kellogg, 'The Death', 5.

[177] Wang edited thirty-three court rulings containing citations of the constitution that were decided before the death of the *2001 SPC Interpretation*. The constitution is cited in these rulings in three ways: as the basis of the claimants' right avocations, for part of the judges'

The NPCSC's abstract review mechanism is primarily based on the *Constitution* and the *Law on Legislation*. In addition to the constitutional provisions that establish the NPC's and NPCSC's constitutional review authority, the *Law on Legislation* further stipulates its constitutional review operation in more detail.

There are three ways to initiate constitutional review. The first is NPC and NPCSC initiation. The NPC can change or repeal inappropriate laws passed by the NPCSC and unconstitutional local autonomous regulations as well as specific regulations approved by the NPCSC. The NPCSC has the power to repeal administrative regulations and local legislation that conflict with the constitution and upper-level legislation.[178] This power does not only concern constitutional review. It concerns two review powers: one includes reviewing the constitutionality of laws and regulations; a second power includes reviewing the legality of non-constitutional laws to ensure that lower-level legislation does not conflict with upper-level legislation. Together, these two review powers are aimed at maintaining unity and harmony at different legal levels through reducing their conflict.

The second way to initiate constitutional review is upon the request of certain authorities. Such authorities that are authorised by the *Law on Legislation* to initiate a constitutional review include the State Council, the Central Military Commission, SPC, Supreme People's Procuratorates, and the standing committees of local people congresses at the provincial level. Where the aforementioned authorities believe that an administrative regulation or local legislation conflicts with the *Constitution* or an upper-level law, they can submit a request to the NPCSC requiring a review.

The third way to initiate constitutional review is upon the suggestion of a government authority, except the aforesaid authorities, social organisations, enterprises or individuals. After the receipt of the suggestion for constitutional review, the working body under the NPCSC researches the matter and submits its suggestion to a specific committee under the NPCSC for review 'when necessary'.[179]

The basic feature of the constitutional review mechanism established by the *Law on Legislation* is that the core agency responsible for constitutional review is the NPCSC. However, the *Law on Legislation* does not mention review of unconstitutional laws passed by the NPC. The NPCSC,

explanation of their rulings and directly as the legal stipulation for making a decision as in the *Qi Yuling* case. See Wang, *Zhongguo Xianfa*, preface.

178 *Law on Legislation*, art. 97.

179 Ibid., art. 99(2).

which is inferior to the NPC, cannot overrule NPC laws, even if they are unconstitutional, similar to the SPC. Because the NPC is supreme in the current political system, which was established by the constitution, it is impossible to form a European-model constitutional court that can overrule any unconstitutional law. The only way to correct unconstitutional NPC laws is revision or changing the law by the NPC upon the NPCSC's suggestion. However, two practical difficulties result from the ineffectiveness of the NPC adjusting its unconstitutional laws. First, the NPC meeting is only held once each year. The annual meeting period is approximately two weeks. The insufficient meeting frequency and short meeting time leads to untimely revision of unconstitutional laws. Second, the NPC adjustment is not a constitutional review mechanism; it is a legislative one and must endure a long and tedious law-making process to revise or repeal unconstitutional NPC laws.

The NPCSC review process has been criticised for its ineffectiveness. Although it clarifies the NPCSC's constitutional review authority, the *Law on Legislation* does not stipulate a detailed and feasible operation mechanism for constitutional review. In practice, both the NPC and NPCSC are ineffective at constitutional review. Although unconstitutional laws are frequent, no case has declared that a law is unconstitutional through the constitutional review mechanism. The unconstitutional law either is enforced for a long time without a timely revision, or it is revised for consistency with the constitution through an alternative to constitutional review. Consider the *2001 Demolition Regulation* as an example. Many provisions of this regulation became unconstitutional after the *2004 Amendment* to the constitution. However, this unconstitutional regulation was enforced for more than six years after 2004, until 2011, when the State Council passed a new regulation to substitute for the old, unconstitutional 2001 regulation. The NPCSC, which is the authority responsible for reviewing unconstitutional administrative regulations, did not initiate the constitutional review to annul the 2001 regulation. The *2004 Amendment* did not play a role in protecting urban house owners' property from the year it went into force to 2011, when the 2001 regulation was repealed. NPCSC constitutional review was ineffective.

The *LAL* also encountered criticism for its unconstitutionality after the 2004 Amendment. This law was enacted by the NPCSC and, thus, its unconstitutional portions should be changed or repealed by the NPC, which is superior to the NPCSC. However, the NPC did not revise the *LAL* for unconstitutionality or inappropriateness. The *LAL* was finally revised by the NPCSC on 28 August 2004, approximately five months after the

2004 Amendment was enacted. However, the revision did not fully render the *LAL* constitutional. The revision is abstract and impractical, which is demonstrated, for example, through insertion of the term 'public interest'. It imposes a public interest requirement in the *LAL* as a premise for land expropriation or requisition. In addition, it substitutes the original term 'requisition' in certain articles (arts 43(2), 45–47, 49, 51, 78–79) with 'expropriation' because use of the term 'requisition' was inconsistent with the usage of the concerned term in the constitution. However, it does not further define 'public interest' or its conditions. The implementation rules and much local legislation on expropriation, which are more practical for governing land expropriation and have been challenged for unconstitutionality, have not been revised through constitutional review or otherwise.

The constitutional review stipulated by both the constitution and *Law on Legislation* has not been developed until 2003, when an accident occurred and shocked the entire nation in the famous *Sun Zhigang* case. Soon after this case, the NPCSC began to advance institutionalisation of constitutional review, which was a small but brave step.

Sun Zhigang (Sun) was a young university graduate from a poor rural family who had just begun his job in Guangzhou and was arrested by the police on 17 March 2003 because he could not show either his identity card or temporary residence card. Although his roommate came to police substation with his ID card several hours later, the police refused to release Sun. The next day, he was compulsorily sent to a Custody & Repatriation Centre (C&R Centre). Two days later, he was found dead in a medical centre after he was severely beaten in the C&R Centre.

After it was reported by the *Southern Metropolitan Daily* (*Nanfang Dushi Bao*), which is a influential local newspaper published in Guangdong Province, this incident quickly attracted nationwide attention.[180] On 14 May, three young scholars who all hold PhD degrees in law and work in law schools submitted a suggestion to the NPCSC for constitutional review of *C&R Measures* under which Sun was placed into compulsory detention. The full name of the *C&R Measures* is *Measures on Custody and Repatriation of Vagrants and Beggars in Cities*, which is an administrative rule enacted by the State Council in 1982.[181] In the beginning, the

[180] Chen and Wang, 'Bei Shourongzhe'.

[181] *Chengshi Liulang Qitao Renyuan Shourong Qiansong Banfa* [*Measures on Custody and Repatriation of Vagrants and Beggars in Cities*], promulgated by the State Council on 12 May 1982. The Chinese text is available at www.law-lib.com/lawhtm/1982/2434.htm.

C&R Measures were only aimed at vagrants and beggars. However, after the issuance of *Opinions on the Questions concerning the Reform of Custody and Repatriation Work* in 1991,[182] the scope of the C&R was extended to include persons without identity cards, a temporary residence permit or a work permit.[183] Even with a legal identity card and work, as with Sun Zhigang, a Chinese citizen would still be detained and repatriated to his original place of *hukou* if he did not apply for a temporary resident permit in a timely manner for a city that is not his original *hukou* residence.[184] According to the petition by the three legal scholars, the *C&R Measures* is unconstitutional because it contravenes art. 37 of the *1982 Constitution of China* which states the following:

> Freedom of the person of citizens of the People's Republic of China is inviolable.
>
> No citizens may be arrested except with the approval or by decision of a people's procuratorate or by decision of a people's court, and arrests must be made by a public security organ.
>
> Unlawful detention or deprivation or restriction of citizens' freedom of the person by other means is prohibited, and unlawful search of the person of citizens is prohibited.

The three scholars' petition letter was soon endorsed by five well-known law professors, including Professor He Weifang, who is from Peking University Law School and a leading scholar in advocating the modern rule of law and civil rights. Even the leading media, including *Xinhua* and *Renmin Daily*, that are run and controlled by the state or the party acted quickly to report the *Sun Zhigang* incident as well as the following social reactions and relevant comments.[185] The social media pushed the NPCSC to the frontier, and the entire society awaited the first constitutional review decision by the NPCSC.

However, to the public's disappointment, the *C&R Measures* was abolished by the State Council on June 20 of 2003, approximately three months

[182] *Guanyu Shourong Qiansong Gongzuo Gaige Wenti de Yijian* [*Opinions on the Questions Concerning the Reform of Custody and Repatriation Work*], promulgated by the State Council in 1991.

[183] Such Opinions was made by the General Office of the State Council. See Zhu, 'Constitutional Review', 641–2.

[184] According to *Guanyu Shourong Qiansong Gongzuo Gaige Wenti de Yijian* [*Opinions on the Questions Concerning the Reform of Custody and Repatriation Work*], non-local residents who stay in a city for longer than three days must apply for temporary residence permit.

[185] Hand, 'Using Law', 122–3.

after Sun's death and one month after scholars' petition. On the same day, a new regulation titled '*Measures of Aid and Management of Urban Vagrants and Beggars Without Life Support*' was enacted to substitute the repealed *C&R Measures*.[186] To the public's surprise, the State Council's reaction was quick, but people who expected the constitutional review mechanism to function were disappointed that the *Sun Zhigang* incident did not lead to the first constitutional review decision. Zhu used a 'black box' operation to explain why the *C&R Measures* was not abolished through constitutional review. He commented that the *Sun Zhigang* incident was internally settled among the state authorities, including the State Council and NPCSC. Compared with an announcement by the NPCSC that the measures are unconstitutional, the State Council's abolishment is an approach that 'minimised the shock by the eventual cancellation of the regulations by the NPCSC'.[187] According to a report by *Xinhua*, which is a state-run media, the *C&R Measures* was abolished because 'such measures cannot meet the need of new situations'. Unconstitutionality was not mentioned in the State Council's abolishment decision of the *C&R Measures*.[188]

Although the expected constitutional review did not occur, the *Sun Zhigang* incident was still regarded as important in facilitating NPCSC institutionalisation of constitutional review. After this case, the NPCSC began to establish a specific agency and design a detailed procedure for enforcing constitutional review.

In May 2004, the NPCSC announced the establishment of a specific agency responsible for maintaining and reviewing laws, administrative regulations and rules that are filed. The agency is The Office of Filing and Reviewing of Laws and Regulations (*fagui shencha bei an shi*, or the Filing and Reviewing Office) under the supervision by the NPCSC's Commission of Legal Work (*fazhi gongzuo weiyuanhui*). According to the head of the NPCSC's General Office, the review and filing job that was previously managed by the office of secretaries was separated and attributed to and dealt with solely by a specific organ. He said: 'It shows that the work of reviewing the constitutionality and legality of the laws and regulations

[186] *Chengshi Shenghuo Wuzhuo de Liulang Qitao Renyuan Jiuzhu Guanli Banfa* [*Measures of Aid and Management of Urban Vagrants and Beggars Without Life Support*], promulgated by the State Council on 20 June 2003. The Chinese text is available at www.gov.cn/zwgk/2005–05/23/content_156.htm.

[187] Zhu, 'Constitutional Review', 643.

[188] *Xin Hua*, 'Chengshi Liulang'.

will be clear-cut in the attribution of job responsibility and much stronger in the enforcement strength.'[189]

In December 2005, the NPCSC revised its work procedure for filing and review work which was enacted in 2000.[190] The current constitutional review mechanism formed by the revised procedure (*2005 Review Procedure*) includes three operation steps: filing, review and correction.

In the first step, 'filing', the State Council and local legislation authorities must submit their legislation to the NPCSC filing. After 2004, the Filing and Review Office is responsible for receiving and maintaining the administrative rules or local legislation filed.

In the second step, 'review', the Filing and Review Office can initiate a review. The review can also be initiated upon request from the government authorities stipulated by the *Law on Legislation* or upon suggestion. The regulations or rules for review should be submitted to the applicable specific commission and Commission of Legal Work under the NPCSC for a written review opinion.

In the third step, 'correction', the NPCSC's written review opinion is then sent to the applicable enacting authority for the authority to correct the questionable regulation or rule. If the notified authority does not provide a correction, the NPCSC can decide to cancel the unconstitutional regulation or rule.

In the same year when this work procedure was revised, a new document titled '*Work Procedure for the Filing and Review of Judicial Interpretations*' was passed.[191] Similar to administrative or local rules, the SPC's judicial interpretations must be submitted to the NPCSC for review. This also reflects the NPC's supreme status over the other national authorities, including the SPC, and solidifies the NPCSC's review function regarding lower-level laws and regulations. One important and inspiring action to note is that by including the SPC's judicial interpretation into its review scope, the NPCSC suggested that it does not want the SPC to gain constitutional review power.

[189] Cui, 'Quanguo Renda'.

[190] *Xingzheng Fagui Difangxing Fagui Zizhi Tiaoli he Danxing Tiaoli Jingji Tequ Fagui Bei-an Shencha Gongzuo Chengxu* [*Work Procedure for Filing and Review of Administrative Rules and Regulations, Local Regulations, Autonomous Regulations and Specific Regulations, and Regulations of Special Economic Zones*], enacted by the Chairmen's Council of the NPCSC on 16 October 2000 and amended on 15 August 2005.

[191] *Sifa Jieshi Bei-an Shencha Gongzuo Chengxu* [*Work Procedure for the Filing and Review of Judicial Interpretations*], enacted by the Chairmen's Council of the NPCSC on 16 December 2005.

However, Cai Dingjian, a constitutional law scholar, argued that the aforementioned review procedure was not a specific review of unconstitutional laws. More precisely, the review examines both unconstitutionality and illegality.[192] He correctly notes that no specific constitutional review system operates independently in China. The constitutional review includes a general review system, which reviews constitutionality and legality. The legality review aims to facilitate consistency between lower-level legislation and higher-level legislation. Mainly, the administrative or local regulations or rules that conflict with the higher-level laws passed by the NPC or NPCSC are filed and reviewed using the aforementioned procedure. Thus, in China, constitutional review is only part of a general review system designed to maintain uniformity within the entire legal system or facilitate consistency among legislation at the different levels of hierarchy.

Revision of the NPCSC's review procedure was acclaimed by the media as a substantial step in facilitating constitutional review and a milestone in China's constitutional history. I believe that these comments are an overstatement. While the revision in 2005 better details the work procedure, it does not substantially change the basic constitutional review mechanism outlined by the 2000 review procedure. The 2005 revision and the specific work office established the previous year show only small progress towards constitutional review (and only on paper rather than in practice), wherein the work procedure (and its effective operation) was improved. Because no rule or regulation has been publicly rendered unconstitutional by the NPCSC after this revision, constitutional review in China faces the same situation as after the 2000 review procedure was enacted. Lacking sufficient information, we cannot arbitrarily conclude that constitutional review by the NPCSC has been slowed in the past few years. It is possible that most reviews focus on legality. Proceedings regarding unconstitutional or illegal regulations or rules by the NPCSC typically include internal consultations between the NPCSC and enactment authorities in question. Although certain reviews were performed by the NPCSC, few of the lower-level regulations or rules that were challenged as unconstitutional or illegal were corrected, or the correction was slow. Moreover, it is reasonable to suggest that the NPCSC has not made substantial reform since 2005, which is demonstrated by the CPC government's reluctant attitude in establishing a more active and effective

192 Wang 'Wanshan'.

constitutional review mechanism. A key drawback of the current constitutional review mechanism that remains uncorrected is that the review does not include laws enacted by the NPC and NPCSC, which renders China's constitutional review fragmentary and unauthoritative.

Can we expect more radical reforms to constitutional review in the near future? Zhu believes that no one can accurately predict future reforms owing to uncertainty in influential factors, such as internal politics, the party leaders' courage and momentum and the maturity of constitutional law theories.[193] In February 2008, Hand and Kellog expressed their conservative judgements that China's constitutional reform prospects were limited. In April 2009, Kellog sadly announced that their analysis 'has been borne out by events of the past year'.[194]

[193] Zhu, 'Constitutional Review', 652. [194] Kellogg, 'The Death', 6.

7

Concluding remarks and suggested reform measures

Effective constitutional review offers an institutional guarantee that the constitution protects private property and other basic constitutional rights. In other words, without this institutional guarantee, the constitutional provisions cannot necessarily play their role in restricting governmental power and protecting the citizens' constitutional rights. To this point, in the text regarding the evolution underlying constitutionalisation of private property, incorporation of public interest, compensation standards and procedural reform, I have identified that the fluctuations and conflicting social forces influence the path of constitutional reform concerning private property. In this chapter, I will generalise the evolution of China's reform in protecting private property as well as the inherent fluctuations of social forces again and offer certain, feasible suggestions for improvement.

7.1 Concluding remarks

The evolutionary path of private property protection in China should be understood from the interaction between domestic reform and the influence of globalisation. The prediction of future development and the suggestions of the feasible reform measures should also be determined through the consideration of the conflict and convergence among the social forces that unfold in such an interaction.

Three forces intervene in the influence of globalisation. These intervening forces include the pressure from the international society to require the rule of law and the strong protection of private property, the FDI investors' demand for land and the FDI investors' request for strong protection of private property. Domestic reform, which is determined at the local level, involves four interacting social forces: the central government's reform tendency towards a market economy and democracy, the local governments' motivation to chase GDP and local revenue growth, the citizens' rights consciousness and the development of interest groups.

In the early stage of China's opening and reform, the citizens' rights consciousness for private property protection was so weak that it could not restrain the ruthless invasion of other social forces, which negatively influenced the protection of private property. To cater to the foreign investors' need for land and to stimulate FDI-driven growth, both the central and local governments tended to transfer the domestic collectives and the citizens' land to the use of foreign enterprises. In addition, to comfort the foreign investors' worry of the possible taking of their property by the government of the host country, the protection of private property or the restraining provisions of government taking was offered to foreign enterprises only in the concerned laws. This further weakened the positive force which required property protection from the local side.

With the advancements in economic development, especially starting in late 1990s, the urbanisation and industrialisation of the development of the real estate industry as a growth engine have resulted in a more massive governmental taking of urban houses and rural land than before the reform. However, as in the early stages of FDI, the protection of private property remains fragile and individuals' property rights are so delicate that they cannot counteract the combined invasion of governmental and business forces. What is different from the previous stage is that the negative force of property protection from the business side is now derived from both FDI and domestic enterprises, and the positive forces have begun to increase. With respect to globalisation and with China's immergence into the globalised society, the international society's requirement for the protection of private property is much stronger than before and China now bears a greater obligation to strengthen the protection of private property as well as other fundamental rights. Regarding localisation, the citizens' rights consciousness has been enhanced during the process of China's opening and reform. Thus, the convergence of the global and domestic positive forces for property protection has led to increasingly stronger resistance to the limitless and unjust governmental taking of private property. The resistance has become so strong, in fact, that it facilitated the birth of the *2004 Amendment* that entrenches the 'taking clause' in the constitution. As for the central government and its role in leading China's reform, it finally acknowledged the *2004 Amendment* because it realised that the deepening of market economy reform would not be successful without a legal system that recognised and protected private property. From the business side, which was a powerful force in the taking of land, the entrepreneurs supported the *2004 Amendment* because it proved beneficial in protecting their properties as well.

The CPC government put itself into a contradictory situation when it approved the incorporation of the *2004 Amendment* into the constitution. On the one hand, both the central and local governments were strongly motivated to take land because doing so increased their revenues and enhanced growth through the resulting urbanisation and industrialisation. On the other hand, however, the governments now had to consider and enforce the requests of the citizens, including individuals and entrepreneurs, to protect their property. The design of the 'taking clause' reflected the CPC government's effort to mitigate its own motivation to take land and the people's requests for protection. The structure of the property clause in the constitution is still fragmentary, however.

First, private property is not incorporated in the section of basic rights, but instead, it is under the title 'General Principles' and forms a part of the property system that is still dominated by public property.

Second, the secondary status of private property still exists. Public property is clearly defined as being sacred and as being the foundation of the country's economic system. The unequal treatment between public property and private property corresponds with the unequal treatment between a public economy and a private economy.

Third, the three prongs of the 'taking clause' are not complete. For example, there is no clear identification or definition regarding compensation. The stipulated compensation without any 'just', 'full' or other limit preceding it indicates that the CPC government wants more flexibility in setting compensation standards in the non-constitutional laws. The principle of 'according to law' is, in essence, more a stipulation of authorisation than a constitutional limit on procedures. The constitution does not have the requirement to impose 'justness' with respect to the 'taking procedure'.

In practice, the function of public interest and compensation as substantive limits on eminent domain has been weak and unsatisfactory in protecting private property from being taken unjustly by the government. Before the *2004 Amendment*, the lack of public interest limits resulted in an overly broad scope of governmental taking activities. In urban areas, the taking of privately owned houses could even be initiated and enforced by business enterprises. In rural areas, local governments used their eminent domain power to aid construction enterprises in acquiring the land they needed as the constitutional principle of public interest was not efficient in substantially restraining the local governments' taking activities. Although the *LAL* governing the governmental taking of rural land was revised to include public interest principle not long after the *2004 Amendment*, it did not constrain the pervasive governmental taking of rural land as there is no clear definition and identification of the term 'public interest' contained within the *LAL*. In a broad sense, the government can include economic growth and development in the scope of public interest, and thus, the expropriated projects that facilitate urbanisation or industrialisation, either directly or indirectly, can be justified as 'in the public interest' even if many of them are executed by enterprises and benefit non-public units. The clarification of public interest was first introduced into the regulation regarding the expropriation of urban houses in 2011, seven years after the *2004 Amendment*. It is indeed laggard legislative progress with respect to the protection of private property. To understand the background of the conflicting social forces that led to the birth of the *2011 Expropriation Regulation*, we find explanations as to why the central government was reluctant to incorporate the constitutional public interest principle into its *2011 Expropriation Regulation* and why such incorporation finally occurred. The angry response from citizens to the hibernating 'taking clause' and the unrestricted taking activities resulted in increasingly more violent incidents. Finally, the death of Tang Fuzhen in 2009 ignited the society-wide opposition to the unrestrained governmental expropriation, which then facilitated the birth of the new *2011 Expropriation Regulation*. By analysing the entire revision process, however, we still find the conflict between government interest and individual property and the influence of the conflict in the production of the finalised version of public interest scope in the 2011 regulation. The detailed limits of public interest scope did not affect the expropriation of rural land, however, as the taking of rural land is of major governmental interest. Furthermore, local governments are far more reluctant to reduce their expropriated rural frontier from inside the domain of private property. Thus, the uneven reform in expropriation between urban areas and rural areas results in an issue of inequality, and hence, one more constitutional issue to be resolved.

With respect to compensation, the progress in the reform of compensation standards also reflects uneven reform. Although not timely, the *2011 Expropriation Regulation* establishes fair market value as the main standard for the calculation of the compensation to the expropriated urban houses, but with respect to the expropriated rural land, the compensation standard is the annual output test, which was stipulated by the 1998 *LAL* and was maintained after the *2004 Amendment*. On the surface, one difficulty is the lack of a mature transaction market for rural land, thus making the use of a comparable market transaction approach impossible. On a deeper level, the real reason the government uses an annual output test, which tends to lead to low compensation and to the failure to develop the transaction market for rural land, is that the government wants to maintain the current land use system because it benefits local governments. The current land use system prohibits direct transactions between the holders of rural land and the demanders of land construction. The change of land use purpose from agriculture to construction and the required transaction process must go through the government. The government, representing the state, transfers the rural land as the land for construction and transfers the collective ownership of the rural land to the state. The government then supplies the land, whose use and transaction right of a certain term of years is conferred to the demanders, and in turn, acquires a huge amount of expropriation surplus. Accordingly, we find that the real reason the government suppresses the compensation available to rural land holders is the fiscal revenue. To raise compensation standards would mean that the government must sacrifice a part of their revenue.

Similar to China, around 2000, India was plagued by frequent social unrest owing to overly broad land expropriation. Facing the farmers' violent protests, the governments in both countries put the reform of rural land expropriation on the agenda. China's reform began in 2004 when the State Council issued its opinions about the land issues in rural areas. Although the scope of land expropriation was not narrowed by the reform, the land compensation amounts were increased mainly by increasing the adjustment of multipliers used for the annual output test. In addition, local governments are required to establish a uniform land section price as the basis for calculating compensation. Although the land section price is required to take into account the annual output and other factors, such as social and economic growth and the farmer's standard of living, the increase in compensation is still far from reasonable as most local governments use annual output as the main criterion when establishing the land section price. A new problem caused by a uniform land section price is the possibility of insufficient compensation to those individual farmers whose output or land quality is much higher than that of other landowners in the same section. These reform measures are not formal laws; instead, they are informally recognised as substantive laws.[1] In India, the reform is much more radical than that of China in that *the 2013 LARR Act* involves substantial impact on both public interest and compensation standards. The scope of public interest justifying the expropriation is narrowed, to a large extent, by requiring public purpose and public use. The increased margin of compensation and resettlement fee is so large that the business sectors are objecting heavily.

On the procedural side, the constitutional provisions of the *2004 Amendment* follow a German style authorisation mode. Although the principle of 'according to law' is more an authorisation clause, in democratic countries such as Germany, the taking procedure stipulated by the laws that are enacted by the democratically elected legislature tends to be less arbitrary and more fair in balancing the power of the government and the involvement of the private owners. In China, the procedure of taking enacted by executive authorities, who are also the expropriation authorities, or by the legislative authorities, who defer to the executive authorities, is certainly deemed unfair to the individual owners of property rights. The taking procedure prior to the *2004 Amendment* was arbitrary and tended to grant advantage to the government side rather than to the private owner. The procedure even lacked the basic elements for composing a fair or due process, such as an opportunity for a advanced notification, hearing, pre-court-decision occupation and advanced payment of compensation. As such, there was no procedure in place to deter the government's unjust expropriation or to ensure that the individuals' private rights were not being violated. Although the reform progress after the *2004 Amendment* provided private parties more bargaining power and more opportunities against government power, the progress was slow and unsatisfactory. The expropriation procedure of urban houses, which was reconstructed by the *2011 Expropriation Regulation* and offers only a conditional and limited hearing opportunity, did make appreciable progress with respect to the timeliness and transparency of information distribution and the requirement of advance payment of compensation before the taking of property. The reform in the expropriation procedure of rural land lagged significantly behind that of the urban policy. Although the notification and hearing opportunities are provided as part of the State Council's decision and the MLR's guidance and opinions, throughout the

[1] Zhu, 'Constitutional Review', 629.

whole procedure, the affected farmers are allowed only to argue the compensation to be awarded for the land. They do not have an opportunity during the hearing to object to the proposed expropriation as it is not in the public interest. Moreover, the advance payment of compensation is not clarified nor is it required.

The reform progress of relevant legislation in executing the three prongs of the 'taking clause' is still limited and not only is far from the common standards of Western countries, but it is also far behind that of India, a comparable big developing economy. In India, although the property clauses were all removed from the constitution by 1979, the democratic mechanism and independent court system serve effectively to push forward the reform of legislation and limit the misuse of the government's expropriation power. China, in the predictable future, cannot match the reform strength reflected by the *2013 LARR Act*. In China, although property clauses were entrenched in the constitution in 2004, the central government and legislature still lack a strong motivation to substantially reform their expropriation laws because the institutional system is characterised by the leadership and policy guidance of the CPC, which is not responsive to the people's request for private property protection very actively. Because of this restraint within the institutional system, even the limited progress incorporated into the constitution with respect to property protection cannot be effectively implemented.

The constitutional review mechanism plays a crucial role in facilitating the enforcement of the constitution and in revising the unconstitutional laws and government activities. Both the U.S. judicial review and the European constitutional court model, although different in the design of review authority, play similar roles in the implementation of the constitution. In the United States, private parties can challenge the unconstitutional expropriation laws and government actions in the courts. In Germany, the decision of the constitutionality of the relevant legislation is referred to the constitutional court. If the legislation based on which the expropriation is made is declared to be unconstitutional, the expropriation decision is invalidated. In China, the constitutional review, which is required by the *1982 Constitution of China* and the *Law on Legislation*, was not implemented until 2004 at which time some implementation steps were initiated. Although a specific review organ and a detailed review procedure were established in 2004 and 2005, respectively, there has been to date no substantial progress in constitutional review. The current NPCSC-centred review mechanism does not review the constitutionality of the NPC or the NPCSC legislation. Although the term 'public interest' was quickly incorporated into the *LAL* through the NPCSC's self-revision process rather than through the constitutional review process after the *2004 Amendment*, the constitutional explanation of the term and the correction of the unconstitutionality of the concerned compensation standards and procedures cannot be expected to be made through the NPCSC's constitutional review. Even the unconstitutional regulations or rules enacted by the State Council or local legislatures cannot be effectively corrected through the current constitutional review. It is difficult for the NPCSC to challenge publicly the enacting authorities of such unconstitutional statutes as both the reviewer and the reviewee are integrated as an inseparable body of the party-country authority.

The current review mechanism has little influence on concrete court suits. Even if the applied regulation or rule has been submitted to the NPCSC for review, the judge can decide the case based on under-review statutes without delaying his decision. In other words, the judge does not have to wait for the NPCSC's review decision. There is no stipulation regarding what remedies are available to the rights holders whose property was taken before the taking regulation was announced as unconstitutional. The SPC's plan to acquire judicial review power of the constitution through the *Qi Yuling* case never developed and, in fact, died in 2008. The NPCSC strengthened its status as the constitutional review authority by placing the SPC under its supervision in 2005 when it promulgated a working procedure for examining the judicial interpretation of the SPC.

The lack of an independent, impartial and active constitutional review authority renders the constitutional protection of private property less meaningful in practice even if such protection is eloquently defined within the constitution. Accordingly, this bottleneck is difficult to break under the current fundamental political system in China. The supremacy of the NPC in the political system has determined that it is impossible for the SPC to be awarded constitutional review power that can be used to restrain the NPC. As a result, the status of the SPC is even lower than that of the State Council in the political system, which means that it is also impossible for the SPC to review the administrative regulations enacted by the State Council.

Thus, the suggestions regarding any future reform that will strengthen private property protection revolve around three issues. One is the improvement of the current constitutional provisions, and the second involves the relevant provisions under the law. The third, and perhaps most important, is the improvement of the constitutional review mechanism, or institutional reform. My suggestions with respect to these issues are given within the current framework of the fundamental property system and political system. In other words, any feasible reform suggestions must take into account that the current property system is not reformed towards privatisation and the Communist Party governance structure has not changed substantially.

7.2 Suggestions for reform

7.2.1 Improvement of the constitutional provisions and the relevant laws

The current constitutional clauses concerning property are incorporated in the section titled 'General Principles' and follow the traditional arrangement in the socialist period, which is to regard the property system as a part of the economic system. Articles 9 and 10, which address the ownership of natural resources and land, adhere to the traditional agreement that corresponds to the economic forms stipulated by arts. 6, 7 and 8. Thus, the logic of such structure is that because the fundamental economic system should be dominated by a public economic form, the main productive resources, including natural resources and land, should be mainly owned by the state and the collectives as they represent the mode of public ownership. Furthermore, because the private economy is secondary to the public economy, individuals are given a secondary right to land, namely, a conditional land use right. According to this logic, public property is announced to be both 'sacred' and 'inviolable', while private property is only considered to be 'inviolable'.

Restrained by this fundamental property structure, the revision of the constitution with the aim of endowing full ownership of land and other natural resources to individuals is nearly impossible in a communist country. Without changing the dominant status of public property to a status characterised by public ownership and thereby strengthening the protection of private property and facilitate the development of a market economy, the constitution may be revised to clarify the independence of private property rights and the equal protection of both public property and private property.

In the first two paragraphs of art. 10, namely art. 10(1)–(2), which concerns the structure of land ownership, only state ownership and collective ownership of land are stipulated. The land use rights of ownership by individuals or units are not listed as an independent land right form.

Accordingly, it is suggested that a new paragraph be inserted as the third paragraph under the art. 10 (1)–(2):

> The units or individuals can enjoy the use rights and other non-ownership property rights of land according to law.

The current art. 10(3) addresses land expropriation. As the original art. 10(2) stipulates only the collective ownership of rural land and the state ownership of urban land, the expropriation of land targets only the owners of land, which leads to an incomplete protection of private property in the specific legislation with respect to expropriation. In urban areas, only those houses that can be owned by private individuals are the target of expropriation. The land use rights attached to the targeted houses are not defined as a property to be expropriated clearly, and thus, they cannot enjoy constitutional protection. In rural areas, the collectives that own land are the ones with whom negotiations must be conducted and they are the ones to directly challenge the law as enforced by the government. The involvement of individual farmers, who own land use rights, is limited in the expropriation process. To clarify that the expropriation of land includes both the expropriation of ownership rights and the expropriation of use rights or any non-ownership right, the term 'land', as stipulated by art. 10(3), as the object of expropriation or requisition can be revised to 'land or its property rights'.

After this revision, the land use rights held by both urban and rural citizens are considered as private property and should, accordingly, be protected directly under the constitution. Thus, we have 'the propertisation of property rights'.

To be consistent with the suggested revision of the constitution, two specific legal documents concerning expropriation should also be revised to include land use rights. It is suggested that the *2011 Expropriation Regulation* clarify that both houses and land use rights are the objects of expropriation. Thus, the valuation should be the valuation of both the house and the land use rights. The current valuation is mainly for houses, while land use rights are only one factor considered when valuing houses. However, if land use rights are independently valued, the compensation will be based on the comparable transaction price of such land rights in the land market, and as a result, this would increase the total compensation awarded to the takees.

The propertisation of land property rights also influences the individual owners' procedural rights. If land use right is established as an independent right by the constitution and by specific laws, the rights holders can act as independent parties and directly challenge the government. This would then require the adoption of additional rights related to expropriation procedures. This is especially important for farmers who have use rights of rural land and are currently given fewer procedural rights than those given to collectives.

It is also recommended that private property be included as part of the citizens' basic rights. There are two ways to accomplish this. The first is to move the clauses that address private property and expropriation from the current section to the section that covers basic rights. The second option is to add a clause to the section on basic rights without moving the original private property and expropriation clauses. The second option is preferable for two reasons. First, removing the clause about private property from the section titled 'General Principle' would result in incomplete stipulations of the property system, which should include state ownership, collective ownership and private property. Second, the expropriation of rural land in China, unlike that in other countries, is not for private rights only. Instead, it involves the land for which state or collective ownership and private use rights coexist. Under situations in which rural land is used for public facilities, the expropriation might concern collective ownership only. Thus, the current expropriation clause, which addresses more than just private property rights, does not belong to the section on basic rights as this section is concerned only with the rights of the individual citizen.

It is notable that the clarification of private property as one person's basic right cannot elevate private property as a fundamental right or as a status of liberty as is found in the constitutions of some western countries. Even if private property is defined as a basic or fundamental right in China's constitution, it is still confined by the fundamental property system as stipulated by the general principles. Nevertheless, such a revision can play an active role in facilitating the protection of private property. First, it ranks property rights with other citizens' basic rights, such as liberties in speech, assembly, residence and so on. In other words, the revision would mean that property rights are on the same level as human rights. The constitutional principles as identified within the section on basic rights and the relevant international treaties concerning human rights can be combined to shelter private property. Second, even if in practice the constitution does not effectively protect the current basic rights or liberties, the definition of private property as a basic right can focus society's attention on the protection of private property, which, in turn, may indirectly and informally restrain the government's ruthless expropriation activities.

Based on the propertisation of land use rights and the fundamentalisation of private property, the next suggested revision is the clarification of the compensation doctrine. The current use of compensation allows the executive authorities substantial discretionary power in deciding its exact standards. Moreover, the application of different standards for different land rights further results in the discriminative treatment of property holders. Accordingly, it is necessary to use a much more specific term such as 'just compensation' or 'full compensation' to better reflect the basic intent of constitutional protection, which is to compensate the takee for his loss. This revision, on the one hand, is consistent with the requirement of private property being 'inviolable', as stated in the constitution. On the other hand, this revision can limit the ruthless explanation by government. Another suggestion is to borrow from Germany's experience and thereby deem any legislation or regulation concerning expropriation, if there exist no exact standards for full or just compensation, is not applicable.

Finally, as to the revision about the equal protection of private property, two types of discrimination should be eliminated through constitutional equal protection. The first discrimination is based on the right holder's ownership or non-owner identity, while the second is based on the public or private nature of the concerned property. The strength of the legal protection in restraining individuals from violating public property should be the same as that in restraining the government or state from infringing on private property. The right holders with non-ownership of private property should be protected by the same standards as those with ownership rights. Thus, a suggested new paragraph should be inserted into the constitution in the section concerning basic rights as an addition to the private property clause. It is:

> The citizens' private property shall not be discriminated against with respect to constitutional and legal protection based on its non-public or its non-ownership nature.

To be consistent with this new constitutional provision, two main revisions to the specific laws regarding expropriation are recommended. First, farmers with non-ownership rights and collectives with ownership rights should be treated equally under the law. Second, farmers with non-ownership rights of land and urban residents who own houses and are with use right of urban land should be treated equally in expropriation procedures. The current discriminatory treatment from both the substantive and the procedural sides should be corrected. Specifically, the main revisions to the specific laws include (1) the farmers' procedural rights should be adjusted to be at the same level as those of collectives and urban residents, and (2) the compensation standard or level should be the same for both affected farmers and urban residents.

The next issue for reform is that of the legislative level of expropriation. The constitution stipulates that the expropriation shall be enforced according to 'law', and the 'law' of expropriation, according to *Law on Legislation*, should be determined by NPC or NPCSC legislation.[2] Thus, the regulation on expropriation enacted by the State Council gives rise to questions with respect to its legality and constitutionality. After the enforcement of the *Law on Legislation* on 1 July 2000, the State Council continued to enforce its regulation on expropriation in the subsequent year. To respond to the questioning of the State Council's legislation authority regarding the expropriation of urban houses, in 2007, the *LUREA* was revised to include an authorisation clause in art. 6 that stipulates that the State Council can enact 'detailed measures' with respect to the expropriation of urban houses. However, the legality and even constitutionality of the regulation on expropriation remains questionable. The *LUREA* is enforced by the NPCSC, which has less legislative authority than the NPC, which enacted the *Law on Legislation*. In addition, the *Property Law* authorised by the NPC in 2007 requires that expropriation must be in accordance with the laws of the NPC or NPCSC.[3] As both the *Law on Legislation* and the *Property Law* require that only the NPC or NPCSC legislation is authorised to govern expropriation, the NPCSC's authorisation clause in the *LUREA* conflicts with the higher level of the NPC law. The right to property is a basic individual right guarded by the constitutional expropriation clauses intended to prevent the government, from exercising expropriation through the executive authorities led by the State Council. Thus, it is inconsistent with the legislative purpose of the constitution's expropriation clause if the executive expropriation authority is allowed to make laws regarding expropriation.

There is no authoritative explanation in the constitution, at this time, as to what public interest and compensation involve. The State Council's

[2] According to the *Law on Legislation*, the issues concerning the expropriation of non-state-owned property shall be stipulated only by the 'law' enacted by the NPC or NPCSC. See *Law on Legislation*, art. 8.

[3] *Property Law*, art. 42(1).

2011 Expropriation Regulation is the only one country-level legislation that stipulates both the scope of public interest and the compensation standard. However, this legislation has been challenged and is considered questionable in its legality as it lacks legislative authority and it covers only the expropriation of urban houses. With respect to the expropriation of rural land, there has been no legislative explanation of public interest, and the constitutionality of average annual output as a compensation standard, which was adopted by the *LAL* before the *2004 Amendment*, remains controversial. The most suitable resolution is that the NPCSC, as the authority in explaining the constitution, should issue its authoritative interpretation regarding these two important constitutional principles on the expropriation of private property. While the NPCSC, because of its long-term delay in providing an explanation of the expropriation clauses, is subject to criticism for not taking the responsibility to enforce the constitution and protect the property rights of the citizens, the inherent reason for this delay is the conflict between the executive government and the individual citizens.

The most difficult issue in the explanation of public interest is whether economic development should be a public interest that justifies expropriation. In the *2011 Expropriation Regulation*, which stipulates public interest situations for the expropriation of urban houses, the State Council retains vast discretion regarding projects to stimulate the economy under the scope of public interest, either directly or indirectly. For the construction of essential facilities, public utilities and affordable housing, it is sufficient to satisfy the requirement of public interest if the government works as an organiser. There is no specification on whether such construction should be completed by a public entity. The incorporation of the reconstruction of old city areas within the scope of public interest gives the government the discretion to use its expropriation power to support a great number of business projects that can both stimulate the economy and benefit private developers. Moreover, the State Council authorises itself unlimited power to add new public interest possibilities to expropriate by enforcing its own administrative regulations. As to the expropriation of rural land, which is a main source of fiscal revenue, local governments are reluctant to limit their scope of expropriation by clarifying and narrowing public interest opportunities.

It is unrealistic to eliminate all economic development projects from the scope of public interest. A feasible resolution is to set limits in the evaluation of the appropriateness of economic development as a public interest for expropriation. In addition to the government's planning and organisation, government regulation and ex-post supervision of the projects that are executed by non-government bodies should be required. When private entities participate in expropriation projects, the role of public interest should be examined with respect to necessity and proportionality.

Given the difficulty in narrowing the scope of public interest and then reducing the government's expropriation activities, I suggest more consideration be given to reforming the compensation awarded to those who experience loss owing to expropriation. If the first threshold, public interest, is too weak to restrain the government's expropriation power, the second threshold, compensation, should bear greater weight in restraining the government's power to take private property. In urban areas, in addition to compensation based on the transaction price of the expropriated house, the compensation to the attached land use rights should also be considered. If the expropriated houses fall within the urban planning for specific development projects, the reasonably expected increase in the value of such land use rights should be part of the compensation awarded to the rights holders. Even if there is no such reasonable expectation and even if it is difficult to evaluate the value of such land use rights as they are not reflected in the price of the expropriated house, a minimum percentage of the compensation for the expropriated house, as a solatium, can be offered to the affected owner. As such, this serves as recognition of and payment for the holder's land use rights. In addition, a percentage of solatium should be offered to the takee whose property is expropriated for the purpose of economic growth or for the projects which are with significant participation of private bodies. For the expropriation of rural land, it is appropriate to use 'no-worse-off' as the basic principle for the decision of compensation as it satisfies the constitutional spirit of the compensation principle, which requires that the property holder's financial situation be restored as if the expropriation had not occurred. Accordingly, the current compensation standards should be reformed to be consistent with this basic value of the compensation principle.

First, the annual output and original use standard should serve only as the minimum compensation standard. Considering the involuntary nature of taking and the right of the displaced farmers in sharing the expropriation surplus, a percentage of the minimum compensation as the solatium should be paid to the affected farmers. The NPC can establish the range of the solatium and authorise the local congresses to determine the exact percentage of such solatium according to the local economic development situation and the growth in the value of such land use rights.

Second, the land section price promulgated by local governments should serve only as the reference and the minimum compensation standard. The final compensation should whichever is greater: the compensation based on land section price or the compensation based on the individual evaluation of the annual output of the expropriated land. If the property holder has sufficient evidence that his land should be compensated with a greater number than the compensation calculated based on the land section price, the greater amount should be paid.

Third, in some places, where the transaction of rural land use rights is allowed and the information offered by the transaction market is sufficient in the calculation of the comparable market price of the expropriated land, the compensation can be based on the transaction price only if the compensation amount is greater than the aforementioned compensation number.

Improving the system to provide appropriate compensation to the affected farmers must be part of the reform of rural land rights. Although the private ownership of rural land is not expected in the near future, the strengthening of the protection of the farmers' rural land rights is an obvious need as evidenced by the recently issued *No. 1 Document* of the CPC Central Committee. The No. 1 document is the first document issued by the CPC Central Committee at the start of the year, and the theme or issue in this document is always perceived as the most important job of the CPC for the upcoming year. There were five No. 1 documents issued between 1982 and 1986 and twelve No. 1 documents issued between 2004 and 2015. All of these No. 1 documents address farmers' rights and interests and/or the development of rural areas. The continuous occurrences of group unrest among farmers resulted in the realisation of the CPC that the protection of farmers' rights and interests is necessary to stabilise the leadership status of the CPC and to ensure social stability. The question here is the motivation behind the Communist Party's reform. That is, the reason for the reform is more to minimise the farmers' discontent passively than to respect the private individual property rights of each citizen actively. Correspondingly, the process of reform will must be slow and discreet.

The most recent CPC policies show that the reform in the area of rural land is and will be still a cautiously gradual one, with the future progress reflected by the limited enlargement of the scope of individual farmers' land rights and the unification of the construction land market between rural and urban areas. Relevant with the research of this book, three key aspects especially attract our attention. First, more property rights will be given to collectively owned profit-oriented construction land. The land for construction will be allowed for more transactional uses including the ones to be sold, leased and appraised as shares. Second, rural construction land will be allowed to be transacted and then to be unified with urban construction land to develop a unified market of construction land, where rural construction land will be given the treatment the same as that to urban land, or in other words, 'the same rights and the same prices'. Third, the scope of expropriation will be narrowed and the relevant procedure will be more strictly regulated. Compensation and resettlement measures will be improved to protect farmers' land rights better.[4] After the fulfillment of these reform measures, it is expected that collectives and their members will receive more benefits from the transaction of their construction land. However, the non-construction land is excluded from the enlargement of rights bundle and the unification of land market. Expropriation will be further narrowed and regulated and the compensation to land-loss farmers will be improved. A security mechanism which is 'reasonable, regulative and multiple' will be established for land-loss farmers. Thus, what will be achieved is a 'reasonable' security or safeguard mechanism which does not fully satisfy the 'just' or 'full' compensation required by constitutional value.

The current legal framework, which limits the farmers' use of their land for agricultural purposes, only allows farmers to collect the interest within the scope of limited agricultural use. After a parcel of farmland is urbanised, the original collective ownership of such land should be converted to state ownership as the constitution stipulates that all land in urban areas should be owned by the state. This implies that the

[4] *Zhonggong Zhongyang guanyu Quanmian Shenhua Gaiga Ruogan Zhongda Wenti de Jueding* [*The CPC Central Committee's Decision on Major Issues Concerning Comprehensively Deepening Reforms*], adopted by the Third Plenary Session of the Eighteenth CPC Central Committee on 12 November 2013. The Chinese text is available at news.xinhuanet.com/fortune/2013–11/15/c_118164235.htm. An English version is available at www.china.org.cn/china/third_plenary_session/2014–01/16/content_31212602.htm. See also *Guanyu Quanmian Shenhua Nongcun Gaige Jiakuai Tuijin Nongye Xiandaihua de Ruogan Yijian* (2004 *Nian Zhongyang Yihao Wenjian*) [*Several Opinions on Comprehensively Deepening Reforms in Rural Areas and Facilitating the Modernisation of Agriculture* (The *CPC Central Committee No. 1 Document* in 2004)], adopted by the CPC Central Committee and the State Council on 31 December 2013 and promulgated on 19 January 2014. The Chinese text is available at www.ce.cn/xwzx/gnsz/szyw/201201/30/t20120130_23027787.shtml.

expropriation surplus based on the new construction purpose of the expropriated rural land should belong to all people including both farmers and urban residents represented by the government. If the government allocates a substantial part of such expropriated surplus to the affected farmers, this would result in a new problem – that is, the fair and constitutional distribution of such surplus should include all people rather than only the farmers. If the affected farmers are allowed to convert their land use purpose to construction according to the zoning laws and then to transfer their land directly to construction developers, this new reform cannot be completed until the constitution is revised and a new property system is established. In other words, the state-ownership requirement for urban land must be revised. It would be extremely difficult, however, to enact such a revision as the reform would result in a conflict of interest between farmers and urban residents and it would significantly reduce the government's revenue and greatly weaken the socialist public-economy-dominate feature of the CPC's governance.[5] A feasible resolution is to clarify the allocation of the expropriation surplus under the current property system as established by the constitution. The expropriation surplus can be divided into two parts. The first part can serve as a solatium to supplement the insufficient compensation to the affected farmers and as a social security fee for maintaining the displaced farmers' basic living standards. The second part can be retained by the government to be used for public expenditures for all citizens.

7.2.2 *Procedural and institutional reforms*

The procedural and institutional reforms are among the most difficult to accomplish. In addition to the reform of the expropriation procedures, which include timely notification, full transparency of information, overall participation of rights holders to dissent against non-public-interest and demand just compensation, prohibition of government occupation before compensation and judicial remedy that makes the whole procedure consistent with the constitutional value of procedural justice, what is

[5] A precondition or bottom line of the CPC-leading rural land reform is that 'the public ownership of land should be secured and not be changed'. See *Guanyu Jiada Gaige Chuangxin Lidu Jiakuai Nongye Xiandaihua Jianshe de Ruogan Yijian* (2015 *Nian Yihao Wenjian*) [*Several Opinions on Enlarging the Reform and Innovation and Fastening Agricultural Modernisation* (*No. 1 Document* of 2015)], jointly released by the CPC Central Committee and the State Council on 1 February 2015. The Chinese text is available at money.163.com/15/0201/19/AHD3KP9Q00251OB6.html.

more important in the constitutional protection of private property is the reform of the corresponding institutional system to effectively enforce the constitution in practice. The overall constitutional protection of private property should include two levels. The first level involves the abstract review of the unconstitutional legislation, and the second level includes the application of constitutional principles in concrete cases.

The current NPCSC-centred review mechanism is not sufficient in correcting the possible unconstitutional legislation. It is not difficult for the NPC to enact legislation or revise the *Law on Legislation* to authorise the NPCSC to review all unconstitutional legislation, including the NPC legislation. This is not very significant, however, as the current NPCSC still serves as the review body, nor is it important in establishing a new review body, such as a constitutional court, or in authorising courts to have the power of review. The problem that is most difficult to correct, however, is in convincing the NPCSC or another constitutional review body to review and announce the unconstitutionality of the legislation and regulations enacted by the NPC, the NPCSC, the State Council and the local governments. Can the CPC tolerate the existence of an independent and impartial constitutional review body that may endanger the supremacy of the party's leadership status?

A similar problem involves the courts' judicial solution. Currently, the courts play only a minimal role in applying the constitution to protect private property rights. As a result of the *2008 SPC Decision*, the SPC and the lower-level courts are prohibited from directly applying the constitution to cases. The courts are also precluded from conducting constitutional review of any legislation. However, the courts cannot refuse to apply the NPC laws, the NPCSC laws or the State Council's administrative rules, even if the laws/rules are unconstitutional, as such laws and rules are still applicable in courts until they have been revised by their appropriate bodies or have been declared invalid by the constitutional review body. Even if the courts submit the issue of constitutionality for review to the NPCSC, they cannot suspend the proceeding of the cases to wait for the NPCSC's response. Even if they could suspend the case, they may not receive a response from the NPCSC as the current laws do not require that the NPCSC respond within a certain period of time. Worse, however, is that the courts are suspected of bias in challenging the government's expropriation decision. Similar to the SPC's inferior status under the supervision of the NPC and the NPCSC and the SPC's deference to the State Council, whose leader has greater status within the Communist Party than the leader of the SPC, the local courts are under the local congresses and their standing committees, and are also under the local governments. Taking it one step further, the local governments are often led by officials who are of a higher ranking than the heads of the local courts within the party organisation. Thus, the reform to create a wholly independent and impartial court system definitely conflicts with the current fundamental political system, and the CPC is greatly reluctant to make any substantial change to the current political system.

A partial and substantial reform can still be accomplished, however. First, a body specialising in constitutional review can be established and charged with the constitutional review of all non-constitutional laws and rules. Without conflict with the current fundamental political system, this body can be a special committee titled 'Committee of Constitutionality Review' under the NPC and NPCSC in the beginning.[6] Considering its lower status than NPCSC, it is mainly for examining the unconstitutionality of the legislation by the authorities which are lower than the NPCSC. It should be given the authority of overruling the legislation that is found unconstitutional. If the legislation by the NPC or NPCSC is found unconstitutional, this committee can submit a report to the NPC or the NPCSC to suggest the revision of the concerned legislation. A much braver reform is to establish a specialised review committee under the NPC that is given the same level of authority as the NPCSC and is authorised by the NPC to review the constitutionality of legislation enacted by NPCSC and the NPC. This specialised review committee could overrule the NPCSC legislation, if found unconstitutional, and require the NPC to initiate the revision of its unconstitutional legislation. Or, a double-level review mechanism can be established: the special committee under the NPCSC for the review of lower-level legislation by local legislators and the State Council, and the specialised committee under the NPC for the review of NPC/NPCSC legislation. More importantly, the review body should be required to respond in a timely manner to the constitutional review as requested by the SPC, the courts or others.

The establishment of such review body can also be gradual: in the beginning, the one under the NPCSC, and later, the one under the NPC.

[6] Currently there are nine special committees under the NPC/NPCSC: Ethnic Affairs Committee; Law Committee; Internal and Judicial Affairs Committee; Financial and Economic Affairs Committee; Education, Science, Culture and Public Health Committee; Foreign Affairs Committee; Overseas Chinese Affairs Committee; Environment Protection and Resources Conservation Committee; and Agriculture and Rural Affairs Committee. They are under the supervision of the NPC, and when the NPC is not in session, they are under the leadership of the NPCSC.

The most radical reform is to establish one constitutional court or committee at the supreme level, whose authorisation even includes the direct overruling of the NPC legislation. However, this demands the fundamental change of the existing structure of political system through the revision of the constitution.

Second, the courts hearing the cases should be allowed to submit their request for review directly to the review body without having to go through the SPC if an issue of constitutionality arises. The courts should be allowed to suspend the proceedings of a case until the constitutional review body issues its decision.

Third, the SPC should be allowed to issue the judicial interpretation regarding the constitutional provisions jointly with the NPCSC and/or the constitution review body. If the NPCSC does not supply the interpretation regarding constitutional principles, the SPC can, upon the local court's request or by itself, issue an interpretation only if it does not conflict with the interpretation of the NPCSC.

Fourth, to afford the courts greater independence in offering a judicial remedy to the affected individuals, the cases concerning expropriation decisions should be heard by a court that is less restrained by the local governments that enact the expropriation decisions. If the expropriation decision is enacted by the local government at a level that is lower than the provincial level, the concerned case should be heard by a court that is higher than the expropriating government at the territorial level. For instance, the expropriation decision made by a municipality-level government should be heard by a provincial court in the first instance. However, an expropriation decision made by a provincial government can still be heard by a provincial level court, and the appealing decision will be made by the SPC. If the decision is made by the ministries under the State Council, it can be challenged in a provincial-level court where the expropriated property is located and the decision can then be appealed to the SPC. By adopting this suggestion, the current structure of the court system is maintained. Of course, a better resolution for facilitating the courts' independence is to eliminate their political link with the party and with the executive governments. This, however, is not feasible at the present time or at any time in the near future as it would be incompatible with the CPC's leadership.

China's reform has been gradual. Similarly, the citizens' consciousness of and need for the protection of their property rights is also progressing gradually. The gradual reform led by the CPC is liberating people's voices and they are beginning to demand better protection of their private property rights. If the Communist Party does not respond to such demands in a timely manner, the anger of the people may be manifested in the form of violence and at the expense of their lives, which would destroy the foundation of the party's leadership. Thus, the protection of private property and other liberties would certainly progress far more quickly. The aforementioned reform measures are suggested under the premise of not reforming the current fundamental political system, but instead within the space that can be tolerated by the Communist Party. However, as the reform gradually moves forward, the day will come when the people's demand for private property and its protection will be incompatible with the party's bottom line. The question is, when that time comes, will the CPC abort the progress towards private property protection in its path or will the CPC reform itself and the political system and thereby substantially improve the protection of citizens' private property? I contend that China will choose the latter of the two approaches because – as Lincoln asserted – any enduring government must be and should be the one 'of the people, by the people, for the people'.[7] I further add and emphasise that here, people refer to 'everyone', not 'most ones' (majority), let alone 'minority ones' or 'someone'. To tame the tyranny of monarch, the democracy is established. Moreover, to tame the misuse of power by government and the tyranny of majority, the rule of law society featured with the guarantee of individual fundamental rights by the constitution and its justiciability should be developed.

[7] The cited words are from Abraham Lincoln's speech 'Gettysburg Address', delivered on 19 November 1863. The sentence which ends such address is 'government of the people, by the people, for the people, shall not perish from the earth'. This speech is available at www.abrahamlincolnonline.org/lincoln/speeches/gettysburg.htm.

BIBLIOGRAPHY

ADB, 'Compensation and Valuation in Resettlement: Cambodia, People's Republic of China, and India', 2007, available at www.adb.org/Documents/Reports/Capacity-Building-Compensation-Valuation/default.asp.

ADB, 'People's Republic of China Thematic Reports', 2007, available at www2.adb.org/Documents/Reports/Capacity-Building-PRC-Thematic/.

F. Afridi and S. X. Li, 'Social Identity and Inequality: The Impact of China's *Hukou* System', available at http://paa2008.princeton.edu/papers/80183.

A. Akinsanya, 'International Protection of Direct Foreign Investments in the Third World', *International and Comparative Law Quarterly*, 36 (1987), 58–75.

A. A. Alchian, 'Some Economics of Property Rights', *Il Politico*, 30 (1965), 816–29.

A. Aleinikoff, 'Constitutional Law in the Age of Balancing', *Yale Law Journal*, 96 (1987), 943–1005.

G. S. Alexander, 'Property as a Fundamental Constitutional Right – The German Example', *Cornell Law Review*, 88 (2003), 733–78.

G. S. Alexander, *The Global Debate over Constitutional Property: Lessons for American Takings Jurisprudence* (The University of Chicago Press, 2006).

L. Alexander, 'The Relationship between Procedural Due Process and Substantive Constitutional Rights', *University of Florida Law Review*, 39 (1987), 323 13.

A. Alvaro, 'Why Property Rights Were Excluded from the Canadian Charter of Rights and Freedoms', *Canadian Journal of Political Science*, 24 (1991), 309–29.

K. Anderson, 'On the Complexities of China's WTO Accession', *The World Economy*, 20 (1997), 749–72.

A. Appadurai, *Modernity at Large: Cultural Dimensions of Globalization* (Minneapolis: University of Minnesota Press, 1996).

A. Aslund, 'Russia's WTO Accession', available at www.iie.com/publications/papers/paper.cfm?ResearchID=686.

S. Baer, 'Equality: The Jurisprudence of the German Constitutional Court', *Columbia Journal of European Law*, 5 (1999), 249–79.

P. Banerjee, 'Land Acquisition and Peasant Resistance at Singur', *Economic and Political Weekly*, 18 (November 2006), 4718–20.

F. Banerjee, 'Singur Votes for Return of Nano', *The Times of India*, 4 May 2011.

A. Bell and G. Parchomovsky, 'The Uselessness of Public Use', *Columbia Law Review*, 106 (2006), 1412–49.

J. Bentham, *The Theory of Legislation (1690)* (New York: Oceana Publications, Inc., 1975).

L. Berger, 'The Public Use Requirement in Eminent Domain', *Oregon Law Review*, 57 (1978), 203–46.

T. Besley and R. Burgess, 'Land Reform, Poverty Reduction, and Growth: Evidence from India', *Quarterly Journal of Economics*, 115 (2000), 389–430.

W. Blackstone, *Commentaries on the Laws of England*, available at ebooks.adelaide.edu.au/b/blackstone/william/comment/contents.html.

C. Bramall, 'Chinese Land Reform in Long-Run Perspective and in the Wider East Asian Context', *Journal of Agrarian Change*, 4 (2004), 107–41.

J. M. Buchanan, 'Property as a Guarantor of Liberty' in C. K. Rowley (ed.), *Property Rights and the Limits of Democracy* (Aldershot, Hants: Edward Elgar, 1993), chap. 1.

K. B. Bucknall, 'Why China Has Done Better than Russia since 1989', *International Journal of Social Economics*, 24 (1997), 1023–37.

J. L. Campbell, *Institutional Change and Globalization* (Princeton University Press, 2004).

J. L. Campbell and O. K. Pedersen (eds.), *The Rise of Neoliberalism and Institutional Analysis* (Princeton University Press, 2001).

Q. Cha, 'Qiyuling-an: Xuezhe de Huiying, Ji Yici Beijing Daxue Faxueyuan Xianfa yu Xingzhengfa Xuezhe de Taolun' ['The Scholars' Responses to Qiyuling Case: The Discussion among the Scholars of Constitutional Law and Administration Law in the Law School of Peking University'], *Fazhi Ribao* [*Legal Daily*], 16 September 2001.

W. Cha, 'Xin Quandi Yundong Yanjiu' ['Research on New Enclosure Movement'], unpublished PhD thesis, Jinan University (2010).

S. Chakravorty, *The Price of Land: Acquisition, Conflict, Consequence* (Oxford University Press, 2013).

N. Chan, 'Land Acquisition Compensation in China: Problems & Answers', *International Real Estate Review*, 6 (2003), 136–52.

N. Chan, 'Recent Reform of China's Rural Land Compensation Standards', *Pacific Rim Property Research Journal*, 12 (2006), 3–21.

H. Chen, 'Qi-an Pifu de Feizhi yu Xianfa Sifahua he Fayuan Yuanyin Xianfa Wenti' ['The Annulment of Reply to Qi Yuling Case and the Issue on the Adjudication of Constitution and the Judicial Direct Application of Constitution'], *Faxue Zazhi* [*Law Science Magazine*], Issue 3 (2009), 11–14.

J. Chen, 'The Revision of the Constitution in the PRC', *China Perspectives*, 53 (May–June 2004), available at www.chinaperspectives.revues.org/2922.

X. Chen, 'Tudi Chubei Bingbu Youbei Gonggong Liyi' ['Land Reserve is not against the Public Interest'], available at www.lcrc.org.cn/publish/portal0/tab101/info31318.htm.

F. Chen and L. Wang, 'Bei Shourongzhe Sunzhigang zhi Si' ['Death of Sun Zhigang, the Detained'], *Nanfang Dushi Bao* [*Southern Metropolitan Daily*], 25 April 2003, available at news.sina.com.cn/s/2003–04–25/11111016223.html.

S. Chen and P. Zhang, 'Guojia Ji Pinkun Xian de Kuayue' ['A Big Leap in a Country-level Poverty County'], *Nongmin Ribao* [*Farmer Daily*], 22 August 2005, available at www.farmer.com.cn/wlb/nmrb/nb1/200508220132.htm.

B. Cheng, 'The Rationale of Compensation for Expropriation', *Transactions of the Grotius Society*, 44 (1958), 267–310.

T. Chen, and M. Seldon, 'The Origins and Social Consequences of China's Hukou System', *The China Quarterly*, 139 (1994), 644–68.

S. V. Ciriacy-Wantrup and R. C. Bishop, 'Common Property as a Concept in Natural Resources Policy', *Natural Resources Journal*, 15 (1975), 713–27.

C. Clague (ed.), *Institutions and Economic Development* (Baltimore and London: The Johns Hopkins University Press, 1997).

D. C. Clark, 'China's Legal System and the WTO: Prospects for Compliance', *Washington University Global Studies Law Review*, 2 (2003), 97–118.

R. Coase, 'The Federal Communications Commission', *Journal of Law and Economics*, 2 (1959), 1–40.

R. Coase, 'The Nature of the Firm', *Economica*, 4 (1937), 386–405.

R. Coase, 'The Problem of Social Cost', *Journal of Law and Economics*, 3 (1960), 1–44.

M. Cohen-Eliya and I. Porat, 'American Balancing and German Proportionality: The Historical Origins', *International Journal of Constitutional Law*, 8 (2010), 263–86.

E. Coke, *The Second Part of the Institutes of the Laws of England*, available at www.constitution.org/18th/coke2nd1797/.

E. Coke, *The Third Part of the Institutes of the Laws of England: Concerning High Treason, and Other Pleas of The Crown, and Criminal Causes [1817]* (Clark, NJ: Lawbook Exchange, 2002).

J. E. Cribbet, 'Concepts in Transition: The Search for a New Definition of Property', *University of Illinois Law Review*, 1986 (1986), 1–42.

W. Cuddihy and B. C. Hardy, 'A Man's House Was Not His Castle: Origins of the Fourth Amendment to the United States Constitution', *William and Mary Quarterly*, 37 (1980), 371–400.

Z. Cui, 'A Comparative Study of the Relationship between Constitution and Property Rights', 1 November 2003, available at chinastudygroup.net/2003/11/a-comparative-study-of-the-relationship-between-constitution-and-property-rights/.

L. Cui, 'Quanguo Renda Fagongwei Sheli Fagui Shencha Bei-an Shi Weifa Weixian Shencha Naru Chengxu' ['NPCSC's Commission of Legal Work Established the Office of Filing and Reviewing of Laws and Regulations to Start the Review of Constitutionality and Legality'], *Zhongguo Qingnian Bao* [*China Youth Daily*], 20 June 2004, available at zqb.cyol.com/gb/zqb/2004–06/20/content_891710.htm.

D. P. Currie, 'Lochner Abroad: Substantive Due Process and Equal Protection in the Federal Republic of Germany', *The Supreme Court Review*, 1989 (1989), 333–72.

A. Day, 'Legal Reform and Economic Development in Vietnam and China: A Comparative Analysis', unpublished MA thesis, Tufts University (2004).

R. de Chowdhuri, 'Rising Star Mamata Battles Communist Bastion in West Bengal', *Reuters*, 18 April 2011, available at in.reuters.com/article/2011/04/18/idINIndia-56400120110418.

K. Deininger, S. Jin and S. Rozelle, 'Dynamics of Legal Change in a Decentralized Setting: Evidence from China's Rural Land Contracting Law', available at www.aeaweb.org/annual_mtg_papers/2006/0108_1300_0201.pdf.

H. Demsetz, 'The Exchange and Enforcement of Property Right', *Journal of Law and Economics*, 7 (1964), 11–26.

H. Demsetz, 'Towards a Theory of Property Rights', *American Economic Review*, 57 (1967), 347–59.

L. Deng, Q. Shen and L. Wang, 'The Emerging Housing Policy Framework in China', *Journal of Planning Literature*, 26 (2011), 168–83.

R. G. Dierks, *Introduction to Globalization: Political and Economic Perspectives for the New Century* (Chicago: Burnham Inc., Publishers, 2001).

C. Ding, 'Policy and Praxis of Land Acquisition in China', *Land Use Policy*, 24 (2007), 1–13.

J. A. Dorn, 'Trade and Human Right: The Case of China', *Cato Journal*, 16 (1996), 77–98.

W. Du and S. Huang, *Shidi Nongmin Quanyi Baozhang de Jingjixue Yanjiu* [*The Economic Research on the Guarantee of the Displaced Farmers' Interest*] (Beijing: Kexue Chubanshe [Science Press], 2009).

X. Du and X. Ren, 'Lifa Taolun Canyuzhe Jianyan Xin Chaiqian Tiaoli' ['The Suggestions to the New Expropriation Regulation from the Participants of Legislation Discussion'], *Fazhi Ribao* [*Legal Daily*], 1 February 2010, available at www.legaldaily.com.cn/zt/content/2010–02/01/content_2050312.htm.

J. G. Durham, 'Efficient Just Compensation as a Limit on Eminent Domain', *Minnesota Law Review*, 69 (1985), 1277–313.

J. W. Ely, *The Guardian of Every Other Right: A Constitutional History of Property Rights* (Oxford University Press, 2008).

E. Engel, 'The History of the General Principle of Proportionality', available at ssrn.com/abstract=1431179.

R. A. Epstein, *Supreme Neglect: How to Revive Constitutional Protection for Private Property* (New York: Oxford University Press, 2008).

R. A. Epstein, *Takings: Private Property and the Power of Eminent Domain* (Cambridge, MA: Harvard University Press, 1985).

K. Ewing, 'The Coolest Nail House in History', *Asia Times*, 31 March 2007, available at www.atimes.com/atimes/China_Business/IC31Cb01.html.

FAO, 'Compulsory Acquisition of Land and Compensation', 2008, available at www.fao.org/docrep/011/i0506e/i0506e00.htm.

J. Fee, 'Reforming Eminent Domain' in D. H. Merriam and M. M. Ross (eds.), *Eminent Domain Use and Abuse: Kelo in Context* (Chicago: American Bar Association, 2006).

M. Fegan, 'Just Compensation Standards and Eminent Domain Injustices: An Underexamined Connection and Opportunity for Reform', *Connecticut Public Interest Law Journal*, 6 (2006), 269–97.

Y. Feng, 'Power, Rights and Interests: A Legal and Economic Analysis of Urban Housing Demolition and Relocation in China' in X. Huang (ed.), *The Institutional Dynamics of China's Great Transformation* (Abington: Routledge, 2011).

S. Fischer, 'Globalization and Its Challenges', *American Economic Review*, 2 (1993), 1–30.

F. Frankfurter, *Mr. Justice Holmes and the Supreme Court* (Cambridge, MA: Harvard University Press, 1938).

E. Freund, *The Police Power: Public Policy and Constitutional Rights* (Chicago: Callaghan & Company, 1904).

J. Fu, 'Shanghai Maiqili Chaiqianqu 1.9 Zonghuo-an Diaocha' ['Investigation on 1.9 Arson Case in the Demolition and Removal Area of Maiqili'], *Nanfang Dushi Bao* [*Southern Metropolitan Daily*], 3 March 2005, A17–18.

W. Fu, 'Tongdi Tongjia Youzhuyu Baohu Shidi Nongmin de Liyi ma' ['Can the Principle of "Same Land Same Price" Protect the Interest of Land-loss Farmers?'], *Nanfang Dushi Bao* [*Southern Metropolitan Daily*], 15 July 2010, available at view.news.qq.com/a/20100715/000004.htm.

M. E. Gallagher, *Contagious Capitalism: Globalization and the Politics of Labor in China* (New Jersey: Princeton University Press, 2005).

C. Gan, 'Xinzhongguo Xianfa Caichan Zhidu de Lishi Huigu' ['A Historical Review of Property System in the Constitutions of New China'], *Zhongguo Faxue* [*China Legal Science*], No. 4 (2010), 132–57.

H. Gao, *Jiti Chanquan xia de Zhongguo Nongdi Zhengshou Wenti Yanjiu* [*Research on the Expropriation of Collectively Owned Farmland in China*] (Shanghai Renmin Chubanshe [Shanghai People's Press], 2009).

S. Gardbaum, 'The "Horizontal Effect" of Constitutional Rights', *Michigan Law Review*, 102 (2003), 387–459.

N. S. Garnett, 'The Neglected Political Economy of Eminent Domain', *Michigan Law Review*, 105 (2006), 101–50.

German Law Journal, 'Federal Constitutional Court Affirms Horizontal Effect of Constitutional Rights in Private Law Relations and Voids a Marital Agreement on Constitutional Grounds', *German Law Journal*, 2 (2001), available at www.germanlawjournal.com/index.php?pageID=11&artID=61/para 11.

A. Gibbard, 'Natural Property Rights', *Noûs*, 10 (1976), 77–86.

A. Giddens, *Runaway World* (New York: Routledge, 2000).

X. Gong 'Yibu Weibei Xianfa he Beili Shehui Zhuyi Jiben Yuanze de Wuquan Fa Cao-an' ['A Draft of Property Law that Violates the Constitution and Departs from the Basic Principles of Socialism'], an open letter delivered online on 12 August 2005, available at news.qq.com/a/20061221/002288.htm.

G. S. Goodpaster, 'The Constitution and Fundamental Rights', *Arizona Law Review*, 15 (1973), 479–519.

S. P. Green, 'Castles and Carjackers: Proportionality and the Use of Deadly Force in Defense of Dwellings and Vehicles', *University of Illinois Law Review*, 1999 (1999), 1–42.

S. Gupta, 'An Overview of Land Acquisition in Singur', available at ssrn.com/abstract=1346911.

J. L. Hafetz, 'A Man's Home is His Castle?: Reflections on the Home, the Family, and Privacy During the Late Nineteenth and Early Twentieth Centuries', *William & Mary Journal of Women and the Law*, 8 (2001–2), 175–242.

W. T. Hagan, 'Private Property, the Indian's Door to Civilization', *Ethnohistory*, 3 (1956), 126–37.

D. Han, 'The Hukou System and China's Development', *The Journal of Developing Areas*, 3 (1999), 355–78.

J. Han (ed.), *Zhongguo Nongcun Tudi Wenti Diaocha* [*Survey on China's Rural Land Issues*] (Shanghai Yuandong Chubanshe [Shanghai Far East Press], 2009).

D. Han, and D. Wang, 'Zhongguo Gongmin Xianfa Yishi Diaocha Baogao' ['Investigation Report on Chinese Citizens' Consciousness of Constitution'], *Zhengfa Luntan* [*Tribune of Political Science and Law*], 6 (2002), 114.

K. J. Hand, 'Using Law for a Righteous Purpose: The Sun Zhigang Incident and Evolving Forms of Citizen Action in the People's Republic of China', *Columbia Journal of Transnational Law*, 45 (2006), 114–95.

G. Hardin, 'The Tragedy of the Commons', *Science*, 162 (1968), 1243–8.

F. A. Hayek, *The Fatal Conceit: The Errors of Socialism* (W. W. Bartley III, ed.) (University of Chicago Press, 1991).

Q. He, 'The Land-Enclosure Movement of the 1990s: Inaugurating China's New "Land Enclosure"', *Chinese Economy*, 33 (2000), 57–88.

M. Heller, 'The Tragedy of the Anticommons: Property in the Transition from Marx to Markets', *Harvard Law Review*, 111 (1998), 621–88.

T. A. Hippler, 'Reexamining 100 Years of Supreme Court Regulatory Taking Doctrine: The Principles of "Noxious Use", "Average Reciprocity of Advantage", and "Bundle of Rights" from *Mugler* to *Keystone Bituminous Coal*', *Boston College Environmental Affairs Law Review*, 14 (1987), 653–727.

W. N. Hohfeld, 'Some Fundamental Legal Conceptions as Applied in Judicial Reasoning', *Yale Law Journal*, 23 (1913), 16–59.

R. G. Holcombe, 'A Theory of the Theory of Public Goods,' *Review of Austrian Economics*, 10 (1997), 1–22.

T. Hsia, 'The Constitution of Red China', *The American Journal of Comparative Law*, 4 (1955), 425–35.

S. Huang, 'Xianfa Sifahua jiqi Yiyi–cong Zuigao Renmin Fayuan de yige Pifu Tanqi' ['The Adjudication of Constitution and Its Significance: Discussion of a SPC Response Enacted Today'], *Renmin Fayuan Bao* [*People's Court Daily*], 13 August 2001.

X. Huang and Y. Zhao, 'Pan Rong: Shouchi Ranshaoping de Yonggan Nvren' ['Pan Rong: A Brave Woman with a Petrol Bottle in Her Hand'], *Nanfang Zhoumo* [*Southern Weekend*], 2 December 2009, available at www.infzm.com/content/38292.

D. Z. Hudson, 'Eminent Domain Due Process', *Yale Law Journal*, 119 (2010), 1280–327.

H. Hunter, 'Soviet Agriculture with and without Collectivization, 1928–1940', *Slavic Review*, 47 (1988), 203–16.

Z. I. Husami, 'Marx on Distributive Justice', *Philosophy & Public Affairs*, 8 (1978), 27–64

Internal Displacement Monitoring Centre, 'India-Large Numbers of IDPs', 3 May 2007, available at www2.ohchr.org/english/bodies/cescr/docs/info-ngos/IDMC2India40.pdf.

H. M. Jacobs and E. M. Bassett, 'All Sound, No Fury? The Impacts of State-Based *Kelo* Laws', *Planning & Environmental Law*, 63 (2011), 3–8.

JCER, *China's Market in 5 to 10 Years*, available at www.jcer.or.jp/eng/pdf/china02.pdf.

X. Jiang and S. Liu, 'Tudi Jiemi' [Uncover the Secret of Land'], *Caijing Magazine*, No. 4 (2006).

D. Johansen, 'Property Rights and the Constitution', available at dsp-psd.pwgsc.gc.ca/Collection-R/LoPBdP/BP/bp268-e.htm.

K. Jurow, 'Untimely Thoughts: A Reconsideration of the Origins of Due Process of Law', *The American Journal of Legal History*, 19 (1975), 265–79.

W. Kasper, *Economic Freedom & Development: An Essay about Property Rights, Competition, and Prosperity* (New Delhi: Centre for Civil Society, 2002).

S. N. Katz, 'Thomas Jefferson and the Right to Property in Revolutionary America', *Journal of Law and Economics*, 19 (1976), 467–88.

T. E. Kellogg, 'The Death of Constitutional Litigation in China?', *China Brief*, Issue 7 (2009), 4–7.

H. H. Khondker, 'Globalization Theory: A Critical Analysis', Department of Sociology working paper, National University of Singapore (1994).

H. H. Khondker, 'Glocalization as Globalization: Evolution of a Sociological Concept', *Bangladesh e-Journal of Sociology*, No. 2 (2004), 1–9.

M. U. Killion, 'China's Amended Constitution: Quest for Liberty and Independent Judicial Review', *Washington University Global Studies Law Review*, 4 (2005), 43–80.

D. P. Kommers, 'The Federal Constitutional Court in the German Political System', *Comparative Political Studies*, 26 (1994), 470–91.

Q. Kong, *China and the World Trade Organization: A Legal Perspective* (Singapore: World Scientific Publishing Company, 2002).

H. Li, 'Chaiqian Jingjixue' ['Economics of Demolition and Removal'], *Sanlian Shenghuo Zhoukan* [*Sanlian Life Weekly*], No. 1 (2010), 37–9.

L. C. Li, 'Path Creation? Processes and Networks: How the Chinese Rural Tax Reform Began', *Policy and Society*, 25 (2006), 61–84.

Q. Li, 'Tax Incentive Policies for Foreign-Invested Enterprises in China and their Influence on Foreign Investment', *Revenue Law Journal*, 18 (2008), 1–41.

M. Li and J. Shi, 'Zhengdi Qupian Zonghe Dijia Buchang Zhidu Chuangxin Yanjiu' ['Research on the Innovation of the Institutions Concerning Comprehensive Land Section Price'], *Hongguan Jingji Yanjiu* [*Research on Macro Economy*], No.8 (2010), 58–60.

W. Li and Y. Wang, 'Gushi Xianwei Shuji de Jingjixue Guandian: Lianjia Laodongli Shi Liqi' ['The Economics Opinion of Gushi County CPC Secretary: Cheap Labor Resource is Significant for Growth'], available at finance.sina.com.cn/g/20060405/22482477267.shtml.

H. Liang, 'Zhongguo Wuquan Fa de Qicao' ['Drafting of Chinese Property Law'], a lecture delivered at Waseda University on 15 January 2002, *Shanxi Daxue Xuebao* [*Journal of Shanxi University*], No.2 (2002), 24–30.

J. Y. Lin, 'Collectivization and China's Agricultural Crisis in 1959–1961', *Journal of Political Economy*, 98 (1990), 1228–52.

G. C. S. Lin, 'Land Development, Municipal Finance, and Urban Expansion in Globalizing China: A Study of Guangdong Province, 2000–2005', Lincoln Institute of Land Policy working paper (2010), available at www.lincolninst.edu/pubs/dl/1812_1044_LinFinal.pdf.

H. Lin and X. Yu, 'Rang Beizhengdi Nongmin Yuanyou Shenghuo Yougaishan Changyuan Shengji Youbaozhang: Jiedu Tudi Guanli Fa Xiuzheng-an Cao An Sida Liangdian' ['To Improve the Original Lives and to Secure the Future Lives of Land-loss Farmers: The Four Noticeable Revisions in the Draft of the Amendment to Land Administration Law'], *Xinhua*, 24 December 2012, available at news.xinhuanet.com/legal/2012–12/24/c_114141344.htm?_fin.

D. Lipton and S. Jeffrey, 'Creating a Market Economy in Eastern Europe: The Case of Poland', *Brookings Papers on Economic Activity*, 1990 (1990), 75–147.

D. Lipton and S. Jeffrey, 'Privatization in Eastern Europe: The Case of Poland', *Brookings Papers on Economic Activity*, 1990 (1990), 293–341.

S. Liu, 'Zhongguo de Tudi Chanquan yu Tudi Shichang Fazhan' ['Development of Rural Land Ownership Rights in China and the Emergence of the Land Market'] in CASS Institution of Rural Development (ed.), *Nongcun Tudi Zhidu Gaige: Guoji Bijiao Yanjiu* [*Reform on Rural Land System: International Comparison*] (Beijing: Shehui Kexue Wenxian Chubanshe [Social Science Academic Press], 2009).

J. Locke, *Two Treatises of Government*, available at www.efm.bris.ac.uk/het/locke/government.pdf.

S. Lubman, *Bird in a Cage: Legal Reform in China after Mao* (CA: Stanford University Press, 1999).

C. Luo, 'Chaiqian Yinfa Jiemei Tongri Lihun' ['The Two Sisters Divorced at the Same Day Because of Demolition and Removal'], *Xinjing Bao* [*Beijing News*], 8 May 2004, available at www.bjnews.com.cn/news/2011/11/09/163185.html.

C. Luo, 'Hunan Jiahe Chaiqian Shijian Zhuizong Baodao' ['The Follow-up Report of the Demolition and Removal Incident in Jiahe of Hunan'], *Xinjing Bao* [*Beijing News*], 17 May 2004, available at www.china.com.cn/chinese/law/565431.htm.

P. Lv, X. Liu and S. Long, 'Zhengdi Qupian Zonghe Dijia Queding Fangfa Shizheng Yanjiu' ['Empirical Research on the Measurement Methods of Comprehensive Land Section Price'], *Zhongguo Tudi Kexue* [*China Land Science*], No. 6 (2005), 30–5.

H. Ma and S. Sun (eds.), *Zhongguo Jingji Jiegou Wenti Yanjiu (Diyi Juan)* [*Research on China's Economic Structure Issues (Volume 1)*] (Beijing: Renmin Chubanshe [People's Publishing House], 1980).

A. Mahalingam and A. Vyas, 'Comparative Evaluation of Land Acquisition and Compensation Processes across the World', *Economic & Political Weekly*, No. 32 (2011), 94–102.

J. Marangos, 'The Political Economy of Shock Therapy', *Journal of Economic Surveys*, 16 (2002), 41–76.

M. Mate, 'The Origins of Due Process in India: The Role of Borrowing in Personal Liberty and Preventive Detention Cases', *Berkeley Journal of International Law*, 28 (2010), 216–60.

F. I. Michelman, 'Socio-Political Functions of Constitutional Protection for Private Property Holdings' in G. E. van Maanen and A. J. van der Walt (eds.), *Property Law on the Threshold of the 21st Century* (Antwerpen: Maklu, 1996), pp. 433–50.

A. S. Miller, 'Protection of Private Foreign Investment by Multilateral Convention', *The American Journal of International Law*, 53 (1959), 371–8.

B. Milanovic, 'The Two Faces of Globalization: Against Globalization as We Know It', *World Development*, 31 (2003), 667–83.

S. Morris and A. Pandey, 'Towards Reform of Land Acquisition Framework in India', *Economic and Political Weekly*, 42 (2007), 2083–90.

H. Mostert, 'Does German Law Still Matter?', *German Law Journal*, Vol. 3, No. 9 (2002), available at www.germanlawjournal.com/article.php?id=183.

J. Nedelsky, 'Should Property be Constitutionalized? A Relational and Comparative Approach' in G. E. van Maanen and A. J. van der Walt (eds.), *Property Law on the Threshold of the 21st Century* (Antwerpen: Maklu, 1996), pp. 417–32.

V. Nee, 'Organizational Dynamics of Market Transition: Hybrid Forms, Property Rights, and Mixed Economy in China', *Administrative Science Quarterly*, 37 (1992), 1–27.

P. Nichols, *Nichols on Eminent Domain* (J. Sackman, R. van Brunt and et al., eds.), 3rd ed., (New York: Matthew Bender, 1997).

P. Nichols, 'The Meaning of Public Use in the Law of Eminent Domain', *Boston University Law Review*, 20 (1940), 615–41.

D. C. North, 'The New Institutional Economics', *Journal of Institutional and Theoretical Economics*, 142 (1986), 230–7.

S. W. Norton, 'Poverty, Property Rights, and Human Well-Being: A Cross National Study', *Cato Journal*, 18 (1998), 233–45.

D. M. O' Brien, *Constitutional Law and Politics*, 1st ed., 2 vols. (New York: W. W. Norton & Company, 1991), vol. II.

M. V. Onufrio, 'The Constitutionalization of Contract Law in the Irish, the German and the Italian systems: Is Horizontal Indirect Effect Like Direct Effect?', 2007, available at www.indret.com/pdf/481_en.pdf.

L. J. Oswald, 'Property Rights Legislation and the Police Power', *American Business Law Journal*, 37 (2000), 527–62.

Our Bureau, 'Red-hand Buddha: 14 Killed in Nandigram Re-entry Bid', *The Telegraph*, 15 March 2007, available at www.telegraphindia.com/1070315/asp/frontpage/story_7519166.asp.

Our Legal Reporter, 'Public Purpose Tag on Singur-Nano Plant Zips Past Legal Hurdle', *The Telegraph*, 19 January 2008, available at www.telegraphindia.com/1080119/jsp/frontpage/story_8801520.jsp.

L. Paler, 'China's Legislation Law and the Making of a More Orderly and Representative Legislative System', *The China Quarterly*, 182 (2005), 301–18.

J. Pan, *Chengshihua Jincheng zhong Tudi Zhengshou Falv Wenti Yanjiu* [*Research on the Legal Issues Concerning Land Expropriation in the Progress of Urbanisation*] (Beijing: Renmin Chubanshe [People's Publishing House], 2009).

Alok Pandey, 'Mamata Wins This Round against Ratan Tata over Singur', 29 September 2011, available at www.ndtv.com/article/india/mamata-wins-this-round-against-ratan-tata-over-singur-136870.

E. F. Paul, *Property Rights and Eminent Domain* (New Brunswick, NJ: Transaction Publishers, 2008).

R. Peerenboom, *China's Long March toward Rule of Law* (Cambridge University Press, 2002).

E. M. Penalver, 'Property Metaphors and *Kelo v. New London*: Two Views of the Castle', *Fordham Law Review*, 74 (2005–2006), 2971–6.

E. M. Penalver, and L. J. Strahilevitz, 'Judicial Takings or Due Process?', *Cornell Law Review*, 97 (2011), 305–68.

Z. Peng, 'Guanyu Zhonghua Renmin Gongheguo Xianfa Xiuzheng Cao-an de Shuoming' ['The Report on the Revision Draft of the PRC Constitution'], 26 November 1982, available at www.iolaw.org.cn/showLaws.asp?id=20686.

R. Pomfret, *Constructing a Market Economy: Diverse Path from Central Planning in Asia and Europe* (Cheltenham and Northampton: American International Distribution Corporation, 2002).

V. Popov, 'Shock Therapy versus Gradualism Reconsidered: Lessons from Transition Economies after 15 Years of Reforms', *Comparative Economic Studies*, 49 (2007), 1–31.

P. B. Potter, 'Globalization and Economic Regulation in China: Selective Adaptation of Globalized Norms and Practices', *Washington University Global Studies Law Review*, 2 (2003), 119–50.

P. B. Potter, 'Legal Reform in China: Institutions, Culture, and Selective Adaptation', *Law & Social Inquiry*, 29 (2004), 465–95.

P. B. Potter, *The Chinese Legal System: Globalization and Local Legal Culture* (New York: Routledge, 2001).

V. Ramnani, 'End of Affordability, Land Costs Will Increase 80 per cent, Say Developers Unhappy with LARR 2011', *Hindustan Times*, 10 September 2011, available at ncrhomes.com/2011/land-acquisition-bill-approved-by-cabinet/.

K. S. Rao, 'Property Rights Under the Constitution', lecture delivered in the Forum of Free Enterprise in Bombay on 26 October 1968, (1969) *2 SCC (Jour)* 1, available at www.ebc-india.com/lawyer/articles/69v2a1.htm.

J. K. Raymond, 'Stopping *Kelo* One Year Later: Legislative Efforts to Reverse Eminent Domain Abuse', June 2006, available at www.sbecouncil.org/uploads/Keloone.pdf.

C. Richter, 'State Based Anti-*Kelo* Laws: Full of Sound & Fury, Signifying Nothing', 1 March 2011, available at northwestlandlawforum.com/2011/03/state-based-anti-kelo-laws-full-of-sound-fury-signifying-nothing.

R. Robertson, *Globalization: Social Theory and Global Culture* (London: Sage, 1992).

D. Rodrik, 'Trade Policy Reform as Institutional Reform' in B. Hoekman, A. Mattoo, and P. English (eds.), *Development, Trade and the WTO: A Handbook* (World Bank, 2002), pp. 3–10.

C. M. Rose, 'Possession as the Origin of Property', *University of Chicago Law Review*, 52 (1985), 73–88.

S. Rosefielde, 'Excess Collectivization Deaths 1929–1933: New Demographic Evidence', *Slavic Review*, 43 (Spring 1984), 83–88.

E. Rothschild, 'Globalization and the Return of History', *Foreign Policy*, No. 115 (1999), 106–16.

C. K. Rowley, 'Limits of Democracy' in C. K. Rowley (ed.), *Property Rights and the Limits of Democracy* (Aldershot and Brookfield: Edward Elgar, 1993).

C. F. Runge, 'Common Property and Collective Action in Economic Development', *World Development*, 14 (1986), 623–35.

J. D. Sachs, 'Accelerating Privatization in Eastern Europe: The Case of Poland', *New Europe Law Review*, 1 (1992–1993), 71–89.

J. D. Sachs, 'Why Russia has failed to stabilize', in A. Aslund, (ed.), *Russian Economic Reform at Risk* (London and New York: Pinter, 1995), pp. 53–63.

J. D. Sachs and W. T. Woo, 'Reform in China and Russia', *Economic Policy*, 9 (1994), 101–45.

P. A. Samuelson, 'The Pure Theory of Public Expenditure', *The Review of Economics and Statistics*, 36 (1954), 387–9.

B. Schwarzwalder, R. Prosterman, J. Ye and J. Riedinger, 'An Update on China's Rural Land Tenure Reforms: Analysis and Recommendations Based on a Seventeen-Province Survey', *Columbia Journal of Asian Law*, 16 (2002–2003), 141–225.

G. W. Scully, 'The Institutional Framework and Economic Development', *Journal of Political Economy*, 96 (1988), 652–62.

I. Sened, *The Political Institution of Private Property* (Cambridge University Press, 1997).

K. Shen, 'Is It the Beginning of the Era of the Rule of the Constitution? Reinterpreting China's "First Constitutional Case"', translated by Liu Yuping, *Pacific Rim Law & Policy Journal*, 12 (2003), 200–32.

B. Shi, 'Buyuan Ku-ao de Guojiaji Pinkun Xian' ['National Impoverished County which Wants to Get Rid of Long Term Hard Slog'], *Nanfengchuang* [*South Reviews*], No. 15 (2009), available at www.nfcmag.com/article/1563.html.

A. Shourie, 'The Manu of Our Times?', available at arunshourie.voiceofdharma.com/text/ambedkar.txt.

B. H. Siegan, *Property and Freedom* (New Brunswick and London: Transaction Publishers, 1997).

M. Spoor and X. Shi, 'Cotton and Rural Income Development in Xinjiang' in M. Spoor (ed.), *The Political Economy of Rural Livelihoods in Transition Economy: Land, Peasants and Rural Poverty in Transition* (London: Routledge, 2009), pp. 225–44.

J. G. Sprankling, *Understanding Property Law* (New York: Matthew Bender & Company, 2000).

J. E. Stiglitz, *Whither Socialism?* (Reprint Edition) (Cambridge, MA: MIT Press, 1996).

M. E. Storme, 'Property Law in a Comparative Perspective (Part I)', 2004, available at www.law.kuleuven.be/web/mstorme/comprop1.pdf.

G. M. Struve, 'The Less Restrictive Alternative Principle and Economic Due Process', *Harvard Law Review*, 80 (1967), 1464–88.

R. M. Sullivan 'Eminent Domain in the United States: An Overview of Federal Condemnation Proceedings' in G. M.Erasmus (ed.), *Compensation for Expropriation: A Comparative Study* (Oxford: Jason Reese in association with the United Kingdom National Committee of Comparative Law, 1990), vol. I.

H. Sun, *Zhengdi Jiufen de Zhengzhixue Fenxi* [*Political Analysis on Land Expropriation Disputes*] (Beijing: Zhishi Chanquan Chubanshe [Intellectual Property Press], 2011).

C. R. Sunstein, 'On Property and Constitutionalism', *Cardozo Law Review*, 14 (1993), 907–35.

A. S. Sweet, 'Why Europe Rejected American Judicial Review and Why It May Not Matter', *Michigan Law Review*, 101 (2003), 2744–80.

X. Tang, 'Citizens Express Anger toward Local Governments by Committing Suicide', *Economic Observer*, 17 September 2010, available at www.eeo.com.cn/ens/homepage/briefs/2010/09/17/181152.shtml.

S. Tang and W. Xie (eds.), *Zhongguo Fangdichan Shiwu Quanshu* [*Handbook of China's Housing and Real Estate*] (Beijing: Xinshidai Chubanshe Press (New Times Press), 1992).

X. Tao, 'Guanyu Guojia Jianshen Zhengyong Tudi Banfa Xiuzheng Cao-an de Shuoming' ['Explanation on the Revision of Measures on Requisition of Land for National Construction'], available at www.npc.gov.cn/wxzl/gongbao/2000–12/23/content_5000446.htm.

The Times of India, 'Assocham seeks review of Land Acquisition Bill', *The Times of India*, 6 September 2011, available at articles.timesofindia.indiatimes.com/2011-09-06/india-business/30118358_1_land-acquisition-bill-favour-of-land-owners-acquisition-for-public-purpose.

W. M. Treanor, 'The Origins and Original Significance of the Just Compensation Clause of the Fifth Amendment', *Yale Law Journal*, 94 (1985), 694–716.

Z. Tong, 'A Comment on the Rise and Fall of the Supreme People's Court's Reply to Qi Yuling's Case', *Suffolk University Law Review*, 43 (2010), 669–79.

A. J. van der Walt, *Constitutional Property Clauses: A Comparative Analysis* (Cape Town: Juta, 1999).

K. J. Vandevelde, 'The New Property of the Nineteenth Century: The Development of the Modern Concept of Property', *Buffalo Law Review*, 29 (1980), 325–67.

W. Voss, 'Appropriate Compensation in terms of Compulsory Purchase in Germany' in Polish Real Estate Scientific Society (ed.), *Some Aspects of Compulsory Purchase of Land for Public Purposes* (Olsztyn, 2010), available at www.tnn.org.pl/tnn/publik/18/TNN_monografia_2010.pdf.

A. Walker and L. Li, 'Land Use Rights Reform and the Real Estate Market in China', *Journal of Real Estate Literature*, Vol. 2, No. 2 (1994), 199–211.

A. Walker, and K. McKinnell, 'Economic Reform and the Future for Real Estate in PRC', *Journal of Property Valuation & Investment*, Vol. 13, No. 5 (1995), 39–49.

D. Wang, 'Complex Households, a Fading Glory: Household Formation During the Collective Period in the People's Republic of China', *Journal of Family History*, 25 (2000), 527–44.

C. Wang, 'From the Rule of Man to the Rule of Law' in D. Cai and C. Wang (eds.), *China's Journey toward the Rule of Law* (Leiden: Brill, 2010), pp. 1–50.

Z. Wang, 'Guanyu Zhonghua Renmin Gongheguo Xianfa Xiuzheng-an (Cao-an) de Shuoming' ['Explanation of the Draft of the 2004 Amendment to the Constitution'], *Renmin Ribao* [*People Daily*], 9 March 2004, available at news.xinhuanet.com/newscenter/2004–03/08/content_1352469.htm.

X. Wang, 'Thirty Years of Reform and Transition in China and Russia: A Comparative Analysis', *China Economist*, Vol. 4, No. 2 (2009), 52–60.

Y. Wang, 'Wanshan Fagui Beian Shenchan Weihu Guojia Fazhi Tongyi' ['To Maintain the Unification of China's Legal System through the Improvement of Filing and Reviewing of Laws and Regulations'], *Zhongguo Qingnian Bao* [*China Youth Daily*], 22 December 2005, available at zqb.cyol.com/content/2005–12/22/content_1221995.htm.

L. Wang, 'Wuquan Fa Lifa de Ruogan Wenti Tantao' ['Several Issues on the Legislation of Property Rights Act'], *Zhengfa Luntan* [*Tribune of Political Science and Law*], No. 4 (2001), 3–7.

L. Wang, *Wuquan Fa Yanjiu* [*Research on Property Law*] (Beijing: Renmin Daxue Chubanshe [People's University Press], 2002).

K. Wang, 'Xinzhongguo Xianfa Baozhang Caichanquan de Lishi Bianqian (1949–2004)' ['The Historical Change of the Provisions Concerning the Protection of Property Right in New China's Constitutions (1949–2004)'], *Fazhi Luntan* [*Nomocracy Forum*], No. 1 (2006).

Y. Wang, *Zhongguo Xianfa Sifahua: Anli Pingxi* [*The Adjudication of China's Constitution: Comments on Typical Cases*] (Beijing Daxue Chubanshe [Peking University Press], 2005).

K. Wang and Z. Li, *Xinzhongguo Tudi Zhengshou Zhidu Yanjiu* [*Research on the Land Expropriation System of New China*] (Beijing: Shehui Kexue Wenxian Chubanshe [Social Sciences Academic Press], 2009).

Y. Wang and A. Murie, 'The Process of Commercialisation of Urban Housing in China', *Urban Studies*, 33 (1996), 971–89.

S. L. Wasby, 'History of the Court: Rights Consciousness in Contemporary Society' in K. L. Hall, J. W. Ely, J. B Grossman and W. M. Wiecek (eds), *The Oxford Companion to the Supreme Court of the United States* (Oxford University Press, 1992).

V. J. Washburn, 'Regular Takings or Regulatory Takings?: Land Expropriation in Rural China', *Pacific Rim Law & Policy*, 20 (2011), 71–124.

O. E. Williamson, *Markets and Hierarchies* (New York: Free Press, 1975).

J. Williamson and P. Lindert, 'Does Globalization Make the World More Unequal?' in M. D. Bordo, A. M. Taylor and J. G. Williamson (eds.), *Globalization in Historical Perspective* (The University of Chicago Press, 2003), pp. 227–76.

M. Wolfe, 'Social Integration: Institutions and Actors', occasional paper No. 4 (UNRISD world summit for social development), 1994.

World Bank, 'China's Rapid Urbanization: Benefits, Challenges & Strategies', available at www.worldbank.org/en/country/china.

World Bank, *World Development Report 1999/2000: Entering the 21st Century* (New York: Oxford University Press, 1999).

J. Wu, Building New China's Legal System, *Columbia Journal of Transnational Law*, 22 (1983–4), 1–40.

K. M. Wyman, 'The Measure of Just Compensation', *UC Davis Law Review*, 41 (2007), 239–87.

J. Xia, 'Jiedu Xin Zhengdi Buchang Guiding: Baohu Beizhengdi Nongmin Hefa Quanyi' [The Illustration of the New Provisions about the Compensation Concerning Land Expropriation: the Protection of Land-loss Farmers' Legal Rights], *Renmin Ribao* [*People Daily*], 17 November 2004, available at www.people.com.cn/BIG5/shehui/1063/2993002.html.

W. Xiao, 'Xianfa shi Shenpan Gongzuo de Genben Falv Yijv' ['The Constitution is the Fundamental Legal Basis of Court Trying Job'], *Faxue Zazhi* [*Law Science Magazine]*, No. 3 (2002), 3–4.

Y. Xin, 'Nongye Liushitiao de Xiuding yu Renmin Gongshe de Zhidu Bianqian' ['Revision of "the Sixty Articles for Agriculture" and the Evolution of the System of the People's Commnunes'], *Zhongguo Dangshi Yanjiu* [*Chinese Communist Party History Studies*], No. 7 (2012), 39–52.

Xinhua, 'Chengshi Liulang Qitao Renyuan Shourong Qiansong Banfa Feizhi' ['Abolishment of Measures on Custody and Repatriation of Vagrants and Beggars in Cities'], *Xinhua*, 19 June 2003, available at www.china.com.cn/chinese/law/349194.htm.

Xinhua, 'China's 4 Trillion Yuan Stimulus to Boost Economy, Domestic demand', *Xinhua*, 9 November 2008, available at news.xinhuanet.com/english/2008–11/09/content_10331324.htm.

Xinhua, 'Guowuyuan Changwu Huiyi Shenyi bing Yuanze Tongguo Guoyou Tudi shang Fangwu Zhengshou yu Buchang Tiaoli' ['The State Council's Regular Meeting Reviewed and Passed in Principle the Regulation on the Expropriation and Compensation Concerning the Houses Built on the State Owned Land'], *Xinhua*, 19 January 2011, available at news.xinhuanet.com/politics/2011–01/19/c_121000691.htm.

Xinhua, 'Xin Zhongguo Dang-an: Xin Zhongguo de Tudi Gaige Yundong' ['Archive of New China: Land Reform Movement in New China'], available at www.gov.cn/test/2009–08/20/content_1397342.htm.

C. Xu, 'Xianfa Sifahua Zhiyi' ['Questioning the Adjudication of Constitution'], *Zhongguo Renda* [*China People Congress*], No. 11 (2006), 44–5.

J. Yang, '2009 Nian Quanguo Maidi Jinzhang 1.5 Wan Yi' ['1.5 Trillion Yuan from the Sale of Land in 2009'], *Xinjingbao* [*Beijing News*], 9 January 2010, available at epaper.bjnews.com.cn/html/2010–01/09/content_53367.htm?div=-1.

K. Yang, 'Jianguo Qianhou Zhongguo Gongchandang dui Zichan Jieji Zhengce de Yanbian' ['The Evolution of the Chinese Communist Party's Policy toward the Bourgeoisie before and after the Establishment of the People's Republic of China'], *Jindaishi Yanjiu* [*Modern Chinese History Studies*], No. 2 (2006), 1–25.

H. Yang, 'Xin Chaiqian Tiaoli Zheng Yijian guo Wantiao, Fei Gonggong Liyi Tiaokuan bei Zhiyi' ['The Feedback Opinions to New Demolition Regulation Are More than 10,000 Pieces and the Clause about Non-public Interest Is Questioned'], *Xin Jingbao* [*Beijing News*], 13 February 2010, available at news.qq.com/a/20100213/000070.htm.

Y. Yang, 'Tudi Guanli Fa Xiugai Gongzuo Qidong' ['The Revision of Land Administration Law was Initiated'], *Xin Jingbao* [*Beijing News*], 20 April 2011, available at epaper.bjnews.com.cn/html/2011–04/20/content_222715.htm?div = -1.

X. Yin, 'Xianfa Sifahua Wenti de Jidian Zhiyi he Sikao' ['Some Questions and Thoughts on the Adjudication of the Constitution'], *Huadong Zhengfa Xueyuan Xuebao* [*ECUPL Journal*], No. 6 (2001), 8–10.

X. Yin and X. Cheng, 'Gushi Xian Qiangzheng Tudi Wushi Mu Liaohuang Qinian' ['The 50 mu Land Expropriated by Gushi County Has Been Left Vacant for Seven Years'], *Henan Ribao* [*Henan Daily*], 10 May 2011, available at news.dahe.cn/2011/05–10/100705598.html.

S. Young, 'Wealth but Not Security: Attitudes towards Private Business in China in the 1980s', *The Australian Journal of Chinese Affairs*, No. 25 (1991), 115–37.

C. Yu, Y. Shi and Z. Zuo, 'Zhongguo Disibo Quandi Yundong yu Chaiqian Xue-an' ['China's Fouth Enclosure Movement and the Bloody Cases of Demolition and Removal'], *Nanfang Dushi Bao* [*Southern Metropolitan Daily*], 2 June 2010.

Y. Zhang, 'Chongqingshi Nongcun Tudi Shichang Fayu Chengdu Yanjiu' ['Evaluation of the Development of Rural Land Market in Chongqing'], unpublished Master thesis, Southwestern University (2011).

L. Zhao, 'Tudi Falv Xiugai jiang Jiasu Baozhang Nongmin Quanyi Shi Zhongxin' ['The Revision of Land Law is Fastened and is with the Protection of the Farmers' Interest as the Focus'], *Nanfang Zhoumo* [*Southern Weekend*], 16 October 2008.

Y. Zhong and R. A. Hays, 'The Transformation of the Urban Housing System in China', *Urban Affairs Review*, 31 (1996), 625–57.

S. Zhong and J. Huang, 'Zhengdi Tongyi Nianchanzhi Biaozhun he Qupian Zonghe Dijia Yinfa de Xinkunjing' ['The New Dilemma Caused by Uniform Annual Output Standard and Comprehensive Land Section Price'], *Guotu Ziyuan* [*National Land Resource*], No. 6 (2007), 42–5.

Zhongguo Gaige Fazhan Yanjiuyuan [China Institute of Reform & Development], *Zhongguo Nongcun Tudi Zhidu de Biange yu Chuangxin* [*History of Changes and Innovations of China's Rural Land System*] (Haikou: Nanhai Chuban Gongsi [Nanhai Press], 1999).

G. Zhu, 'Constitutional Review in China: An Unaccomplished Project or a Mirage?', *Suffolk University Law Review*, 43 (2010), 625–53.

X. Zou, and A. J. Oskam, 'New Compensation Standard for Land Expropriation in China', *China & World Economy*, Vol. 15, No. 5 (2007), 107–20.

Z. Zuo, 'Huangcheng Gushi: Bei Liaohuang de Chengjian Mingxing Xian' ['A Deserted City Gushi: The Abandoned Model County for Urban Construction'], *Nanfang Dushi Bao* [*Southern Metropolitan Daily*], 2 June 2010, available at gcontent.oeeee.com/5/7c/57c0531e13f40b91/Blog/ba2/4c0dc2.html.

INDEX

Lightning Source UK Ltd.
Milton Keynes UK
UKHW02n2204270518
323278UK00012B/149/P

9 781107 125438